Study Guide

FINANCIAL REPORTING & ANALYSIS

Third Edition

Lawrence Revsine
Daniel W. Collins
W. Bruce Johnson

Charles Fazzi
St. Vincent College

PEARSON

Prentice
Hall

Upper Saddle River, New Jersey 07458

VP/Editorial Director: Jeff Shelstad
Acquisitions Editor: Bill Larkin
Associate Editor: Sam Goffinet
Manager, Print Production: Christy Mahon
Production Editor & Buyer: Wanda Rockwell
Printer/Binder: Courier, Bookmart Press

10 9 8 7 6 5 4 3 2 1
ISBN 0-13-143024-6

Contents

CHAPTER 1

THE ECONOMIC AND INSTITUTIONAL SETTING FOR FINANCIAL REPORTING

Chapter Review

Learning Objective 1: Why financial statements are a valuable source of information about companies, their current health, and their prospects for the future.

Users of financial statements are decision makers. To make informed decisions, investors and other users rely on a variety of qualitative and quantitative information. Usually, the starting point of quantitative information is the firm's **financial statements**. **Reliable, relevant** financial statements present the best information about a company's economic history, current financial health, and prospects for the future. Because most financial statements possess a reasonable degree of **comparability** among firms in the same industry, decision makers use financial statements to more efficiently allocate capital and resources, encourage innovation, provide markets for securities, and grant credit.

Learning Objective 2: How investors, creditors, securities analysts, and auditors use financial statements.

Financial statements reflect the quantitative results of **economic events** that affect a company. The **balance sheet** reflects a picture of a firm's economic position at a point in time. The **income statement, statement of cash flow,** and **statement of changes in stockholders' equity** describe the changes that occurred in producing income, cash, and equity during the year. Most financial statement users utilize them as a/an:

1. **analytical tool** for trends, growth rates, asset quality, and productivity.
2. **management report card** for profitability and efficiency.
3. **early warning signal** of profitability, liquidity, and solvency problems.
4. **basis for prediction** of future earnings and stock prices.
5. **measure of accountability** for the stewardship of the assets.

Learning Objective 3: How accounting rules are established and why

Accounting financial statements disclose the economic history of the company and can be used to gauge company performance. Statements can also be manipulated by fraudulent managers to hide fraud. Decision makers must analyze data presented in financial statements to ascertain the degree to which the statements **faithfully represent** the economic events and activities affecting the company.

Learning Objective 4:
How the demand for financial information comes from its ability to improve decision making and monitor managers' activities.

Learning Objective 5:
How the supply of financial information is influenced by the costs of producing and disseminating it, and by the benefits it provides.

are established and why management can shape the financial information communicated to outsiders and still be within the rules.

events and activities affecting the company.

Financial statements are demanded because of their value as a source of information about a company's performance, financial condition, and stewardship of its resources.

Statement readers must be able to :
1.   understand current financial reporting standards and guidelines.
2.   recognize that management can shape information given to others, and
3.   distinguish between **reliable** and **judgmental** information.

Five major groups of decision makers create demand for financial statements:
1.   **Shareholders and investors** (potential shareholders):
      a. To select investments consistent with individual preferences for risk, return, dividend yield, and liquidity.
      b.   To **evaluate management's performance**.
2.   **Managers and employees**:
      a.   To measure benefits from employment contracts.
      b.   To value the benefits from **Employment Stock Ownership Plans** (ESOPs).
      c.   To monitor the health of pension and profit-sharing plans.
      d.   To negotiate union contracts.
      e.   To gauge future profitability, stability, and solvency.
3.   **Lenders and suppliers**:
      a.   To judge credit worthiness, interest rates, and collateral.
      b.   To monitor compliance with loan **covenants**.
      c.   To monitor continued health of firms with whom they do business.
4.   **Customers:** To be sure that suppliers can be relied upon in the future.
5.   **Government and regulatory agencies**:
      a.   To assess and collect tax revenue.
      b.   To establish new tax laws designed to enhance social welfare.
      c.   To negotiate and monitor compliance with contract suppliers.
      d.   To regulate public utilities and monopolies.
      e.   To monitor the banking and insurance industries.
      f.   To monitor securities markets.

An integral part of financial statements is disclosures that appear with the statements but not on the statements. Such disclosures may be **mandatory** or **voluntary**.

Financial statement users make disclosure decisions within the scope of **cost/benefit** analysis. The **Securities and Exchange Commission (SEC),** the **Financial Accounting Standards Board (FASB),** and the **International Accounting Standards Board (IASB)** require some mandatory disclosures to ensure minimum levels of financial disclosure.

These organizations do encourage other disclosures which firms may choose to implement. Companies must weigh the benefits of disclosure against the costs of disclosure.

Benefits of disclosure include dissemination of information that:
1. is beneficial to the firm in the form of "good news," financial information.
2. Helps raise required capital at favorable terms in the market.
3. Establishes a reputation for supplying credible information to users.

Disclosures have four potential **economic costs**:
1. **Information collection, processing and dissemination costs**
   a. Expensive information collection costs such as retirement benefits, post-retirement benefits.
   b. Auditing costs.
2. **Competitive disadvantage costs**
   a. Information that signals competitors about future plans, and tactics, such as, pricing strategies, or new products and customer markets.
   b. Information about technological or managerial innovations.
   c. Detailed information about company operations, sales, and production costs, or marketing strategies.
   d. Information that improves the bargaining position of customers, suppliers, employees, or unions.
3. **Litigation costs**
   a. Cost of defending the claims of shareholders, creditors, or competitors.
   b. Damage to corporate or management reputation.
4. **Political costs**
   a. Taxes placed on unpopular industries.
   b. Anti-trust litigation.
   c. Environmental regulation.
   d. Rescinding protective import quotas.

Professional **analysts** consist of :
1. **Equity investors** who utilize

    a. **fundamental analysis** approach to assess the discounted cash flow per share and compare it to the current stock price.

    b. **technical analysis** to chart the price and volume movements of the stock.

    c. **liquidation value** as a minimum value.

    d. the **price earnings ratio** as a multiplier of current or projected earnings.

2. **Creditors** who focus on assessing the

    a. firm's ability to meet debt obligations in a timely manner.

    b. company's **credit risk** or credit worthiness.

    c. firm's **financial flexibility** to raise additional cash from selling assets, issuing stock, or borrowing more.

    d. need for protective loan **covenants**.

3. **Financial advisors** (security analysts) who utilize all of the practices of equity investors and creditors with a high level of expertise to provide information to those groups.

4. Independent **auditors** who examine management's financial statements to choose audit procedures designed to detect major improprieties.

Analysts rely on three types of information:

1. quarterly and annual financial statements with non-financial operating and performance data;

2. **management's discussion and analysis (MD&A)** of financial and non-financial data with key trends and a discussion of those trends; and

3. information that makes it possible to identify future opportunities, risks, and plans.

Development of Generally Accepted Accounting Principles (GAAP)

In the past century, the accounting profession has developed a network of conventions, rules, guidelines, and procedures collectively referred to as **generally accepted accounting principles (GAAP)**. The overriding goal of GAAP is to assure that financial statements represent faithfully and clearly the economic condition and performance of the company. The conceptual framework of accounting includes qualitative characteristics of accounting information that statements must possess to assure this. These include:

- **Relevance** – Financial information capable of making a difference in a decision.
  - ❖ **Timeliness** – Information that is available to decision makers   when it is current.
  - ❖ **Predictive value** – Information that improves the decision makers ability to forecast the outcomes of past or present events.
  - ❖ **Feedback value** – Information that confirms or alters the

decision maker's earlier expectations.

* ❖ **Reliability** – Information that is free from error and bias
* ❖ **Verifiability** – Independent measurers should get similar results when using the same measurement methods.
* ❖ **Representational faithfulness** – The degree to which the accounting actually represents the underlying economic event.
* ❖ **Neutrality** – Information should not be presented that favors one party over another.
* ❖ **Comparability** – Information must be measured and reported in a similar manner across companies.
* ❖ **Consistency** – The same accounting methods are used to describe similar methods from period to period.

Two additional accounting conventions are used by accounting professionals in evaluating whether financial reports are complete, understandable and helpful to readers:

* **Materiality** – Information that contains omissions or misstatements that would alter the judgment of a reasonable person.
* **Conservatism** – Financial reports adequately reflect business risks and uncertainties.

GAAP is determined by a partnership of the public and private sectors. In 1933, Congress gave the SEC statutory authority to determine accounting standards. SEC delegates this authority to the accounting profession. It currently rests with the FASB, created in 1970. GAAP is imprecise and allows necessary flexibility to choose specific accounting procedures. Wily managers can manipulate financial statements by careful selection of procedures to produce desirable results. Examples of manipulations are **income smoothing**, timing of recognition of expenses and revenues, advantageous interpretation of **contingent liabilities**, and carefully disclosing only required items. GAAP governs only U.S. companies

Financial statement information is more complex and more widely available than ever before. Documents filed with the SEC are available on the internet through Electronic Data Gathering and Retrieval system (**EDGAR**). Information is cheap and easy to obtain but the world is more complex. Analysts are expected to be professionally skeptical about the information they have and recognize that financial statement can both conceal and reveal.

International accounting standards are set by the International Accounting Standards Board (IASB). The IASB represents 153 accounting organizations from 112 countries and has issued 41 standards and 33 interpretations of existing standards. The IASB has developed a core set of accounting standards that have been endorsed by the International Organization of Securities Commissions (IOSCO) of which the SEC is a member. These core standards are to be used for cross-border capital raising and stock exchange listing purposes but have not been adopted by the SEC. IOSCO has also developed disclosure standards for multinational companies, and these have been adopted by the SEC.

**APPENDIX:
GAAP in the United States**

GAAP developed in the United States from a series of events beginning with the establishment of the **New York Stock Exchange** in 1792, the establishment of income tax in 1913, the stock market crash of 1929, and the creation of the SEC in 1933. SEC has the power to establish and enforce the accounting policies and practices of registered companies. The **Securities and Exchange Act of 1934** required the independent audit of publicly traded firms' financial statements. SEC delegated most of the authority to the **American Institute of Certified Public Accountants (AICPA)**, who developed the **Committee on Accounting Procedure (CAP)** in 1938. In 1959, AICPA established the **Accounting Principles Board (APB)** to succeed the CAP, which, in turn, was succeeded by FASB in 1973.

The CAP issued 51 **Accounting Research Bulletins (ARBs)** and four **Accounting Terminology Bulletins** to narrow the areas of differences and inconsistencies in accounting practice. These pronouncements were not binding on corporations or auditors.

The APB issued 31 **Opinions** and four Statements from 1959 to 1973 to resolve current accounting controversies and develop a conceptual foundation for accounting. In October 1964 the governing body of the AICPA adopted **Rule 203** requiring audit opinions to certify conformity with GAAP. Dissatisfaction with the APB led to the formation of the FASB.

In 1973 the FASB began its reign over accounting standard formation. The FASB differed from its predecessors in that it has seven paid full-time members, independent from their employers, who were not required to be CPAs, and represented members of the financial community. FASB also provides members with staff and advisory support. **Accounting Series Release No. 150**, issued by the SEC in 1973, formally acknowledged that FASB pronouncements had **"substantial authoritative support"** as the SEC standard of financial reporting and disclosure.

FASB follows a **due process** procedure to establish accounting standards. The three main steps in the process are:

1. A **discussion memorandum** is issued to outline key issues involved and the preliminary view of FASB. The public is free to respond to FASB with their views and FASB sometimes holds public forums.

2. After further consideration, FASB issues an **exposure draft** and invites further public comment.

3. FASB votes on whether to issue the standard or modify the exposure draft and reissue another draft. Passage requires the approval of five of the seven board members.

Many groups, including special interest groups, accounting firms, government agencies, preparing organizations, and trade organizations, appeal for alternative standards in the due process procedures. Arguments center around cost-benefit concerns, theoretical soundness, implementation issues, and adverse social costs.

Auditing standards, previously set by the AICPA, are the responsibility of the Public Company Accounting Oversight Board (PCAOB). The PCAOB, funded by mandatory fees from public companies, operates under the oversight of the SEC. The board was created by the Sarbanes-Oxley Act of 2002 and is empowered to establish auditing standards and to conduct periodic quality reviews of auditors work.

Glossary of Terms

Accounting Principles Board (APB)
Established in 1959 by the AICPA to replace the Committee on Accounting Procedure. Existed from 1959 to 1973, issued thirty-one Opinions and four Statements designed to improve financial reporting and disclosure.

American Institute Of Certified Public Accountants (AICPA)
A voluntary professional organization comprised of Certified Public Accountants. Established the Generally Accepted Auditing Standards.

Analyst
Anyone who uses financial statements to make decisions including investors, creditors, financial advisors, and auditors.

Analytical Review Procedure Tools
Used by the auditors to illuminate relationships among financial statement data. The tools include trend analysis, ratio analysis, and other forms of comparative analysis.

Committee on Accounting Procedure (CAP)
Established in 1938 by the AICPA, the CAP was responsible for narrowing the areas of differences and inconsistencies in accounting practice. The CAP functioned until 1959.

Comparability	A qualitative characteristic of financial information that states that financial information should be measured and reported in a similar manner among different companies.
Conservatism	An accounting convention that strives to ensure that business risks and uncertainties are adequately reflected in the financial reports.
Consistency	A qualitative characteristic of financial information that states that the same accounting methods should be used to describe similar events from period to period.
Competitive Disadvantage	A disclosure cost that arises as a result of a competitor using proprietary information about a firm's strategies, technology, innovations, or operations gained from disclosures in public financial reports.
Disclosure Costs	Four potential costs that can arise from informative financial disclosures are: 1) information, processing, and dissemination costs; 2) competitive disadvantage costs; 3) litigation costs; and 4) political costs.
Efficient Markets Hypothesis	A school of stock market analysis that presumes that analysts have no insights about the value of a company beyond the current security price.
Financial Accounting Standards Board (FASB)	The organization to whom the Securities and Exchange Commission (SEC) currently delegates the authority to set accounting standards in the United States. The SEC monitors the activities of the FASB.
Financial Advisors	Those who provide information and advice to investors and creditors including securities analysts, brokers, portfolio strategists, and industry consultants.
Fundamental Analysis	A method of financial analysis that relies on balance sheet and income statement information, along with macro-economic data, to forecast future stock price movements.
Generally Accepted Accounting Principles (GAAP)	A network of conventions, rules, guidelines, and procedures that serve as the principles and rules that govern financial reporting.
International Accounting Standards Board	The organization responsible for developing international accounting standards.
Litigation Costs	The disclosure costs that arise when financial statements users initiate lawsuits against a firm.
Materiality	An accounting convention that ensures that omissions and misstatements in the financial reports will not affect the judgment of a reasonable person.

Neutrality	A qualitative characteristic of financial information that states that information cannot be selected to favor one set of interested parties over another.
New York Stock Exchange	Established in 1792 as the primary mechanism for trading ownership in corporations.
Political Costs	The disclosure cost that arises from operating in a highly visible industry giving rise to potential political vulnerability. The result of a political cost is often a political initiative designed to penalize or hinder the firm.
Public Company Accounting Oversight Board	The organization that has the authority to establish auditing standards.
Relevance	A qualitative characteristic of financial information that states that the financial information must be capable of making a difference in a decision.
Reliability	A qualitative characteristic of financial information that states that the information must be verifiable, faithfully represented, and reasonably free of error and bias.
Representational Faithfulness	A qualitative characteristic of financial information that is the degree to which the information represents what it purports to represent.
Securities and Exchange Commission (SEC)	Agency created by the Federal Government having the ultimate authority to establish the rules for the preparation of financial statements of companies whose securities are sold to the general public.
Technical Analysis	A school of stock market analysis that relies on price and volume movements of stocks and does not utilize financial statement data.
Timeliness	A qualitative characteristic of financial information that states that making information available to decision makers before it loses its capacity to influence their decisions is important.
Verifiability	A qualitative characteristic of financial information that states that independent measurers, using the same measurement methods, should get similar results.

Test Yourself

True or False Questions

T   F   1.   The best source of information about the current health of a company is the board of directors.

T   F   2.   Financial statements may be used as an analytical tool and as a measure of accountability.

T   F   3.   Financial statements provide an economic history which is comprehensive and quantitative.

T   F   4.   Accounting is an exact science.

T   F   5.   Users demand financial statements because of their value as an information source about a firm's performance, financial condition, and stewardship of its resources.

T   F   6.   The supply of financial information is determined by the cost-benefit rule.

T   F   7.   An investor using technical analysis to determine over-priced or under-priced securities relies on price and volume movements of stocks.

T   F   8.   An investor using fundamental analysis to determine over-priced or under-priced securities relies heavily on price and volume movements of stocks.

T   F   9.   The efficient market hypothesis proponents believe that it is not futile to forecast the market price of undervalued or overvalued stocks using financial statements.

T   F   10.   Employees use financial information to value the benefits from employee stock ownership plans.

T   F   11.   The requirement that Fox Co. maintain a 2:1 current ratio to avoid loan default is called a loan covenant.

T   F   12.   Government agencies use financial statement information from suppliers to resolve contract disputes.

T   F   13.   Financial statement information has value because it enhances uncertainty about a company's economic health.

T   F   14.   The Securities and Exchange Commission is a private agency that helps to regulate and enforce financial reporting requirements.

T   F   15.   The Financial Accounting Standards Board is a private agency that helps to regulate financial reporting requirements.

T   F   16.   Public and private regulatory agencies establish and enforce financial reporting requirements to ensure that companies meet certain minimum levels of financial disclosure.

T F 17. Financial statement disclosures may provide economic benefits to firms with zero cost.

T F 18. The cost of determining post-retirement health care costs to employees is a political cost.

T F 19. Antitrust litigation against a company is referred to as a litigation cost.

T F 20. Disclosure of information that provides a benefit to a firm's competitor is referred to as a political cost.

T F 21. Financial statement users have diverse information needs because they might each face different decisions.

T F 22. The determination of the total value of a company's assets if sold individually less the debt the company owes is the price-earnings ratio.

T F 23. The application of standards promulgated by the Financial Accounting Standards Board is always free from the need for professional judgment.

T F 24. Timeliness is one of the quantitative characteristics of financial information.

T F 25. The ultimate authority for financial statement rules affecting publicly traded companies is the Financial Accounting Standards Board.

T F 26. Managers are often driven by their own self interest to manipulate reported financial statement information.

T F 27. Prior to 1900, corporate financial reporting practices in the United States were primarily intended for third party users.

T F 28. The International Accounting Standards Board is responsible for developing international accounting standards.

T F 29. The Securities and Exchange Act of 1934 required the audit of financial statements of publicly traded companies.

T F 30. AICPA's Rule 203 - Accounting Principles forced corporations and their auditors to implement accounting standards prescribed by the Accounting Principles Board.

Multiple-Choice Questions
Select the best answer from those provided.

_____ 1. A company's financial statements provide investors with information about
a. the health of the industry in which the company operates.
b. economic events that affected a company which can be translated into accounting numbers.
c. future projections of revenues and expenses.
d. the relative position of competitors.

_____   2.   The financial data provided to prospective investors is the responsibility of the company's
a.   auditors.
b.   board of directors.
c.   stockholders.
d.   Management.

_____   3.   Investors use financial statements as a/an
a.   stockholder report card.
b.   late warning signal.
c.   management report card.
d.   guarantee against fraud.

_____   4.   Which one of the following accounts would a financial statement user expect to be measured with a high degree of precision and a high degree of reliability?
a.   Accumulated Amortization
b.   Warranty Liability
c.   Common Stock
d.   Contingent Liability

_____   5.   Which one of the following accounts would a financial statement user expect to be measured with a moderate degree of precision and reliability because the amounts are based on management's judgment?
a.   Accounts Receivable
b.   Allowance for Doubtful Accounts
c.   Cash
d.   Common Stock

_____   6.   The school of stock market analysis known as _technical_ analysis relies on
a.   cash flow information
b.   sales
c.   price and volume movements of stock
d.   product acceptance.

_____   7.   Employees demand financial statement information because the firm's performance is often linked to
a.   employee stock ownership plans.
b.   social security benefits.
c.   disability plan benefits.
d.   workmen's compensation benefits.

_____ 8. Suppliers monitor the financial statements of their customers to
   a. learn trade secrets of their competitors.
   b. determine their selling prices.
   c. assess the financial strength of their customers.
   d. report its customers' financial performance to credit bureau services.

_____ 9. A governmental agency responsible for regulating financial reporting in the
   United States is the
   a. Securities and Exchange Commission.
   b. Financial Accounting Standards Board.
   c. National Association of Securities Dealers.
   d. New York Stock Exchange.

_____ 10. Which one of the following types of disclosure costs is the cost of the audit of the
   financial statements?
   a. political cost
   b. litigation cost.
   c. information collection and dissemination cost.
   d. competitive disadvantage cost

_____ 11. The imposition of the Windfall Profits Tax on the oil industry created a/an
   a. litigation cost.
   b. information collection and dissemination cost.
   c. political cost.
   d. competitive disadvantage cost.

_____ 12. A firm's book value of assets minus liabilities owed is
   a. stockholder's equity.
   b. market equity.
   c. net present value.
   d. liquidation value.

_____ 13. A firm is financially flexible if it can
   a. exchange assets for newer technology.
   b. make required payments on liabilities in a timely manner.
   c. extend repayment terms of debts.
   d. raise cash by selling bonds.

_____ 14. Professional analysts find the necessary information to give a complete picture of
   a company in the
   a. quarterly payroll reports.
   b. annual proxy statements.
   c. auditor's report.
   d. annual report, business press, and other trade information sources.

_____ 15. Reliable information is
a. relevant.
b. unbiased.
c. comparable.
d. timely.

_____ 16. If a company fails to disclose information about a transaction because it might be embarrassing to the company, it is violating
a. comparability.
b. verifiability.
c. consistency.
d. neutrality.

_____ 17. When a company changes from FIFO to weighted average method of accounting for inventory, it violates
a. consistency.
b. comparability.
c. neutrality.
d. faithful representation.

_____ 18. Which one of the following has been granted authority to determine accounting rules by the SEC?
a. American Institute of Certified Public Accountants
b. State Boards of Accountancy
c. New York Stock Exchange
d. Financial Accounting Standards Board

_____ 19. In 1973 the pronouncements of the Financial Accounting Standards Board were formally acknowledged by the SEC as having
a. the weight of law.
b. substantial authoritative support.
c. guidance use only.
d. no real significance.

_____ 20. The Financial Accounting Standards Board has the responsibility for establishing accounting standards for the
a. United States.
b. United States and Canada.
c. United States and Europe.
d. United States and Mexico.

Solutions

Answers to True or False Questions

True answers: 2, 3, 5, 6, 7, 10, 11, 12, 15, 16, 21, 26, 28, 29, 30
False answers explained:
1.   The best source of information is the <u>financial statements</u>.
4.   Accounting is <u>not</u> an exact science.
8.   An investor using <u>technical analysis</u> relies on price and volume movements of stock.
9.   Efficient market hypothesis proponents believe it is futile to forecast stock market prices using financial statements.
13.   Financial statement information <u>reduces</u> uncertainty about a company's economic health.
14.   The Securities and Exchange Commission is a <u>government</u> agency.
17.   Financial statement disclosures provide economic benefits to firms and result in <u>disclosure costs</u> to the firm.
18.   The cost of determining post-retirement health care costs for employees is an <u>information collection, processing, and dissemination</u> cost.
19.   Anti trust litigation against a company is a political cost.
20.   Disclosure of information that provides a benefit to a firm's competitor is referred to as a <u>competitive disadvantage</u> cost.
22.   The determination of the total value of a company's assets if sold individually less the debt the company owes is the <u>liquidation</u> value.
23.   The application of standards promulgated by the Financial Accounting Standards Board is <u>never</u> free from the need for professional judgment.
24.   Timeliness is one of the <u>qualitative</u> characteristics of financial information.
25.   The ultimate authority for financial statement rules affecting publicly traded companies is the <u>SEC</u>.
27.   Prior to 1900 corporate financial reporting practices in the United States were primarily intended for <u>management</u>.

Answers to Multiple-Choice Questions

1.	B	6.	C	11.	C	16.	D
2.	D	7.	A	12.	A	17.	A
3.	C	8.	C	13.	D	18.	D
4.	C	9.	A	14.	D	19.	B
5.	B	10.	C	15.	B	20.	A

CHAPTER 2

ACCRUAL ACCOUNTING
AND INCOME DETERMINATION

Chapter Review

Learning Objective 1:
The distinction between cash-basis versus accrual-basis income, and why accrual income is a better measure of operating performance.

There are two different approaches to measuring income for an entity; accrual basis and cash-basis accounting.

Under **accrual-basis** accounting, **revenues** are recorded in the period in which they are **earned** and become **measurable**. **Expenses** are **expired costs** or assets used in producing the revenues reported. The matching principle requires that related revenues and expenses be recognized in the same accounting period. The measurement base is the economic or **critical event**.

FYI. . . A cash-basis entity's income statement is entitled **Statement of Receipts and Disbursements**.

Under **cash-basis** accounting, revenues and expenses are recorded in the period in which the cash is received or paid. The measurement base is **time**. Differences between accrual-basis and cash-basis accounting can be large. Both measure an important reality. The accrual-basis method reports the reality of economic value added (or performance) during an accounting period. The cash-basis method reports the reality of cash flows. Both are important in financial reporting. In accrual accounting, we report accrual-basis measurement of revenue on the income statement, and cash-basis measurement on the statement of cash flows.

The reality of cash flows is important to the cash management in an organization. Companies unable to manage cash flow do not remain in business very long. However, accrual accounting better matches economic benefit with economic effort, thereby producing a more realistic measure of operating performance than cash flows produce. Accrual accounting income also provides a better basis for predicting the future performance of an organization.
(See Demonstration Problem 1)

The heart of the matter. . .

The first lesson in accounting should be to distinguish between **recording** and **reporting**. **Recording** refers to the bookkeeping (data entry) portion of accounting. Accuracy is important. This represents the history of the economic events of the firm. **Reporting** refers to the transformation of the recorded data into intelligent **information** for the benefit of users.

Net Assets = Equity
because if
A = L + E, then
A — L = E. Net assets
is defined as A — L,
which equals equity.

FYI. . .
A measure of value at a
point in time is a **stock**.
A measure of a change
in values between two
points in time is a **flow**.
Balance sheets are
stocks and income
statements are flows.

The key issues of **revenue recognition** are the **timing** and **amount** of the recognition. Revenue recognition evokes **expense recognition**. The **matching principle** requires that the costs used in producing the revenue be recognized in the same accounting period. Properly matched revenues and expenses provide **income recognition**.

The **accounting equation**
        Assets = Liabilities + Equity
is the basis of the recording process in accounting. Because equations have two sides and must remain in equilibrium, the **recording process** is defined as **double-entry** accounting to record the change in both sides of the equation to maintain its balance.

The **reporting process** is also an expression of the accounting equation.
The **balance sheet** is a pure expression of the accounting equation:
        Total Assets = Total Liabilities + Equity.

Some changes in the balance sheet are expressed by the income statement, statement of cash flow, and the statement of changes in equity.
            Δ Assets = Δ Liabilities + Δ Equity
and   Assets = Cash + Noncash assets
and   Equity = Owner transactions + Prior Earnings + Current income

The **income statement** expresses:
            Current income = Revenues — Expenses.
Revenues and expenses create changes in assets and liabilities.
The **cash flow statement** expresses:
            Δ Cash = Δ Liabilities + Δ Equity — Δ Non-cash assets
The **statement of changes in equity** expresses:
            Δ Equity = Δ Owner transactions + Prior Earnings + Current income

Learning Objective 2:
The criteria for revenue
recognition under
accrual accounting and
how they are used in
selected industries.

Revenue recognition has two criteria that <u>must both</u> be met:
1.   The **critical event** has taken place.
2.   The amount is reasonably **measurable** and **collection is reasonably assured.**

The **critical event** can occur during the revenue producing process at one of four times:
1.   During the production phase.
        a. Must meet three conditions:
            1) Requires specific customer and agreed upon price.
            2) Significant performance and future costs readily estimated.
            3) Reasonably accurate estimate of cash collections.

4) Generally used by the long-term construction industry (ships, roads, buildings, military contracts, etc.).

2.   At the completion of production.
   a.   Justified when:
      1)   Product immediately saleable at quoted market prices.
      2)   Units are homogeneous.
      3)   No significant uncertainty about distribution costs.
   b.   Normally used by natural resource and agricultural industries.
3.   At the time of sale.
   b.   Requires substantial completion of product or services and relative certainty about the timing and amount of cash flows.
   c.   Most often used for retail and manufacturing industries.
4.   After the time of sale.
   a.   Used when either of the following conditions exists:
      4)   Extreme uncertainty about cash collections.
      5)   Substantial work remains and cost cannot be reasonably estimated.
   b.   Used by real estate developers, start-up franchisors, and home appliance rent-to-own marketers.

Learning Objective 3: The matching principle, and how it is applied to recognize expenses under accrual accounting.

No matter which method of revenue recognition is employed, the recognition of expenses (**expired costs**) must always follow the **matching principle** by recording the expenses in the period in which the revenue is recognized. Payment can occur:
1.   before costs are used, creating **prepaid expenses** or **inventories**.
2.   at the same time costs are used.
3.   after the costs are used, creating **accrued liabilities.**

Learning Objective 4: The difference between product and period costs.

Costs are either **traceable costs** (product costs) or period costs. **Product costs** are easily traced to the product to be recognized at the time of revenue recognition. **Period costs** are not traceable to specific products but generally benefit the business during a time period. Period costs are recognized in the time period they benefit. Examples of each type of cost:

Product Costs	Period Costs
Purchase of inventory	Administrative expenses
Transportation-in	Administrative salaries
Production costs	Advertising sales salaries
Warranty costs	

Learning Objective 5: The format and classifications for a multiple step income statement and how the statement format is

Preparers organize income statements to separate the **sustainable** types of income activities from those that are **transitory**. Sustainable income possesses the most predictive value of future income or future cash flows. Transitory income is unlikely to occur in future periods and

designed to differentiate earnings components that are more sustainable from those that are more transitory.

consists of four types: special or unusual items, discontinued operations, extraordinary items and the cumulative effect of a change in accounting principle. The income statement is divided into the following major categories:

1. **Income from continuing operations:** Includes normal operating activities of the enterprise and special or unusual items. Income tax expense attributable from this income is deducted as a line item.
2. **Discontinued operations:** Includes income from the discontinued operations and gains or losses on disposal of business components, both shown net of tax effects.
3. **Extraordinary items:** Gains and losses that are both unusual in nature and infrequently occur, shown net of tax effects.
4. **Cumulative effect of changes in accounting principle:** Shown net of tax effects.

Learning Objective 6: The distinction between special and unusual items, discontinued operations, extraordinary items, and the cumulative effect of accounting changes.

Special or unusual items are material items that are **either** unusual in nature **or** unlikely to recur. Determinations are made based on the specific circumstances of each occurrence for the time and place in which they occur. **Extraordinary items** are **both** unusual in nature **and** unlikely to recur taking into account the environment in which the business operates. Therefore, a tornado may be unusual for one company and extraordinary for another depending upon the state location. **Discontinued operations** relate to components of an entity that have been discontinued. A component of an entity comprises operations and cash flows that can be clearly distinguished operationally and for financial reporting purposes from the rest of the entity. **Cumulative effect of changes in accounting principles** are also shown net of taxes.

Not all accounting changes are shown on the income statement. There are five basic distinctions in accounting changes:

1. **General rule for accounting principle changes:**
   a. Usually involves the change from one GAAP to another.
   b. Cumulative effect is shown on the income statement with **pro forma** income figures.
2. **Retroactive changes:**
   a. Required in the following instances:
      1) When required by FASB for newly issued standards.
      2) Change from LIFO to another inventory method.
      3) Changes in accounting for long-term construction projects.
   b. All prior years are restated. No pro forma disclosures are needed.

3.   **Retroactive effect indeterminable:**
     a. Required for changes **to** LIFO inventory method.
     b. Requires no changes in prior statements and no cumulative effect.
4.   **Changes in accounting estimates:**
     a.   No special recognition in the financial statements.
     b.   If amounts have material effect on income, disclosure required.
5.   **Change in reporting entity:**
     a.   Usually occurs when previously separate statements are combined into consolidated statements.
     b.   Requires restatement of all prior years to reflect the new entity.

Learning Objective 7:
The distinction between basic and diluted earnings per share (EPS) and required EPS disclosures for certain income statement components.

Earnings per share is a common measure of operating performance. There are potentially two sets of EPS numbers reported. **Basic EPS** is computed by dividing income available to common shareholders by the weighted average common shares outstanding. **Diluted EPS** reflects the EPS that would result if all potentially diluted securities were converted to common stock. Firms that report diluted EPS have a complex capital structure, that is firms that have convertible debt, convertible preferred stock, stock options or warrants outstanding. The calculations of EPS will be covered in later chapters.

Learning Objective 8:
What comprises comprehensive income and alternative formats for displaying this amount, in the financial statements.

Comprehensive income is the change in equity during the period arising from transactions with non-shareholders. Not all increases in net assets are currently recognized in the income statement. The income statement usually reflects all **closed transactions**. **Open transactions** are often reported as a separate section of stockholders' equity. SFAS No. 130 requires that non-owner generated increases in equity from open transactions be reported as **other comprehensive income** components. There are three general types:
1.   Unrealized gains and losses on available-for-sale marketable securities.
2.   Unrealized gains and losses on foreign currency translations.
3.   Unrealized losses on recognition of minimum pension obligations under SFAS No. 87.
Net Income + Other Comprehensive Income = Total Comprehensive Income

SFAS No. 130 further requires companies to report comprehensive income in a statement that is displayed with the same prominence as the other financial statements. This can be accomplished with:
     1. A combined statement of income and comprehensive

income.

2.   Separate statements of income and comprehensive income.
3.   As a part of the statement of changes in stockholders' equity.

APPENDIX:
Learning Objective 9:
The basic procedures for preparing financial statements and how to conduct T-account analysis

The basic accounting equation is the foundation for the financial recording and reporting model as represented by the Balance Sheet.

ASSETS = LIABILITIES + OWNERS EQUITY

Revenue and expense accounts are tied to owners' equity. Revenues cause owners' equity to increase while expenses cause owners equity to decrease. The income statement presents the relationship of revenues and expenses in arriving at net income in the following manner.

REVENUES – EXPENSES = NET INCOME

Net income flows into owners' equity at the end of a period by a process known as closing the books which will be described later.

Recording accounting information system is based on a double entry system and each T-account has two sides, a debit (DR) side and a credit (CR) side. The debit side is the left side and the credit side is the right side.

ACCOUNT

Debit	Credit
DR	**CR**
Left	Right

Combining the rules of debit and credit with the accounting equation yields the following basic recording rules:

Asset accounts		=	**Liability Accounts**		+	**Owner's Equity Accounts**	
Debits	Credits		Debits	Credits		Debits	Credits
(DR)	**(CR)**		**(DR)**	**(CR)**		**(DR)**	**(CR)**
increase	**decrease**		**decrease**	**increase**		**decrease**	**increase**
the	the		the	the		the	the
balance	balance		balance	balance		balance	balance

Since revenue are positive owners' equity and expenses are negative owners' equity, the following basic recording rules emerge:

Revenue Accounts		**Expense Accounts**	
OE increases		OE decreases	
Debits	Credits	Debits	Credits
(DR)	(CR)	(DR)	(CR)
decrease	**increase**	**decrease**	**increase**
the	the	the	the
balance	balance	balance	balance

The accounting equation must always be "in balance" i.e., the total assets equal the total liabilities and owners' equity. Adherence to the rules of debit/credit will automatically keep the accounting equation in balance.

A journal entry is used to record a transaction in the journal. The basic format for an entry is:

(DR) Account Title   XXX
    (CR) Account Title   XXX

The dollar total of the debits will always equal the dollar total of the credits for each transaction. **See Demonstration Problem 2.**

The DRs and CRs that are made in each journal entry are posted to T-accounts. The process of transferring these numbers to the left (DR) or right (CR) side of the T-accounts is known as **posting**. A separate T-account is maintained for each asset, liability and owners' equity account including revenues and expenses.

Recording accounting information is a routine process that follows the following path:

Economic Event Occurs
↓
Debits and Credits are recorded in the **journal**
↓
Posting to the T-accounts.

Adjusting entries are journal entries that must be made at the end of the period to update the T-accounts for economic events that are not reflected in them. This is necessary so that all economic events of the period are included in the financial statements.

Adjusting entries fall into the following four categories:

1. Adjustments for **prepayments** – Prepayments are assets that have been purchased and paid for that are now used to some degree. The

use of this asset must be reflected as an expense and the asset must be decreased in amount. The adjusting entry will debit an expense account and credit an asset account. Examples are prepaid insurance, prepaid rent, supplies, and depreciation on buildings and equipment.

2. Adjustments for unearned revenues – Unearned revenues represent cash that has been collected from a client or customer but the work has not been performed or the product delivered. The unearned revenue represents a liability for the company when the cash is collected. As this revenue is earned through the delivery of product or providing services, revenue must be recorded to reflect what has been earned. The adjusting entry will debit an unearned revenue account and credit a revenue account. Examples are fees received in advance, and magazine subscriptions.

3. Adjustments for **accrued expenses** – Accrued expenses are expenses that the company has incurred but has not yet paid for them. These expenses must be recorded in that accounts with an accompanying liability to reflect what is owed and will be paid in the future. The adjusting entry required is to debit an expense and credit a liability. Examples are salaries and wages, utilities, and interest expense.

4. Adjustments for **accrued revenues** – Accrued revenues are revenues the company has earned but has not yet collected the cash because the payment will occur later. The adjusting entry required is to debit a receivable and credit a revenue account. Examples are interest revenue and services provided.

(See Demonstration Problem 3.)

Once adjusting entries have been prepared and posted to the T-accounts, the financial statements can be prepared. The next step in the recording model is to **close the books**. This entails placing a "zero" balance in each revenue and expense account and update the owner's equity account, retained earnings. In order to achieve this, **a closing entry** is prepared that will debit each revenue account and credit each expense account. The entry will be balanced with a debit or credit to retained earnings. If the company had net income, retained earnings will be credited to complete the entry. If the company incurred a loss, retained earnings will be debited. **(See Demonstration Problem 3)**

T-accounts can be a very useful device to analyze and understand how an individual account balance has changed. The general model to follow is:

Beginning Account Balance + Increases – Decreases = Ending Account Balance

Combined with knowledge regarding how the specific accounts are

related will enable you to effectively analyze individual financial
statement items.

Glossary of Terms

Accrual Accounting	The cornerstone of earnings measurement. A method of reporting revenues when they are "earned" and become "measurable".
Adjusting entries	Journal entries which update the accounting records prior to the preperation of financial statements.
Cash Basis Accounting	A method of recording revenues and expenses based on the actual receipt and payment of cash.
Closed Transactions	A transaction whose ultimate "payoff" results from events that have already occurred and whose dollar flows can be predicted fairly accurately.
Closing entries	Journal entries which "zero" out revenue and expense accounts and update the retained earnings of the entity.
Component of an Entity	Operations and cash flows that can be clearly distinguished, operationally and for financial reporting purposes from the rest of an entity when assessing discontinued operations.
Credit	The right side of a T-account
Comprehensive Income	The change in equity (net assets) of a business entity during a period from transactions and other events and circumstances from nonowner sources.
Critical Event	In terms of revenue recognition this is the one event considered to be absolutely essential to the ultimate increase in net asset value.
Debit	The left side of a T-account
Discontinued Operation	A non-recurring item of income or loss that involves the discontinuance or disposal of an component of readily distinguishable operations and cash flows.
Earned Revenue	Revenues are considered earned when the entity has substantially accomplished what it must do to be entitled to the benefits represented by the revenues.
Earnings per Share	Income available to common shareholders divided by the weighted average common shares outstanding for the period.
Expenses	The expired costs or assets used up in the production of revenues. Expenses are recorded in the same accounting period in which revenues are recognized.

Extraordinary Item	A non-recurring item of gain or loss reported on the income statement that is both unusual in nature and infrequent in occurrence.
Income from Continuing Operations	A component of income that includes only the normal, recurring, more sustainable, ongoing economic activities of the entity.
Intra-Period Tax Allocation	A method of reporting items on the income statement that matches the income tax with the item that gave rise to it.
Matching Principle	An accounting convention that calls for the recognition of revenues in the same period as the expenses that helped to produce them.
Net Assets	Gross assets minus gross liabilities.
Open Transactions	Transactions which are not "closed" (complete) giving rise to unrealized gains or losses that by-pass the income statement and are reported as direct adjustments in the balance sheet.
Period Costs	A method of revenue recognition applied to long-term construction contracts that calls for revenue recognition as the construction process progresses.
Product Costs	Costs incurred that can be directly traced to the revenues that they helped produce.
Pro Forma	Term applied to financial statements prepared on an "as if" basis, i.e. as if the new accounting principle had been applied during all periods presented.
Realizable Revenues	Revenues are realizable when related assets received or held are readily convertible to known amounts of cash or claims to cash.
Special or Unusual Items	Gains and losses that occur relatively infrequently, but that arise from a firm's ongoing operations.
Sustainable Items	Income statement items that are expected to be repeated in future periods.
Transitory Items	Income statement component items that are not likely to be repeated in future periods.

Demonstration Problems

1.   Cash v. Accrual Income Measurement

The Xavier Computer Corporation has the following events occur during June, its first month of operations:

Sales orders from customers	$300,000
Computers delivered to customers	180,000
Cash collected from customers	100,000
Purchase orders sent to vendors	160,000
Purchases received from vendors	140,000
Cost of computers delivered to customers	84,000
Cash paid to vendors on account	60,000
General operating expenses incurred during the month	60,000
General operating expenses paid during the month	50,000
Rent prepaid for one year	24,000
Salaries paid to employees	30,000

Required: Determine (A) the cash-basis income and (B) the accrual-basis income (cash collection is reasonably assured).

(A)   **First Step:** Determine the **critical event** for revenue recognition.
Application: Under the cash-basis of revenue recognition, the critical event is cash collection.
Solution: Revenue from customers is $100,000.

Second Step: Determine the expense recognition under the cash-basis method.
Application: Under the cash-basis of expense recognition, the critical event is cash payment.
Solution: Cash paid to vendors was $60,000.
    Cash paid for general operating expenses was $50,000.
    Cash paid for rent was $24,000.
    Cash paid to employees for salaries was $30,000.

(A) Final Solution:

Xavier Computer Corporation
Cash-Basis Income Statement
For the Month Ended June 30, XXXX

Revenue from Customers	$100,000	
Cost of Goods Sold	60,000	
Gross Profit	$ 40,000	
Operating Expenses:		
Rent	$24,000	
General Expenses	50,000	
Salaries	30,000	104,000
Net Income		$ (64,000)

(B)   **First Step:** Determine the **critical event** for revenue recognition.
Application: Under the accrual-basis of revenue recognition, the critical event is the delivery of the computers to the customers when cash collection is reasonably assured.
Solution: Revenue from customers is $180,000.

Second Step: Determine the expense recognition under the accrual-basis method.

Application: Under the accrual-basis of expense recognition, the matching principle is applied.
Solution: Cost of inventory delivered to customers was $84,000.
　　　　Cost of general operating expenses incurred was $60,000.
　　　　Cash paid for rent was $24,000 but only $2,000 was an expense for June.
　　　　Cash paid to employees for salaries was $30,000.

(B) Final Solution:　　　　　Xavier Computer Corporation
　　　　　　　　　　　　　　Income Statement
　　　　　　　　　　　　　　For the Month Ended June 30, XXXX

Sales	$180,000	
Cost of Goods Sold	84,000	
Gross Profit	$ 96,000	
Operating Expenses:		
Rent	$ 2,000	
General Expenses	60,000	
Salaries	30,000	92,000
Net Income	$ 4,000	

2. Recording Journal Entries

Travelers Service Company, Inc., organizes and leads small group tours to the Hawaiian Islands. During the month of January, Year 2 (the first month of operations), the following transactions occurred:

1/1　Sold 1000 shares of stock to investors for $50,000
1/1　An office was located in town and rent of $1,500 was paid for the first month.
1/3　Office supplies costing $600 were purchased for cash.
1/5　A computer and laser printer were purchased on account for $2,800
1/8　Commissions of $8,500 were billed to clients for services performed.
1/14　Paid for the computer and printer purchased on 1/5
1/20　Cash in the amount of $4,800 is collected from clients for services billed on 1/8
1/30　The electric utility bill in the amount of $225 is received for January.

Required: Prepare journal entries for the month of January.

First Step: Decide which accounts were affected, the dollar amounts, and apply the rules of debit and credit.
Second step: Prepare the journal entry.

Solution:
1/1　　　Cash in the amount $50,000 is received in exchange for capital stock.
　　　　Cash, an asset is increased and debited; capital stock, an owners' equity account is increased and credited

        (DR) Cash   50,000

              (CR) Capital Stock   50,000

Rent is an expense for $1,500 is incurred and cash is paid.
Rent, an expense is increased and debited; cash, an asset is decreased and credited.

        (DR) Rent Expense   1,500

            (CR) Cash   1,500

Office supplies are increased for $600 and cash is paid.
Office supplies, an asset is increased and debited; an asset is decreased and credited.

        (DR) Office Supplies   600

            (CR) Cash   600

A computer is purchased for $2,800 and payment will occur later.
Equipment, an asset is increased and debited; Accounts payable, a liability is Increased and credited.

        (DR) Equipment   2,800

            (CR) Accounts Payable   2,800

Services are performed for clients for $8,500 and will be received later.
Accounts receivable, an asset is increased and debited for $8,500; Service Revenue, a revenue account is increased and credited.

        (DR) Accounts Receivable   8,500

            (CR) Service Revenue   8,500

Cash of $4,200 is received from clients for services rendered.
Cash, an asset is increased and debited; Service Revenue, a revenue account Is increased and credited.

        (DR) Cash   4,200

            (CR)Service Revenue   4,200

The $2,800 owed on the computer is paid.
Accounts payable, a liability is decreased and debited; cash, an asset is decreased and credited.

        (DR) Accounts Payable   2,800

            (CR) Cash   2,800

Cash in the amount of $4,800 is received from clients for amounts owed to the company. Cash, an asset is increased and debited; accounts receivable, an asset is decreased and credited.

(DR) Cash	4,800	
(CR)Accounts Receivable		4,800

The electric utility bill for $225 is received for the month of January, it will be paid in the future. Utility expense, an expense is increased and debited; accounts payable, a liability is increased and credited.

(DR) Utility Expense	225	
(CR) Accounts Payable		225

3. Recording Adjusting and Closing Entries

Fortune's Videos, Ins. Is in the business of renting videos. A partial list of account balances at December 31, Year 5 appears below.

	DR	CR
Supplies	$600	
Rental Tape Library	24,000	
Accumulated Depreciation – Library		9,000
Furniture and Fixtures	8,000	
Accumulated Depreciation – Furniture		3,200
Salary Payable		
Unearned Tape Rental Revenue		900
Retained Earnings	6,800	
Tape Rental Revenue	38,000	
Salary Expense	9,200	
Rent Expense	3,800	
Utilities Expense	1,600	
Depreciation Expense – Library		
Depreciation Expense – Furniture		
Advertising Expense	2,400	
Supplies Expense		

Adjusting Entry information:
1. Depreciation on the rental library, $6,000: on the furniture $1,400
2. Accrued salary expense at December 31, $240
3. Unearned tape revenue earned this year, $600
4. Supplies on hand at December 31, $150

Required A: Prepare adjusting entries at December 31
B: Prepare closing entries at December 31

A: First Step – Determine what type of adjusting entry is required.
  Second Step – Determine the dollar amount to be recorded and the accounts affected.
  Third Step – Prepare the adjusting entry.

1. Depreciation is a prepayment adjustment. The asset has been acquired and must be adjusted for its use. The dollar amount is $6000 for the rental library and $1,400 for the furniture. Accounts affected are depreciation expense and accumulated depreciation. The expense is increased and debited; the asset is used and decreased by a credit to accumulated depreciation (A **contra account** that is deducted from the asset account).

    (DR) Depreciation Expense – Tape Library   6,000
    (DR) Depreciation Expense - Furniture   1,400
        (CR) Accumulated Depreciation – Tape Library   6,000
        (CR) Accumulated Depreciation – Furniture   1,400

2. Accrued salary expense is an accrued expense adjustment for salaries that are part of this period's expense but will be paid for in the future (at the next pay day). The dollar amount of $240 must be recorded as an expense, a debit, and an increase in a payable must be recorded, a credit.

    (DR) Salary Expense   240
        (CR) Salaries Payable   240

3. Unearned tape rental revenue is an adjustment for unearned revenue. This revenue has been collected in cash already but has not been recognized as earned. The dollar amount of $600 has to be recorded as revenue, a credit, and the liability, unearned revenue, must be decreased, a debit

    (DR) Unearned Tape Rental Revenue   600
        (CR) Tape Rental Revenue   600

4. The adjustment for supplies records the supplies used this period as an expense. It is a prepayment adjustment. Supplies purchased earlier cost $600 but only $150 of supplies are on hand at the end of the period. This means supplies in the amount of $450 have been used and must be recorded as an expense. An expense account must be increased, a debit, and an asset account must be decreased, a credit.

    (DR) Supplies Expense   450
        (CR) Supplies   450

B. Prepare the Closing entries

First Step – select the accounts that must be closed.
Second Step – Account balances must be changed to reflect the impact of the adjusting entries.
Third Step – Prepare the closing entry and "zero" out revenue and expense accounts.

Solution:

First Step: Revenue and expense accounts must be closed.
Second Step: The revenue and expense accounts have the following adjusted balances:

	DR	CR
Tape Rental revenue		38,600
Salary Expense	9,440	
Rent Expense	3,800	
Utilities Expense	1,600	
Depreciation Expense – Library	6,000	
Depreciation Expense – Furniture	1,400	
Advertising Expense	2,400	
Supplies Expense	450	

Third Step :

	DR	CR
(DR) Tape Revenue Rental	38,600	
(CR) Salary Expense		9,440
(CR) Rent Expense		3,800
(CR) Utilities Expense		1,600
(CR) Depreciation Expense – Library		6,000
(CR) Depreciation Expense – Furniture		1,400
(CR) Advertising Expense		2,400
(CR) Supplies Expense		450
(CR) Retained Earnings		13,430

Test Yourself

True or False Questions

T F 1.   Accrual accounting recognizes revenue when the cash is collected.

T F 2.   Assets that have been used up in the production of revenues are called liabilities.

T F 3.   The use of accrual accounting may produce large discrepancies between reported profits and the amount of cash generated from operations.

T F 4.   Cash accounting earnings provide a more accurate measure of the economic value added during a period than do the operating cash flows.

T F 5.   The decoupling of measured earnings from operating cash flows is a consequence of accrual accounting.

T F 6.   For most firms, income is earned as a result of a single activity.

T F 7.   The key issue surrounding the recognition of revenue is the issue of timing.

T F 8.   Revenue recognition and the matching of expenses against revenue are the two steps involved in the accounting process of income recognition.

T F 9.   Owner's equity is decreased when income is recognized.

T F 10. When the "critical event" takes place in the revenue earning process, revenue should be recognized.

T F 11. For revenue recognition to take place there must be objective, verifiable evidence of the amount of value that has been added.

T F 12. When John Deere Co. manufactures a tractor it has met both conditions for revenue recognition and should immediately record a sale.

T F 13. Depreciation on factory equipment is a period cost

T F 14. The dominant practice for revenue recognition in most retail and manufacturing businesses is at the time of sale.

T F 15. The recognition of expenses must adhere to the matching principle unless the entity is using the percentage-of-completion method.

T F 16. Costs that are easily traceable to the revenues they helped to produce are called product costs.

T F 17. Costs that are expensed over the time frame benefited are called product costs.
T F 18. Advertising expense is treated as a product cost.

T   F   19.   Income from continuing operations should include only the normal, recurring, more sustainable, ongoing economic activities.

T   F   20.   Gains and losses that occur relatively infrequently and arise from continuing business activities are classified as extraordinary items on the income statement.

T   F   21.   "Special or unusual items" are reported net of income taxes on the income statement.

T   F   22.   Extraordinary items on the income statement are reported net of income taxes.

T   F   23.   Discontinued operations are reported after the cumulative effect of accounting changes on the income statement.

T   F   24.   Disposals of assets and alterations of product lines in response to changes in consumer tastes are usually referred to as discontinued operations.

T   F   25.   A discontinued component of a business is one being eliminated that comprises operations and cash flows that can be clearly distinguished operationally and for financial reporting purposes from the rest of the entity.

T   F   26.   An extraordinary item must meet the criteria of being usual in nature and infrequent in occurrence.

T   F   27.   A moving van is sold by Ace Transfer and Storage and this results in an extraordinary gain.

T   F   28.   A material item that is "special or unusual" is required to be disclosed separately as part of pre-tax income from continuing operations.

T   F   29.   Prior period financial statements are always restated for the income effect of changing to a new principle.

T   F   30.   Past income is never adjusted upon the change of an accounting estimate.

T   F   31.   A change in the reporting entity requires restatement of comparative financial statements for prior years.

T   F   32.   Unrealized gains and losses from translating foreign currency financial statements of majority-owned subsidiaries into U.S. dollar amounts for preparation of consolidated financial statements is an item of other comprehensive income.

T   F   33.   "Other comprehensive income" components that are considered open are reported as direct adjustments to stockholders' equity.

T   F   34.   Comprehensive income provides a measure of all changes in equity of an enterprise that result from transactions with the owners.

Multiple-Choice Questions

Select the best answer from those provided.

_____   1.   Revenues are recognized under the accrual method of accounting when
a. cash is received.
b. cash is received and the revenues are earned.
c. revenues are earned and become measurable.
d. revenues are received and become measurable.

_____   2.   Revenues are recognized under the cash basis when the revenue is
a. received.
b. received and earned.
c. earned and becomes measurable.
d. received and becomes measurable.

> The Howard Corporation sells 200 cases of paper to the Bill Company on December 26 for $2,000. Howard delivers the paper to Bill on December 30, Leo pays $800, and agrees to pay the balance on January 5.

Table 2-1

_____   3.   Refer to Table 2-1.   Under the cash basis, how much revenue is recognized in December?
a. $ 0
b. b. $2000
c. c. $1200
d. d. $800

_____   4.   Refer to Table 2-1. Under the accrual basis, how much revenue is recognized in January?
a. $ 0
b. b. $2,000
c. c. $1,200
d. d. $800

5. Refer to Table 2-1. Using the cash basis, which one of the following entries would record the revenue recognition for December?

a. DR Cash   800
        CR Sales   800

b. DR Cash   2000
        CR Sales   2000

c. DR Cash   800
        DR Accounts Receivable   1,200
            CR Sales   2,000

d. DR Accounts Receivable   2,000
        CR Sales   2,000

6. Refer to Table 2-1. Using the accrual basis, which one of the following entries would properly record the revenue recognition for December?

a. DR Cash   2,000
        CR Sales   2,000

b. DR Cash   800
        CR Sales   800

c. DR Cash   800
        DR Accounts Receivable   1,200
            CR Sales   2,000

d. DR Accounts Receivable   2,000
        CR Sales   2,000

7. An increase in net assets always arises from the
a. payment of an expense.
b. recognition of income.
c. accrual of a liability.
d. investment in new equipment.

8. The "critical event" for revenue recognition is
a. fixed GAAP for every situation.
b. the same for every business.
c. dependent upon the exact nature of the business and industry.
d. easily defined by the FASB.

9. Smith Used Airplanes purchases a plane for $300,000 in the month of May. It sells the plane in the month of August. Which one of the following principles requires that the $300,000 be recognized as an expense in August?
a. revenue recognition principle
b. matching principle
c. historical cost principle
d. full disclosure principle

Mae's Dress Shop had the following costs paid during the month of June
      Inventory purchases $5,000
      Marketing costs   1,000
      Delivery costs   250
Ida sold $4,000 of the inventory in May.

Table 2-2

10.   Refer to Table 2-2. What is the amount of Mae's cash-basis expense for the month of June?
        a. $6,500
        b. $6,250
        c. $6,000
        d. $5,000

11.   Refer to Table 2-2. What is the amount of Mae's June expense when applying the matching principle?
        a. $6,500
        b. $6,250
        c. $5,250
        d. $1,000

12.   Refer to Table 2-2. What type of cost is the delivery expense?
        a. period cost
        b. traceable cost
        c. inventory cost
        d. product cost

13.   Which one of the following costs would be a product cost?
        a. rent of office equipment
        b. factory payroll
        c. sales salaries
        d. office salaries

14.   The process of reporting discontinued operations net of tax on the Income Statement is known as
        a. inter-period income tax allocation.
        b. intra-period income tax allocation.
        c. deferred tax recognition.
        d. accrued tax recognition.

15.   An event that is both unusual in nature and infrequent in occurrence is a/an
   a. ordinary item.
   b. special item.
   c. extraordinary item.
   d. discontinued item.

16.   When a company changes from LIFO to weighted-average inventory method, the change is reported as a/an
   a. cumulative effect change.
   b. error correction.
   c. change in an accounting estimate.
   d. retroactive adjustment.

17.   When a company changes from sum-of-the-years digits depreciation to straight-line depreciation, the change is reported as a/an
   a. cumulative effect change.
   b. error correction.
   c. change in an accounting estimate.
   d. retroactive adjustment.

18.   Harry's Supply House changed an estimate of its salvage value on fixed equipment items.   This change is
   a. treated as a cumulative effect change.
   b. reported as an error correction.
   c. reported as a retroactive adjustment.
   d. only disclosed if it has a material effect on current and future income.

Exercises

1.   The Whitney Company reported revenues of $275,000 on its accrual basis income statement for the month of April. The following information is available:

Accounts Receivable - March 31	$45,000
Accounts Receivable - April 30	37,000
Uncollected accounts recovered during April	5,000

Required: Prepare a schedule to calculate how much revenue is reportable for April under the cash-basis of income determination.

_____

_____

_____

_____

2.   Merten, Inc. operates a retail clothing store. The company reports on the accrual basis and must record the proper amount of accruals for the following expenses at December 31.

a. Merten leases a fax machine for $200 per month, payable at the beginning of each month. The lease calls for an additional $.10 per fax for faxes in excess of 100 per month payable by the end of the following month. In December, 1,250 faxes were made.

b. Merten received a bill from Sooner Natural Gas on January 10 for $320. The bill was for the month of December.

c. Merten received a bill from General Telephone Company for $260 on January 5 with the following charges:

   1.   Normal Monthly Charge - January $100
   2.   Long-distance calls for December   160

Required: Determine the proper amount of December expense for the income statement and accrued liabilities at December 31 for the balance sheet for each of these items.

_____

_____

_____

_____

_____

_____

_____

3.   As the controller of Will International, you are approached by one of your staff who tells you that she needs help in classifying the following accounts as product or period costs.

Required: Identify each of the following as product or period cost by filling in the proper title in the blank.

_____   1.   Depreciation of office equipment.

_____   2.   Factory telephone expense.

_____   3.   Salary of the secretary to the plant foreman.

_____   4.   Transportation charges to deliver finished product to customers.

_____   5.   Fuel for factory machinery.

_____   6.   Rent for the factory building.

_____   7.   Rent for the administrative building.

_____   8.   Administrative salaries expense.

_____   9.   Office electricity.

_____   10.   Freight expense on purchase of raw materials.

4.   Information for the Zipper Company for the year ended December 31, XXXX is presented below.

Sales	$850,000
Administrative Expenses	100,000
Selling Expenses	130,000
Tornado Loss (unusual for the area)	45,000
Cumulative Effect of a Change in Accounting Principle	
(Increase to income)	50,000
Cost of Goods Sold	415,000
Other Revenues	10,000
Other Expenses	5,000

Required: Prepare a multiple-step income statement in proper form for the fiscal year ending December 31, XXXX. Assume a 35% tax rate.

_____

_____

_____

_____

_____

_____

_____

_____

_____

_____

_____

5.   For each of the following items, indicate whether the item is:
      a. Special or unusual item
      b. Discontinued operations
      c. Extraordinary item
      d. Cumulative effect of accounting change
      e. Retroactive change
      f. Change in accounting estimate
      g. Other items

_____   1.   A change from weighted average to LIFO inventory method.

_____   2.   A change in the useful life of an asset from 5 years to 7 years due to changes in technology.

_____   3.   A change from LIFO to FIFO inventory method.

_____   4.   A tornado loss in Maine.

_____   5.   The discontinuance of producing televisions by Sony, Inc.

_____   6.   An earthquake loss in California.

_____   7.   The gain on equipment sold to purchase more updated equipment.

_____   8.   A change in the method of reporting long-term construction projects.

_____   9.   The sale of some of its restaurant chains by Pepsico.

_____   10.   A change from straight-line to double-declining-balance depreciation.

_____   11.   A fire loss of $500,000 in a company whose net income is $1,000,000.

_____   12.   A volcano eruption loss in Hawaii.

_____   13.   A change from FIFO to specific identification inventory method.

_____   14.   A change in the charge for health-care expense due to improved insurance rates.

6.   Harris Learning Systems Inc., engaged in the following transactions during June, Year 3, its first month of operations:

June 1	Received $36,00 from investors and issued capital stock
2	Purchased $800 of office supplies on account
6	Performed services for customers and received cash of $4,00
9	Paid $400 of the accounts payable for supplies
18	Performed services for customers on account, $2,400
26	Received $1,600 from customers on account
27	Paid the following expenses: salaries $1,400; rent $900.

Required : Prepare journal entries for the month of June.

7.   An accountant discovered the following adjustments on December 31, Year 6:

1. Prepaid Insurance, beginning, $800, Payments made during the period $1,200.
    Prepaid insurance, ending $900

2. Interest revenue accrued $600.

3. Unearned service revenue, beginning, $1,800. Unearned service revenue ending $600

4. Depreciation, $4,500

5. Wages expense owed to employees at end of year $9,000 (To be paid on payday).

Required: Prepare adjusting entries for these items.

_____

_____

_____

_____

_____

_____

_____

_____

_____

_____

_____

_____

_____

_____

_____

_____

_____

_____

_____

_____

_____

_____

_____

_____

_____

_____

_____

_____

_____

_____

_____

_____

_____

_____

_____

Solutions

Answers to True or False Questions

True Answers: 3, 5, 7, 8, 11, 14, 16, 19, 22, 25, 28, 30, 31, 32, 33,
False answers explained:
1.   Revenue is recognized when <u>earned and measurable</u>.
2.   Assets used in production of revenues are <u>expenses</u>.
4.   <u>Accrual</u> accounting is a more accurate measure.
6.   Income is earned as a result of <u>many</u> activities.
9.   Owner's equity is <u>increased</u> when income is recognized.
10.   <u>Both</u> the critical event and the <u>condition of measurability</u> must be present to recognize revenue.
12.   Completion of manufacturing does not meet both conditions for revenue recognition.
13.   Depreciation on the factory equipment is a <u>product</u> cost.
15.   Recognition of expenses must <u>always</u> adhere to matching principle.
17.   Costs related only to time are <u>period</u> costs.
18.   Advertising expense is a <u>period</u> cost.
20.   Continuing operations are <u>not</u> an <u>extraordinary</u> item.
21.   Special or unusual items are part of <u>operating</u> income and <u>not</u> shown net of tax.
23.   Discontinued operations are reported <u>before</u> extraordinary items and cumulative effect.

24.   Consumer taste modifications are treated as a normal, <u>recurring</u> part of doing business.
26.   Extraordinary items are <u>unusual</u> in nature and infrequent in occurrence.
27.   Sale of a productive asset is <u>not</u> an extraordinary item as both conditions are not met.
29.   Prior period financial statements are <u>generally not</u> restated for changes in accounting principle.
34.   Comprehensive income <u>excludes</u> transactions with owners.

Answers to Multiple-Choice Questions

1.	C	4.	A	7.	B	10.	B
2.	A	5.	A	8.	C	11.	C
3.	D	6.	C	9.	B	12.	A

13.   B   Cash expenses: Purchases $10,000, Marketing $2,000, Delivery Costs $500.

14.   B   Accrual expenses: Cost of Goods Sold $8,000, Marketing $2,000, Delivery Costs $500.

15.	C	17.	A
16.	D	18.	D

Solutions to Exercises

1.

Whitney Company
Reconciliation of Accrual to Cash-Basis Income
For the Month Ended April 30, XXXX

Accrual-Basis Revenues	$275,000	
Add: Decrease in Accounts Receivable		8,000
Uncollectible Accounts Recovered		5,000
Cash-Basis Revenues	<u>$288,000</u>	

2.

December Expenses		December 31 Liabilities:	
Fax Expense	$315	Account Payable on Fax	$215
Utilities Expense	320	Utility Payable	320
Telephone Expense	260	Account Payable on Telephone	160

3.   Product costs: 2, 3, 5, 6, 10
       Period costs: 1, 4, 7, 8, 9

4.

Zipper Company

Income Statement

For the Year Ended December 31, XXXX

Sales		$ 850,000
Cost of Goods Sold		415,000
Gross Profit		$ 435,000
Administrative Expenses	$100,000	
Selling Expenses	130,000	230,000
Income from Operations		$ 205,000
Other Revenue	$ 10,000	
Other Expenses	(5,000)	5,000
Income before Taxes		$ 210,000
Income Tax Expense		(73,500)
Income before Extraordinary Item		$ 136,500
Tornado Loss (net of $36,000 tax effect)		(29,250)
Cumulative Effect of Accounting Principle Change (net of $40,000 tax effect)		32,500
Net Income		$ 139,750

5.

1.	G	6.	A	11.	C
2.	F	7.	A	12.	A
3.	E	8.	E	13.	D
4.	C	9.	A	14.	F
5.	G	10.	D		

6.

June	1	(DR) Cash	36,000	
		(CR) Capital Stock		36,000
	2	(DR) Supplies	800	
		(CR) Accounts Payable		800
	6	(DR) Cash	4,000	
		(CR) Service Revenue		4,000
	9	(DR) Accounts Payable	400	
		(CR) Cash		400
	18	(DR) Accounts Receivable	2,400	
		(CR) Service Revenue		2,400
	26	(DR) Cash	1,600	
		(CR) Accounts Receivable		1,600
	27	(DR) Salaries Expense	1,400	
		(DR) Rent Expense	900	
		(CR)		2,300

7.

1.	(DR) Insurance Expense	1,100	
	(CR) Prepaid Insurance		1,100
2.	(DR) Interest Receivable	900	
	(CR) Interest Payable		900
3.	(DR) Unearned Service Revenue	1,200	
	(CR) Service Revenue		1,200
4.	(DR) Depreciation Expense	4,500	
	(CR) Accumulated Depreciation		4,500
5.	(DR) Wages Expense	9,000	
	(CR) Wages Payable		9,000

CHAPTER 3

Additional Topics in
Income Determination

Chapter Review

Learning Objective 1:
The conditions under which it is appropriate to recognize revenue and profits either before or after the point of sale.

Revenue is usually recognized at the point of sale because it is the earliest point when the conditions of having the critical event take place, the amount is measurable and collection is reasonably assured have occurred. However there are cases when these conditions are met either before or after the sale. In these cases, revenue and profit recognition can occur before the sale at production or after the sale when the cash is collected.

Learning Objective 2:
The procedures for recognizing revenue and adjusting associated asset values in three specific settings – long-term construction constructs, agricultural commodities and installment sales.

Long-term construction project revenue is recognized under two methods:
1. Percentage-of-completion method: Preferred GAAP method which recognizes a proportional amount of the revenue each year based on the percentage of costs incurred to date. (Recognition is <u>during</u> production.)
2. Completed-contract method: Used only when costs cannot be reliably estimated. Revenue is recognized only at the contract completion.
(See Demonstration Problem 1.)

Agricultural commodities are often recognized at the <u>completion</u> of production under two different assumptions:
1. Completed transaction (sales) method: Recognizes income only on transactions completed within the period.

Example: Jones harvests 5,000 bushels of wheat at a time when the market price is $2.00/bushel. The wheat cost $1.00/bushel to produce. His inventory cost is $1.00/bushel. If he sells 3,000 bushels on the harvest date in Period 1, he records:

Revenues	$6,000	(3,000 x $2.00)
Expenses	3,000	(3.000 x $1.00)
Income from Sale	$3,000	

If he sells the remaining bushels for $3.50 in Period 2, he will recognize in that period:

Revenues	$7,000	(2,000 x $3.50)
Expenses	2,000	(2.000 x $1.00)
Income from Sale	$5,000	

2. Market price (production) method: Recognizes income earned at the completion of production based on the market price for that date. Sales after that time report the difference between the harvest price and the subsequent price as a holding gain or loss on speculation.

Example: Same as above. In period 1 Jones recognizes income at the point of harvest for all bushels produced.

Revenues	$10,000	(5,000 x $2.00)
Expenses	5,000	(5.000 x $1.00)
Income from Sale	$ 5,000	(Production revenue)

His inventory cost of the 2,000 remaining bushels is $4,000 or the market price at the date of harvest.
In Period 2, he records the following additional income:

Revenues	$7,000	(2,000 x $3.50)
Expenses	4,000	(2,000 x $2.00)
Income from Sale	$3,000	(Speculation gain)

Installment sales recognize income after the sale as cash is collected when the risk of non-collection is high and there is no reasonable basis for estimating the uncollectable portions. Revenue recognition is based on the gross profit percentage of the original sale times the cash collected. (See **Demonstration Problem 2**.)

Learning Objective 3: Specialized application of revenue recognition principles for franchise sales, sales with right of return, and "bundled" software sales with multiple deliverables.

In a **franchise** arrangement, the franchisor gives the exclusive right to sell a product or service in a given area and use the franchisor's name to the franchisee. Typically there are two types of payments involved in the arrangement:
1.   An initial franchise fee, all or part of which is paid to the franchisor when the agreement is signed with the remainder due in installments (with interest) over a specified period.
2.   Continuing or periodic fees that are generally based on a percentage of sales generated by the franchisee.

Accounting for periodic fees received by the franchisor are recorded as revenue in the period they are received and earned. Initial franchise fees pose a greater challenge. The initial franchise fee is composed of two elements:
1. Payment for the right to operate a franchise in a given area.
2. Payment for services to be performed by the franchisor.
SFAS No. 45 specifies that revenue from initial franchise fees should be recognized when all material services or conditions relating to the sale have been substantially performed or satisfied by the franchisor. This is

not easily discernable, opening the way for revenue recognition abuses to occur.

In certain industries companies experience high rates of return of their products. Due to the magnitude of the returns, questions arise concerning the recognition of revenue. Should revenue be recognized at the time of sale or be deferred until the product returns are resolved? *SFAS No. 45* specifies that for a seller to record revenue at the time of sale when **right of return** exists, the following criteria must be met:

1. The seller's price to the buyer is fixed or determinable at the time of sale.
2. The buyer has paid the seller, or the buyer is obligated to pay the seller and the obligation is not contingent on the resale of the product.
3. The buyer's obligation to the seller does not change in the event of theft or physical destruction or damage of the product.
4. The buyer acquiring the product for resale has economic substance and exists separate and distinct from the seller.
5. The seller does not have significant obligations for future performance to directly bring about resale of the product to the buyer.
6. The amount of future returns can be reasonably estimated.

When **all** six conditions are met, the seller can estimate sales returns for the period and properly record them. When any of these conditions are not met, then sales revenue and related cost of sales are deferred and recognized when the return privilege has expired or when the conditions are met, whichever occurs first.

Bundled sales occur when vendors bundle products and sell them for a lump-sum price. The key accounting issue related to bundled sales is the timing of the revenue recognition. How much of the revenue should be recognized at time of sale and how much should be deferred and recognized as the seller satisfies its commitment for other deliverables as specified in the contract.

SOP 97-2 states that if a software sales arrangement includes multiple, distinct elements, then the revenue from the arrangement should be allocated to the various elements based on vendor specific objective evidence of the element's relative fair value.

Learning Objective 4: How the flexibility in GAAP for income determination invites managers to manipulate or manage earnings.

Management must use judgment in applying the criteria for revenue and expense recognition. This can lead to exploitation of the flexibility in GAAP to manipulate reported earnings and hide the "true" performance of the company. Research seems to indicate that some companies are using these tactics to manage earnings upward to meet or beat earning projections.

Learning Objective 5:
The various techniques used to manage earnings.

Five different vehicles have been identified as ploys used by firms to manage earnings:

1. **"Big Bath" restructuring charges** – Excessive restructuring charges have been taken by management, thereby leading to large one-time write-offs that are not viewed adversely by stock prices. These charges can be reversed in future years when a boost to the bottom line is needed.

2. **Creative acquisition accounting and purchased R & D** – Purchased research and development costs are immediately expensed resulting in an economic asset that never appears on the balance sheet. If revenues materialize from these projects in the future, there are no offsetting charges to expense leading to a classic mismatching of revenues and expenses that appears as future excessive profits. Goodwill, on the other hand, must be capitalized and amortized under present GAAP. To avoid the goodwill drag on future earnings, some firms allocate as much as possible to in – process R&D activities that are written off immediately.

3. **Miscellaneous "cookie jar reserves"** – Estimated expenses with accrued liabilities are unrealistic in amount so that a firm can over-reserve in good times and cut back, or even reverse previous charges, when times are bad. These reserves become an income smoothing device.

4. **International errors deemed to be "immaterial" and international bias in estimates** – Management intentionally misapplies GAAP and when caught by the auditor argues the item is immaterial and not worth correcting. A series of these immaterial errors could have a material affect on the bottom line. Companies can also intentionally misstate estimates to achieve a desired earnings target.

5. **Premature or aggressive revenue recognition** – Revenues can be recognized before they have been "earned" (critical event criterion) or become "realized" (measurability criterion).

Learning Objective 6:
SEC guidance on revenue recognition designed to curb earnings management.

The SEC in *Staff Accounting Bulletin 101,* identifies the following criteria for revenue recognition:
1. Persuasive evidence of an exchange arrangement exists.
2. Delivery has occurred or services have been rendered.
3. The seller's price to the buyer is fixed or determinable, and
4. Collectibility is reasonably assured.

These criteria are intended to close some loopholes in how GAAP is applied in practice.

Learning Objective 7:
How error corrections and restatements of

Accounting errors and irregularities can occur due to simple oversight, disagreement on how to account for a given transaction, or if management attempts to exploit the flexibility in GAAP or commit

| prior period financial statements are reported. | financial fraud to overstate income and inflate assets. Material errors discovered after the year in which the error is made are corrected through a **prior period adjustment.** This results in an adjustment of the company's beginning retained earnings balance and correction of related asset or liability balances. |

Glossary of Terms

Completed-Contract Method	A method of revenue recognition on long-term projects that delays revenue recognition until the project has been completed.
Franchise	An arrangement where the franchisor (seller) gives the franchisee (buyer) the exclusive right to sell a product or service in a given locale and use the franchisor's name for a specified period of time.
Installment Sales Method	A method of revenue recognition used when the risk of non-collection is high or it is impractical to estimate the amount of uncollectibles. Under this method of revenue recognition, the gross profit on sales is deferred and recognized in subsequent periods when the installment receivables are collected in cash.
Market Price Method	A method of revenue recognition whereby revenue is recognized when the product is ready to go to market not when actually sold. A readily determinable market price must be available.
Percentage-of-Completion Method	A method of revenue recognition applied to long-term construction contracts, that calls for revenue recognition as the construction process progresses.
Point of Sale Revenue Recognition	Revenue is recognized when product is sold or services provided. This is the earliest point to determine the criteria for revenue recognition.
Prior Period Adjustment	An adjustment to the beginning balance of retained earnings to correct an error of a previous time period.

Demonstration Problems

1.   Long-term Construction Projects

Philadelphia Ship Yard is building a large military ship for a contract price of $60,000,000. This is estimated to be a two-year project with an estimated cost of $48,000,000. The following information is available:

	Year 1	Year 2
Costs Incurred	$20,000,000	$26,000,000
Estimated Completion Costs	$28,000,000	$0
Billings on Construction in Progress	16,000,000	$44,000,000
Cash Collected	$10,000,000	$50,000,000

Required: Make the journal entries required each year assuming (A) the percentage-of-completion method and (B) the completed-contract method.

(A)   **First Step:** Determine the **critical event** for revenue recognition.
Application: Under the percentage-of-completion method, revenue recognition is measured by a computation of the costs incurred during the period divided by the total estimated costs of the project times the estimated gross profit on the project.
Solution:

	Year 1	Year 2
Costs Incurred To Date	$20,000,000	$46,000,000
Estimated Completion Costs	$28,000,000	$0
Total Estimated costs	$48,000,000	$46,000,000
Project Contract Price	$60,000,000	$60,000,000
Total Estimated Costs	$48,000,000	$46,000,000
Estimated Gross Profits	$12,000,000	$14,000,000

Revenue recognized: Year 1
Cost incurred to date x Estimated gross profit = Revenue Recognition
Total estimated costs
$20,000,000   x $12,000,000 = $5,000,000
$48,000,000

Revenue recognized: Year 2
Cost incurred to date x Estimated gross profit = Revenue — Prior Recognition = Current Revenue

Total estimated costs
$46,000,000   x $14,000,000 = $14,000,000 — $5,000,000 = $9,000,000

$46,000,000

Second Step: Record the journal entries for Year 1 and Year 2
Year 1
1. Record the costs incurred:
   DR Inventory: Construction in Progress   20,000,000
   CR Accounts Payable, Cash, etc.   20,000,000

2. To record customer billings:
   DR Accounts Receivable   16,000,000
          CR Billings on Construction in Progress   16,000,000

3. To record cash received:
   DR Cash   10,000,000
          CR Accounts Receivable   10,000,000

4. To record income recognized:
   DR Inventory: Construction in Progress   5,000,000
          CR Income on Long-term Construction Contract   5,000,000

Year 2
1. Record the costs incurred:
   DR Inventory: Construction in Progress   26,000,000
          CR Accounts Payable, Cash, etc   26,000,000

2. To record customer billings:
   DR Accounts Receivable   44,000,000
          CR Billings on Construction in Progress   44,000,000

3. To record cash received:
   DR Cash   50,000,000
          CR Accounts Receivable   50,000,000

4. To record income recognized:
   DR Inventory: Construction in Progress   9,000,000
          CR Income on Long-term Construction Contract   9,000,000

5. To record completion and acceptance of project:
   DR Billings on Construction in Progress   60,000,000
          CR Inventory: Construction in Progress   60,000,000

(B)   First Step: Determine the **critical event** for revenue recognition.
      Application: Under the completed contract method, revenue recognition recognized at
      the completion of the project.

Solution:

	Total contract price
	$60,000,000
Total costs	$46,000,000
Total profit	$14,000,000

Second Step: Record the journal entries for Year 1 and Year 2
<u>Year 1</u>
1. <u>Record the costs incurred:</u>
   DR Inventory: Construction in Progress   20,000,000
   CR Accounts Payable, Cash, etc   20,000,000

2. <u>To record customer billings:</u>
   DR Accounts Receivable   16,000,000
       CR Billings on Construction in Progress   16,000,000

3. <u>To record cash received:</u>
   DR Cash   10,000,000
       CR Accounts Receivable   10,000,000

<u>Year 2</u>
1. <u>Record the costs incurred:</u>
   DR Inventory: Construction in Progress   26,000,000
       CR Accounts Payable, Cash, etc   26,000,000

2. <u>To record customer billings:</u>
   DR Accounts Receivable   44,000,000
       CR Billings on Construction in Progress   44,000,000

3. <u>To record cash received:</u>
   DR Cash   50,000,000
       CR Accounts Receivable   50,000,000

4. <u>To record completion and acceptance of project:</u>
   DR Billings on Construction in Progress   60,000,000
       CR Inventory: Construction in Progress   46,000,000
       CR Income on Long-term Construction Contract   14,000,000

> **The heart of the matter . . .**
> The only difference in the journal entries between the percentage-of-completion and the completed-contract method is that there is no annual charge to the inventory account and recognition of revenue in the completed-contract method. Therefore, in the final entry, the credit to Inventory: Construction in Progress is for the amount of the total costs and the income is recognized in full.

2. Installment Sales Method

The Stone Company sells appliances to low income families on the installment basis. There is a high rate of non-collection on these contracts.

Required:

A. Complete the following table by filling in all blank information.
B. Prepare all journal entries for Year 2.

	Year 1	Year 2	Year 3
Installment Sale	$600,000	$800,000	$900,000
Cost of Installment Sales	$450,000	560,000	585,000
Gross Profit	$_____	$_____	$_____
Gross Profit %	_____%	_____%	_____%
Cash Collections:			
Year 1	$200,000	$240,000	$120,000
Year 2		280,000	240,000
Year 3			360,000
Gross Profit Recognized:			
Year 1	$_____	$_____	$_____
Year 2		$_____	$_____
Year 3			$_____
Total Gross Profit Recognized			
for the year	$_____	$_____	$_____

A. First Step: Compute gross profit for each year.
   Application: Gross Profit = Sales - Cost of Goods Sold

Solution:	Year 1	Year 2	Year 3
Sales — Cost of Goods Sold	$150,000	$240,000	$315,000

Second Step: Compute gross profit percentage.
Application: Gross Profit % = Gross Profit / Sales

Solution:	Year 1	Year 2	Year 3
Gross Profit/Sales	25%	30%	35%

Third Step: Compute gross profit recognized.
Application: Gross profit recognized = Cash collected for Year A sales x Year A gross profit %

Solution:	Year 1	Year 2	Year 3
Year 1	$200,000 x 25%	$240,000 x 25%	$120,000 x25%
Year 2	$280,000 x 30%	$240,000 x 30%	$360,000 x35%

A.   **Final Solution:** Complete table by adding the recognized gross profit amounts for each year.

	Year 1	Year 2	Year 3
Installment Sales	$600,000	$800,000	$900,000
Cost of Installment Sales	450,000	560,000	585,000
Gross Profit	150,000	240,000	315,000
Gross Profit %	25 %	30 %	35 %
Cash Collections:			
Year 1	$200,000	$240,000	$120,000
Year 2		280,000	240,000
Year 3			360,000
Gross Profit Recognized:			
Year 1	$ 50,000	$ 60,000	$ 30,000
Year 2		84,000	72,000
Year 3			126,000
Total Gross Profit Recognized for the year	$ 50,000	$ 144,000	$228,000

B.   Record the journal entries for Year 2:
       Application: Use the information from the table to complete the journal entries.

1. Record the installment sales for the current year.
    DR Accounts Receivable-Year 2 Sales   800,000
        CR Installment Sales   800,000

2. Record the cost of the installment sales removed from inventory for the current year.
    DR Cost of Installment Sales   560,000

            Inventory   560,000

3. Record the cash received from all customers during the current year. Separate the cash collections by the year of sale.

DR Cash	520,000	
CR Accounts Receivable - Year 1 Sales		240,000
CR Accounts Receivable - Year 2 Sales		280,000

4. Record the deferral of gross profit for the current year sales.

DR Installment Sales	800,000	
CR Cost of Installment Sales		560,000
CR Deferred Gross Profit-Year 2 Sales		240,000

5. Recognize the realized gross profit related to cash collections during the year.

DR Deferred Gross Profit-Year 1 Sales	60,000	
DR Deferred Gross Profit-Year 2 Sales	84,000	
CR Realized Gross Profit on Installment Sales		144,000

Test Yourself

True or False Questions

T F 1. The construction of a cruise ship would probably qualify to use the percentage-of-completion method for revenue recognition.

T F 2. The completed contract method is often used when it is possible to determine expected long-term construction costs with a high degree of reliability.

T F 3. The "critical event" for revenue recognition in the mining of gold is the actual extraction of the gold ore.

T F 4. Revenue recognition may be deferred where the risk of non-collection is unusually low and where there is no reasonable basis for estimating the proportion of accounts likely to prove uncollectable.

T F 5. Interest on installment contracts should be reported separately on the financial statements.

T F 6. The difficulty in franchise accounting arises from the recognition of the initial franchise fee.

T F 7. Sales with rights of return must meet six conditions to avoid deferral of sales and cost of sales until the return period expires.

T F 8. A prior period adjustment is recorded as an adjustment to the ending retained earnings balance.

Multiple-Choice Questions

Select the best answer from those provided.

_____ 1. Which one of the following businesses is likely to recognize revenue during the production phase?
a. potato farmer
b. silver mining company
c. cruise ship builder
d. rent-to-own appliance dealer

_____ 2. Which one of the following businesses is likely to recognize revenue at the completion of production?
a. home builder
b. potato farmer
c. military aircraft contractor
d. rent-to-own appliance dealer

_____ 3. Which one of the following businesses is likely to recognize revenue after the time of the sale?
a. oil well drilling contractor
b. potato farmer
c. home builder
d. rent-to-own appliance dealer

_____ 4. When losses occur on long-term contracts using the percentage-of-completion method, they are recognized
a. proportionately over the contract period using costs incurred as a base.
b. evenly over the contract period.
c. in their entirety as soon as is becomes known that a loss will be suffered.
d. at the completion of the project.

_____ 5.   Which one of the following entries would be made in the last year of a long-term construction contract to record the completion and acceptance of a $10,0000,000 project that cost $7,500,000 using the completed-contract method of revenue recognition?

a. DR Construction in Progress   10,000,000
        CR Billings on Construction in Progress   10,000,000

b. DR Billings on Construction in Progress   10,000,000
        CR Construction in Progress   7,500,000
        CR Income on Long-Term Construction Contract
        Contract   2,500,000

c. DR Construction in Progress   7,500,000
    DR Income on Long-Term Construction
        Contract   2,500,000
        CR Billings on Construction in Progress   10,000,000

d. DR Billings on Construction in Progress   2,500,000
        CR Construction in Progress   2,500,000

_____ 6.   When losses occur on long-term contracts using the completed-contract method, they are recognized
a. proportionately over the contract period using costs incurred as a base.
b. evenly over the contract period.
c. in their entirety as soon as is becomes known that a loss will be suffered.
d. at the completion of the project.

Table 3-1
The Sims Potato Company has completed the fall harvest with 5,000,000 pounds of premium potatoes. The potatoes cost $150,000 from planting to harvest and the market price of the potatoes on the day they are placed in storage is $.50 per pound. Sims sells 3,200,000 pounds in Year 1 and holds the remaining 1,800,000 until Year 2 when it sells for $.75 per pound.

_____ 7.   Refer to Table 3-1. Using the completed transaction sales method, how much net revenue should Sims recognize in Year 1?
a. $1,504,000
b. $1,600,000
c. $2,500,000
d. $3,200,000

_____ 8.   Refer to Table 3-1. Using the market price production method, how much net revenue should Sims recognize in Year 1?
a. $150,000
b. $2,350,000
c. $2,500,000
d. $3,200,000

Exercises

1.   The Lion Company sells retirement homes in a coastal area and properly reports revenues on the installment basis.

Required:
A.   Complete the following table by filling in all blank information.

	Year 1	Year 2	Year 3
Installment Sales	$1,200,000	$1,400,000	$1,600,000
Cost of Installment Sales	800,000	990,000	1,200,000
Gross Profit	$400,000	$_____	$_____
Gross Profit %	33.33 %	_____%	_____%
Cash Collections:			
Year 1	$408,000	$360,000	$480,000
Year 2		480,000	440,000
Year 3			560,000
Gross Profit Recognized:			
Year 1	$ 136,000	$_____	$_____
Year 2		$_____	$_____
Year 3			$_____

Total Gross Profit Recognized
           for the year $ 136,000 $_____ $_____

B.   Prepare all journal entries required in Year 2.

_____

_____

_____

_____

_____

_____

_____

_____

_____

_____

_____

_____

_____

_____

_____

_____

_____

_____

_____

_____

_____

2.   United Ship Yard is building a large cruise ship for a contract price of $200,000,000.
        This is estimated to be a three-year project with an estimated cost of $168,000,000.
        United uses the percentage-of-completion method of revenue recognition. The following
        information is available:

(In $ Thousands)	Year 1	Year 2	Year 3
Costs Incurred during year	$42,000	$90,000	$44,000
Estimated Completion Costs	126,000	42,000	0
Billings on Construction-in-Progress	40,000	80,000	80,000
Cash collected	20,000	80,000	100,000

Required: (Round all answers to the nearest thousand.)

A. Compute the amount of gross profit to be recognized in Year 1, Year 2, and Year 3.

Show computations in good form.

B. Prepare all the journal entries required in Year 2.

C. Prepare the journal entry required in Year 3 to acknowledge completion and acceptance of the project.

_____

_____

_____

_____

_____

D.   Indicate the Balance Sheet presentation of current assets (omit Cash) for these items at the end of Year 2.

_____

_____

_____

_____

_____

_____

Solutions

Answers to True or False Questions

True Answers: 1, 3, 5, 6, 7.
False answers explained:
2.   Completed contract method is permissible when it is <u>not</u> possible to determine expected costs with a high degree of certainty.
4.   Revenue recognition can be deferred when the risk of non-collection is <u>high</u>.
8.   A prior period adjustment is recorded as an adjustment to the beginning retained earnings balance.

Answers to Multiple-Choice Questions

1.   C
2.   B
3.   D
4.   C
5.   B
6.   C

7.   A   Cost per bushel $150,000/5,000,000 pounds = $.03
            Sales = 3,200,000 pounds x $.50 = $1,600,000

Cost = 3,200,000 pounds x $.03 =   96,000
Net Income $1,504,000

8.   B   Sales = 5,000,000 pounds x $.50 = $2,500,000
             Cost = 5,000,000 pounds x $.03 =   150,000
             Net Income $2,350,000

Solutions to Exercises

1.

A.	Year 2	Year 3
Installment Sales	$1,400,000	$1,600,000
Cost of Installment Sales	910,000	1,200,000
Gross Profit	$490,000	$400,000
Gross Profit %	35%	25%
Cash Collections:		
Year 1	$360,000	$480,000
Year 2	480,000	440,000
Year 3		560,000
Gross Profit Recognized:		
Year 1	$ 120,000	$ 160,000
Year 2	$ 168,000	$ 154,000
Year 3		$ 140,000
Total Gross Profit Recognized for the year	$288,000	$554,000

B.DR Accounts Receivable-Year 2 Sales   1,400,000
        CR Installment Sales   1,400,000

DR Cost of Installment Sales   910,000
        Inventory   910,000

    DR Cash   840,000
            CR Accounts Receivable - Year 1 Sales   360,000
            CR Accounts Receivable - Year 2 Sales   480,000

    DR Installment Sales   1,400,000
            CR Cost of Installment Sales   910,000
            CR Deferred Gross Profit-Year 2 Sales   490,000

DR Deferred Gross Profit-Year 1 Sales	120,000	
DR Deferred Gross Profit-Year 2 Sales	168,000	
CR Realized Gross Profit on		
Installment Sales		288,000

2.

A. Year 1 Gross Profit recognized: $8,000,000
$$\frac{42,000}{168,000} \times \$32,000,000 = \$8,000,000$$

Year 2 Gross Profit recognized: $5,862,000
$$\frac{132,000}{174,000} \times \$26,000,000 = \$19,724,000 — \$8,000,000 = \$11,724,000$$

Year 3 Gross Profit recognized: $4,276,000
$$\frac{176,000}{176,000} \times \$24,000,000 = \$24,000,000 — \$19,274,0000 = \$4,276,000$$

B. DR Inventory: Construction in Progress	90,000,000	
CR Cash, Accounts Payable, etc.		90,000,000
DR Accounts Receivable	80,000,000	
CR Billings on Construction in Progress		80,000,000
DR Cash	80,000,000	
CR Accounts Receivable		80,000,000
DR Inventory: Construction in Progress	11,724,000	
CR Income on Long-term Construction		
Contract		11,724,000
C. DR Billings on Construction in Progress	200,000,000	
CR Inventory: Construction in Progress		200,000,000

D.

United Ship Yard
Balance Sheet
December 31, Year 2

<u>Current Assets</u>

Accounts Receivable	$20,000,000
Inventory: Construction in Progress	151,724,000
Less: Billings on Construction in Progress	(120,000,000)

CHAPTER 4

STRUCTURE OF THE BALANCE SHEET
AND STATEMENT OF CASH FLOWS

Chapter Review

Learning Objective 1:
How the various asset,
liability and stockholders'
equity accounts on a
typical corporate balance
sheet are measured and
classified.

The balance sheet presents an expansion of the **accounting equation**.

Assets = Liabilities + Stockholders' Equity

Assets present the resources of the firm (assets), while the liabilities and equity represent the financing provided by creditors and owners. Thus, the balance sheet presents the capital structure of the entity, ie., how much of a company's assets are financed from debt versus equity sources. Management must address various capital structure issues in determining corporate strategy. The balance sheet also provides information for assessing the short-term liquidity of an enterprise, as well as long-term solvency.

FYI. . .
Balance sheets are
economic stocks — values
at a given point in time.

A number of different valuation techniques are used to present balance sheet accounts. The following is a summary of the evaluation methods used for reporting each type of balance sheet account:

Account	Valuation Method
Cash	**Current market price**
Short-term debt investments	**Current market value**
Short-term equity investments	Current market value
Net accounts receivable	**Net realizable value**
Inventories	**Lower of cost or market**
Property, plant and equipment	**Depreciated historical cost**
Accounts payable	Historical cost
Accrued liabilities	Historical cost
Long-term debt	**Discounted present value**
Deferred income taxes	Historical cost
Common stock	Par value
Additional paid-in capital	Historical sales price minus par value
Retained earnings	Mixture of values

Learning Objective 2:
How to use balance sheet
information to understand
key differences in the
nature of the firm's
operations and how those

A common-size balance sheet is prepared by expressing all items as a percentage of total assets or, equivalently as a percentage of total liabilities, plus stockholders' equity. By comparisons between balance sheet items, the conclusions drawn demonstrate how users can learn about the underlying economics and nature of the firm's operations that generated those numbers.

operations are financed.

Learning Objective 3:
Differences in balance sheet terminology and presentation format in countries outside the United States.

Balance sheet formats and account titles can be very different in other countries. Many European countries present assets beginning with fixed assets followed by the current assets displayed in order of increasing liquidity. Different sub-totals are sometimes presented in order to make liquidity and solvency assessments.

Account titles on foreign balance sheets can have different meanings and may be unique to the GAAP of the country. In the United Kingdom, stocks is the common term for inventory and the "Debtors" account is the equivalent of accounts receivable in the United States. In the stockholders' equity section the financial statement user may find accounts that have no U.S. counterpart. This includes the "capital redemption reserve" tied to treasury stock, and the "revaluation reserve" which results from a revaluation of fixed assets.

Financial statement users must be aware of differences they will encounter in statement format terminology, and in measurement and recognition criteria when working with non-U.S. financial statements.

Learning Objective 4:
The information provided in footnotes on significant accounting policies, subsequent events and related party transactions.

Footnotes are an integral part of companies' financial statements that provide a wealth of information to better understand and interpret the numbers presented. Three important notes typically found in companies reports are:

1. The **summary of significant accounting policies:** which explains the important accounting choices that the reporting entity uses to account for selected transactions and accounts.
2. The disclosure of **subsequent events**: transactions that occur after the close of a companies' fiscal year, but before the financial statements are issued. These events must be disclosed when they are material and likely to influence an investors' appraisal of the risk and return prospects of the entity
3. A **related party transaction** occurs when a company enters into a transaction with individuals or other businesses that are in some way connected with it or its management. Due to the risk of these transactions, they must be disclosed in a footnote

Learning Objective 5:
How successive balance sheets and the income statement can be used to determine cash inflows and outflows for a period.

Although the <u>recording</u> of accounting data for balance sheet accounts is usually historical cost, the <u>reporting</u> of balance sheet accounts is often a mixture of measurement bases. Users should recognize the effects that different measurement bases have when aggregating numbers across accounts and computing ratios used in inter-company comparisons.

As we have seen, the balance sheet represents the basic accounting equation:

$$\text{Assets} = \text{Liabilities} + \text{Stockholders' Equity}$$

Learning Objective 6:
How information provided in the cash flow statement can be used to explain changes in non-cash accounts on the balance

Because balance sheets measure stocks, they are presented at a point in time. Two successive balance sheets (1 and 2) compared to each other provide the following mathematical representation:

$$\text{Assets}_{(2)} = \text{Liabilities}_{(2)} + \text{Stockholders' Equity}_{(2)}$$

minus

sheet.

$$\text{Assets}_{(1)} = \text{Liabilities}_{(1)} + \text{Stockholders' Equity}_{(1)}$$

equals

$$\Delta \text{ Assets} = \Delta \text{ Liabilities} + \Delta \text{ Stockholders' Equity}$$

If the assets are separated into cash and non-cash assets, the equation reads:

$$\Delta \text{ Cash} + \Delta \text{ Non-cash Assets} = \Delta \text{ Liabilities} + \Delta \text{ Stockholders' Equity}$$
and
$$\Delta \text{ Cash} = \Delta \text{ Liabilities} - \Delta \text{ Non-cash Assets} + \Delta \text{ Stockholders' Equity}$$

Therefore, the change in the cash account during the period can be explained by the changes in the other components of the balance sheet during the period. Two successive balance sheets and the income statement for the period that bridges the two balance sheets are used to prepare the cash flow statement. Therefore, the cash flow statement will explain the changes in the non-cash accounts on the balance sheet from the beginning to the end of the period.

The heart of the matter. . .

To get a quick picture of where a company is investing its resources, and the source of the funds the company is using to make these investments, read the cash flow statement carefully. The cash flow statement gives a good synopsis of the company's activities because it explains all the changes in the non-cash accounts on the balance sheet.

Net income is <u>not</u> equal to the net change in cash because of three reasons:

1.   The income statement is prepared on the accrual basis of accounting and not all operating transactions are cash transactions.

2.   Changes in cash are also a result of capital transactions from investments.

3.   Some changes in cash are related to changes in liabilities and owners' transactions.

Learning Objective 7:
The distinction between operating, investing, and financing sources and uses of cash.

The cash flow statement presents the cash inflows and outflows in the three major activity areas of the firm. Firms operate, invest in, and finance operations and investments. For cash flow purposes, these activities are defined as:

1.   **Operating Activities**: cash inflows and outflows from the normal business activities that produce revenue. Normal

business activities include extending credit to customers and using credit terms for purchases and expenses.

2.   **Investing Activities**: cash inflows and outflows related to buying and selling investments, making loans to others, and buying and selling assets used to generate revenues.

3.   **Financing Activities**: cash inflows and outflows from issuing and repurchasing stocks and bonds, borrowing and repaying loans, and paying dividends.

The heart of the matter. . .

Operating cash flows should provide for the needs of investing and financing activities because both investing and financing activities have a finite limit. The only renewable source of cash is from the operations of the company, which is limited only by the capacity to produce and/or sell products or services.

Learning Objective 8: How changes in current asset and liability accounts can be used to adjust accrual earnings to obtain cash flows from operations.

The **indirect approach** to presenting operating cash flows adjusts net income to cash flow from operations by reflecting the changes in various current asset and current liability accounts. The general rule is that increases in current assets and decreases in current liabilities (excluding Notes Payable) use more cash than the income statement reflects, <u>and</u> decreases in current assets and increases in current liabilities (excluding Notes Payable) become sources of cash by retaining cash in the company. Depreciation, amortization, and depletion are expenses without cash payments that must be added to net income to compute cash flow from operations.

The heart of the matter. . .

To adjust income to net cash flow from operations:

	Net income	
Plus:	Depreciation, amortization, and depletion	
	Decreases in current assets	
	Increases in current liabilities	
Minus:	Increases in current assets	
	Decreases in current liabilities	
Equals:	**Cash flow from operations**	

(See Demonstration Problem 1)

Investing activities describe changes in long-term assets, investments, and loans made to non-customers. Inflows result from sales of these assets or collections of loans. Cash outflows are used to purchase non-current assets or make loans. Financing activities describe changes in loans (both short-term and long-term Notes Payable), other long-term liabilities, and stockholders' equity. Financing inflows include cash borrowings, sale of common or preferred stock, or resale of treasury stock. Financing outflows include payment of dividends, repayment of loans, and purchase of treasury stock. Although interest expense represents the cost of borrowing, *SFAS No. 95* specifically defines interest expense as an operating cash outflow. **(See Demonstration Problem 2)**

Glossary of Terms

Additional Paid-in Capital	An account that reflects the amounts in excess of par or stated value that were received by the corporation when the shares of stock were originally sold.
Balance Sheet	The financial statement that summarizes the assets of the entity, the liabilities incurred to finance the assets, and the shareholders' equity representing the amount of financing provided by the owners of the entity.
Contra-Asset Account	An account that appears in the balance sheet as a deduction from an asset account.
Current Assets	Assets expected to be converted into cash within the next twelve months or within the operating cycle if the operating cycle is longer than twelve months.
Current Liabilities	Debts or obligations expected to be settled from current assets within the next twelve months or within the operating cycle if longer.
Deferred Income Taxes	Taxes on income recognized in current and prior periods that will not be paid to the government until future periods.
Direct Method	A method of preparing the statement of cash flows which reports the individual operating cash inflows and outflows in a direct manner.
Fair Value	The amount at which an asset could be bought or sold in a current transaction between willing parties, that is, other than a forced liquidation or sale.
Historical Cost	The expression of the amount of net dollar units arising from past transactions.
Indirect Method	A method used for preparing the statement of cash flows that attempts to derive cash flows from operations by adjusting earnings for the differences between accrual basis revenues and expenses and cash inflows and outflows.
Lower of Cost or Market	The measurement base applied to assets which depends upon the relationship between historical cost and current market price (fair value).
Monetary Assets	Those assets which are fixed in dollar amounts irrespective of price changes.
Non-Monetary Assets	Those assets such as inventory or buildings that are not fixed in dollar amounts.

	It is this potential for changing value that is the distinguishing characteristic of non-monetary items.
Operating Cycle	The elapsed time beginning with the initiation of production and ending with the eventual cash collection of the receivables generated from the sale of the finished product.
Par Value	A dollar amount determined in articles of incorporation which establishes the carrying amount for the common stock on the balance sheet.
Related Party Transaction	A transaction that occurs between a company and individuals or businesses that are connected to it or its management.
Retained Earnings	The account that measures the cumulative earnings less dividend distributions of the company since its inception.
Statement of Cash Flow	The financial statement that provides a detailed summary of the cash inflows and cash outflows derived from the three primary activities of operations, financing and investing.
Subsequent Event	An event or transaction that occurs after the close of the fiscal year but before the financial statements are issued.
Summary of Significant Accounting Policies	The footnote that explains the important accounting choices that the reporting entity uses to account for selected transactions and accounts.
Translation	The use of the current rate of exchange for foreign currency units to convert monetary assets into dollars.

Demonstration Problems

1.   **Preparing an Indirect Method Operating Section of the Cash Flow Statement**

Jupiter Corporation
Comparative Balance Sheets
December 31, Year 1 and Year 2

Assets	Year 1	Year 2
Cash	$ 40,000	$ 12,000
Accounts Receivable	80,000	140,000
Inventory	460,000	420,000
Prepaid Expenses	20,000	48,000
Plant & Equipment (net)	900,000	980,000
Total Assets	$1,500,000	$1,600,000

Liabilities and Stockholders' Equity		
Accounts Payable	$ 72,000	$ 48,000

Accrued Liabilities	12,000	40,000
Long-term Debt	300,000	260,000
Common Stock	600,000	700,000
Retained Earnings	516,000	552,000
Total Liabilities and Stockholders' Equity	$1,500,000	$1,600,000

Additional Information for Year 2:

Depreciation Expense	$ 40,000
Net Income for Year 2	80,000

Required: Prepare the indirect method operating activities section of the Cash Flow Statement for Year 2.

First Step: Determine which balance sheet accounts provide information for the operating section of the cash flow statements.

Application: Current assets (except investments and loans to non-customers) and current liabilities (except for Notes Payable) will provide information necessary for computing cash flow from operations.

Solution:

Assets	Year 1	Year 2
Cash	$ 40,000	$ 12,000
Accounts Receivable	**80,000**	**140,000**
Inventory	**460,000**	**420,000**
Prepaid Expenses	**20,000**	**48,000**
Plant & Equipment (net)	900,000	980,000
Total Assets	$1,500,000	$1,600,000

Liabilities and Stockholders' Equity		
Accounts Payable	**$ 72,000**	**$ 48,000**
Accrued Liabilities	**12,000**	**40,000**
Long-term Debt	300,000	260,000
Common Stock	600,000	700,000
Retained Earnings	516,000	552,000
Total Liabilities and Stockholders' Equity	$1,500,000	$1,600,000

Second Step: Compute the change in the affected balance sheet accounts.

Application: Subtract Year 1 from Year 2 to determine the change.

Solution:	Year 1	Year 2	Difference
Accounts Receivable	80,000	140,000	+ 60,000
Inventory	460,000	420,000	— 40,000
Prepaid Expenses	20,000	48,000	+ 28,000
Accounts Payable	72,000	48,000	— 24,000
Accrued Liabilities	12,000	40,000	+ 28,000

Third Step: Determine other information needed to compute the operating cash flows.

Application: Preparing the indirect method operating section of the cash flow statement requires

net income and depreciation from the income statement.
Solution: Net income is $80,000 and depreciation expense is $40,000.

Final Solution: Apply the formula on page 46.

Jupiter Corporation
Statement of Cash Flows
For the Year Ended December 31, Year 2

Operating Cash Flows:

Net Income			$80,000
Plus: Depreciation		$ 40,000	
Decrease in inventory		40,000	
Increase in accrued liabilities		28,000	108,000
Minus: Increase in accounts receivable		$(60,000)	
Increase in prepaid expenses		(28,000)	
Decrease in accounts payable		(24,000)	(112,000)
Cash Flows from Operations			$76,000

2.   Preparation of the Cash Flow Statement

Prepare the whole cash flow statement for Jupiter Corporation for Year 2.

First Step: Identify the balance sheet accounts that contain evidence of investing activities.
Application: Investing activities describe changes in long-term assets, investments, and loans made to non-customers.
Solution:

Assets	Year 1	Year 2
Cash	$ 40,000	$ 12,000
Accounts Receivable	80,000	140,000
Inventory	460,000	420,000
Prepaid Expenses	20,000	48,000
Plant & Equipment (net)	**900,000**	**980,000**
Total Assets	$1,500,000	$1,600,000

Second Step: Compute the cash flow from investing activities.
Application: Determine the change in the net plant and equipment account.

Solution: Prepare a T-account to analyze the change in net plant and equipment.

	Plant & Equipment (net)		
Beginning Balance	900,000		
Purchase of Assets	120,000		
		40,000	Year 2 Depreciation
Ending Balance	980,000		

The purchase of assets is backed into with the following computation:

Beginning Balance — Current Depreciation = Ending Balance — Equipment Purchases

$900,000 — $40,000 = $980,000 — Equipment Purchases

Therefore: Purchases = $980,000 — $900,000 + $40,000 = $120,000

Third Step: Determine the balance sheet accounts that contain evidence of financing activities.

Application: Financing activities describe changes in loans, other long-term liabilities, and stockholders' equity.

Solution:

Liabilities and Stockholders' Equity	Year 1	Year 2
Accounts Payable	$ 72,000	$ 48,000
Accrued Liabilities	12,000	40,000
Long-term Debt	300,000	260,000
Common Stock	600,000	700,000
Retained Earnings	512,000	552,000
Total Liabilities and Stockholders' Equity	$1,500,000	$1,600,000

Fourth Step: Compute the cash flow from financing activities.

Application: Subtract Year 1 from Year 2 to determine the change.

Solution:

	Year 1	Year 2	Difference
Long-term Debt	300,000	260,000	— 40,000
Common Stock	600,000	700,000	+ 100,000
Retained Earnings	516,000	552,000	+ 36,000

The decrease in long-term debt is evidently a repayment of the debt. The increase in common stock indicates a new issuance of common stock. The change in retained earnings is a combination of net income and dividends paid. Prepare a T-account to analyze the change in retained earnings.

	Retained Earnings	
Beginning Balance		516,000
		80,000 Net Income
Dividends Declared	44,000	
Ending Balance		552,000

Back into the amount of dividends with the following computation:

Beginning Balance + Net Income = Ending Balance + Dividends

$516,000 + $80,000 = $512,000 + Dividends

Therefore: Dividends = $516,000 + $80,000 — $552,000 = $44,000

Final Solution:

Jupiter Corporation
Statement of Cash Flows
For the Year Ended December 31, Year 2

Operating Cash Flows:

Net Income			$ 80,000
Plus:	Depreciation	$ 40,000	
	Decrease in inventory	40,000	
	Increase in accrued liabilities	28,000	108,000
Minus:	Increase in accounts receivable	$(60,000)	
	Increase in prepaid expenses	(28,000)	
	Decrease in accounts payable	(24,000)	(112,000)
	Cash Flows from Operations		$ 76,000

Investing Cash Flows:

Purchase of long-term assets		(120,000)

Financing Cash Flows:

Repayment of long-term loans	$(40,000)	
Issuance of common stock	100,000	
Payment of dividends	(44,000)	
Cash Flow from Financing Activities		16,000
Net Change in Cash		$(28,000)

Test Yourself

True or False Questions

T F   1.   The cash account for a company that consists exclusively of U. S. dollar amounts is reported at current market value.

T F   2.   Property, plant and equipment is reported at acquisition cost.

T F   3.   Long term debt is reported on the balance sheet at discounted present value.

T F   4.   Debt and equity securities held for short-range investment purposes are to be carried at cost.

T F   5.   Net accounts receivable are reported at their original historical cost.

T F   6.   Accounts payable are reported on the balance sheet at their historical cost.

T F   7.   Retained earnings measures the cumulative earnings of a corporation minus dividends since inception.

T F   8.   A subsequent event must be disclosed in a footnote in all circumstances.

T F   9.   A related party transaction footnote should include the nature of the relationship, a description of the transaction, and the dollar amount involved.

T F 10.   The statement of cash flows shows why the financial structure of the firm has changed between two balance sheet dates.

T F 11.   Reported net income will usually equal cash flow from operating activities.

T F 12.   Cash flow statements are not required to be prepared to have a complete set of financial statements.

T F 13.   The sale of merchandise inventory for cash gives rise to cash flow from operations.

T F 14.   The cash purchase of a delivery truck for a pizza shop is an example of an investing activity.

T F 15.   The issue of bonds for cash represents a financing activity.

T F 16.   Cash dividends paid by a corporation are classified as cash flows from operations.

T F 17.   The purchase of treasury stock for cash is a financing activity.

T F 18.   To adjust accrual earnings to cash flow from operations, a decrease in accounts receivable should be added to the accrual basis income.

T F 19.   A decrease in merchandise inventory should be added to accrual basis income to change it to cash flows from operations.

T F 20.   An increase in deferred revenues should be subtracted from accrual basis income to determine cash flow from operations.

T F 21.   An increase in accrued expenses should be subtracted from cash flow from operations to arrive at accrual basis income.

T F 22.   The indirect approach in preparing the statement of cash flows does not show individual operating cash inflows and outflows.

T F 23.   Depreciation expense should be added to net income to arrive at cash flow from operations.

T F 24.   Amortization expense should be subtracted from net income to arrive at cash flow from operations.

Multiple-Choice Questions

Select the best answer from those provided.

_____ 1.   The accounting equation is expressed in the
  a. income statement.
  b. Statement of cash flow.

    c. balance sheet.

    d. Statement of changes in stockholders' equity.

_____ 2.   The conversion to cash within one year is a requirement for an asset to be classified as

    a. fixed.

    b. long-term.

    c. current.

    d. intangible.

_____ 3.   Land is always measured on the balance sheet at

    a. liquidation value.

    b. current market price.

    c. realizable future value.

    d. historical cost.

_____ 4.   Which one of the following is a monetary asset?

    a. Notes Receivable

    b. Investment in Equity Securities

    c. Timber Reserves

    d. Inventory

_____ 5.   A delivery truck owned by a moving company is reported on the balance sheet at

    a. current market value.

    b. historical cost.

    c. historical cost minus accumulated depreciation.

    d. net realizable value.

_____ 6.   Accounts Payable are reported on the balance sheet at

    a. current market value.

    b. historical cost.

    c. discounted present value.

    d. future value.

_____ 7.   A note payable to First State Bank, due in five years, is reported on the balance sheet at

    a. current market value.

    b. historical cost.

    c. discounted present value.

    d. future value.

_____ 8.   The Common Stock account is reported on the balance sheet at the

    a. par value.

    b. current market value.

    c. net realizable value.

      d. discounted present value.

_____ 9.   A combination of different valuation bases is always used for reporting
      a. Cash.
      b. Land.
      c. Accounts Payable.
      d. Retained Earnings.

_____ 10.   The acquisition of equipment in exchange for common stock of the corporation gives rise to
      a. cash flow from operating activities.
      b. cash flow from investing activities.
      c. cash flow from financing activities.
      d. no cash activities.

_____ 11.   The payment of a dividend by Smith Corporation gives rise to a cash outflow from
      a. operating activities.
      b. investing activities.
      c. financing activities.
      d. no cash activities.

_____ 12.   The cash purchase of the stock of another company gives rise to a cash outflow from
      a. operating activities.
      b. investing activities.
      c. financing activities.
      d. no cash activities.

The Matthew Smith Company provides the following information from its Year 1 and Year 2 balance sheets:

	Year 1	Year 2
Accounts Receivable	$240,000	$200,000
Inventory	280,000	260,000
Prepaid Insurance	24,000	8,000
Prepaid Rent	80,000	40,000
Accounts Payable	200,000	160,000

The following information is available from the Year 2 income statement:

Sales	$900,000
Cost of Goods Sold	500,000
Insurance Expense	16,000
Rent Expense	80,000

Table 4-1

_____   13.   Refer to Table 4-1. How much cash did Smith collect from customers in Year 2?
        a. $460,000
        b. $940,000
        c. $900,000
        d. $860,000

_____   14.   Refer to Table 4-1. How much cash did Smith pay for inventory during Year 2?
        a. $400,000
        b. $480,000
        c. $520,000
        d. $500,000

_____   15.   Refer to Table 4-1. How much cash did Smith pay for insurance during Year 2?
        a. $40,000
        b. $ 8,000
        c. $24,000
        d. $ 0

_____   16.   Refer to Table 4-1. How much cash did Smith pay for rent during Year 2?
        a. $80,000
        b. $60,000
        c. $40,000
        d. $ 0

_____   17.   Refer to Table 4-1. Assuming that the information provided from the income
               statement represents all of the pre-tax income of the Matthew Smith Company,
               what is the difference between the accrual-basis and cash-basis income in Year 2?
        a. Accrual exceeds cash basis by $76,000.
        b. Cash exceeds accrual basis by $76,000.
        c. Accrual exceeds cash basis by $60,000.
        d. Cash exceeds accrual basis by $60,000.

Table 4-2

> The following information is available from Harry Ames, Inc. comparative balance sheets for Years 3 and 4:
>
> | | Year 4 | Year 3 |
> |---|---|---|
> | Land | $70,000 | $55,000 |
> | Buildings (net) | 200,000 | 150,000 |
> | Notes Payable to Banks | 112,500 | 100,000 |
> | Common Stock | 112,500 | 100,000 |
> | Additional Paid-in Capital | 95,000 | 75,000 |
> | Retained Earnings | 300,000 | 120,000 |
>
> Additional information is available:
> 1. The Year 4 income statement shows Depreciation Expense of $25,000.
> 2. Net income for Year 4 is $225,000.
> 3. Land was acquired for 1,000 shares of common stock at a market price of $15 per share. The stock has a par value of $10.
> 4. Harris borrowed $62,500 during the year from its bank.

_____ 18.   Refer to Table 4-2. How much cash did Ames pay to purchase land if no land was disposed of during Year 4?
    a. $20,000
    b. $10,000
    c. $15,000
    d. $ 0

_____ 19.   Refer to Table 4-2. How much cash did Ames repay to the bank on loans during Year 4?
    a. $100,000
    b. $625,000
    c. $ 50,000
    d. $ 10,000

_____ 20.   Refer to Table 4-2. How much cash did Ames pay to purchase buildings if no building was disposed of during Year 4?
    a. $ 75,000
    b. $ 25,000
    c. $ 50,000
    d. $200,000

_____ 21.   Refer to Table 4-2. What was the sales price per share of Ames' common stock sold in Year 4?
    a. $10
    b. $15

               c. $18
               d. $20

_____   22.   Refer to Table 4-2. How much cash did Ames pay to stockholders in the form of dividends during Year 4?
               a. $ 50,000
               b. $ 0
               c. $125,000
               d. $225,000

Exercises

1.   For the balance sheet items listed below, indicate how they are measured on the year-end balance sheet. Select the appropriate letter from the following list:
     A   Historical Cost
     B   Amortized (or Depreciated) Cost
     C   Market (Fair) Value
     D   Lower of Cost or Market
     E   Discounted Present Value
     F   Combination of all bases

_____   1.   Accounts Payable

_____   2.   Bonds Payable

_____   3.   Short-term Investment in stock of competitor

_____   4.   Short-term Investment in Bonds

_____   5.   Deferred Income Taxes

_____   6.   Retained Earnings

_____   7.   Goods to be resold to customers

_____   8.   Accrued Liabilities

_____   9.   Buildings

_____   10.   Land

2.   For each of the following selected transactions of the Hisker Corporation, indicate whether the transaction is a cash flow operating activity (O), investing activity (I), financing activity (F), or other activity (N).

_____   1.   Sale of treasury stock.

_____   2.   Declaration of a cash dividend.

_____   3.   Purchase of supplies.

_____   4.   Borrowing from the bank to purchase land.

_____   5.   Exchange of common stock for the acquisition of land.

_____   6.   Collection of an account receivable.

_____   7.   Purchase of a competitor's company.

_____   8.   Repurchase of common stock.

_____   9.   Payment of accrued liabilities.

_____   10.   Purchase of equity securities classified as current assets.

_____   11.   Purchase of equipment for cash.

_____   12.   Conversion of a bond investment into a common stock investment.

3.   Bob Beaves Company is a sole proprietorship that sells chemical supplies to college
     science labs. The following is the comparative balance sheets for Years 1 and 2 with
     additional information.

Bob Beaves Company
Comparative Balance Sheets
December 31, Year 1 and Year 2

Assets	Year 1	Year 2
Cash	$ 15,000	$ 12,000
Accounts Receivable	25,000	38,000
Inventory	120,000	115,000
Prepaid Expenses	5,000	7,000
Plant & Equipment (net)	250,000	240,000
Total Assets	$415,000	$412,000

Liabilities and Capital	Year 1	Year 2
Accounts Payable	$ 8,000	$ 7,000
Accrued Liabilities	3,000	2,000
Long-term Debt	88,000	85,000

Capital	316,000	311,000
Total Liabilities and Capital	$415,000	$412,000

Additional Information for Year 2:

Depreciation Expense	$ 4,000
Net Income for Year 2	12,500

Required: Prepare the operating activities section of the Cash Flow Statement for Year 2 using the indirect method.

_____

_____

_____

_____

_____

_____

_____

_____

_____

_____

_____

_____

_____

4.   King Corporation engaged in the following transactions during Year 4:

Cash purchase of equipment	$600,000	Sale of 10-year bonds	$800,000
Long-term bank borrowing	500,000	Cash purchase of land	120,000
Sale of treasury stock	100,000	Payment of cash dividend	140,000
Declaration of cash dividend	200,000	Cash purchase of long-term	
Acquisition of equipment in		debt securities	120,000
exchange for common stock	400,000		

Required: Prepare the investing and financing sections of the Statement of Cash Flows for the King Corporation for Year 4.

_____

_____

_____

_____

_____

_____

_____

_____

_____

_____

5.   The controller of Clark, Inc. presents you with the following information and asks you to prepare a schedule showing the cash flow from operations for the company for Year 5.

Increase (Decrease) in account balance:

Cash	$ 10,000
Accounts receivable	200,000
Inventory	(150,000)
Prepaid expenses	(20,000)
Accounts payable	(15,000)
Wages payable	20,000
Long-term debt	10,000
Common stock	300,000
Retained earnings	35,000
Net income	$ (85,000)
Depreciation	25,000
Amortization	120,000

Required: Prepare the cash flow from operations section of the Statement of Cash Flows using the indirect method.

_____

_____

_____

_____

_____

_____

_____

_____

_____

_____

_____

_____

_____

_____

_____

_____

6.

Moser Corporation
Balance Sheet (in $ Thousands)
December 31, Year 3

Assets		
Cash		$ 200
Accounts Receivable (net)		1,000
Inventory		1,200
Land		200
Building	$400	
Allowance for Depreciation	(200)	200
Equipment	$1,600	
Allowance for Depreciation	(800)	800
Total Assets		$3,600
Liabilities and Stockholders' Equity		
Accounts Payable		$ 224
Accrued Liabilities		136
Long-Term Notes Payable		800
Common Stock ($1 Par Value)		800
Additional Paid-in Capital		500
Retained Earnings		1,140
Total Liabilities and Stockholders' Equity		$3,600

Moser Corporation
Statement of Cash Flows (in $ Thousands)
For the Year Ended December 31, Year 3

Operating Cash Flows:		
Net Income		$ 300
Plus: Depreciation ($40,000 Building)	$ 240	
Decrease in Inventory	140	
Increase in Accounts payable	88	468

Minus: Gain on sale of equipment	$ (40)	
Increase in Accounts receivable	(180)	
Decrease in Accrued liabilities	(24)	(244)
Cash Flow from Operations	$ 524	
Investing Cash Flows:		
Purchase of equipment	$(400)	
Purchase of land	(100)	
Sale of equipment (Cost $50,000)	40	
Cash Flow from Investing		(460)
Financing Cash Flows:		
Payment of long-term debt	$(200)	
Sale of common stock (200,000 shares)	400	
Payment of dividend	(124)	
Cash Flow from Financing		76
Net Change in Cash		$ 140

Required: From the financial statements provided, prepare the balance sheet for December 31, Year 2.

_____

_____

_____

_____

_____

_____

_____

_____

_____

_____

_____

_____

_____

_____

_____

_____

_____

_____

_____

_____

_____

_____

_____

_____

Solutions

Answers to True or False Questions

True answers: 1, 3, 6, 7, 9, 10, 13, 14, 15, 17, 18, 19, 22, 23
False answers explained:
2.   Property, plant and equipment is reported at depreciated historical cost..
4.   Debt and equity securities should be carried at <u>market value</u>.
5.   Net accounts receivable are reported at <u>net realizable value</u>.
8.   A subsequent must be disclosed when <u>material.</u>
11.   Reported net income will usually <u>not</u> equal cash flow from operations.
12.   Cash flow statements <u>are required</u> along with the balance sheet and the income statement.
16.   Dividends are classified as <u>financing</u> activities.
20.   An increase in accrued expenses should be added to determine cash flow from operations.
21.   The decrease in accrued expenses should be <u>added</u> to obtain cash flow.
24.   Amortization should be added back.

Answers to Multiple-Choice Questions

1.	C	4.	A	7.	C	10.	D
2.	C	5.	C	8.	A	11.	C
3.	D	6.	B	9.	D	12.	B

13.   B   Sales $900,000 + A/R Decrease $40,000 = $940,000

14.   B   COGS $500,000 + decrease in Inventory $20,000 — decrease in A/P $40,000 = $480,000

15.   D   Insurance Expense $16,000 — Decrease in Prepaid Insurance $16,000 = $0

16.   C   Rent Expense $80,000 — Decrease in Prepaid Rent $40,000 = $40,000

17.   B

	Cash Basis	Accrual Basis
Revenue	$940,000	$900,000
Cost of Goods Sold	(520,000)	(500,000)
Insurance	(0)	(16,000)
Rent	(40,000)	(80,000)
Net Income	$380,000	$304,000

18.   D   Common Stock (1,000 sh. @ $15) $15,000 — net change in account $15,000 = $0

19.   C   N/P Beg. Balance $100,000 + Borrowing $62,500 — Ending N/P Balance $112,500 = $50,000

20.   A   Ending Building Balance $200,000 + Depr. Expense $25,000 — Beg. Building Balance $150,000 = $75,000

21.   D

Common Stock Ending Balance	$ 125,000
+ Additional Paid in Capital Ending Balance	95,000
— Land (1,000 shares)	(15,000)
— Common Stock Beg. Balance	(100,000)
— Additional Paid in Capital Beg. Balance	(75,000)
Amount received for stock sold	$ 30,000

Change in Common Stock Account = $25,000 / Par Value $10 = 2,500 shares issued.
Amount received $30,000 /1,500 shares = $20 each

22.   A   Beg. R/E Balance $125,000 + Net Income $225,000 — Ending R/E Balance $300,000 = $50,000 dividend

Solutions to Exercises

1.
1.	A	5.	A	9.	B
2.	E	6.	F	10.	A
3.	C	7.	D		
4.	C	8.	A		

2.
1.	F	5.	N	9.	O
2.	N	6.	O	10.	I
3.	O	7.	I	11.	I
4.	F	8.	F	12.	N

3.

Bob Beaves Company
Statement of Cash Flows

For the Year Ended December 31, Year 2

Operating Cash Flows:

Net Income		$ 12,500
Plus:		
Depreciation	$ 4,000	
Decrease in Inventory	5,000	
Increase in Accounts Payable	6,000	15,000
Minus:		
Increase in Accounts Receivable	$(13,000)	
Increase in Prepaid Expenses	(2,000)	
Decrease in Accrued Liabilities	(1,000)	(16,000)
Cash Flow from Operations		$ 11,500

4.

King Corporation
Statement of Cash Flows
For the Year Ended December 31, Year 4

Investing Cash Flows:

Purchase of equipment	$(600,000)	
Purchase of securities	(120,000)	
Purchase of Land	(120,000)	
Investing Cash Flow	$(840,000)	

Financing Cash Flows:

Bank borrowings	$ 500,000	
Sale of bonds	800,000	
Sale of treasury stock	100,000	
Payment of cash dividends	(140,000)	
Financing Cash Flows		1,260,000

5.

Clark, Inc.
Statement of Cash Flows
For the Year Ended December 31, Year 5

Operating Cash Flows:

Net Income		$(85,000)
Plus: Depreciation	$ 25,000	
Amortization	120,000	
Decrease in Inventory	150,000	
Decrease in Prepaid expenses	20,000	

Increase in Wages payable	20,000	335,000
Minus: Increase in Accounts receivable	$(200,000)	
Decrease in Accounts payable	(15,000)	(215,000)
Cash flow from operations		$ 35,000

6.

Moser Corporation
Balance Sheet (in $ Thousands)
December 31, Year 3

Assets

Cash		$ 60
Accounts Receivable (net)		820
Inventory		1,340
Land		100
Building	$400	
Allowance for Depreciation	(160)	240
Equipment	$1,300	
Allowance for Depreciation	700)	600
Total Assets		$3,160

Liabilities and Stockholders' Equity

Accounts Payable		$ 136
Accrued Liabilities		160
Long-Term Notes Payable		1000
Common Stock ($1 Par Value)		600
Additional Paid-in Capital		300
Retained Earnings		964
Total Liabilities and Stockholders' Equity		$3,160

Explanations:

	Ending Balance	Change	Beginning Balance
Cash	$ 200	— $ 140	$ 60
Accounts Receivable	1000	— 180	820
Inventory	1200	+ 140	1340
Land	200	— 100	100
Building	400	+ 0	400
Accum. Depr.	200	— 40	160
Equipment	1600	— 400 + 100	1,300
Accum. Depr.	800	— 120 + 20	700
Accounts Payable	224	— 88	136
Accrued Liabilities	136	+ 24	160
Long-term Notes	800	+ 200	1000
Common Stock	800	— 200	600
Paid-in Capital	5000	— 200	300
Retained Earnings	1140	— 300 + 124	964

CHAPTER 5

ESSENTIALS OF
FINANCIAL STATEMENT ANALYSIS

Chapter Review

Learning Objective 2: Why analysts worry about the quality of financial statement information, and how quality is determined.

Financial analysts use three main tools to analyze a company's financial statements:

1. **common size statements,**
2. **trend statements, and**
3. **financial ratios.**

Analysts use three main types of analysis techniques.

1. **Time-series analysis** identifies trends over time for a business unit. For example, trend statements are a time-series analysis and comparing the ratios of a company over a length of time becomes a time-series analysis.

2. **Cross-sectional analysis** identifies similarities and differences across companies or business units for the same point in time. Examples include comparing the common-size statements or the ratios of two companies for the same time periods.

3. **Benchmark comparisons** measure a company's performance against a predetermined standard. For example, comparing a firm's ratios against the industry average uses the industry statistics as a benchmark.

FYI. . .
Raw accounting data is **disaggregated** data. Financial statements condense or **aggregate** this data into meaningful information. The process of aggregating the data serves as a filter.

The quality of the analysis depends upon the underlying integrity of the accounting data and reporting. Management's choice of accounting principles also affects the reporting and analysis results and serves as a filter between the raw data and the financial reports. Accounting alternatives allow management to plan the results of its financial reporting. However, the full disclosure principle requires management to disclose its accounting policies. Through full disclosure, analysts can adjust the reported numbers to mitigate distortions caused by management-selected accounting policies.

Knowledge of the company and its industry is critical for informed

FYI. . .
Companies such as
**Moody's, Standard &
Poors, Value Line**, and
**Robert Morris &
Associates** provide
industry information
and averages.

financial statement analysis. An analyst gains knowledge of the
company from studying company history and **time-series** financial
information such as comparative **common-size** and **trend** statements,
and the company's **financial ratios** over a period of time. **(See
Demonstration Problem 1.)** The analyst gains industry information
from published materials or industry associations. **Cross-sectional**
comparisons with major competitors can be made by careful
examination of competitor's common-size and trend statements, and
financial ratios for the same period of time. **Benchmark comparisons**
can be made for the firm and competitors by contrasting the company's
ratios to the industry averages. **(See Demonstration Problem 2.)**

The heart of the matter . . .
Common-size statements and ratio analysis provide the easiest comparison
methods of two companies of relatively different sizes. Trend statements
provide a clear indication of growth and decline for one company. Ratio
analysis indicates changes in the composition of the financial statement
elements for one company or differences in the financial statement elements
between two companies.

Learning Objective 1:
How competitive forces
and a company's
business strategy
influence its
profitability and the
composition of its
balance sheet.

Successful companies strive to outperform the competition. The
strategies adopted by firms give rise to differences in cost structures
which create differences in the financial ratios. Two strategies that
consistently provide superior performance results are:
1.   product and service **differentiation**, and
2.   **low-cost leadership**.

A product and service **differentiation** seeks to focus customers on the
quality, value, or uniqueness of the firm's offering to build customer
loyalty. Some companies distinguish themselves by offering superior
service with quality products that can be purchased from others. Such
companies differentiate the service delivery instead of the product.
Differentiation allows the company to maintain or increase the profit
margin on such products or services.

FYI. . .
Differentiation
strategies are used by
the most successful
companies. Look at the
Fortune list of the "best
companies" for
examples.

The **low-cost leadership** strategy focuses customers on product pricing.
 Some customers are willing to sacrifice service and luxury for cost
savings. Successful firms utilize high sales volume to generate cost
savings from quantity discounts, economies of scale, an efficient
administrative structure, and zealous cost containment. A low-cost
leadership strategy requires constant vigilance because of the highly
competitive industry environment.

Most successful companies are able to combine the two strategies to
some degree. The quest is to achieve a **competitive advantage** over

some degree. The quest is to achieve a **competitive advantage** over rivals. Analysts find evidence of competitive advantage in the financial ratios.

Analysts rely on four major types of ratios:
1.   profitability;
2.   asset utilization (or activity);
3.   short-term liquidity risk; and
4.   long-term solvency risk.

The heart of the matter...
There is a connection between profitability, liquidity, and solvency. Poor profitability leads to illiquidity. Illiquidity leads to bankruptcy or insolvency. Insolvency leads to liquidation. Profitable companies can become illiquid without good cash management. Profitability, liquidity, and solvency problems can be cured with vigilant financial management and strong strategic planning.

Profitability ratios are divided into two major areas:
1.   measuring the profitable employment of the firm's assets; and
2.   measuring the profitable employment of the equity provided by investors.

Learning Objective 3: How return on assets (ROA) can be used to analyze a company's profitability, and what insights are gained from separating ROA into its profit margin and asset turnover components.

Return on Assets (ROA) examines the profitable use of the firm's assets. The firm wants to measure how well it employs the assets to create sustainable after-tax profits, ignoring interest expense, and including some adjustments related to accounting quality concerns.

$$ROA = \frac{\textbf{Net Operating Profit After Taxes (NOPAT)}}{\textbf{Average Total Assets}}$$

Notice that Net Income is not used as the numerator. NOPAT adjusts three items of net income:
1.   removes nonoperating and nonrecurring items;
2.   adds back after-tax interest expense; and
3.   adjusts for distortions caused by off-balance sheet items that might affect both earnings and assets.

The ROA calculation has two components:
1.   **Operating Profit Margin = NOPAT / Sales** and
2.   **Asset Turnover = Sales / Average Total Assets**.

$$ROA = \frac{NOPAT}{Sales} \quad x \quad \frac{Sales}{Average\ Total\ Assets}$$
$$= Operating\ Profit\ Margin\ x \quad Asset\ Turnover$$

This illustrates mathematically that the only two ways to increase ROA are to increase the Operating Profit Margin or the Asset Turnover.

are to increase the Operating Profit Margin or the Asset Turnover. Operating Profit can be further decomposed to examine different components of revenue and expenses. Asset Turnover can be decomposed to examine current and long-term asset utilization.

Analysts compare the company's ROA to the benchmark of the **competitive floor**. Intense competition tends to drive the ROA of its members toward the competitive floor. A firm that performs above its industry's competitive floor possesses a competitive advantage. A firm must vigorously pursue low-cost leadership and differentiation strategies to maintain its superior performance.

Learning Objective 5: How short-term liquidity risk differs from long-term solvency risk, and what financial ratios are used to assess these two dimensions of credit risk.

Creditors pay particular attention to asset utilization (activity), short-term liquidity, and long-term solvency ratios. Credit risk is a combination of the:

1. **ability to repay** a loan from cash generated by operations, asset sales, or other borrowings, <u>and</u>
2. management's **willingness to pay** the debt after prioritizing cash needs.

Cash flow statements are an important source of information for those assessing credit risk because the statement breaks down cash flow into cash provided by operating, investing, and financing activities. Such information aids in assessing credit risk.

Analysts compute and analyze the following ratios:
<u>Short-term Liquidity Ratios</u>

1. **Current Ratio** — indicates the ability to meet short term obligations from cash, marketable securities, receivables, and inventory.
   Current Ratio = Current Assets / Current Liabilities

2. **Quick Ratio** (also called the Acid Test Ratio)— indicates the immediate ability to meet short-term obligations from cash, marketable securities, and receivables.
   Quick Ratio = <u>Current Assets — Inventory</u>
   Current Liabilities

3. **Days Receivable Outstanding** — measures the number of days on average it takes to collect accounts receivable. This ratio also provides information about the quality of receivables management. The days should be slightly higher than the normal sales terms to reflect good management.
   Days Receivable Outstanding = 365 days / A/R Turnover

4. **Days Inventory Outstanding** — measures the number of days

it takes the firm to sell its inventory. The higher the number of days, the greater the risk of inventory obsolescence.
Days Inventory Outstanding = 365 days /Inventory Turnover

5.   **Days Accounts Payable Outstanding** — measures the number of days it takes the firm to pay its accounts payable. The number of day should match the credit terms of suppliers as closely as possible.
Days Accounts Payable Outstanding = 365 days / A/P Turnover

Learning Objective 6:
How to interpret the results of an analysis of profitability and risk.

Cash inflows and outflows should be sufficiently matched in a healthy company.
Days Spread in Cash Flows = Days A/R + Days Inventory — Days Payable

When the spread is positive, the firm must cover this mismatch of cash flows through other financing means or with other operating cash inflows.

Activity Ratios
1.   **Accounts Receivable Turnover** — indicates how frequently the firm collects its receivables each year.
A/R Turnover = Net Sales / Average Accounts Receivable
2.   **Inventory Turnover** — indicates how many times per year the firm sells (or turns) its inventory.
Inventory Turnover = Cost of Goods Sold/Average Inventory
3.   **Accounts Payable Turnover** — indicates how many times per year the company repays its payables.
A/P Turnover = Inventory Purchases/Average Accounts Payable

Long-term Solvency Ratios
1.   **Long-term Debt to Assets** — measures the percentage of assets that are funded by long-term debt. This higher this ratio, the greater the solvency risk.
Long-term Debt to Assets = Long-term Debt / Total Assets

2.   **Long-term Debt to Tangible Assets** - measures the percentage of tangible assets that are funded by long-term debt. This higher this ratio, the greater the solvency risk.
Long-term Debt to   =   Long-term Debt
Tangible Assets   Total Assets — Intangible Assets
3.   **Interest Coverage** — indicates the number of times a firm can

pay its interest expense from operating income. The coverage is indicative of debt servicing abilities.

Interest Coverage = Operating Income before Interest and Taxes

Interest Expense

4. **Operating Cash Flows to Total Liabilities** — indicates the ability to service short-term and long-term debt from operating cash flows. The higher this ratio, the lower the credit risk.

Operating Cash Flows = Operating Cash Flows to Total Liabilities

Avg. Current Liabilities + Long-term Debt

Learning Objective 4:
How return on common equity (ROCE) can be used to assess the impact of financial leverage on a company's profitability.

Investors gauge the profitability of an investment in a firm's common stock by measuring the profitability of the company against shareholders' investments.

Return on Common Equity (ROCE) measures the net income as a percentage of common shareholders' equity.

ROCE   = Net Income Available to Common Shares

Average Common Shareholders' Equity

Income Available to common shareholders is net income less preferred dividends. Common Shareholders' Equity (CSE) is comprised of common stock, capital contributed in excess of par on common stock, and retained earnings.

The ROCE calculation has three components:

1. Return on Assets (ROA) — **NOPAT / Average Assets**
2. Common Earnings Leverage — **Net Inc. Avail. to Common / NOPAT**
3. Financial Structure Leverage — **Average Assets / Average CSE**

ROCE =   NOPAT   x   Net Inc. to Common   x   Average Assets

Average Assets   NOPAT   Average CSE

ROCE   = ROA   x Common Earnings   x   Financial

Structure

Leverage   Leverage

Return on Common Equity examines how the assets are financed. ROCE looks at the profitable use of assets (ROA), the percentage of the earnings that belong to the common shareholders (Common Earnings Leverage), and the degree to which the company uses common shareholders' investments to finance the assets. A company that successfully uses borrowed capital to finance its long-range activities (leverages) will have a higher rate of return on shareholders' equity than a company that uses more invested capital because less stockholder investment is required to achieve the same amount of profits. Likewise, a company that incurs losses in a leveraged position will see those losses (negative profits) higher than a company that uses more invested capital.

Learning Objective 7: Why EBITDA (earnings before interest, taxes, depreciation, and amortization) can be a misleading indicator of profitability and cash flow.

Earnings before interest, taxes, depreciation, and amortization, (EBITDA), is being highlighted by some companies in public announcements and forums. This non- GAAP earnings figure is also referred to as cash earnings and pro-forma earnings. Companies are selectively choosing those income statement items they wish to include in these earnings numbers. This can be terribly misleading.

It is important to remember:
1. There are no standard definitions for non-GAAP earnings numbers.
2. Some real costs of the business are ignored resulting in an incomplete picture of profitability.
3. Using these non-GAAP earnings as a measure of cash flow can be misleading.

(See Demonstration Problem 3 for computations of financial ratios and Demonstration Problem 4 for analysis of financial ratios.)

Glossary of Terms

Activity Ratios	A set of ratios that provide information on how efficiently the company is using its assets.
Asset Utilization	The measure of an entity's sales generated from each asset dollar.
Benchmark Comparison	An analytical tool that measures a company's performance or health against some predetermined standard.
Common Size Statements	Income statements that have been recast with each item on the statement shown as a percent of sales.
Cross-Sectional Analysis	A financial analysis tool that identifies similarities and differences across companies or business units at a single moment in time.
Debt Ratios	A set of ratios that provide information about the long-term debt in a company's financial structure.
Differentiation of Product and Service	A business strategy that focuses customer attention on unique product or service attributes to gain customer loyalty and attractive profit margins.
Financial Leverage	A term that relates to the ability of an entity to use debt to increase the

shareholders' returns when the company earns more on each borrowed dollar than it pays out in interest.

Financial Ratios	An analytical tool used to evaluate profit performance and assess credit risk based on a comparison of financial statement numbers.
Goodwill	The amount in the acquisition price that represents a premium paid for the target company over and above the value of its identifiable assets.
Gross Domestic Product	A measure of a nation's economic growth defined as the dollar value of all final goods and services produced in a given year.
Liquidity	A company's ability to generate cash for working capital and immediate debt repayment needs.
Low-Cost Leadership	A business strategy which focuses customer attention on product pricing.
Operating Profit Margin	The profit yield based on sales dollars.
Return on Common Equity	A measure of a company's performance in using capital provided by shareholders to generate earnings.
Solvency	A company's long term ability to generate cash internally or from external sources to satisfy plant capacity needs, fuel growth, and repay debt when due.
Time-Series Analysis	A financial analysis tool that identifies financial trends over time for a single company or business unit.
Trend Statements	A financial analysis tool that recasts income statements in percentage terms using a base year rather than sales.

Demonstration Problems

1.   Preparing a Common Size Income Statement, Balance Sheet, and Cash Flow Statement.

Ferrara Corporation
Income Statement
For the Years Ended December 31,

(In millions)	Year 5	Year 4	Year 3
Sales	$32,400	$23,000	$17,600
Cost of Goods Sold	15,600	11,200	6,600
Operating Expenses	5,400	4,600	3,800
Interest Expense	100	120	100
Income Taxes	4,200	2,600	2,400
Net Income	$ 7,100	$ 4,480	$ 4,700

Ferrara Corporation
Balance Sheet
December 31,

(In millions)	Year 5	Year 4	Year 3
Assets			
Cash	$ 3,000	$ 2,400	$ 3,400
Accounts Receivable	8,400	6,400	4,200
Inventory	5,000	3,600	3,000
Plant, Property & Equipment (net)	18,000	15,200	12,000
Total Assets	$35,000	$27,600	$22,600
Liabilities and Shareholders' Equity			
Accounts Payable	$ 1,800	$ 1,200	$ 1,000
Other Current Liabilities	5,400	4,800	4,400
Long-term Liabilities	3,600	3,000	2,200
Common Stock	5,200	4,600	4,400
Retained Earnings	19,000	14,000	10,600
Total Liabilities and Shareholders' Equity	$34,000	$27,600	$22,600

Ferrara Corporation
Statement of Cash Flows
For the Years Ended December 31,

(In millions)	Year 5	Year 4	Year 3
Cash Provided by Operating Activities	$ 8,000	$ 6,000	$ 5,600
Cash Used by Investing Activities	(5,400)	(5,800)	(6,600)
Cash Provided (Used) by Financing Activities	(2,000)	(1,200)	800
Net Change in Cash	$ 600	$ (1000)	$ (200)

Required: Prepare a common size income statement, balance sheet, and statement of cash flows for Ferrara Corporation for Year 3, Year 4, and Year 5. What information do the common size statements provide about Ferrara Corporation?

First Step: Determine the denominator to use to recast the income statement as a common size statement. **Application:** In a common size income statement, each item is recast as a percent of sales for that year.
Solution: Divide each item in the income statement by Sales.

Ferrara Corporation
Common Size Income Statement
For the Years Ended December 31,

	Year 5	Year 4	Year 3
Sales	100.00%	100.00%	100.00%
Cost of Goods Sold	48.15%	48.70%	37.50%
Operating Expenses	16.67%	20.00%	21.59%
Interest Expense	.31%	.52%	.57%
Income Taxes	12.96%	11.30%	13.64%
Net Income	21.91%	19.48%	26.70%

Second Step: Determine the denominator to use to recast the balance sheet as a common size statement. **Application:** In a common size balance sheet, each item is recast as a percent of the total assets for that year.
Solution: Divide each item in the balance sheet by Total Assets.

Ferrara Corporation
Common Size Balance Sheet
December 31,

	Year 5	Year 4	Year 3
Assets			
Cash	8.57%	8.70%	15.05%
Accounts Receivable	24.00%	23.19%	18.58%
Inventory	14.29%	13.04%	13.27%
Plant, Property & Equipment (net)	53.14%	55.07%	53.10%
Total Assets	100.00%	100.00%	100.00%
Liabilities and Shareholders' Equity			
Accounts Payable	5.14%	4.35%	4.43%
Other Current Liabilities	15.43%	17.39%	19.47%
Long-term Liabilities	10.29%	10.87%	9.73%
Common Stock	14.86%	16.67%	19.47%
Retained Earnings	54.28%	50.72%	46.90%
Total Liabilities and Shareholders' Equity	100.00%	100.00%	100.00%

Third Step: Determine the denominator to use to recast the statement of cash flows as a common size statement.

Application: In a common size cash flow statement, each item is recast as a percent of the sales for that year.

Solution: Divide each item in the cash flow statement by sales for the year.

Ferrara Corporation
Common Size Statement of Cash Flows
For the Years Ended December 31,

	Year 5	Year 4	Year 3
Cash Provided by Operating Activities	24.69 %	26.09 %	31.81%
Cash Used by Investing Activities	(16.67)%	(25.22)%	(37.50)%
Cash Provided (Used) by Financing Activities	(6.17)%	(5.22)%	4.55 %
Net Change in Cash	1.85 %	(4.35)%	(1.14)%

Fourth Step: Analyze the information provided by the common size statements.

Application: Look at the common size income statement. Cost of goods sold rose significantly in Year 4 and declined somewhat in Year 5, reducing its gross profit on product sales by over 10% of sales. Operating expenses declined as a percentage of sales by 5% from Year 3 to Year 5. Interest expense and income taxes remained about the same percentage of sales.

Look at the common size balance sheet. Inventory and plant assets remain relatively the same percentage of total assets for the three years. Cash and accounts receivable remain about the same combined percentage of total assets but cash decreased and accounts receivable increased by about 7% of total assets. This happened at the same time that there was a change in gross profit. This may indicate that Ferrara began selling to a different class of customers who required credit terms and lower prices.

Look at the common size cash flow statement. Cash provided by operations fell as a percentage of sales from Year 3 to Year 5 corresponding to the increase in accounts receivable. Ferrara used less sales dollars for investing activities by 21% of sales and increased the use of cash for financing activities by about 11% of sales during the three year period.

2.   Preparing a trend income statement, balance sheet, and statement of cash flows.
        Required: Prepare a trend income statement, balance sheet, and statement of cash flows
        for the Ferrara Corporation using Year 3 as the base year.

First Step: Determine the denominator to use to recast the income statement as a trend statement.

Application: In a trend income statement, each item is recast as a percent of the base year item.

Solution: Divide each item in the income statement by the base year item.

Ferrara Corporation
Trend Income Statement
For the Years Ended December 31,

	Year 5	Year 4	Year 3
Sales	184.09%	130.68%	100.00%
Cost of Goods Sold	236.36%	169.70%	100.00%
Operating Expenses	142.11%	121.05%	100.00%
Interest Expense	100.00%	120.00%	100.00%
Income Taxes	175.00%	108.33%	100.00%
Net Income	151.06%	95.32%	100.00%

Second Step: Determine the denominator to use to recast the balance sheet as a trend statement.
Application: In a trend balance sheet, each item is recast as a percent of the base year item.
Solution: Divide each item in the balance sheet by the base year item.

Ferrara Corporation
Trend Balance Sheet
December 31,

	Year 5	Year 4	Year 3
Assets			
Cash	88.24%	70.59%	100.00%
Accounts Receivable	200.00%	152.38%	100.00%
Inventory	166.67%	120.00%	100.00%
Plant, Property & Equipment (net)	155.00%	126.67%	100.00%
Total Assets	154.87%	122.12%	100.00%
Liabilities and Shareholders' Equity			
Accounts Payable	180.00%	120.00%	100.00%
Other Current Liabilities	122.73%	109.09%	100.00%
Long-term Liabilities	163.64%	136.36%	100.00%
Common Stock	118.18%	104.55%	100.00%
Retained Earnings	179.25%	132.08%	100.00%
Total Liabilities and Shareholders' Equity	154.87%	122.12%	100.00%

Third Step: Determine the denominator to use to recast the statement of cash flows as a trend statement.
Application: In a trend cash flow statement, each item is recast as a percent of the base year item.
Solution: Divide each item in the cash flow statement by the base year item.

Ferrara Corporation
Trend Statement of Cash Flows
For the Years Ended December 31,

	Year 5	Year 4	Year 3
Cash Provided by Operating Activities	142.86 %	107.14 %	100.00%
Cash Used by Investing Activities	81.82 %	87.88 %	100.00%
Cash Provided (Used) by Financing Activities	(250.00)%	(150.00)%	100.00%
Net Change in Cash	(300.00)%	500.00 %	100.00%

3.   **Computing profitability, asset utilization, short-term liquidity, and long-term solvency ratios.**

Required: Compute the following ratios for the Ferrara Corporation for Year 5 assuming a 35% tax rate:
   A. Return on Assets
   B. Operating Profit Margin
   C. Total Asset Turnover
   D. Current Ratio
   E. Quick Ratio
   F. Accounts Receivable Turnover
   G. Days Receivable Outstanding
   H. Inventory Turnover
   I. Days Inventory Held
   J. Accounts Payable Turnover
   K. Days Accounts Payable Outstanding
   L. Long-term Debt to Assets
   M. Long-term Debt to Tangible Assets
   N. Interest Coverage
   O. Operating Cash Flows to Total Liabilities
   P. Return on Common Equity
   Q. Common Earnings Leverage
   R. Financial Structure Leverage

   A.   Compute Return on Assets
First Step: Determine the formula.
Solution: ROA = $\dfrac{\text{Net Operating Profit After Taxes (NOPAT)}}{\text{Average Total Assets}}$

Second Step: Determine the components from the financial statements.
Application: NOPAT = Net Income + After-tax Interest
        Average Total Assets = (Beginning Assets + Ending Assets) / 2
Solution: ROA = $\dfrac{\text{Net Income }\$7{,}100 + \text{After-tax Interest Expense }\$100 \times (1 - .35)}{\text{Average Assets }(\$27{,}600 + \$35{,}000)/2)} = \dfrac{\$7{,}165}{\$31{,}300} = 22.89\%$

B.   Compute Operating Profit Margin
First Step: Determine the formula.
Solution: Operating Profit Margin   = $\dfrac{\text{NOPAT}}{\text{Sales}}$

Second Step: Determine the components from the financial statements.
Application: NOPAT (from part A) = $7,165   Sales = $32,400
Solution: Operating Profit Margin = $\dfrac{\text{NOPAT \$7,165}}{\text{Sales \quad \$32,400}}$ = 22.11%

C.   Compute Total Asset Turnover
First Step: Determine the formula.
Solution: Total Asset Turnover = $\dfrac{\text{Sales}}{\text{Average Total Assets}}$

Second Step: Determine the components from the financial statements.
Application: Sales = $32,400   Average Total Assets (from part A) = $31,300
Solution: Total Assets Turnover = $\dfrac{\text{Sales} \quad \$32,400}{\text{Average Total Assets \$31,300}}$ = 1.04 times

D.   Compute the Current Ratio.
First Step: Determine the formula.
Solution: Current Ratio = $\dfrac{\text{Current Assets}}{\text{Current Liabilities}}$

Second Step: Determine the components from the financial statements.
Application: Current Assets = Cash $3,000+ Accounts Receivable $8,400 + Inventory $5,000 = $16,400
     Current Liabilities = Accounts Payable $1,800 + Other Current Liabilities $5,400 = $7,200
Solution: Current Ratio = $\dfrac{\text{Current Assets \$16,400}}{\text{Current Liabilities \$7,200}}$ = 2.28 to 1

E.   Compute the Quick Ratio.
First Step: Determine the formula.
Solution: Quick Ratio = $\dfrac{\text{Current Assets — Inventory}}{\text{Current Liabilities}}$

Second Step: Determine the components from the financial statements.
Application: Current Assets (from part D) = $16,400   Inventory = $5,000
     Current Liabilities (from part D) = $7,200
Solution: Quick Ratio = $\dfrac{\text{Current Assets \$16,400 — Inventory \$5,000}}{\text{Current Liabilities \$7,200}}$ = $\dfrac{\$11,400}{\$7,200}$ = 1.58 to 1

F.   Compute the Accounts Receivable Turnover.

First Step: Determine the formula.

Solution: _____Sales_____

Average Accounts Receivable

Second Step: Determine the components from the financial statements.

Application: Sales = $32,400   Average A/R = Beginning A/R $6,400 + Ending A/R $8,400)/2 = $7,400

Solution: _____Sales $32,400_____ = 4.4 times

Average Accounts Receivable $7,400

G.   Compute the Days Receivable Outstanding.

First Step: Determine the formula.

Solution: Days Receivable Outstanding =   365 days / Accounts Receivable Turnover

Second Step: Determine the components from the financial statements.

Application: Accounts Receivable Turnover (from part G) = 4.4 times

Solution: Days Receivable Outstanding = _____365 days_____ = 82.95 days

Accounts Receivable Turnover 4.4

H.   Compute the Inventory Turnover.

First Step: Determine the formula.

Solution: _Cost of Goods Sold_

Average Inventory

Second Step: Determine the components from the financial statements.

Application: Cost of Goods Sold = $15,600

Average Inventory = (Beginning Inventory $3,600 + Ending Inventory $5,000) / 2 = $4,300

Solution: _Cost of Goods Sold $15,600_   = 3.63 times

Average Inventory $4,300

I.   Compute the Days Inventory Held.

First Step: Determine the formula.

Solution: Days Inventory Held =   365 days / Inventory Turnover

Second Step: Determine the components from the financial statements.

Application: Inventory Turnover (from part H) = 3.63 times

Solution: Days Inventory Held = _____365 days_____ = 100.55 days

Inventory Turnover 3.63

J.   Compute Accounts Payable Turnover when inventory purchases are $17,000.

First Step: Determine the formula.

Solution: Accounts Payable Turnover =_ Inventory Purchases_

Average Accounts Payable

Second Step: Determine the components from the financial statements.

Application: Purchases are given $17,000   Average A/P = (Beginning $1,200 + Ending $1,800)/2 = $1,500
Solution: Accounts Payable Turnover = $\underline{\text{Inventory Purchases} \quad \$17,000}$ = 11.33 times
$\qquad\qquad\qquad\qquad\qquad$ Average Accounts Payable $ 1,500

K.   Compute Days Accounts Payable Outstanding.

First Step: Determine the formula.
Solution: Days Accounts Payable Outstanding = 365 days / Accounts Payable Turnover
Second Step: Determine the components from the financial statements.
Application:
Solution: Days Accounts Payable Outstanding = $\underline{\qquad\qquad 365 \text{ days} \qquad\qquad}$ = 32.22 days
$\qquad\qquad\qquad\qquad\qquad$ Accounts Payable Turnover 11.33

L.   Compute Long-term Debt to Assets Ratio.

First Step: Determine the formula.
Solution: $\underline{\text{Long-term Debts}}$
$\qquad$ Total Assets

Second Step: Determine the components from the financial statements.
Application: Long-term debt = $3,600   Total Assets = $35,000
Solution: $\underline{\text{Long-term Debts } \$ 3,600}$ $\qquad$ = 10.29%
$\qquad\qquad$ Total Assets $35,000

M.   Compute Long-term Debt to Tangible Assets.

First Step: Determine the formula.
Solution: Long-term Debt to Tangible Assets = $\underline{\qquad\quad \text{Long-term Debts}}$
$\qquad\qquad\qquad\qquad\qquad$ Total Assets — Intangible Assets
Second Step: Determine the components from the financial statements.
Application: Long-term Debts and Total Assets from Step L. There are no Intangible Assets listed on the balance sheet.
Solution: $\underline{\qquad\qquad \text{Long-term Debts } \$3,600 \qquad\qquad}$ $\qquad$ = 10.29%
$\qquad\qquad$ Total Assets $35,000 — Intangible Assets $-0-

N.   Compute Interest Coverage Ratio.

First Step: Determine the formula.
Solution: Interest Coverage = $\underline{\text{Net Income + Interest Expense + Income Taxes}}$
$\qquad\qquad\qquad\qquad\qquad$ Interest Expense

Second Step: Determine the components from the financial statements.
Application: Net Income = $7,100   Interest Expense = $100   Income Tax = $4,200
Solution: $\underline{\text{Net Income } \$7,100 + \text{Interest Expense } \$100 + \text{Income Tax } \$4,200}$ = 114.00 times
$\qquad\qquad\qquad\qquad\qquad$ Interest Expense $100

O.   Compute Operating Cash Flows to Total Liabilities.

First Step: Determine the formula.

Solution: Operating Cash Flows   = $\dfrac{\text{Operating Cash Flows}}{\text{Average Current Liabilities } + \text{ Long-term Liabilities}}$

to Total Liabilities

Second Step: Determine the components from the financial statements.

Application: Operating Cash Flows = $8,000   Long-term Liabilities = $3,600

Average Current Liabilities = $\dfrac{\text{Beginning (\$1,200 + \$4,800) + Ending (\$1,800 + \$5,400)}}{2} = \$6,600$

Solution: Operating Cash Flows = $\dfrac{\text{Operating Cash Flows \$8,000}}{\text{Avg. Current Liab. \$6,600 } + \text{ Long-term Liab. \$3,600}} = 78.43\%$

to Total Liabilities

P.   Compute Return on Common Equity.

First Step: Determine the formula.

Solution: ROCE = $\dfrac{\text{Net Income}}{\text{Average Common Equity}}$

Second Step: Determine the components from the financial statements.

Application: Net Income = $7,100, Common Equity = Common Stock + Retained Earnings

Average Common Equity = $\dfrac{\text{Beginning (\$4,600 + \$14,000) + Ending (\$5,200 + \$19,000)}}{2} = \$21,400$

Solution: ROCE = $\dfrac{\text{Net Income \$7,100}}{\text{Average Common Equity \$21,400}} = 33.18\%$

Q.   Compute Common Earnings Leverage.

First Step: Determine the formula.

Solution: Common Earnings Leverage = $\dfrac{\text{Net Income Available to Common}}{\text{NOPAT}}$

Second Step: Determine the components from the financial statements.

Application: Net Income = $7,100 (There is no preferred stock so all earning are attributable to common shares.) NOPAT (from part A) = $7,165

Solution: Common Earnings Leverage = $\dfrac{\text{Net Income Available to Common \$7,100}}{\text{NOPAT \$7,165}} = 99.09\%$

R.   Compute Financial Structure Leverage.

First Step: Determine the formula.

Solution: $\dfrac{\text{Average Total Assets}}{\text{Average Common Equity}}$

Second Step: Determine the components from the financial statements.

Application: Total Assets (from part A) = $31,300   Average Common Equity (from part P) = $21,400

Solution: $\dfrac{\text{Average Total Assets   \$31,300}}{\text{Average Common Equity \$21,400}} = 1.46$ times

4.   Analyzing a firm's ratios.

Required: List Ferrara's ratios and analyze the results.

First Step: Prepare a table of the profitability, asset utilization, short-term liquidity, and long-term solvency ratios.

Solution:

Profitability Ratios

Return on Assets	22.89%
Operating Profit Margin	22.11%
Total Assets Turnover	1.04 times
Return on Common Equity	33.18%
Common Earnings Leverage	99.09%
Financial Structure Leverage	1.46 times

Asset Utilization (Activity) Ratios

Accounts Receivable Turnover	4.40 times
Inventory Turnover	3.63 times

Short-term Liquidity Ratios

Current Ratio	2.28 to 1
Quick Ratio	1.58 to 1
Days Receivable Outstanding	82.95 days
Days Inventory Held	100.55 days
Accounts Payable Turnover	11.33 times
Days Accounts Payable Outstanding	32.22 days

Long-term Solvency Ratios

Long-term Debt to Assets	10.29%
Long-term Debt to Tangible Assets	10.29%
Interest Coverage	114.00 times
Operating Cash Flows to Total Liabilities	78.43%

Second Step: Evaluate Ferrara Corporation's financial performance.

Application: Examine each set of ratios and compare to the benchmark industry ratios or to normative (rule of thumb) standards. Because there are no industry ratios and we are unaware of the industry in which Ferrara operates, we can only compare Ferrara to normative standards. Look for conflicting or corroborating indications among the ratios.

Solution: Profitability: Ferrara enjoys a high Operating Profit Margin, ROA, and ROCE. With no preferred stock and little interest expense, the Common Earnings Leverage is near 100% and because debt is small, the Financial Structure Leverage is low at 1.46 times.

Asset Utilization (Activity): The Accounts Receivable Turnover is low indicating that the firm sells on longer than 30-day terms. Inventory Turnover is lower than the receivables turnover. Because these are both low, we would need to investigate the industry averages to determine if these are within a normal range of the industry average.

<u>Short-term Liquidity Ratios</u>: Ferrara is a very liquid company. The rule of thumb for the Current Ratio and Quick Ratio are 2:1 and 1:1 respectively. Ferrara exceeds these by 10% to 60%. Ferrara pays its payables within 32 days giving it an excellent credit reputation.   This information combined with the low level of leverage may indicate that this company's management is fiscally conservative.

<u>Long-term Solvency Ratios</u>: Ferrara is extremely solvent. Only 10% of its assets are financed with long-term debt and interest coverage is outstandingly high. Operating cash flows can pay <u>all</u> liabilities in 15 months.

Bottom Line: Ferrara is highly profitable, liquid, and solvent. This may be a good investment.

Test Yourself

True or False Questions

T   F   1.   Time-series analysis helps identify financial trends over time for a single company.

T   F   2.   Cross-sectional analysis helps identify similarities and differences across companies over a period of time.

T   F   3.   The measure of a company's performance against some predetermined standard is a benchmark comparison.

T   F   4.   Time-series analysis is not influenced by distortions of financial statement data.

T   F   5.   The "raw" data needed for a complete financial picture always reaches the financial report.

T   F   6.   Management would never intentionally exceed the minimum reporting or disclosure requirements for GAAP that would provide excess details useful to the financial analyst.

T   F   7.   The basic tools of financial statement analysis are completely immune to distortions caused by GAAP.

T   F   8.   Common-size balance sheets recast each item as a percent of total assets.

T   F   9.   Financial analysts use common-size financial statements to help them spot changes in a company's cost structure and profit performance.

T   F   10.   Trend statements recast each income statement item in percentage terms using sales as the base.

T   F   11.   Common-size statements provide a clearer indication of growth and decline than trend statements.

T   F   12.   Informed financial statement analysis begins with knowledge of the company and its industry.

T F 13. The return on common equity ratio is often the starting point for an evaluation of profit performance.

T F 14. The return on assets analysis allows for no adjustments to the company's reported earnings and assets.

T F 15. An adjustment to earnings and assets for distortions related to accounting quality concerns might involve an off-balance sheet operating lease.

T F 16. Decreasing the intensity of asset utilization is one alternative for increasing the rate of return on assets.

T F 17. The current asset turnover ratio enables the analyst to spot efficiency gains from accounts receivable and inventory management.

T F 18. An erosion of profitability and competitive advantage may occur as a company consistently earns rates of return lower than the industry floor.

T F 19. Two strategies for achieving superior business performance include product and service differentiation and low cost leadership.

T F 20. Differences in business strategies that a company adopts give rise to differences in cost structures.

T F 21. Credit risk is the ability of an organization to borrow money.

T F 22. Ability to repay debt is based on the ability of the company to generate cash only from operations.

T F 23. Credit risk analysis using financial ratios typically involves an assessment of liquidity and solvency.

T F 24. Short-term liquidity problems may arise as a result of long-term solvency problems.

T F 25. Activity ratios are used to analyze how efficiently a company produces revenues.

T F 26. A cash flow statement is often the first statement the analyst will review when assessing a company's credit risk.

T F 27. A high credit risk company generates cash flows substantially in excess of what is required to sustain its business activities.

T F 28. Financial leverage benefits shareholders whenever the cost of debt is less than what the company earns on borrowed debt.

T F 29. A company's profit performance, from the viewpoint of the shareholder, can be gauged using the return on common equity.

T   F   30.   Return on Common Equity measures a company's performance in using capital provided by shareholders to generate earnings.

Multiple-Choice Questions
Select the best answer from those provided.

_____   1.   A tool used to measure a company's performance against a predetermined standard is a/an
a.   time-series analysis.
b.   common size statement.
c.   benchmark comparison analysis.
d.   profitability analysis.

_____   2.   To remove the effects of an information filter an analyst will use the
a.   financial statements.
b.   form 10K.
c.   trend analysis.
d.   footnote disclosures.

_____   3.   A common size income statement recasts expenses as a percent of
a.   net income.
b.   total assets.
c.   sales.
d.   equity.

_____   4.   A trend income statement recasts each expense on the income statement item as a percentage of
a.   total assets.
b.   the base year item.
c.   sales.
d.   equity.

_____   5.   In a common size balance sheet, accounts receivable is expressed as a percentage of
a.   total equity.
b.   total liabilities.
c.   total assets.
d.   total sales.

_____   6.   In a trend balance sheet, accounts payable is expressed as a percentage of
a.   total assets.
b.   the base year item.
c.   sales.
d.   equity.

_____   7.   On a common size cash flow statement, net operating cash flows are expressed as a percentage of
a.   ending cash balance.
b.   total equity.
c.   total assets.
d.   sales.

_____   8.   On trend cash flow statements, net financing cash flows are recast as a percentage of
a.   the ending cash balance.
b.   sales.
c.   the base year item.
d.   total equity.

_____   9.   Which one of the following items is removed from Net Income to arrive at Net Operating Profit After Taxes (NOPAT)?
a.   after-tax depreciation.
b.   after-tax interest.
c.   after-tax advertising.
d.   after-tax amortization.

_____   10.   Which one of the following measures the profitable use of a firm's assets?
a.   Return on Common equity
b.   Current Ratio
c.   Quick Ratio
d.   Return on Assets

_____   11.   Net Operating Profit After Taxes / Average Assets is the correct formula for the
a.   Current Ratio.
b.   Quick Ratio.
c.   Return on Assets.
d.   Interest Coverage.

_____   12.   A competitive advantage is enjoyed by companies that consistently earn rates of return
a.   above the industry's competitive floor.
b.   below the industry's competitive floor.
c.   equal to the industry's competitive floor.
d.   equal to one-half of the industry's competitive floor.

_____ 13.   A company that desires superior performance in its industry would choose which
one of the following strategies?
a. price leadership
b. niche marketing
c. low-cost leadership
d. market segmentation

_____ 14.   Credit risk is the borrower's ability to repay debt and
a. the willingness to pay.
b. earn a profit.
c. remain solvent.
d. borrow additional monies.

_____ 15.   Analysts use liquidity and solvency ratios to determine
a. profitability.
b. credit risk.
c. return on assets.
d. cash flow.

_____ 16.   The disparity of cash inflows and cash outflows cause problems with
a. profitability.
b. asset utilization.
c. long-term financing.
d. short-term liquidity.

_____ 17.   The Quick Ratio is a measure of the most immediate
a. profitability of a company.
b. liquidity of a company.
c. cash flow of a company.
d. asset utilization of a company.

_____ 18.   The efficiency with which a firm uses its assets is measured by
a. profitability ratios.
b. cash flow ratios.
c. solvency ratios.
d. activity ratios.

_____ 19.   The Macon Company buys from suppliers on a net 90 day basis, experiences an
Accounts Receivable Turnover of 6 times, and has an Inventory Turnover of 8
times. Cash inflows and outflows are
a. evenly matched.
b. negatively mismatched by 15 days.
c. positively mismatched by 15 days.
d. negatively mismatched by 75 days.

_____ 20.   Solvency is the ability to generate sufficient cash flows to maintain productive
capacity and
   a. make a profit.
   b. service long-term debt.
   c. service short-term debt.
   d. pay dividends.

Exercises

1.   The following is a condensed Income Statement for Years 1, 2, and 3 for the Millie
Andrews Corporation.

Millie Andrews Corporation			
Comparative Income Statements			
For the Years Ended December 31,			
	Year 3	Year 2	Year 1
Sales	$356,800	$325,000	$301,000
Cost of Goods Sold	240,000	215,000	200,000
Operating Expenses	90,000	90,000	80,000
Net Income	$ 26,800	$ 20,000	$ 21,000

Millie Andrews Corporation

Comparative Income Statements
For the Years Ended December 31,

	Year 3	Year 2	Year 1
Sales	_____	_____	_____
Cost of Goods Sold	_____	_____	_____
Operating Expenses	_____	_____	_____
Net Income	_____	_____	_____

Required: Prepare comparative common size income statements for years 1, 2, and 3.

2.   Required: Using the comparative income statements in Exercise 1, prepare trend income
statements for the Millie Andrews Corporation for Years 1, 2, and 3 using Year 1 as the
base year.

Millie Andrews Corporation
Comparative Income Statements
For the Years Ended December 31,

	Year 3	Year 2	Year 1
Sales	_____	_____	_____
Cost of Goods Sold	_____	_____	_____
Operating Expenses	_____	_____	_____
Net Income	_____	_____	_____

3.   The Herr Corporation's condensed balance sheets appear below for Year 4, Year 5, and Year 6.

Herr Corporation
Balance Sheet
For the Years Ended December 31,

Assets	Year 6	Year 5	Year 4
Current Assets	$ 27,500	$ 23,250	$ 35,000
Plant and Equipment (net)	245,000	210,000	225,000
Intangible Assets (net)	12,500	13,750	15,000
Total Assets	$ 285,000	$ 247,000	$ 275,000
Liabilities & Stockholders' Equity			
Current Liabilities	$ 20,000	$ 17,500	$ 16,250
Long-Term Liabilities	200,000	150,000	187,500
Stockholders' Equity	65,000	79,500	71,250
Total Liabilities & Equity	$ 285,000	247,500	$ 275,000

Required: Prepare Herr Corporation's common size balance sheet for Year 4, Year 5 and Year 6.

Herr Corporation
Common Size Balance Sheet
For the Years Ended December 31,

Assets	Year 6	Year 5	Year 4
Current Assets	_____	_____	_____
Plant and Equipment (net)	_____	_____	_____
Intangible Assets (net)	_____	_____	_____
Total Assets	_____	_____	_____
Liabilities & Stockholders' Equity			
Current Liabilities	_____	_____	_____
Long-Term Liabilities	_____	_____	_____
Stockholders' Equity	_____	_____	_____
Total Liabilities & Equity	_____	_____	_____

4. Required: Using Year 4 as the base year, complete the trend balance sheet for Year 4, Year 6

Herr Corporation
Trend Balance Sheet
For the Years Ended December 31,

Assets	Year 6	Year 5	Year 4
Current Assets	_____	_____	_____
Plant and Equipment (net)	_____	_____	_____
Intangible Assets (net)	_____	_____	_____
Total Assets	_____	_____	_____
Liabilities & Stockholders' Equity			
Current Liabilities	_____	_____	_____
Long-Term Liabilities	_____	_____	_____
Stockholders' Equity	_____	_____	_____
Total Liabilities & Equity	_____	_____	_____

5.   The following information is available for the Stephens Corporation.

Condensed Balance Sheet

Assets	Year 10	Year 9
Cash	$40,000	$37,500
Accounts Receivable (net)	125,000	112,500
Merchandise Inventory	75,000	67,500
Plant, Property, & Equipment (net)	360,000	322,500
Total Assets	$600,000	$540,000

Liabilities and Stockholders' Equity		
Accounts Payable	$80,000	$ 60,000
Long-term Notes Payable	150,000	125,000
Common Stock	150,000	150,000
Additional Paid-in Capital	40,000	40,000
Retained Earnings	180,000	165,000
Total Liabilities and Stockholders' Equity	$600.000	$540,000

Net Income Year 10	$ 80,000
Cost of Goods Sold	570,000
Net Credit Sales	900,000

Required: Compute the following ratios for Year 10 from the information provided.

A. Total Asset Turnover   _____

B. Quick Ratio   _____

C. Current Ratio   _____

D. Inventory Turnover   _____

E. Long-Term Debt to Assets _____

F. Return on Common Equity_____

G. Financial Structure Leverage_____

H. Accounts Receivable Turnover_____

Solutions

Answers to True or False Questions

True Answers: 1, 3, 8, 9, 12, 15, 17, 19, 20, 23, 24, 26, 28, 29, 30
False answers explained:
2.   Cross-sectional analysis identifies similarities and differences at a single moment in time.
4.   All types of comparisons are influenced by distortions in the data.
5.   The raw data for financial reports does not always reach the financial.
6.   Management sometimes does provide much more than a minimum of information that might help the analyst.
7.   No tool is immune from distortions caused by GAAP.
10.   Trend analysis utilizes a base year for a comparison base.
11.   Trend statements actually provide the clearer indication of growth and decline.
13.   The return on assets ratio is often the starting point for an evaluation of profit performance.
14.   There are three categories of adjustments before computing return on assets.
16.   Increasing the intensity of asset utilization is one alternative for increasing the rate of return on assets.
18.   The erosion of profits and loss of advantage may occur if the rates of return are consistently higher than the industry floor as this will bring about greater competition.
21.   Credit risk refers to the ability and willingness to pay ones debts.
22.   Ability to repay debt is determined by an entity's ability to generate cash from many sources that are in excess of its other cash needs.
25.   Activity ratios are used to analyze how efficiently a company uses its assets.
27.   This company would be a low credit risk company.

Answers to Multiple-Choice Questions

1.	C	6.	A	11.	C	16.	D
2.	D	7.	D	12.	A	17.	B
3.	C	8.	C	13.	C	18.	D
4.	C	9.	B	14.	A	19.	B (90 — 60 — 45)
5.	C	10.	D	15.	B	20.	B

Answers to Exercises

1.

Millie Andrews Corporation

Common Size Income Statements
For the Years Ended December 31,

	Year 3	Year 2	Year 1
Sales	100.0%	100.0%	100.0%
Cost of Goods Sold	67.3%	66.2%	66.4%
Operating Expenses	25.2%	27.7%	26.6%
Net Income	7.5%	6.1%	7.0%

2.

Millie Andrews Corporation

Trend Income Statements
For the Years Ended December 31,

	Year 3	Year 2	Year 1
Sales	118.5%	108.0%	100.0%
Cost of Goods Sold	120.0%	107.5%	100.0%
Operating Expenses	112.5%	112.5%	100.0%
Net Income	127.6%	95.2%	100.0%

3.

Herr Corporation
Common Size Balance Sheet
For the Years Ended December 31,

Assets	Year 6	Year 5	Year 4
Current Assets	9.6%	9.4%	12.7%
Plant and Equipment (net)	86.0%	85.0%	81.8%
Intangible Assets (net)	4.4%	5.6%	5.5%
Total Assets	100.0%	100.0%	100.0%

Liabilities & Stockholders' Equity			
Current Liabilities	7.0%	7.1%	5.9%
Long-Term Liabilities	70.2%	60.7%	68.2%
Stockholders' Equity	22.8%	32.2%	25.9%
Total Liabilities & Equity	100.0%	100.0%	100.0%

Herr Corporation
Trend Balance Sheet
For the Years Ended December 31,

Assets	Year 6	Year 5	Year 4
Current Assets	78.6%	66.4%	100.0%
Plant and Equipment (net)	108.9%	93.3%	100.0%
Intangible Assets (net)	83.3%	91.7%	100.0%
Total Assets	103.6%	89.8%	100.0%

Liabilities & Stockholders' Equity			
Current Liabilities	123.1%	107.7%	100.0%
Long-Term Liabilities	106.7%	80.0%	100.0%
Stockholders' Equity	91.2%	111.6%	100.0%
Total Liabilities & Equity	103.6%	89.8%	100.0%

5.

A.   Total Asset Turnover = $\dfrac{\text{Sales } \$900{,}000}{\text{Average Total Assets (\$600{,}000 + \$540{,}000)/2}}$ = 1.58 times

B.   Quick Ratio = $\dfrac{\text{Current Assets (\$240{,}000)} - \text{Inventory (\$75{,}000)}}{\text{Current Liabilities \$80{,}000}}$ = 2.06 to 1

C.   Current Ratio = $\dfrac{\text{Current Assets } \$240{,}000}{\text{Current Liabilities \$80{,}000}}$ = 3.0 to 1

D.   Inventory Turnover = $\dfrac{\text{Cost of Goods Sold \$570{,}000}}{\text{Average Inventory (\$75{,}000 + \$67{,}500) / 2}}$ = 8.0 times

E.   Long-Term Debt to Assets = $\dfrac{\text{Long-term Debt } \$150,000}{\text{Total Assets } \$600,000}$ = 25.0 %

F.   Return on Common Equity = $\dfrac{\text{Net Income } \$81,000 \text{ — Preferred Dividends } \$0}{\text{Average Common Equity } (\$370,000 + 355,000) / 2}$ = 22.3

G.   Financial Structure Leverage = $\dfrac{\text{Average Total Assets } (\$600,000 + \$540,000)/2}{\text{Average Common Equity } (\$370,000 + 355,000) / 2}$ = 1.57 times

H.   Accounts Receivable Turnover = $\dfrac{\text{Sales } \$900,000}{\text{Average A/R } (\$125,000 + \$112,500) / 2}$ = 7.6 Times

CHAPTER 6

THE ROLE OF FINANCIAL INFORMATION IN VALUATION, CASH FLOW ANALYSIS AND CREDIT RISK ASSESSMENTS

Chapter Review

Learning Objective 1:
The basic steps in corporate valuation.

Corporate valuation is a process of estimating the net worth or intrinsic value of a company or one of its operating units, or its ownership's shares. Fundamental analysis techniques are frequently used by investors and analysts. Estimates of cash flow and earnings from operations become the focal point of the analysis. Corporate evaluation follows this three step process:
1. Forecasting the future value of value-relevant attributes of
   a. free cash flows or distributable cash flows;
   b. accounting earnings; and
   c. balance sheet book values.
2. Determining the risk associated with the forecasted future amounts.
3. Computing the discounted present value of the expected future amounts using a discount rate that reflects the risk of uncertainty from step 2.

Learning Objective 2:
What free cash flows are and how they are used to value a company.

Free cash flow is operating cash flow minus cash outlays necessary to maintain current operating capacity by replacing plant and equipment. Therefore, free cash flow represents the capacity to finance expansion to repay debt, distribute cash dividends, and repurchase stock. The discounted free cash flow valuation model asserts that investors depend upon current expectations of future free cash flows to value the stock. The model computes the current value at the discounted present value of the estimated future distributable cash flows using a discount rate that reflects the risk and timing of the cash flows.

Discounted Free Cash Flow Valuation Model:

$$P_O = \frac{CF_O}{r}$$

Where P_O = Current Price
CF_O = Current Free Cash Flow per share
r = discount rate

Learning Objective 3:

The FASB asserts that current accrual **accounting earnings** are a better

How accounting earnings are used in valuation and why current earnings are considered more useful than current cash flows for assessing future cash flows.

predictor of future cash flows than are current cash flows because of the forward-looking nature of accrual accounting. Accrual accounting takes a long-horizon, multi-period view of capital expenditure transactions which smoothes the effect over a number of periods. By nature, cash flows are "lumpy" and fluctuate annually. Empirical data suggest that stock returns are correlated better with accrual earnings than operating cash flows. Accrual accounting is the better measure of sustainable annualized long-run future free cash flows.

Assuming that current earnings are a better predictor of future cash flows than current cash flows, current earnings can be substituted into the discounted free cash flow valuation model. The simplified model becomes:

Learning Objective 4: What an earnings multiple is and what factors contribute to variation in price to earnings multiples

$$P_O = \frac{X_O}{r} \quad \text{or} \quad \frac{P_O}{X_O} = \frac{1}{r}$$

where P_O = Current Price
X_O = Current earnings per share
r = discount rate

The left side of the equation is the **Price/Earnings** (PE) ratio, also called the **earnings multiplier**. The right side of the equation is the reciprocal of the risk-adjusted discount rate which represents the rate of return demanded by shareholders on their investments. The risk-adjusted rate of return is the equity cost of capital. This valuation approach computes the stock price as a multiple of current period earnings where the multiple is the reciprocal of the firm's equity cost of capital.

Since investors use the current period earnings per share to value the stock, differences in earnings across firms must help to explain the differences in stock prices. Accrual accounting earnings are, therefore, value-relevant. Cross-sectional studies employing regression analysis indicate that earnings explain some, but not all, of the cross-sectional variation in stock prices. The regression equation is:

$P_i = \alpha + \beta X_i + e_i$ where P_i = closing stock price for firm i at period end
X_i = the firms accrual earnings for the period
α = intercept of the line
β = slope of the line
e_i = random error

Permanent earnings are **sustainable** earnings.

When β is positive and statistically significant, the correlation between earnings and prices explains some of the variation in prices. The adjusted R^2 for the regression will identify the proportion of the share price explained by earnings.

Other sources of variation in prices are **risk differences** and **growth opportunities**. Riskier firms have higher costs of equity capital. The higher the cost of equity capital, the lower the share price. Growth opportunities increase the share prices by the net present value of future growth opportunities (NPVGO). The valuation model then expands to:

$$P_O = \frac{X_O}{r} + NPVGO$$

Where $\frac{X_O}{r}$ = present value from assets in place.

NPVGO = net present value of future growth opportunities.

The present value of the earnings assumes no growth potential from a firm that distributes all of its earnings to shareholders as dividends. The NPVGO assumes that a firm retains earnings to fund new investment projects that have positive net present values. Stock prices will increase because the retained earnings will grow at a higher rate than required by investors. **(See Demonstration Problem 1.)**

The growth rate in earnings depends upon the **retention ratio** (the portion of earnings reinvested each period) and the rate of return on the new investment. When the retention ratio is positive and the rate of return on the new investment exceeds the cost of equity capital, the NVPGO will be positive and contribute to an above average earnings multiple. A firm's return on equity (ROE) indicates whether the firm can expect to earn more than the cost of capital on reinvested earnings.

Learning Objective 5: How the distinction among permanent, transitory, and valuation-irrelevant components of earnings affects price-earning multiples.

When analysts use the earnings multiplier to value stock, the earnings amount becomes an important quantity. Income statements are divided into important categories of income:
1.   **Income from continuing operations**, including some unusual or non-recurring items;
2.   **Income from discontinued operations**;
3.   **Extraordinary gains and losses**; and
4.   **Cumulative effect of changes in accounting principles**.

Permanent earnings are value-relevant and expected to continue in future periods. Permanent earnings include income from continuing operations minus any unusual or non-recurring items. The multiplier for permanent earnings (β_P) should approach $1/r$ or the reciprocal of the risk-adjusted cost of capital. (If the cost of capital is 12.5%, the multiplier (β_P) is 8.)

Transitory earnings are value-relevant but not expected to continue in future periods. Transitory earnings include unusual or non-recurring items, discontinued operations, and extraordinary gains and losses. The multiplier for transitory earnings (β_T) should approach 1.

Value-irrelevant earnings (or noise) are not related to future earnings and should be ignored. **Cumulative effect of changes in accounting principles** are noise. The multiplier (β_O) is zero.

The earnings regression model can be rewritten as the sum of the earnings components:

$$P_i = \alpha + \underset{\substack{\text{Permanent} \\ \text{Earnings}}}{\beta_P X_i^P} + \underset{\substack{\text{Transitory} \\ \text{Earnings}}}{\beta_T X_i^T} + \underset{\substack{\text{Value-irrelevant} \\ \text{Earnings}}}{\beta_O X_i^O} + e_i$$

(See Demonstration Problem 2.)

Learning Objective 6: The notion of earnings quality and what factors influence the quality of earnings.

Sustainable earnings are high quality earnings. Therefore, the higher the proportion of permanent earnings in the earnings regression model, the higher the firm's stock price. As the transitory or value-irrelevant earnings components rise, the quality of earnings erodes. Earnings quality is eroded by:

1. transitory income items;
2. gains or losses from extraordinary items;
3. restructuring gains and losses;
4. accounting principles and methods chosen; and
5. subjectivity of accounting estimates.

Research indicates that investors recognize these differences and translate them into share prices.

Learning Objective 7: The abnormal earnings approach to valuation and how it is applied to practice.

If an ordinary firm can produce normal earnings that are equal to the cost of capital, investors will pay for the book value of that firm. Investors are willing to pay a premium above book value for firms that earn more than the cost of capital by producing **positive abnormal earnings**. Conversely, firms that produce **negative abnormal earnings** have share prices below book value. The abnormal earnings valuation model is:

∞

Valuing a Business

Opp0rtunity

$$P_O = BV_O + \sum_{t=1} \frac{E_O \text{ (\textbf{Abnormal Earnings}}_t)}{(1+r)^t}$$

Where BV = equity book value per share

E_O = expectation of future abnormal earnings per share

r = cost of equity capital

The cost of equity capital is the amount required by stockholders on investment. Abnormal earnings (AE) are the actual earning that exceed required earnings.

$$AE = X_t - (r \times BV_{t-1}) \quad \text{Where } X_t = \text{Actual earnings}$$
$$r = \text{cost of equity capital}$$
$$BV_{t-1} = \text{Book value at beginning of year}$$

(See Demonstration Problem 3.)

When a firm's return on equity (ROE) exceeds its return on assets (ROA), the firm can earn a higher return on its investments that the cost of debt financing. Firms that consistently earn a higher ROE than the industry average will usually have shares that have a higher market value to book value ratio.

Learning Objective 8:
The notion of "earnings surprises" and how stock returns relate to "good news" and "bad news" earnings surprises.

Earnings surprises happen when the expected future earnings are different than expected. The efficient market theory suggests because the market incorporates all information into prices, stock values reflect investors unbiased expectations about the firm's future earnings and cash flow. Information comes from a variety of sources including financial statements. As new information is released, stock prices change. Earnings announcements either confirm investors' expectations, provide surprises by exceeding expectations ("good news"), or fall short of expectations ("bad news"). Stock behavior is predictable:
1.   "Good news" — stock drifts upward before the earnings announcement and rises again after the announcement.
2.   "Bad news" — stock drifts downward before the earnings announcement and falls again after the announcement.
3.   "Confirming news" — prices tend to remain about the same.
Small companies that are not closely followed by analysts tend to exhibit little pre-announcement price drifts because of lack of information.

Valuing a Business

Analysts value businesses in a variety of ways but the two most

Opportunity

FYI. . .
Cash provided by operations is the only renewable source of cash. Investing and financing cash flows have finite limits.

common are:
1.   Expected future free cash flows; and
2.   Expected abnormal earnings.

Information required under both methods includes:
1.   Expected future free cash flows for each year;
2.   Approximation of the cost of equity capital;
3.   Terminal value estimate; and
4.   Present value interest factors for the cost of equity capital.

Using information contained in pro forma financial statements, one can compute the expected value of future cash flows and the present value of the business. If these exceed the investment required, the investment should be considered as meeting minimum criteria for demanded rate of return.
(See Demonstration Problem 4.)

Learning Objective 9:
The importance of cash flow analysis and credit risk assessment in lending decisions.

While investors try to determine share value, creditors need to assess the firm's ability to meet debt obligations to pay interest and repay principal. Lending options include:
1.   **Short-term loans** — mature in one year or less and usually finance working capital. These are often secured by inventory or receivables.
2.   **Long-term loans** — mature in one to five years and usually finance fixed assets, investments in subsidiaries, refinance existing long-term debt, or provide long-term working capital. These are often secured by the assets purchased with the proceeds.
3.   **Revolving loan** — a credit line that is committed for more than one year. Borrowers usually borrow and repay as necessary to meet seasonal needs. Interest floats with prime rate and the borrower pays a commitment fee to secure the line of credit.
4.   **Commercial paper** — short-term notes issued by large corporations maturing in 270 days or less that pay a fixed interest rate.
5.   **Bonds** — publicly held long-term notes payable. Bonds may be secured or unsecured (**debenture** bonds). A **bond indenture** contains numerous protective covenants such as **sinking fund** requirements, **call provisions** or conversion features.

Loan officers prepare a financial analysis of a company to determine the firm's ability to repay that includes the following steps:

1.   Gain an understanding of the firm's business, risk, profitability, industry position, and financial strength;
2.   Preparation of **pro forma** (forecasted) financial statements to indicate the effect of the loan on the financial statements in expected and worst- case scenarios;
3.   Conduct a **due diligence** assessment of management's ethics; and
4.   Prepare a comprehensive risk assessment.

Cash flow analysis provides the loan officer with valuable information to assess a client's credit worthiness. Operating cash flows should be positive and sufficient to cover the debt service and other financing and investing needs of the firm. This will not happen each year in a company's history, but must occur regularly over the long term.

A firm normally experiences negative investing cash flows indicating that the firm is making investments. Positive investing cash flows are from disinvestment of assets. Emerging companies make substantial investments to begin and grow the business. Growing companies make substantial expansion investments. Mature companies replace assets to sustain current operations.

A firm uses financing cash flows to fund investments that cannot be funded from operations. Equity and debt financing provide cash flow and dividends and debt repayment use cash. Sustained positive financing cash flows from debt indicate that the company continues to borrow.

APPENDIX A

An estimate of share price can be derived from analysts' earnings forecasts and the abnormal earnings valuation model using the following five steps:

1. Obtain earnings per share (EPS) estimates for some future time horizon from analysts.
2. Combine the EPS estimates with projected dividends to forecast common equity book value for the time horizon.
3. Compute annual abnormal earnings by subtracting normal earnings from analysts' EPS estimates.
4. Forecast the perpetual abnormal earnings flow that will occur beyond the explicit time horizon.

5. Add the current book value and the present value of the two abnormal earnings components to obtain an intrinsic value estimate of the company's share price.

APPENDIX B
Learning Objective 10:
How to forecast a company's financial statements

Financial statement forecasts are an essential ingredient of equity valuation and credit risk analysis. The starting point for a forecast is a detailed understanding of the company, its recent financial performance and health.

There are six steps to preparing a comprehensive financial statement forecast:

1. Project sales revenue for each period in the forecast horizon.
2. Forecast operating expenses and derive projected pre-tax operating income before depreciation and amortization.
3. Forecast the level of operating assets and liabilities.
4. Forecast the company's financial structure and dividend policy each period.
5. Forecast depreciation expense and tax expense each period.
6. Derive projected cash flow statements from the forecasted income statements and balance sheets.

Glossary of Terms

Abnormal Earnings	Earnings that are either above or below a stated benchmark such as cost of capital.
Bond Seniority	A feature that specifies which bondholders will be paid off first in the event of bankruptcy.
Bond Sinking Fund	A fund established to accumulate funds over the life of a bond issue that insures the repayment of the bondholders.
Call Provision	A provision in a bond indenture that allows a company to repurchase part or all of a bond issue at stated prices over a specific period.
Commercial Paper	Short-term notes sold directly to investors by large highly-rated companies.
Corporate Valuation	An estimate of the worth or price of a company, one of its operating units, or its ownership shares.
Distributable Cash Flow	Operating cash flow minus cash outlays for the replacement of existing buildings, equipment and furnishings. The amount available to finance planned expansion of operating capacity, reduce debt, pay dividends, or

repurchase stock.

Earnings Multiple	The price/earnings ratio, a measure of the relationship between a firm's current earnings and its share price, expressed mathematically as the reciprocal of the equity cost of capital.
Earnings Quality	A measure of how much the reported profits of a company diverge from their true operating earnings.
Earnings Surprises	A deviation in reported earnings from the expectations of investors.
Free Cash Flow	Distributable Cash Flow.
Indenture	A written agreement between the borrowing company and its creditors.
Net Cash Flows	The difference between cash inflows and outflows.
Permanent Earnings Component	A component of the income statement that is valuation relevant and expected to continue into the future.
Price/Earnings Ratio	The Earnings Multiple.
Risk-Adjusted Discount Rate	Equity cost of capital.
Secured Bonds	Bonds that specify collateral used to protect bondholders in the event of default.
Sensitivity Analysis	An analysis that examines "best case" and "worst case" scenarios for alternative assumptions concerning financial statement information and competitor behavior.
Transitory Earnings Component	A component of the income statement that is valuation relevant but is not expected to persist into the future.
Value Irrelevant Earnings (Noise) Component	A component of earnings that is unrelated to future free cash flows or future earnings and, therefore not pertinent to assessing current share price.
Value-Relevant Attribute	An item of data or other financial information that drives a firm's value.
Zero-Growth Perpetuity	An assumption for a mature firm with stable cash flow that the current level of cash flows will continue in perpetuity.

Demonstration Problems

1. **Discounted Free Cash Flow Valuation Model**

The table below contains the expected future free cash flows of the Alpha Corporation along with the appropriate discount factors at 16%.

	Year 1	Year 2	Year 3	Beyond Year 3
Expected Free Cash Flows	$(10,000)	$16,000	$20,000	$24,000
Discount Factor at 16%	.86207	.74316	.64066	.64066

Required: Calculate the present value of the expected free cash flows and determine if Alpha should make a $100,000 investment assuming that the required rate of return is 16%.

First Step: Compute the expected value of all years beyond Year 3.
Application: Divide the annual expected free cash flows for all years beyond Year 3 by the discount factor.
Solution: $24,000 / .16 = $150,000

Second Step: Compute the discounted expected cash flow.
Application: Multiply each cash flow by the discount factor and sum the totals.
Solution: Complete the table below:

Alpha Corporation
Valuation of Expected Future Cash Flows

	Year 1	Year 2	Year 3	Beyond Year 3
Expected Free Cash Flows	$(10,000)	$16,000	$20,000	$150,000
Discount Factor at 16%	.86207	.74316	.64066	.64066
Present Value of Each Flow	$(8,620)	$11,891	$12,813	$96,099

Estimated Value = $112,183

Third Step: Determine if a $100,000 investment is acceptable if the required rate of return is 16%.
Application: If one discounts the future free cash flows at the minimum required rate of return and the value is greater than the investment required, the investment is acceptable.
Solution: The estimated value is more than the investment, so this investment is acceptable.

2. **The Earnings Regression Model.**

The following information is available for the Register Company, which experiences a risk-adjusted equity cost of capital of 12%.

EPS	$4	EPS Components:	
		Permanent	80%
		Transitory	15%
		Value-Irrelevant	5%

Required: Determine the implied total earnings multiple and the implied share price for the Register Company.

First Step: Decompose the earnings per share.
Application: The earnings per share comprises three separate types of earnings.
Solution: Multiple the earnings per share by each of the components.

EPS Decomposition:

Permanent component	80% x $4 = $3.20
Transitory component	15% x $4 = $ .60
Value-irrelevant component	5% x $4 = $ .20

Second Step: Apply the earnings multiple to compute the implied share price.
Application: Permanent earnings should have a multiplier of the reciprocal of the risk-adjusted cost of capital, transitory earnings should have a multiplier of 1, and value-irrelevant earnings should have a multiplier of zero.
Solution: Multiply the earnings by the Beta of each component.

Earnings Multiple Applied:

Permanent component ($\beta_P = 8.33$)	8.33 x $3.20 = $26.66
Transitory component ($\beta_T = 1$)	1.00 x .60 = .60
Value-irrelevant component ($\beta_O = 0$)	0 x .20 = ___.00
Implied Share Price	$27.26

Third Step: Determine the implied total earnings multiplier.
Application: Divide the implied share price by the earnings per share.
Solution: $27.26 / $4 = 6.82

3.   **Computing Abnormal Earnings**

Assume the following information for the Carlini Corporation:
NOPAT = $50,000   r = 20%   Book Value = $220,000

Required: Calculate abnormal earnings.

First Step: Determine the formula for abnormal earnings.
Application: Abnormal Earnings = Actual Earnings — (r x Book Value)
Solution: Abnormal Earnings = Actual Earnings — (r x Book Value)
                      = $50,000 — (.20 x $220,000)
                      = $50,000 — $44,000 = $6,000

4.   **Valuation of Firms.**
Brad Patton has an opportunity to invest $50,000 for a franchise sandwich shop. The franchiser provided an analysis of pre-tax earnings and estimated free cash flows based on twenty years of experience for similar installations. Research on the franchiser indicates that it is known for honesty in its business dealings.

Deli Sandwich Shop

Estimated	Year 1	Year 2	Year 3	Year 4	Beyond Year 4
Pre-tax Earnings	$(5,000)	$5,000	$9,000	$13,000	$14,000
Free Cash Flows	(2,500)	7,500	12,500	15,000	14,000
PVIF: 15%	0.86957	0.75614	0.65752	0.57175	0.57175

Required: Determine the value of the sandwich shop using
1.   the expected future free cash flows approach.
2.   the expected abnormal earnings approach.

Part A: Expected future free cash flows approach
First Step: Determine the information needed to use the expected future free cash flows approach.
Application: The expected future free cash flows approach requires the estimated future free cash flows, the expected rate of return, and the present value interest factors for the rate of return.
Solution:

Estimated	Year 1	Year 2	Year 3	Year 4	Beyond Year 4
Free Cash Flows	$ (2,500)	$7,500	$12,500	$15,000	$14,000
Expected rate of return 15%					
PVIF: 15%	0.86957	0.75614	0.65752	0.57175	0.57175

Second Step: Compute the present value of the expected free cash flows to value the company.
Application: Multiply each year's estimated free cash flows by the PVIF. (For years 4 and beyond, find the terminal value.)
Solution: Terminal value = $\dfrac{\text{Estimated annual free cash flow} \quad \$14,000}{\text{Discount rate .15}}$ = $93,333

Deli Sandwich Shop

Estimated	Year 1	Year 2	Year 3	Year 4	Beyond Year 4
Free Cash Flows	$(2,500)	$7,500	$12,500	$15,000	$93,333
PVIF: 15%	0.86957	0.75614	0.65752	0.57175	0.57175
Present Value	$(2,174)	$5,671	$8,219	$8,576	$53,363

Present Value = $73,655

Part B: Expected abnormal earnings approach
First Step: Determine the information needed to use the expected abnormal earnings approach.
Application: The expected abnormal earnings approach requires the estimated normal earnings, the expected rate of return, the estimated pre-tax earnings, and the present value interest factors for the rate of return.
Solution:
Estimated normal earnings = Discount rate (15%) x Investment $50,000 = $7,500

Estimated	Year 1	Year 2	Year 3	Year 4	Beyond Year 4
Pre-tax Earnings	$(5,000)	$5,000	$9,000	$13,000	$14,000
Expected rate of return 15%					
PVIF: 15%	0.86957	0.75614	0.65752	0.57175	0.57175

Second Step: Compute the present value of the abnormal earnings to value the company.
Application: Multiply each year's estimated abnormal earnings by the PVIF. Abnormal earnings are the estimated pre-tax earnings minus the normal earnings. (For years 4 and beyond, find the terminal value.) Add the present value of the abnormal earnings to the investment to find the value of the company.
Solution: Terminal value = $\dfrac{\text{Estimated abnormal earnings } \$6,500}{\text{Discount rate } .15}$ = $43,333

Deli Sandwich Shop

Equity	Year 1	Year 2	Year 3	Year 4	Beyond Year 4
Book Value	$50,000	$50,000	$50,000	$50,000	$50,000
Cost of Capital	0.15	0.15	0.15	0.15	0.15
Normal Earnings	$ 7,500	$ 7,500	$ 7,500	$ 7,500	$ 7,500

Estimated	Year 1	Year 2	Year 3	Year 4	Beyond Year 4
Pre-tax Earnings	$ (5,000)	$ 5,000	$ 9,000	$ 13,000	$ 14,000
Normal Earnings	7,500	7,500	7,500	7,500	7,500
Abnormal Earn.	$ (12,500)	$ (2,500)	$ 1,500	$ 5,500	$ 43,333*
PVIF: 15%	0.86957	0.75614	0.65752	0.57175	0.57175
Present Value	$(10,870)	$ (1,890)	$ 986	$ 3,145	$ 24,776

Present Value = $16,147   *Terminal value = $6,500/0.15 = $43,333
Investment   50,000
Estimated Value $66,147

Test Yourself

True or False Questions

T F   1.   Balance sheet book values serve as a value-relevant attribute that drive a firm's value.

T F   2.   The determination of the risk associated with a value-relevant attribute is not a
requirement when valuing a company.

T F   3.   Dividends are a value-relevant attribute, but they represent the creation of wealth rather
than the distribution of wealth.

T F   4.   Equity investors and analysts use fundamental analysis to estimate the value of a company.

T F   5.   Free cash flow is the operating cash minus cash outlays for the replacement of existing
operating capacity.

T F   6.   The price of stock in the market today is equal to the sum of the stream of expected future
free cash flows per share of stock discounted back to the present.

T F   7.   The equity cost of capital should not be adjusted to reflect the uncertainty or riskiness of
the cash flow stream.

T F   8.   According to the FASB, accrual accounting generally provides a better indication about a
firm's performance than information on cash receipts and disbursements.

T F   9.   Cash accounting produces an earnings number that smoothes out the unevenness in year-
to-year cash flows.

T F   10.   A measure of the relation between a firm's future earnings and its share price is the
earnings multiple.

T F   11.   A cross-sectional study of earnings and stock prices is a method used to test whether
earnings are value-relevant.

T F   12.   Two firms with the same level of current and future earnings will always sell for the same
price.

T F   13.   The portion of a firm's earnings reinvested each period is the reinvestment ratio.

T F   14.   Income from continuing operations is generally regarded as a transitory component of
earnings.

T F   15.   A change in accounting principle that has no future cash flow consequence is regarded as
valuation-irrelevant.

T   F   16.   Permanent earnings should have a higher earnings multiple than transitory earnings.

T   F   17.   Earnings are considered high quality when they are sustainable.

T   F   18.   Earnings quality is not affected by the accounting methods chosen by management.

T   F   19.   A firm that produces negative abnormal earnings would have a share price above book value.

T   F   20.   Any difference between actual earnings for a period and the investor's required dollar return on invested capital at the beginning of the period represents abnormal earnings.

T   F   21.   When estimates of future earnings prove to be incorrect, an "earnings surprise" is the end result.

T   F   22.   Research evidence has shown that quarterly earnings announcements have no bearing on stock prices.

T   F   23.   Sensitivity analysis involves constructing "best case" and "worst case" scenarios that incorporate alternative assumptions about sales, costs, and competitors' behaviors.

T   F   24.   Creditors analyze financial statements primarily to assess the adequacy of per share prices.

T   F   25.   Sinking fund provisions require the borrower to make payments to a trustee who in turn uses these funds to retire debt.

Multiple-Choice Questions
Select the best answer from those provided.

_____   1.   Free cash flow is operating cash flow
  a.   minus accrual income.
  b.   plus accrual income.
  c.   minus cash outlays to replace existing operating capacity.
  d.   plus cash outlays to replace existing operating capacity.

_____   2.   The equity cost of capital is the discount rate used for the
  a.   present value model.
  b.   discounted accrual earnings model.
  c.   combined cost of capital model.
  d.   discounted free cash flow valuation model.

_____ 3.   FASB believes that current accrual accounting earnings are the best predictor of
            a. current cash flows.
            b. future cash flows.
            c. past accrual accounting earnings.
            d. future cash-basis accounting earnings.

_____ 4.   The price earnings ratio is the
            a. earnings multiple.
            b. return on assets.
            c. profit on sales.
            d. return on common equity.

_____ 5.   The most significant explanations for variations in the earnings multiples are
            growth opportunities and
            a. length of time in business.
            b. maturity of the firm.
            c. risk differences.
            d. rank within the industry.

_____ 6.   An example of permanent earnings is
            a. income from continuing operations excluding special or non-recurring items.
            b. Non-recurring items.
            c. extraordinary gains and losses.
            d. prior period adjustments.

_____ 7.   Discontinued operations gains or losses are regarded as
            a. permanent earnings.
            b. value-irrelevant earnings.
            c. transitory earnings.
            d. noise.

_____ 8.   Sustainable earnings are considered
            a. discretionary earnings.
            b. low quality earnings.
            c. high quality earnings.
            d. value-irrelevant earnings.

_____ 9.   As transitory components become a less important part of a firm's reported
earnings, the reported earnings are
a.   a less reliable indicator of sustainable cash flows.
b.   less quality enhanced.
c.   a less reliable indicator of fundamental value.
d.   a more reliable indicator of sustainable cash flows.

_____ 10.   Negative abnormal earnings are produced when a firm earns
a.   more than the cost of equity capital.
b.   less than the cost of equity capital.
c.   the equivalent of the cost of equity capital.
d.   superior earnings.

_____ 11.   Firms that have a share price below book value earn
a.   below the industry average.
b.   equal to the cost of equity capital.
c.   below the cost of equity capital.
d.   above the cost of equity capital.

_____ 12.   If the Return on Equity exceeds the Return on Assets, the earnings are
a.   below the cost of debt financing.
b.   equal to the cost of debt financing.
c.   above the cost of debt financing.
d.   at least one-half of the cost of debt financing.

_____ 13.   Earnings in excess of stockholders' required dollar return on invested capital are
a.   value-irrelevant earnings.
b.   transitory earnings.
c.   noise.
d.   abnormal earnings.

_____ 14.   A company with a Return on Equity that consistently exceeds the industry average
will generally have shares that sell at a
a.   market-to-book ratio equal to the industry average.
b.   higher market-to-book ratio than the industry average.
c.   lower market-to-book ratio than the industry average.
d.   lower market price than its competitors.

_____ 15. Incorrect estimates of future earnings give rise to
   a. negative abnormal earnings.
   b. positive abnormal earnings.
   c. negative cash inflows.
   d. an earnings surprise.

_____ 16. Prior to the announcement of lower than expected earnings, stock returns exhibit
   a. a negative drift downward.
   b. a positive drift upward.
   c. no change in stock returns.
   d. a negative drift downward followed by an immediate upward drift.

_____ 17. The interest rate on a bond will usually
   a. remained fixed.
   b. float.
   c. be below prime interest.
   d. float below prime interest.

_____ 18. Commercial paper represents
   a. long-term notes from highly rated corporations.
   b. long-term notes from lowly rated corporations.
   c. short-term notes from highly rated corporations.
   d. secured bonds.

_____ 19. A debenture bond is a/an
   a. senior bond.
   b. callable bond.
   c. sinking fund bond.
   d. unsecured bond.

_____ 20. Emerging companies typically experience
   a. positive operating cash flows.
   b. negative operating cash flows.
   c. positive accrual accounting income.
   d. negative cost of equity capital.

Exercises

1. The following information is available for two companies:

	Eddy Corporation	Lou Corporation
Cost of Equity Capital	11%	15%
Earnings per Share	$9	$6

Required:
   A. Calculate the earnings multiple for each company.
   B. Assuming that the earnings will continue in perpetuity, calculate the expected share price for each company.

_____

_____

_____

_____

_____

_____

_____

2. The following information is available for the Indiana Corporation, which experiences a risk-adjusted equity cost of capital of 15%.

EPS	$20	EPS Components:	
		Permanent	85%
		Transitory	10%
		Value-Irrelevant	5%

Required: Determine the earnings multiple and the implied share price for the Indiana Corporation.

_____

_____

_____

_____

_____

_____

_____

_____

3.   The controller of Shoes Unlimited asked you to develop an estimate of the amount of
     earnings for last year that exceeded the cost of the firm's equity capital. You were able to
     develop the following information:
           Net Operating Profit Before Taxes = $66,667
           Cost Of Capital = 15%
           Book Value = $200,000
           Tax Rate = 40%.

Required: Compute the earnings that exceeded the cost of equity capital.

_____

_____

_____

_____

_____

_____

_____

4.   Assume the following information for Shasta, Inc.:
           NOPAT = $150,000   r = 11%   Book Value = $400,000

Required:
    A. Calculate abnormal earnings.
    B. If Shasta, Inc. is able to add a new product line at a cost of $140,000, what will happen to
        abnormal earnings?

_____

_____

_____

_____

_____

_____

_____

_____

5.   Terry Sarvas has been asked to invest $80,000 for a franchise gift shop. The franchiser provided an analysis of projected free cash flows based on ten years of experience for similar installations. Research on the franchiser indicates that it is honest in its business dealings.

The Little German Gift Shop

Estimated	Year 1	Year 2	Year 3	Year 4	Beyond Year 4
Free Cash Flows	$(7,500)	$4,000	$9,500	$15,000	$16,000
PVIF: 12%	0.89286	0.79719	0.71178	0.63552	0.63552
16%	0.86207	0.74316	0.64066	0.55229	0.55229

Required:
A.   If Terry expects to earn 12% on his investment, should he make the investment? What is the maximum he should pay for the franchise to earn 12%? As part of the presentation, compute the present value of the free cash flows and the estimated terminal value.

B.   If Terry expects to earn 16% on his investment, should he make the investment? What is the maximum he should pay for the franchise to earn 16%? As part of the presentation, compute the present value of the free cash flows and the estimated terminal value.

_____

_____

_____

_____

_____

Solutions

Answers to True or False Questions

True Answers: 1, 4, 5, 6, 8, 11, 15, 16, 17, 20, 21, 23, 25

False answers explained:

2.   The determination of risk or uncertainty associated with a value-relevant attribute <u>is</u> an important step in the process.

3.   Dividends are a value-relevant attribute, but they represent the <u>distribution</u> of wealth rather than the creation of wealth.

7.   The equity cost of capital <u>should be</u> adjusted to reflect uncertainty.

9.   <u>Accrual</u> accounting smoothes out the unevenness of cash flows.

10.   The relation between a firm's <u>current earnings</u> and its share price is the earnings multiple.

12.   The stock prices may be different because of differences in <u>risk and uncertainty</u>.

13.   The portion of a firm's earnings reinvested each period is the <u>retention ratio</u>.

14.   Income from operations is generally considered a <u>permanent</u> component of earnings.

18.   Earnings quality <u>is affected</u> by the accounting methods chosen by management.

19.   The share price would be <u>below</u> book value.

22.   Quarterly and annual earnings announcements <u>do have</u> a bearing on stock prices.

24.   Creditors analyze financial statements primarily to determine a firm's ability to meet its debt obligations.

Answers to Multiple-Choice Questions

1.	c	6.	a	11.	c	16.	a
2.	d	7.	c	12.	c	17.	a
3.	b	8.	c	13.	d	18.	c
4.	a	9.	d	14.	b	19.	d
5.	c	10.	b	15.	d	20.	b

Answers to Exercises

		Eddy Corporation	Lou Corporation
1.			
A.	Earnings Multiple = 1/r	1 / .11 = 9.1	1 / .15 = 6.7

B.   Expected Share Price = EPS x Earnings Multiplier

		$9 x 9.1 = $81.90	$6 x 6.7 = $40.20

2.

Indiana Corporation
Analysis of Implied Share Price

EPS Decomposition:

Permanent component	85% x $20 = $17.00
Transitory component	10% x $20 = $ 2.00
Value-irrelevant component	5% x $20 = $ 1.00

Earnings Multiple Applied:

Permanent component ($\beta_P = 6.7$)	6.7 x $17.00 = $113.90
Transitory component ($\beta_T = 1$)	1.0 x 2.00 = 2.00
Value-irrelevant component ($\beta_O = 0$)	0 x 1.00 = .00
Implied Share Price	$115.90
Implied Total Earnings Multiple $115.90/$20	5.80

3.

$$\text{Abnormal Earnings} = \text{Actual Earnings} - (\text{r x Book Value})$$
$$= \$40,000 - (.15 \text{ x } \$200,000)$$
$$= \$40,000 - \$30,000 = \$10,000$$

4.

A. $\text{Abnormal Earnings} = \text{Actual Earnings} - (\text{r x Book Value})$
$$= \$300,000 - (.11 \text{ x } \$800,000)$$
$$= \$300,000 - \$88,000 = \$212,000$$

B. $\text{Abnormal Earnings} = \text{Actual Earnings} - (\text{r x Book Value})$
$$= \$300,000 - (.11 \text{ x } \$940,000)$$
$$= \$300,000 - \$103,400 = \$196,600$$

5.

A.   The Little German Gift Shop

Estimated	Year 1	Year 2	Year 3	Year 4	Beyond Year 4
Free Cash Flows	$(7,500)	$ 4,000	$9,500	$15,000	$133,333*
PVIF: 12%	0.89286	0.79719	0.71178	0.63552	0.63552
Present Value	$(6,696)	$ 3,189	$6,762	$9,533	$84,736

Present Value = $97,524   *Terminal value = $16,000/.12

At 12% cost of equity capital, make the investment because it will earn more than 12%, since the present value is higher than $80,000. The maximum payment for the franchise to earn 12% is $97,524.

B.

The Little German Gift Shop

Estimated	Year 1	Year 2	Year 3	Year 4	Beyond Year 4
Free Cash Flows	$(7,500)	$ 4,000	$9,500	$15,000	$100,000*
PVIF: 16%	0.86207	0.74316	0.64066	0.55229	0.55229
Present Value	$(6,466)	$ 2,973	$6,086	$8,284	$55,229

Present Value = $66,106   *Terminal value = $32,000/0.16

At 16% cost of equity capital, do not make the investment because it will earn less than 16%, since the present value is lower than $80,000. The maximum payment for the franchise to earn 16% is $66,106.

CHAPTER 7

THE ROLE OF FINANCIAL INFORMATION
IN CONTRACTING

Chapter Review

Learning Objective 1:
What conflicts of
interest arise between
managers and
shareholders, lenders or
regulators.

Financial accounting numbers are used to determine compliance and outcomes for loan agreement, compensation agreements, and contracts with agencies, supplies, distributors, and customers.. The integrity of financial statement data depends upon the methods used by an entity and the ability of management to change or manipulate the methods.

Businesses are run by people with delegated authority to make decisions. Contractual relationships delegate such authority to various people who may experience **conflicts of interest** in the performance of such duties. A manager is responsible to himself, his company, and the third parties of contracts. Sometimes the interests of each party conflict. Contracts should be written by negotiators to eliminate or reduce the possibility of conflicts of interest by clearly specifying the mutual rights and responsibilities of each party to the agreement. Business decisions affect the value of the firm and the share value of the owners.

FYI. . .
The **risk /reward**
tradeoff provides that
the higher the **risk**, the
greater the **rewards** and
losses.

Lenders must protect themselves by reducing conflicts of interest. Lenders should write contracts with restrictive debt covenants that reduce borrowers' capacity to harm creditors.

FYI. . .
Borrowers should
negotiate carefully both
affirmative and negative
covenants in a lending
agreement to make sure
that compliance is
feasible in the short run
and the long run.

Because covenants protect the lenders, well-constructed covenants also lower the cost of debt financing to the borrower. Debt covenants can be either affirmative or negative. **Affirmative covenants** stipulate actions the borrower must take including:
1.   using the loan for the agreed-upon purpose (no asset substitution);
2.   maintenance of financial covenants and reporting requirements;
3.   compliance with laws;
4.   compliance with rights of inspection; and
5.   maintenance of insurance, properties, and records.

Learning Objective 2:

Financial covenants establish minimum financial tests intended to signal

148

How and why accounting numbers are used in debt agreements, in compensation contracts, and for regulatory purposes.

financial problems and trigger lender intervention long before default becomes a reality. Therefore, the borrower must provide lenders financial statements on a regular and timely basis. Financial covenants usually require minimum ratio maintenance for various liquidity, profitability, and solvency ratios.

Negative covenants place restrictions on managerial decisions that might impair the creditor's claims against cash flow including:

1. limits on the total indebtedness, investments of funds, capital expenditures, leases, and loans;
2. restrictions on dividend payments, share repurchases, mergers, asset sales, prepayment of loans, and new business ventures; and
3. remedies for the creditor in case of default to enable the creditor to recover the maximum amount.

Most lending agreements require borrowers to provide a Certificate of Compliance indicating that management finds no violation of any covenant. When violations occur, management must notify the lender and provide remedies to prevent seizure of collateral, acceleration of debt, or initiation of bankruptcy proceedings. A common remedy is loan agreement renegotiation.

Costly defaults can occur in a number of ways:

1. A **technical default** occurs when all principal and interest payments are made timely but one or more loan covenants are violated.
2. A **payment default** occurs when the borrower cannot meet a principal or interest payment.
3. A **cross default** occurs when the borrower fails to make other required debt payments.

Managers have the ability to choose alternative accounting techniques, make discretionary expenditures and accrual adjustments, and make decisions about the timing of transactions which reduce the likelihood of technical default.

When managers manipulate accounting data with discretionary accruals, timing of gain or loss transactions, or with accounting changes, the changes made in earnings, ratios, and cash flows are seldom sustainable.

The heart of the matter. . .

Learning Objective 3:
How managerial incentives are influenced by the use of accounting-based contracts and regulations.

The Board of Directors hires officers to manage the firm. Professional managers may lack a passion for long-term corporation excellence that comes with long-term affiliation with the firm or substantial ownership in the firm. Separation of ownership and stewardship creates potential conflicts of interest between managers and shareholders. Conflicts of interest can be eliminated if managers are induced to behave like owners. Compensation packages linking managerial pay to the market value of shares help managers to think like shareholders.

Most firms compensate executives with a package consisting of:
1.   **Base salary** commensurate with industry norms and individual talent.
2.   **Short-term incentives** linked to financial performance.
3.   **Long-term incentives** linked to long-term growth and prosperity.

Incentive pay is "at risk" to the executives, which accomplishes the goal of making the managers think like shareholders.

Chief executive officers (CEOs) receive from 21% to 51% of their compensation in the form of incentive pay. Short-term incentives are usually tied to bonuses for achieving certain levels of net income or after-tax rate of return on assets. The most common types of long-term incentives are:
1.   **Stock options** — Stock options allow executives to buy stock at a specified price four to seven years into the future. If the executive helps the company value to grow, the option price will be substantially below the market price in the future.
2.   **Stock appreciation rights (SARs)** — SARs are a cross between a stock option and a bonus. The executive receives a bonus in the future equal to the appreciation in value of a number of shares of stock.
3.   **Restricted stock** — The firm awards an executive restricted stock shares that must be forfeited if the executive terminates

employment.

4. **Performance plans** — Performance plans reward executives with shares or units earned by specific performance of predetermined goals.

5. **Performance unit plans** – The plan allocates a given number of units at the start of the award period. Cash equal to the number of units earned times the fixed dollar value, with the proportion of units determined by the degree to which performance goals have been achieved.

6. **Performance share plans** – These plans are similar to performance unit plans in that each employee is allocated a fixed number of shares with the proportion earned out contingent upon the extent to which financial and strategic plans are met.

Annual **proxy statements** contain information about a company's executive compensation plans and includes a detailed analysis of the type and amount of the five highest paid executives.

Firms' executive incentives were tied to accounting numbers in 1996 by the following percentages:

	Long-term Plans
Return on equity	29%
Earnings per share	35%
Net income	71%
Cash flow	10%
Return on assets	29%
Economic value added	12%
Return on capital	8%
Other	8%

Source: 1996 The Conference Board

FYI. . .
Short-term focus may be one of the worst failings in American business practices.

The widespread use of accounting-based incentives raises four issues:

1. Earnings growth does not always translate into increased shareholder value. Executives can grow earnings with investments that do not exceed the cost of capital. Rewards tied only to earnings may reward executives for earnings growth that does not increase share value.

2. The accrual accounting process can distort traditional measures of company performance. Return on assets (ROA) defined as net operating after tax profit/average total assets can improve due to

real profitability gains. However, some ROA improvements can arise due to the effect of depreciation accounting. Depreciation causes the book value of depreciable assets to decline, which, in turn, causes a decline in the ROA denominator. The smaller ROA denominator leads to a larger ROA percentage. Stockholders do not want to pay an ROA bonus due solely to depreciation.

3.   Incentives tied to earnings encourage managers to focus on the short run. Executives may make decisions that keep short-term profits high and prevent the firm from long-term stable growth, such as keeping old fully depreciated equipment instead of replacing it with more productive new equipment that requires depreciation and reduces current income.

4.   Executives have some discretionary power over accounting policies and procedures. When bonus potential is high, an executive might maneuver earnings by liquidating LIFO layers or reducing research and development expenditures. When bonus potential is low, an executive might further reduce income by accelerating certain write-offs related to asset impairment, restructuring costs, and depreciable or amortizable assets. Such write-offs will improve the possibilities of bonuses in the future.

Firms can ameliorate the short-term focus of annual incentive plans by including substantial long-term incentive plans such as stock option plans. Firms can organize **compensation committees,** comprised of outside (non management) directors, to judge whether the bonus calculations were inflated by manipulation or represent the economic reality of performance.

Learning Objective 4:

What role contracts and regulations play in shaping managers' accounting choices.

FYI. . .

Firms in regulated industries must prepare financial statements for governmental agencies which require **regulatory accounting principles (RAP).**
SFAS No. 71 allows firms to use regulatory assets and liabilities, computed under RAP methods, to determine rates in GAAP financial statements when

1.   the rates recover the costs of providing regulated services, and
2.   the rates can be charged and collected in the competitive

Because many industries have unique accounting practices, the AICPA publishes many industry audit guides to provide accountants with detailed information specific to an industry.

environment.

Financial statement users should understand the methods used to prepare the statements (RAP or GAAP) to evaluate financial performance and condition.

Banks and financial institutions must meet **minimum capital requirements**.
Financial institutions must maintain a minimum capital adequacy ratio defined as:

$$\text{Capital adequacy ratio} = \frac{\text{Invested capital (as defined by RAP)}}{\text{Gross Assets (as defined by RAP)}}$$

An institution with inadequate capital faces serious problems that can range from submitting detailed plans to restore capital adequacy, increased scrutiny by regulators, denial of requests to merge or expand, to dividend restrictions.

FYI. . .
Losses from bad loans are also called **loan charge-offs**.

The best way to avoid problems is to employ profitable operating principles and remain financially sound. Some managers attempt artificial compliance by selecting accounting policies that increase RAP capital or reduce RAP assets.
Loans receivable comprise the bulk of financial institutions' assets, so managers carefully time the recognition of questionable loans. By understating the loan losses and **loan loss provisions**, managers increase net income and help the firm meet its capital adequacy ratio.

Utility firms are granted monopolies by governmental agencies. In exchange for the monopoly privilege, the governmental agencies determine the rates the utilities can charge to avoid profiteering. By setting the rates allowed, the agencies also determine the return on sales, assets, and equity. Typical rate formulas would be:

Allowed revenue =
Operating costs + Depreciation + Taxes + (ROA x Assets)

where ROA is predetermined by the regulator. RAP defines the allowable operating costs and asset base used in computing allowed revenue. Two of the major differences between utilities' GAAP and RAP are:
1.	deferral of expenses that can probably be recovered through

future revenues, and

2.   capitalization of equity costs on construction projects.

GAAP requires that expired costs (expenses) be recognized in the period sustained and that interest be capitalized only on construction projects.

Managers can manipulate rates by either increasing the asset base or by influencing regulators and/or the FASB to make non-allowable operating costs allowable. These can be accomplished by carefully designing contracts to comply with RAP rules for inclusion in the allowable costs or asset base.

FYI. . .
The **LIFO Compliance Rule** requires firms which use the LIFO inventory method for tax purposes to also use it for financial accounting

Internal Revenue Service requires income tax reporting on a tax basis. Many tax-basis rules are consistent with GAAP. The most common departures are depreciation, goodwill amortization, and the **LIFO compliance rule**. Firms and industries that report high profits also draw the attention of legislators who have been known to impose excess profits taxes. Manager have found that it is best to select accounting practices that minimize income to avoid political attention.

Learning Objective 5: What accounting "gimmicks" are sometimes used to hide a company's true performance and how to spot them.

Loan covenants, compensation contracts, regulatory agency oversight, and tax avoidance are powerful incentives that sometimes cause managers to hide a company's true economic performance and financial condition.

The following list identifies some accounting distortions and "gimmicks" used by managers:

- Unexplained changes in accounting methods
- Excessive year-end inventory purchases for LIFO companies when prices are rising
- Change in accounting estimates for useful life, lease residual value and pension benefit assumptions
- Receivables or inventory growth that outpaces sales growth
- Bad debt reserves that are low relative to receivables
- Sudden sale or securitization of receivables
- Unusually long depreciation of amoritization lives
- Capitalizing start up costs rather than expensing
- Increasing gap between earnings and operating cash flows
- Increasing gap between earnings and tax income
- Unexplained large changes in deferred tax balances

- Off-balance sheet financing arrangements
- Unexpected write-offs of assets
- Large changes in discretionary expenses
- Unusual business transactions that increase earnings
- Related-party transactions
- Audit qualifications or unexplained change in outside auditor

Appendix:

Two major conflicts arise in lending agreements.

1. **Asset Substitution** — borrowers use borrowed funds to fund riskier projects than indicated in the borrower's application. Owners are more willing to risk borrowed funds for risky projects than equity funds. High risk projects lower the expected value of the firm and the creditor's claim on assets. Management and owners have incentives to magnify gains by selecting higher risk projects and transferring substantial risk to the creditors. **(See Demonstration Problem 1.)**

2. **Repayment** — borrowers use borrowed funds to pay larger dividends than before the borrowing and risk the inability to repay the principal. Management can use operating cash flows to increase investment in the company, repay debt, pay dividends, or buy treasury shares. Managers who are also owners have strong incentives to use operating capital for dividends or treasury stock and transfer the cash to themselves.

Glossary of Terms

Affirmative Covenants   Covenants that stipulate actions that a borrower must take.

Asset Substitution   Replacing lower risk projects with higher risk projects to harm the creditor and benefit the owners.

Certificate of Compliance   A written statement required by a lender which affirms that management has reviewed the financial statements and found no violations of any covenant provision.

Debt Covenants   Loan provisions specifically designed to address the problems of asset substitution and repayment.

Discretionary

Accounting Accruals	Noncash financial statement adjustments which accrue revenues or expenses.
Events of Default	A section of a loan agreement which describes circumstances in which the creditor has the right to terminate the lending relationship.
Insubstance Defeasance	A transaction that allows a company to treat a liability as if paid off when it irrevocably places cash or other assets in trust solely for the purpose of making all remaining principal and interest payments.
Negative Covenants	Restrictions that prevent actions that might impair the lender's claim against the company's cash flows, earnings, and assets. These covenants place restrictions on managerial decisions.
Payment Default	A situation in which the borrower is unable to make the scheduled interest or principle payment.
Performance Plan	A plan which awards cash or stock earned according to the degree of achievement of predetermined performance goals.
Regulatory Accounting Principles	The methods and procedures that must be used when preparing financial statements for regulatory agencies.
Restricted Stock	An award of stock that is not transferable or subject to forfeiture for a number of years.
Stock Appreciation Rights	Executive compensation that pays an amount equal to the difference between the current stock price and the "exercise" price.
Stock Options	Executive compensation that provides an executive with the right to buy firm shares at a stated price for a period of years.
Technical Default	A situation in which a borrower has made all scheduled payments of principal and interest, but is in violation of one or more loan covenants.

Demonstration Problem

1.　Assessment of the expected value of projects.

Federal Investments is deciding between two alternatives for its next project. The following is a summary of the payoffs for each $1,000,000 investment:

Project	Probability (1)	Net Payoff (1)	Probability (2)	Net Payoff (2)
A	.6	$1,500,000	.4	$700,000
B	.5	1,800,000	.5	400,000

Required: Calculate the expected value of each alternative.

First Step: Determine the expected value of each alternative.
Application: The expected value of each alternative is the sum of the probable outcomes possible.
Solution:

A	.6 ($1,500,000) + .4 ($700,000) = $900,000 + $280,000 = $1,180,000
B	.5 ($1,800,000) + .5 ($400,000) = $900,000 + $200,000 = $1,100,000

Alternative A has the highest expected value and would be selected if all other aspects of the project were acceptable to Federal.

Test Yourself

True or False Questions

T F 1. Financial accounting numbers are rarely used to define contract terms.

T F 2. Conflicts of interest often enter into business relationships.

T F 3. Contract terms can reduce or eliminate conflicting incentives that arise in business relationships.

T F 4. Asset substitution is a source of conflict between a lender and a business owner.

T F 5. Creditor value is increased and shareholder value falls when money borrowed for a low risk project is invested in a higher risk project.

T F 6. A method to reduce conflicts of interest between managers and shareholders is to write contracts that restrict the owner-manager's ability to harm creditors.

T F 7. Loan provisions are specifically designed to address the issue of asset substitution but not repayment.

T F 8. Affirmative covenants stipulate actions that a borrower must take.

T F 9. Compliance with the law is an example of an affirmative covenant.

T F 10. Financial covenants establish maximum financial tests with which a borrower must comply.

T F 11. Negative covenants place direct restrictions on managerial decisions.

T F 12. Debt covenants reduce default risk.

T F 13. A technical default occurs when a borrower makes all principal and interest payments but violates one or more loan covenants.

T F 14.   Managers usually try to make accounting choices that will reduce the risk of technical default.

T F 15.   Stock options are one of the least used long-term incentive devices for managers.

T F 16.   Stock appreciation rights ease the cash flow burden on executives when exercising stock options.

T F 17.   Phantom stock provides executives with the cash value of the shares earned rather than the stock itself.

T F 18.   Research has shown that when annual earnings already exceeded bonus levels, managers used discretionary accounting options to increase earnings.

T F 19.   Regulatory accounting principles never show up in a company's financial statements prepared under Generally Accepted Accounting Principles.

T F 20.   The capital adequacy ratio is calculated by dividing the invested capital by the net assets.

T F 21.   Banking regulators do not have a powerful weapon to encourage compliance with minimum capital guidelines.

T F 22.   Loan charge-offs are receivables that the bank no longer expects to collect.

T F 23.   Regulatory accounting principles for utilities have no effect on the rates customers pay.

T F 24.   Financial statement distortions will be most prevelant when loan covenants are met.

T F 25.   Financial statement footnotes provide valuable information to uncover distortions and "gimmicks".

Multiple-Choice Questions

Select the best answer from those provided.

_____   1.   Financial accounting numbers can be used to
             a. define contract terms.
             b. replace a legal document.
             c. enforce a legal document.
             d. measure the time period of a legal contract.

_____ 2.   The delegation of decision-making authority is an essential feature of
a. all business relationships.
b. most business relationships.
c. all contracts.
d. most contracts.

_____ 3.   A conflict of interest arises when one party to a business relationship can make a decision that
a. benefits both parties.
b. benefits him or her but harms the other party.
c. is detrimental to both parties.
d. is favorable to both parties.

_____ 4.   Asset substitution is a source of conflict that may arise between
a. creditors and lenders.
b. debtors and business owners.
c. creditors and business owners.
d. low risk investment projects.

_____ 5.   A source of conflict between a banker and a business owner is a/an
a. failure to repay debt.
b. debt repayment.
c. reinvestment of profits in the business.
d. decision by the business owner to reduce dividend payments.

_____ 6.   Investment projects with a high dispersion of potential returns are usually preferred by
a. creditors.
b. stockholders.
c. lenders.
d. bankers.

_____ 7.   The transfer of wealth from creditors to shareholders takes place with
a. repayment of debt.
b. reduction of debt.
c. liability reduction.
d. asset substitution.

_____ 8.   The usage of funds for employee bonuses that are held for the repayment of debt gives rise to a/an
a.   source of credit.
b.   source of income.
c.   source of conflict.
d.   source of agreement.

_____ 9.   The restriction of asset substitution is accomplished with the use of provisions in
a.   debt obligation.
b.   credit obligation.
c.   credit covenant.
d.   debt covenant.

_____ 10.   An affirmative covenant stipulates actions that a borrower
a.   must take.
b.   should take.
c.   may take.
d.   must not take.

_____ 11.   The placement of a direct restriction on managerial decisions is a
a.   positive restriction.
b.   negative covenant.
c.   negative restriction.
d.   positive covenant.

_____ 12.   A limit on the payment of employee bonuses by the business entity is an example of a
a.   negative covenant.
b.   negative restriction.
c.   positive covenant
d.   positive restriction.

_____ 13.   The events of default section of a loan agreement describes the circumstances in which the lending relationship may be terminated by
a.   either party to the agreement.
b.   the borrower.
c.   the lender.
d.   the Securities and Exchange Commission.

_____ 14. A certificate of compliance is furnished to the lender by the company's
   a. management.
   b. attorney.
   c. auditor.
   d. stockholders.

_____ 15. When it is probable that the borrower will not be able to cure a default in the debt covenant within the next twelve months the debt must be
   a. removed from the balance sheet.
   b. classified as a long-term liability.
   c. classified as a current liability.
   d. only reported as a footnote disclosure.

_____ 16. A technical loan default occurs when the borrower violates a loan covenant and has made
   a. all interest payments but no principal payments.
   b. all principal payments but no interest payments.
   c. no interest or principal payments.
   d. all interest and principal payments.

_____ 17. Management's efforts to maintain the terms of loan covenants often leads to earnings increases that are likely to be
   a. permanent.
   b. sustainable.
   c. transitory.
   d. of high quality.

_____ 18. Shareholders and managers may be able to overcome potential conflicts of interest if managers are provided with incentives that encourage them to behave as if they were
   a. owners.
   b. auditors.
   c. debtors.
   d. employees.

_____ 19. Long-term incentive devices for managers would include which one of the following?
   a. Boats
   b. Stock options
   c. Cars
   d. Cash bonuses

_____ 20.   Phantom stock is
a.   transferable.
b.   subject to forfeiture.
c.   not transferable and subject to forfeiture for a period of years.
d.   voting stock.

_____ 21.   The ability of executives to use discretion over accounting policies represents a controversy surrounding
a.   materiality.
b.   the cost-benefit constraint.
c.   present value.
d.   the use of accounting based incentive plans.

_____ 22.   The compensation committee of a company should be made up of
a.   high level management.
b.   all the officers of the company.
c.   the president and treasurer.
d.   Members of the Board of Directors who are "outside directors."

_____ 23   The capital adequacy ratio in the banking industry is defined as Invested Capital divided by
a.   Gross Assets.
b.   Net Assets.
c.   Net Liabilities.
d.   Gross Liabilities.

_____ 24.   For regulatory rate setting, image advertising in the utilities industry is considered to be a/an
a.   part of cost of goods sold.
b.   fixed cost.
c.   disallowed operating cost.
d.   allowable operating cost.

_____ 25.   Which of the following is not a potential accounting distortion
a.   receivables that outpace sales growth
b.   bad debt reserves that follow industry norms
c.   unusual business practices that boosts earnings
d.   large changes in discretionary expenses

Exercises

1. The Golf Corporation has a loan with a bank that calls for Golf to maintain a 2.5 to 1 current ratio as of December 31st of each year. At December 1st the corporation is reporting current assets of $1,000,000 and current liabilities of $600,000. Golf expects no change in current liabilities and a $100,000 increase in current assets by December 31st.

    Required:
    A. Will the corporation be in compliance with the loan covenants at the end of the year?
    B. What can management do to correct the potential problem?
    C. What are the ethical implications of management's actions?

2.   The Wire Company is reporting $1,000,000 of total current assets at the fiscal year end, and a current ratio of 2.5 to 1 when the auditor proposes several adjustments. The proposed adjustments will increase current liabilities by $200,000 and will increase current assets by only $25,000. The company is required to maintain working capital of $500,000 for a bank loan.

Required:
   A. Compute the amount of working capital before adjustments.
   B. Compute the amount of working capital after adjustments.
   C. Does the Wire Company meet the covenant restriction if the auditor imposes the adjustments?

_____

_____

_____

_____

_____

_____

_____

_____

_____

3.   Arnold Company is choosing its next major investment and has narrowed it to two alternatives. The alternatives have the following payoffs based on a $1,000,000 investment:
      Alternative 1 has a .5 probability of producing a net payoff of $1,600,000 and a .5 probability of producing a net payoff of $750,000. Alternative 2 has a .7 probability of producing a net payoff of $1,800,000 and a .3 probability of producing a net payoff of $600,000.

Required:
   A. Calculate the expected value of each alternative.
   B. Which project would be preferred by the shareholders?
   C. If the project is to be financed with debt, which of the projects would be preferred by the creditors?

_____

_____

_____

_____

_____

_____

_____

_____

Solutions

Answers to True or False Questions

True Answers: 2, 3, 4, 6, 8, 9, 11, 12, 13, 14, 16, 17, 22, 25
False answers explained:
1. Financial accounting numbers are <u>often</u> used to define contract terms.
5. Creditor value is <u>decreased</u> and shareholder value is <u>increased</u>.
7. Loan provisions are designed to address <u>asset substitution and repayment</u>.
10. Financial covenants establish <u>minimum</u> financial tests.
15. Stock options are the <u>most</u> frequently used item for long-term incentives.
18. When annual earnings exceed bonus levels, managers use discretionary accounting options to <u>reduce</u> earnings.
19. Regulatory accounting principles <u>may</u> show up in a company's financial statements prepared under Generally Accepted Accounting Principles.
20. The capital adequacy ratio is calculated by dividing the invested capital by the <u>gross assets</u>.
21. Banking regulators <u>do have</u> a powerful weapon to encourage compliance with minimum capital guidelines.
23. Regulatory accounting principles for utilities <u>do have</u> an effect on rates charged.
24. Financial statement distortions will be most prevalent when loan covenants are <u>not</u> met.

Answers to Multiple-Choice Questions

1.	A	6.	B	11.	B	16.	D	21.	D
2.	B	7.	D	12.	A	17.	C	22.	D
3.	B	8.	C	13.	C	18.	A	23.	D
4.	C	9.	D	14.	A	19.	B	24.	A
5.	A	10.	A	15.	C	20.	C	25.	B

Answers to Exercises

1.   A.   The corporation will not be in compliance with the loan covenant because the current ratio will be 1.83:1. ($1,100,000/$600,000) = 1.83:1

        B.   Management could pay off some of the liabilities in order to bring the current ratio into line. This would provide an ethical and intelligent response from management. Management might attempt to shift liabilities from the current category to the non-current category by renegotiating the loans into long-term liabilities or reclassifying current liabilities into the non-current liabilities. Management could also attempt to manipulate asset values to increase the current assets by understating Allowance for Uncollectible Accounts or overstating inventory.

        C.   The payment of the liabilities is a sound ethical decision while the other manipulations would call into question the ethical behavior of management. The alternatives would also appear to involve fraudulent financial reporting.

2.   A.   Working Capital = Current Assets — Current Liabilities
            Current Assets $1,000,000/2.5 = Current Liabilities $400,000
            Working Capital = $1,000,000 — $400,000 = $600,000

        B.   After adjustments:
            Current Assets $1,025,000 — Current Liabilities $600,000 = $425,000

        C.   The company will not be in compliance with the loan covenant.

3.   A.   Alternative 1:
            Expected Return
            (.5 x $1,600,000 + .5 x $750,000) = $800,000 + $375,000 = $1,175,000
            Alternative 2:
            Expected Return
            (.7 x $1,800,000 + .3 x $600,000) = $1,260,000 + $180,000 = $1,440,000

        B.   The shareholders would prefer Alternative 2 because of the higher expected return. The debt holders would prefer Alternative 1 because it is a little safer with less dispersion.

CHAPTER 8

RECEIVABLES

Chapter Review

Learning Objective 1:
The methods used to estimate uncollectible accounts in order to determine the expected net realizable value of accounts receivable.

Amounts owed to a firm by outsiders are called **receivables.** Receivables arising from credit sales are **trade** or **accounts receivable** and usually are disclosed separately from other types of receivables if significant. According to GAAP, receivable balances on the balance sheet reflect the **net realizable value.** Net realizable value is the gross receivables minus estimated uncollectible amounts due to 1) customer default on payment and 2) returns or adjustments. The Accounts Receivable account always carries the balances of gross receivables. Two contra-asset accounts (Allowance for Uncollectibles and Allowance for Returns and Adjustments) reflect the balances deemed to not be realizable.

FYI. . .
The **Sales Revenue Method** of estimating uncollectibles is often called the **Income Statement Method.** The **Gross Accounts Receivable Method** is often called the **Balance Sheet Method.**

Uncollectible accounts are estimated in two ways:

1. **Sales Revenue Method** — assumes that bad debts arise as a consistent percentage of sales. This method determines the amount of the Bad Debt Expense for a period and creates an Allowance for Uncollectibles, by estimating the percentage of sales revenue that will never be collected.

2. **Gross Receivables Method** — assumes that bad debts arise as predictable percentages of categories of aged receivables. This method determines the amount of sufficient Allowance for Uncollectibles and adjusts the Bad Debt Expense accordingly. This process requires the use of an **Aging of Accounts Receivable. (See Demonstration Problem 1.)**

Managers that use the Sales Revenue Method appropriately apply the Gross Receivables Method at year end to satisfy themselves that the Allowance for Uncollectibles is adequate.

The allowance for uncollectibles account is a contra-asset account that is deducted from gross accounts receivables on the balance sheet. In this way the acounts receivables appear on the balance sheet at net realizable value.

When a specific receivable becomes uncollectible, the unpaid receivable is written-off (credited) and the Allowance for Uncollectibles is also reduced (debited). Expense recognition occurs in the year of sale, in accordance with the matching principle, when the Bad Debt Expense account is debited. Because the expense recognition is based on estimates, management has the capacity to manipulate earnings or smooth income. Research indicates that companies tend to increase Bad Debt Expense during good income years and decrease it during poor earnings years.

Learning Objective 2: How firms estimate and record sales returns and allowances.

When customers are dissatisfied with their purchases and return them, adjustments are made to their accounts receivable. The contra-revenue account, Sales Returns and Adjustments, is debited and the receivable is credited. Management does not directly reduce the Sales account because the dollar level of activity and quantity of adjustments made to sales provides valuable information about current and potential customer problems. Significant changes in the Sales Returns and Adjustments account relative to Sales may indicate:

1.   a change in the quality of the product;
2.   adoption or cessation of aggressive revenue recognition practices; or
3.   potential problems with or improvement in customer satisfaction.

Learning Objective 3: How to evaluate whether or not reported receivables arose from real sales and how to spot danger signals.

Differences between the growth rate of Sales on the income statement and Accounts Receivable on the balance sheet signal a **red flag**. These two growth rates should remain similar unless the company has changed its:

1.   sales terms;
2.   credit policies;
3.   accounting methods; or
4.   financing method for receivables.

Any time a firm experiences a growth in the Days Receivable Outstanding ratio, the growth rate of accounts receivable will be higher than the growth rate of sales. This is positive when the company elects to offer generous sales terms to attract a new class of customer, such as college students, young marrieds, or start-up firms. It is negative when the ratio increases without changes in sales terms because it indicates an erosion in customer credit-worthiness. In a similar manner, the company may have relaxed its credit policies in the credit approval process to increase its sales or customer base. This is positive when the company remains near the industry average for Days Receivable

Outstanding.

Receivables growth might also exceed sales growth when the company changes its timing of sales recognition. (Although this change raises questions about changes in accounting principles, we will ignore that consideration at this time.)

FYI. . .
Investors rate firms who adopt aggressive revenue recognition policies as higher risk.

The real danger in this situation is that the increased sales and receivables are conditional (not finalized) sales and a high percentage will later be written-off as returns. Practices like "bill and hold" sales where the customer is billed but delivery of merchandise is delayed raises questions about what period such sales should impact. This is an **aggressive revenue recognition policy**. Sales made with substantial rights of return or exchange should not be recognized as revenue unless the amounts of returns can be reasonably estimated. Such an estimate should be included as an **Allowance for Returns and Adjustments**.

It is important to read the Notes to the Financial Statements to assure that the company has not hidden a growth of receivables by **factoring** or selling some of its receivables. A ready market exists to factor or sell receivables. When sold, the receivable balance is reduced, cash is increased, and changes in the growth rate of receivables are masked.

A sales strategy that is often successful is to offer selected customers long-term credit in the form of notes. Notes bear interest and are legally easier to enforce than accounts receivable due to their more formal mature. Sales are recorded at the cash price and interest is recognized as interest revenue and accrued when earned.

Learning Objective 4:
How to impute and record interest when notes receivable yield either no explicit interest or an unrealistically low interest rate.

Some firms construct their terms with no interest or below market interest rates. To be considered an arms length transaction, notes must bear an interest rate that is similar to prevailing borrowing rates for that class of borrower. GAAP requires that notes made with interest terms substantially below prevailing rates have reasonable interest imputed and accounted for by the effective interest method. Sales are recorded at the **implied cash price** which is computed as the present value of the future cash flows of all principal and interest payments discounted at the prevailing borrowing rate. Using the recording techniques for imputed interest clearly separates sales revenue from interest revenue in the financial reports. **(See Demonstration Problem 2.)**

Learning Objective 5:
How companies transfer

In managing its operating cash flows a firm can use receivables as an immediate source of operating cash flows. To accelerate cash

or dispose of receivables in order to accelerate cash collection and how to distinguish between transactions that represent sales of receivables and those that are borrowings.

collections from receivables, companies may employ:

1.   **factoring**, selling the receivables with recourse or without recourse; and
2.   **assignment**, borrowing using the receivables as collateral.

Firms use these techniques because:

1.   Customers need credit but the administrative costs of carrying receivables is higher than the costs of factoring through credit card companies or other commercial factors.
2.   There may be in imbalance between the credit terms of the company's supplies and the time required to collect receivables.
3.   The company is short of operating cash and can accelerate collection cheaper and easier than borrowing operating capital.

FYI. . .
Mortgage companies, automobile finance corporations, and credit card companies use **asset securitization** to finance their operations and spread risk.

Factoring **without recourse** effectively sells the receivable to a third party in a closed transaction. The factor discounts the receivables and the seller recognizes this cost as Interest Expense. If any of the receivables are uncollectible, the factor bears the loss.

Factoring **with recourse** sells the receivable to the third party but the transaction is not completely closed. The factor discounts the receivables and the seller recognizes this cost as Interest Expense. If any of the receivables are uncollectible, the seller bears the loss. Therefore, the factor often withholds an additional amount to cover potential uncollectibles. When all receivables have been paid, the factor then remits any unused reserve for defaulted accounts to the seller.

In the **assignment** process, a firm uses the receivables as collateral for a loan to the company and disclosure of the collateral arrangement is included in the Notes to the Financial Statements. **(See Demonstration Problem 3.)**

Notes Receivable can also be sold or assigned through a **discounting** process, with or without recourse. FASB No. 140 defines a sale as a transfer where the transferor surrenders control over the receivable. The transferor surrenders controls when:

1.   The transferor nor its creditors can reach the receivable.
2.   The transferee has the right to dispose of the assets.
3.   There is no obligation for the transferor to repurchase or redeem the transferred assets in the future nor can the transferor force the holder to return the assets.

When notes are sold, the seller nets the maturity value of the note against the note proceeds and charges the difference to Interest Expense or Interest Revenue. If the notes are assigned, the collateral arrangement is disclosed in the Notes to the Financial Statements. **(See Demonstration Problem 4.)**

The selling of accounts and notes receivables has become a popular method of **asset securitization** where the buyer uses the receivables as collateral for securities it sells to investors. The bundling of receivables reduces the default risk to the investor. In some transfers it is difficult to determine if the transfer is a sale or assignment when the original seller continues to service the accounts. Incorrect reporting of these transfers results in potential understatement of assets and liabilities or misrepresentations of gains and losses.

In order to facilitate the sale of the securities, an SPE (special purpose entity) is created. The SPE is a trust corporation created for this transaction. The transferor sells the receivables to the SPE, who in turn issues debt securities collateralized by the receivables to investors. The cash flow from the collection of the receivables is used to cover periodic interest payments. The creation of the SPE allows for the protection of investors and favorable financial reporting treatment for the transferor.

Securitizations are designed to avoid consolidation of the SPE by the transferor by meeting the following four conditions:

1. It is demonstrably distinct from the transferor
2. Its activities are narrowly limited
3. It holds only rigidly defined types of assets
4. Its ability to dispose of assets is limited to narrowly defined circumstances.

GAAP requires disclosure of <u>all</u> transfers <u>with recourse</u>, but only <u>material</u> transfers <u>without recourse</u>. This makes detection of sales of receivables difficult for transfers without recourse and hides the real growth of receivables.

Learning Objective 6: Why receivables are sometimes restructured when a customer experiences financial difficulty and how to account for the troubled-debt restructuring.

Most lenders recognize that losses are minimized when a customer unable to make payments can avoid bankruptcy. Lenders can make concessions by:
1.   reducing or eliminating scheduled interest or principal payments;
2.   lengthening the repayment period; and
3.   settling the loan for cash or other assets.
Troubled debt restructuring is accomplished either by **settlement** or

continuation with modification of terms.

Settlement requires the transfer of cash and/or other assets to the lender to extinguish the debt. If assets other than cash are transferred, the asset is revalued to its fair market value. The <u>debtor</u> recognizes an:
1.   **ordinary** gain or loss on the asset transfer.
2.   **extraordinary** gain on the debt restructuring.
The <u>lender</u> recognizes an **ordinary** loss on the restructure.
(See Demonstration Problem 5.)

To determine how to account for a **continuation with modification of terms**, we must determine first whether the modification results in the sum of future cash flows of the restructured note are greater than or less than the book value of the note on the restructuring date.

In either case, the accounting treatment of lenders and borrowers is very different for troubled debt restructuring. Let us examine the <u>debtor's</u> results.
1.   When the restructured cash flows are **less** than current book value:
   a. the new loan amount is the <u>total restructured cash flows</u>;
   b. the gain on debt restructuring is <u>extraordinary</u>; and
   c. there is <u>no</u> future interest expense and all payments apply to principal. **(See Demonstration Problem 6.)**

FYI. . .
The **book value** of a debt is the amount owed plus accrued interest to the date of measurement

2.   When the restructured cash flows are **more** than current book value:
   a.   the new loan amount is the current book value;
   b.   there is no gain on debt restructuring; and
   c.   a <u>new interest rate</u> must be calculated to equate the current book value with the restructured cash flows. **(See Demonstration Problem 7.)**

The lender's results are different from the debtor's. The <u>lender</u> recognizes the following:
1.   When the restructured cash flows are **less** than current book value:
   a. the new loan amount is the <u>present value</u> of the restructured cash flows discounted at the <u>original</u> interest rate;
   b. the loss on debt restructuring is <u>ordinary</u>; and
   c. the future interest expense is based on the <u>original</u> interest rate. **(See Demonstration Problem 6.)**

FYI. . .
To find the interest rate

that equates current book value to a single future payment, find r where:

$$(1+r)^n = \frac{\text{Future payment}}{\text{Book value}}$$

n = number of periods

2. When the restructured cash flows are **more** than current book value:
    a. the new loan amount is the present value of the restructured cash flows discounted at the original interest rate;
    b. the loss on debt restructuring is ordinary; and
    c. the future interest expense is based on the original interest rate. **(See Demonstration Problem 7.)**

Glossary of Terms

Accounts Receivable	Amounts owed to a business firm by an outsider that arise from credit sales.
Aging Schedule	A schedule showing how long each receivable has been on the books.
Allowance method	The contra-asset account that is subtracted from accounts receivable to arrive at the net realizable value of the accounts receivable.
Asset Securitization	A method where a buyer uses receivables as collateral for securities it sells to investors.
Assignment of Receivables	A method used to accelerate cash collection by pledging the receivables to collateralize a loan.
Discounting	The term applied to the sale or assignment of notes receivable used to accelerate cash collections on notes receivable.
Factoring of Receivables Net	A method to accelerate cash collections by selling the receivables to a bank in exchange for cash.
Realizable Value	The amount of money a business can reasonably expect to collect from its credit customers.
Notes Receivable	A written promise to pay in the future.
Percentage of Receivables	A method used to estimate uncollectible accounts applying a percentage to gross receivables.
Percentage of Sales	The sales revenue approach used to estimate uncollectible accounts.
Sales Returns and Adjustments	A contra-revenue account.

| Special Purpose Entity | A trust or corporation created to enable a company to utilize asset securitization as a method to sell receivables. |

Special Purpose Entity   A trust or corporation created to enable a company to utilize asset securitization as a method to sell receivables.

Trade Receivables   Accounts Receivable generated by sales in the normal course of business.

With Recourse   Factoring of receivables where the company is willing to buy back any bad receivables.

Without Recourse   Factoring of receivables where the bank cannot collect from the factoring company for bad accounts.

Demonstration Problems

1.   **Estimating bad debt expense by the Sales Revenue and Gross Receivables methods.**

The Ryan Corporation shows the following on its Trial Balance at December 31, Year 5:

Accounts Receivable	$ 675,000
Allowance for Uncollectibles	21,000
Sales	5,280,000
Sales Returns and Adjustments	171,000
Bad Debt Expense	87,500

Ryan Corporation's Receivables manager provides you with the following data:

	Total Amount	Loss Estimate
Currently due receivables	$ 466,000	1%
Receivables 30 days past due	103,000	3%
Receivables 60 days past due	52,500	8%
Receivables 90 days past due	25,500	20%
Receivables >90 days past due	28,000	50%

Required:
A.   Prepare the proper year-end adjusting entry if Ryan uses the Sales Revenue method of accounting for uncollectible accounts based on a rate of 2% of net sales.
B.   Prepare the proper year-end adjusting entry if Ryan uses the Gross Receivables method of accounting for uncollectible accounts based on an aged Accounts Receivable.
C.   If Ryan uses the Sales Revenue method, is the Allowance for Uncollectibles sufficient?

A. Sales Revenue Method
First Step: Determine the formula used by the company to determine Bad Debt Expense.
Solution: Ryan uses 2% of Net Sales

Second Step: Compute Bad Debt Expense as 2% of Net Sales
Application: Net Sales = Sales — Sales Returns and Adjustments

Solution: Bad Debt Expense = 2% (Sales $5,280,000 — Sales Returns and Adjustments $171,000)
Bad Debt Expense = 2% (5,109,000) = $102,180

Third Step: Prepare the adjusting entry.
Application: Using the Sales Revenue Method, the Bad Debt Expense account should be equal to the estimated loss from uncollectibles equal to 2% of net sales.
Solution: Calculated Bad Debt Expense $102,180
      Bad Debt Expense per Trial Balance   87,500
        Increase needed $ 14,680

DR Bad Debt Expense   14,680
CR Allowance for Uncollectibles   14,680
To adjust to 2% of net sales.

B. Gross Receivables Method
First Step: Prepare an Accounts Receivable Aging Statement
Solution:

Ryan Corporation
Accounts Receivable Aging Statement
December 31, Year 5

	Total Amount	Loss Estimate	Provision
Currently due receivables	$ 466,000	1%	$ 4,660
Receivables 30 days past due	103,000	3%	3,090
Receivables 60 days past due	52,500	8%	4,200
Receivables 90 days past due	25,500	20%	5,100
Receivables >90 days past due	28,000	50%	14,000
Totals	$675,000		$31,050

Second Step: Prepare the journal entry.
Application: Compare the calculated Allowance balance to the actual balance and prepare the journal entry.
Solution: Allowance for Uncollectibles balance $21,000
      Calculated balance   31,050
        Adjustment required $10,050

DR Bad Debt Expense   10,050
CR Allowance for Uncollectibles   10,050
To adjust to amount needed per aging schedule.

C. Judging the sufficiency of the Allowance for Uncollectibles

Application: Compute the Allowance for Uncollectibles after the adjustment and compare to estimate.

Solution: $21,000 + $14,680 = $35,680   It is sufficient because it is at least $31,050. Ryan may decide to lower the estimated Bad Debt Expense or leave it as calculated.

2. Selling with Notes Receivable.

Hazlett, Inc. made a $100,000 sale to the White Corporation on a note basis. The total note is due in two years and the prevailing interest rate for this type of loan is 10%.

Required: For each of the following independent assumptions, prepare the journal entries to record (1) the sale, (2) the collection or accrual of interest at the end of year one, and (3) the final collection of the note.

A. The note bears 10% interest payable annually.
B. The note bears no interest and $100,000 is due in two years.
C. The note bears 5% interest payable annually.

A. Note Receivable with reasonable interest.

First Step: Prepare the journal entry to record the sale.

Application: Record the sale at the present value of the note receivable. Because the note bears the prevailing interest rate that is payable annually, the present value of the note is the maturity value.

Solution:

    DR Note Receivable   100,000
        CR Sales   100,000
    To record the sale to White Corporation on a 2 year note at 10% interest.

Second Step: Prepare the journal entry to record the receipt of interest at the end of Year 1.

Application: Compute the interest as: interest = principal x rate x time

Solution: i = $100,000 x 10% x 1 year = $10,000

    DR Cash   10,000
        CR Interest Revenue   10,000
    To record the receipt of interest for the first year on the White Corporation note.

Third Step: Prepare the journal entry to record the receipt of the final payment at the end of Year 2.

Solution:

DR Cash   110,000
  CR Interest Revenue   10,000
  CR Note Receivable   100,000

To record the receipt of interest and principal at the end of the second year
on the White note.

B. Non-interest bearing Note Receivable.

First Step: Prepare the journal entry to record the sale.

Application: Record the sale at the present value of the note receivable. Because the note is non-interest bearing, the present value must be calculated at a discount rate of 10% (the prevailing rate). According to present value tables, the present value factor for the sum of $1, 2 periods, at 10% is .82645.

Solution: PV = PVIF .82645 x Maturity Value $100,000 = $82,645

DR Note Receivable   82,645
  CR Sales   82,645

To record the sale to White Corporation on a two-year note with
imputed interest at 10%..

Second Step: Prepare the journal entry to accrue interest at the end of Year 1.

Application: Prepare an amortization table for the note receivable.

Solution:

Amortization Table

Period	Interest Payment	Interest Revenue	Amortization	Carrying Value
				$82,645
1	$ 0	$8,264*	$8,264	90,909
2	$ 0	9,091*	17,355	100,000

*rounded

DR Note Receivable   8,264
  CR Interest Revenue   8,264

To record interest earned for year one on the White note.

Third Step: Prepare the journal entry to record the receipt of the final payment at the end of Year 2.

Application: Record the accrual of the final interest amount and the receipt of the maturity amount.

Solution:

DR Note Receivable   9,091
  CR Interest Revenue   9,091

To accrue interest for year two on the White note.

DR Cash   100,000
     CR Note Receivable   100,000
To record payment in full of the White note.

C. Note Receivable with unreasonable interest rate.
First Step: Prepare the journal entry to record the sale.
Application: Record the sale at the present value of the note receivable. To calculate the present value of the note, one must compute the present value of the maturity amount <u>plus</u> the present value of the interest payments, discounted at the prevailing interest rate of 10%.
Solution:

Present Value of Maturity value (from Step B, 1)	$82,645.00
Present Value of Interest Payments $5,000 (5% x $100,000):	
Year 1:$5,000 x PVIF(10%, 1 period) .90909	4545.45
Year 2: $5,000 x PVIF (10%, 2 periods) .82645	<u>4,132.25</u>
Total Present Value	<u>$91,322.70</u>

DR Note Receivable   91,322.70
     CR Sales   91,322.70
To record the sale to White Corporation on a two-year note with 5% interest payable annually.

Second Step: Prepare the journal entry to record the receipt of interest at the end of Year 1.
Application: Interest will be paid in the amount of $5,000 but an amortization table must be constructed to properly record the interest expense.
Solution: Amortization Table

Period	Interest Payment	Interest Revenue	Amortization	Carrying Value
				$91,322.70
1	$5,000.00	$9,132.27	$4,132.27	95,454.97
2	$5,000.00	9545.03*	4,545.03	100,000.00

*rounded
DR Cash   5,000.00
DR Note Receivable   4,132.27
     CR Interest Revenue   9,132.27
To record interest earned for year one on the White note.

Third Step: Prepare the journal entry to record the receipt of the final payment at the end of Year 2.
Application: Record the receipt of the final interest amount and the receipt of the maturity amount.

Solution:

DR Cash	5,000.00	
DR Note Receivable	4,545.03	
CR Interest Revenue		9,545.03

To record interest earned for year two on the White note.

DR Cash	100,000	
CR Note Receivable		100,000

To record payment in full of the White note.

3.   Factoring and assigning Receivables

Harris Enterprises wishes to accelerate its cash flow on accounts receivables. The Marker Finance Corporation presents a plan to accomplish this. Harris has $600,000 of receivables that are acceptable to Marker.

Required: Prepare all of the journal entries required in the following unrelated circumstances.

A. Harris factors the receivables to Marker without recourse for a fee of 5%. Andrea collects from the customers.
B. Harris factors the receivables to Marker with recourse for a fee of 3%, a 5% retainer against default, and an actual bad accounts total of $22,000. Marker collects from the customers.
C. Harris assigns the receivables to Marker for three-month loan with a discount fee of 3%. Taylor collects 96% of the receivables.

A. Factoring without recourse.
First Step: Determine the type of arrangement and how to record the journal entry.
Application: Factoring without recourse is a sales arrangement. Marker assumes all losses on bad accounts. The discount fee becomes interest expense to Harris.
Solution:

DR Cash	570,000	
DR Interest Expense	30,000	
CR Accounts Receivable		600,000

To record transfer of receivables to Marker for a 5% discount.
  ($600,000 x 5% = $30,000)

B. Factoring with recourse.
First Step: Determine the type of arrangement and how to record the journal entry.
Application: Factoring with recourse is a sales arrangement. Harris assumes all losses on bad accounts and Marker withholds a loss contingency until all accounts are paid and the loss is known. The discount fee becomes interest expense to Harris.

Solution:

DR Cash	552,000	
DR Interest Expense	18,000	
DR Due from Marker	30,000	
CR Accounts Receivable		600,000

To record transfer of receivables to Marker for a 3% discount ($600,000 x 3% = $18,000), and a loss contingency of 5% ($600,000 x 5% = $30,000).

DR Cash	8,000	
DR Allowance for Uncollectibles	22,000	
CR Due from Andrea		30,000

To record final settlement of factoring with Marker.

C. Assignment of Receivables

Third Step: Determine the type of arrangement and how to record the journal entry.

Application: Assignment is a borrowing arrangement. Harris will use the proceeds of the receivables to repay the loan. Interest is withheld up front by Marker.

Solution:

DR Cash	582,000	
DR Prepaid Interest Expense	18,000	
CR Note Payable — Marker Finance		600,000

To record the borrowing of $300,000 from Marker Finance due in 3 months.

DR Cash	576,000	
DR Allowance for Uncollectibles	24,000	
CR Accounts Receivable		600,000

To record payment by customers on account.

DR Note Payable — Marker Finance	600,000	
DR Interest Expense	18,000	
CR Prepaid Interest Expense		18,000
CR Cash		600,000

To record payment in full of Marker note payable and recognition of interest expense.

4.   **Discounting Notes Receivable.**

Hall Company receives a $40,000, four-month, 9% note from a customer for the sale of merchandise. Two months later Hall discounts the note at the First National Bank at 12% without recourse.

Required: Prepare the journal entries to record these transactions.

First Step: Record the receipt of the note from the customer.
Solution:

DR Note Receivable	40,000	
CR Sales		40,000

To record sale of merchandise on a four-month 9% note.

Second Step: Record the discounting at the bank at 12% without recourse.
Application: Compute the proceeds of the discounted note:
Proceeds =   Maturity value — (Maturity value x Interest Rate x time)
The difference between the face value of the note and the proceeds is either Interest Revenue (when the proceeds are higher) or Interest Expense (when the face is higher). Because the discounting is without recourse, there will be no other entries on Hall's books.

Solution: Proceeds =   Maturity value = $40,000 x 1.03 = $41,200
          — Interest = $41,200 x .12 x 2/12 = _____824_
           Net Proceeds $40,376

DR Cash	40,376	
CR Interest Revenue		376
CR Note Receivable		40,000

To record proceeds of note discounted at 12%.

5.   **Settlement of a troubled debt.**
Nichols, Inc. owes the City National Bank $500,000 plus $30,000 in accrued interest at June 30. The note is due but Nichols cannot make the payment in full. After negotiations, Nichols agrees to give the bank land with a market value of $260,000 (and a cost of $180,000) plus $240,000 in full settlement of the debt.

Required:
1.   Make all journal entries necessary on the Nichols, Inc. books.
2.   Make all journal entries necessary on the City National Bank books.

A. Debt settlement for the borrower.
First Step: Bring the asset to be surrendered to market value.
Application: The land value must be raised to market value and an ordinary gain on disposal of assets recognized.
Solution:

DR Land	80,000	
CR Gain on Disposal of Asset		80,000

To record the appreciation in value of land from $180,000 to $260,000.

Second Step: Record the settlement on Nichols, Inc. books.

Application: Record the assets surrendered in the settlement, the liabilities (both principal and interest payable) settled, and determine if there is an <u>extraordinary</u> gain or loss on the debt restructure.

Solution:

DR Note Payable — City National Bank	500,000	
DR Interest Payable	30,000	
CR Cash		240,000
CR Land		260,000
CR Extraordinary Gain on Debt Restructure	30,000	

To record settlement of the City National Bank loan for $240,000 plus land.

B. Debt settlement for the lender.

First Step: Record the terms of the settlement.

Application: Record the assets received at fair market value, subtract the loan and interest forgiven, and determine if there is an <u>ordinary</u> gain or loss on the settlement.

Solution:

DR Cash	240,000	
DR Land	260,000	
DR Loss on Receivable Restructuring	30,000	
CR Note Receivable		500,000
CR Interest Receivable		30,000

6.   **Troubled debt restructuring when restructured cash flows are less than carrying value.**

Ewing Corporation currently owes Western Bank $600,000 plus $60,000 in accrued interest for one year at 10%. Ewing can pay neither the loan nor the interest at the current time. After extensive negotiations, the bank agrees to extend the note for six months, forgive $40,000 of the interest and accept payment in full for $650,000 at the end of six months.

Required:
A. Make all journal entries necessary on the Ewing Corporation's books.
B. Make all journal entries necessary on the Western Bank books.

A. Debt restructure on the debtor's books.

First Step: Determine if the future cash outflow is greater than or less than the carrying value of the note.

Application: If the carrying value is more than the future cash outflow, the debtor recognizes extraordinary gain on restructure and all future payments are applied to principal. If the future cash outflows exceed the carrying value, the debtor recognizes no gain on restructure and re-computes the interest rate.

Solution: Carrying Value = Principal $600,000 + Interest Payable $60,000 = $660,000

Future Cash Outflows = $650,000

Therefore, carrying value exceeds future cash outflows.

Second Step: Record the journal entry to record the continuation with modification of terms.

Application: The difference between the carrying value and future cash payments is an extraordinary gain on debt restructuring.

Solution:

DR Note Payable — Western Bank	600,000	
DR Interest Payable	60,000	
CR Restructured Note Payable — Western Bank		650,000
CR Extraordinary Gain on Debt Restructure		10,000

To record the restructure of the note to Western Bank.

B. Debt restructure on the lender's books.

First Step: The lender must value the new note at the present value of the future cash flows at the original lending rate.

Application: Compute the present value of $650,000 for six months at 10% interest.

Solution: Present value = PVIF (1 period, 5%) x New note principal

Present value = PVIF .95238 x New note principal $650,000 = $619,047

Second Step: Prepare the journal entry to record the debt restructuring.

Application: Remove the old debt elements and record the new note with any loss recorded as an <u>ordinary</u> loss.

Solution:

DR Restructured Note Receivable — Ewing, Inc.	619,047	
DR Loss on Receivable Restructuring	40,953	
CR Note Receivable — Ewing, Inc.		600,000
CR Interest Receivable		60,000

To record the restructure of the Ewing, Inc. note. Final payment in six months will include principal of $619,047 plus interest at 10% for six months of $30,952.

7.   Troubled debt restructuring when restructured cash flows are more than carrying value.

Assume the same facts as in Problem 6 except that the payment will be $690,000 at the end of one year.

Required:
A. Make all journal entries necessary on the Ewing Corporation's books.
B. Make all journal entries necessary on the Western Bank books.

A. Debt restructure on the debtor's books.
First Step: Determine if the future cash outflow is greater than or less than the carrying value of the note.
Application: If the carrying value is more than the future cash outflow, the debtor recognizes extraordinary gain on restructure and all future payments are applied to principal. If the future cash outflows exceed the carrying value, the debtor recognizes no gain on restructure and re-computes the interest rate.
Solution: Carrying Value = Principal $600,000 + Interest Payable $60,000 = $660,000
                Future Cash Outflows = $690,000
                Therefore, future cash outflows exceed carrying value.

Second Step: Record the journal entry to record the continuation with modification of terms.
Application: The difference between the carrying value and future cash payments is the interest expense to be recognized in the future. A new interest rate must be computed to determine the effective rate.
Solution: New interest rate computation:
                Carrying value = Future payment / (1 + r)
                $(1 + r) = \underline{\text{Future payment } \$690,000}$ = 1.0454545
                            Carrying value $660,000
                r = 4.545%

DR Note Payable — Western Bank   600,000
DR Interest Payable   60,000
    CR Restructured Note Payable — Western Bank   660,000
To record the restructured debt to Western Bank. The new note will
bear interest at 4.545%. Final payment will be $690,000.

B. Debt restructure on the lender's books.
First Step: The lender must value the new note at the present value of the future cash flows at

the original lending rate.
Application: Compute the present value of $690,000 for one year at 10% interest.
Solution: Present value = PVIF (1 period, 10%) x New note principal
Present value = PVIF .90909 x New note principal $690,000 = $627,272

Second Step: Prepare the journal entry to record the debt restructuring.
Application: Remove the old debt elements and record the new note with any loss recorded as an <u>ordinary</u> loss.

Solution:

DR Restructured Note Receivable — Ewing, Inc.		627,272	
DR Loss on Receivable Restructuring		32,728	
	CR Note Receivable — Ewing, Inc.		600,000
	CR Interest Receivable		60,000

To record the restructure of the Ewing, Inc. note. Final payment in one year will include principal of $627,272 plus interest at 10% for one year of $62,727.

Test Yourself

True or False Questions

T F 1.   Net realizable value for receivables is the amount of money a business can reasonably expect to collect from the credit customers.

T F 2.   Selling to customers who are unable to pay is treated as an expense of the period in which the sale takes place.

T F 3.   The trade-off between increased costs and additional profits from credit sales shows that bad debts are unavoidable.

T F 4.   The principle of conservatism requires that some estimate of uncollectible accounts be associated with current period costs.

T F 5.   The gross receivables method of estimating bad debts expense uses a percentage of current period sales.

T F 6.   Estimating bad debts expense for the period using a percentage of sales is the sales revenue method.

T F 7.   The accrual method of accounting for bad debt expense calls for recognition when the non-paying customer is identified.

T F   8.   The Allowance for Uncollectible Accounts is a contra-revenue account.

T F   9.   If the rate of growth of accounts receivable exceeds the rate of growth of sales, it always signifies a problem.

T F   10.   Factoring of receivables refers to the sale of the receivables.

T F   11.   A written promise to pay is evidenced by a note receivable held by the company.

T F   12.   When a note is received that bears no stated interest rate, interest is ignored.

T F   13.   Interest received on a note from the sale of product is considered part of the sales price.

T F   14.   Factoring receivables without recourse means that the bank cannot recover from the customer if the receivable proves uncollectible.

T F   15.   Assigning receivables is another term for factoring the receivables.

T F   16.   Factoring receivables is a method to speed up the collection of the receivables.

T F   17.   Accounts receivable and notes receivable may be factored.

T F   18.   The term for the sale of a note receivable is discounting.

T F   19.   The sales revenue approach to bad debts requires the use of an aging schedule.

T F   20.   SFAS 140 requires that the transferor surrender control over receivables in order to treat the transaction as a sale.

T F   21.   Securitization occurs when receivables are bundled together and sold or transferred to another organization which issues securities collateralized by the receivables.

T F   22.   Financial statement analysts look for disclosures on contingent liabilities with regard to discounted notes receivable.

T F   23.   Materiality is the level of information that if disclosed would change the decision maker's judgment.

T F   24.   By selling receivables to a factor without recourse and not disclosing the transaction, the account representing receivables overstates the true growth of receivables over the period.

T F   25.   Troubled debt restructuring may only be accomplished by continuation with modification.

T F   26.   When the sum of future cash flows is below the restructured note's book value, including accrued interest at the restructuring date, a gain will be recognized.

Multiple-Choice Questions

Select the best answer from those provided.

_____ 1.   Gross accounts receivable minus estimated uncollectibles and returns and adjustments is
a. net realizable value.
b. historical cost.
c. fair market value.
d. present value.

_____ 2.   Bad debts are required to be expensed in the year of sale because of the
a. matching principle.
b. Going concern principle.
c. historical cost principle.
d. conservatism constraint.

_____ 3.   The Allowance for Uncollectibles account is what type of account?
a. Liability
b. Expense
c. contra-asset
d. contra-equity

_____ 4.   The periodic assessment of the reasonableness of the Allowance for Uncollectibles is accomplished with
a. the management of earnings.
b. an aging of Accounts Receivables.
c. the write-off of bad accounts.
d. the percentage of sales method.

_____ 5.   When customers return goods purchased during the current period from a firm, Sales Returns and Adjustments is debited and which one of the following accounts is credited?
a. Allowance for Uncollectibles
b. Allowance for Sales Returns and Adjustments
c. Sales
d. Accounts Receivable

_____ 6.   When a firm utilizes aggressive revenue recognition practices, it overstates
a. Allowance for Uncollectibles.
b. Accounts Receivable.
c. Allowance for Sales Returns and Adjustments.
d. Sales Returns and Adjustments.

_____ 7.   Factoring accounts receivable is one method for disguising the rapid growth of the Accounts Receivables account compared to
  a. Accounts Payable.
  b. Stockholders' Equity.
  c. Sales.
  d. Cost of goods sold.

_____ 8.   Present value is used to express which one of the following accounts on the balance sheet?
  a. Notes Receivable
  b. Equipment
  c. Accounts Receivable
  d. Retained Earnings

_____ 9.   Sales made through notes receivable recognize the revenue
  a. at the time of the sale, for the implied cash price.
  b. after all cash has been collected.
  c. after the final payment, including interest.
  d. in installments, as cash is collected.

_____ 10.   Interest revenue on notes receivable is recognized
  a. when payment is made on the note.
  b. as it is earned.
  c. when the principal payment is due.
  d. as it is collected.

_____ 11.   The factoring of receivables is a transaction with
  a. the customer.
  b. an attorney.
  c. a third party.
  d. a vendor.

_____ 12.   If a note receivable is discounted without recourse and the customer defaults at the final payment, the seller
  a. has no obligation to the bank.
  b. must repay the full amount of the note plus interest to the bank.
  c. must repay the principal only to the bank.
  d. must refund the amount received from the bank at the time of discounting.

_____ 13. Factoring of receivables can serve to hide excessive growth of receivables when
  a. transfers are made with collateral.
  b. transfers are made without recourse.
  c. asset securitization occurs with recourse.
  d. loans are discounted.

_____ 14. Bankruptcy may be avoided by
  a. a net operating loss carryback.
  b. a quasi-reorganization.
  c. an extraordinary loss.
  d. a troubled debt restructuring.

_____ 15. Settlement or continuation with modification of terms may be used to accomplish
  a. bankruptcy.
  b. insolvency.
  c. troubled debt restructuring.
  d. liquidity.

_____ 16. Neither a gain nor a loss is recognized when the sum of the future cash flows of a restructured note is
  a. above the current note's book value.
  b. equal to the current note's fair market value.
  c. below the current note's book value.
  d. below the current note's fair market value.

_____ 17. An extraordinary gain on a debt restructuring is recognized when the sum of the future cash flows of the restructured note is
  a. above the current note's book value.
  b. equal to the current note's fair market value.
  c. below the current note's book value.
  d. above the current note's fair market value.

_____ 18. In a troubled debt restructuring, the new note's value is
  a. the same for the debtor and lender.
  b. always higher for the lender.
  c. different for the debtor and lender.
  d. usually lower for the debtor.

_____   19.   Lenders use which one of the following rates for the restructured note?
a.   recomputed rate
b.   original rate
c.   zero rate because all payments are principal
d.   negotiated rate

Exercises

1.   The Rob Corporation decided to factor its receivables with the Herb Finance Group. Herb charges a 2% fee on the total receivables factored. Rob factors $100,000 of its receivables.

Required: Prepare the journal entries to record the:
A.   transfer of the receivables assuming the transfer is made with recourse and Herb withholds $10,000 for potential uncollectibles, returns, and adjustments.
B.   settlement when uncollectibles are $6,000 and returns and adjustments are $3,500.

_____

_____

_____

_____

_____

_____

_____

_____

_____

_____

_____

_____

2.   The Jade Corporation has assigned $100,000 of its receivables to the Guaranty Bank. The assignment serves as collateral on a $75,000 note. Guaranty Bank charged a 3% fee on the assigned accounts and the interest rate was 10% on the note.

Required: Prepare journal entries to record (A) the assignment of receivables on Jade's books and (B) the collection of $40,000 of the assigned accounts after deducting $500 for the write-off of a bad debt.

_____

_____

_____

_____

_____

_____

_____

_____

_____

_____

3.   On January 2, Year 5, the Howard Company sells a piece of land that originally cost $100,000 to Rachel Plecha for a $300,000, four-year, non-interest bearing note. There is no established selling price for the land and notes of this type normally are at 10% interest.

Required:
A. Determine the selling price of the land and prepare an amortization schedule for this transaction.
B. Prepare the entry to record the sale.
C. How much interest revenue will Howard recognize at the end of the first year of the contract?

_____

_____

_____

_____

_____

_____

_____

_____

_____

_____

_____

4.   The Wenner Company has a $300,000 note due on July 1, Year 3 plus accrued interest of $6,000, but is unable to pay the debt when due. The bank agrees to settle the debt in full by accepting a piece of equipment that has a net book value of $175,000 (cost of $225,000) and a fair market value of $160,000 along with a cash payment of $100,000. **Required:** Prepare the journal entries to record this transaction on the books of Wenner Company and the bank.

5.   Silver, Inc. currently owes the Commerce Bank $100,000 plus 10% interest of $10,000. It is unable to pay this amount and asks for a restructure of the loan to extend the payment time for two years, forgive the current interest, and pay $120,000 at the end of two years from the proceeds of a contract that will be due at that time. The bank agrees to take the contract as additional collateral and accept the proposed terms.

Required: Prepare entries for the restructure, recognition of interest at the end of year one, and final settlement at the end of year two for (A) Silver, Inc. and (B) Commerce Bank.

Solutions

True or False Questions

True answers: 1, 2, 3, 6, 10, 11, 14, 16, 17, 18, 20, 21, 22, 23, 26
False answers explained:

4. The principle of <u>matching</u> requires that some estimate of uncollectible accounts be associated with current period costs.
5. The <u>sales revenue</u> method uses a percentage of current period sales.
7. The accrual method of accounting for bad debt expense calls for recognition in the period when the <u>sale is made</u>.
8. The Allowance for Uncollectibles is a contra-asset account.
9. The rate of growth of receivables exceeding the rate of growth of sales could be the result of a <u>policy change concerning receivables</u>.
12. When a note receivable bears no stated interest rate, interest is imputed.
13. Interest received on a note from the sale of product is considered <u>interest income</u>.
15. <u>Assigning</u> receivables is pledging them as collateral on a loan whereas factoring is the sale of receivables.
19. The <u>gross receivables</u> approach to bad debts requires the use of an aging schedule.
24. If receivables sold to a factor without recourse are not disclosed, the receivables account <u>understates </u>the true growth of receivables over the period.
25. Troubled debt restructuring may <u>also be </u> accomplished by settlement of the obligation.

Answers to Multiple-Choice Questions

1.	A	6.	B	11.	C	16.	A
2.	A	7.	C	12.	A	17.	C
3.	C	8.	A	13.	B	18.	C
4.	B	9.	A	14.	D	19.	B
5.	D	10.	B	15.	C		

Exercises

1. A. DR Cash   93,000
        DR Interest Expense   2,000
        DR Due from Herb   5,000
            CR Accounts Receivable   100,000
        To record transfer of receivables to Herb Finance Group.

B. DR Cash   250
    DR Allowance for Uncollectibles   3,000
    DR Sales Returns and Adjustments   1,750
        CR Due from Herb   5,000
    To record the completion of the Herb factoring arrangement.

2. A. DR Cash   72,750
        DR Interest Expense   2,250
            CR Note Payable — Guaranty Bank 75,000
        To record the assignment of Accounts Receivable for the Guaranty note payable.

    B. DR Cash   40,000
        DR Allowance for Uncollectibles   500
            CR Accounts Receivable   40,500
        To record the collection of receivables.

3. A. Present Value = Maturity Value x PVIF (4 periods, 10%)
        Present Value = Maturity Value $300,000 x PVIF .68301 = $204,903

Amortization Table

Period	Interest Payment	Interest Revenue	Amortization	Carrying Value
				$204,903
1	$0	$20,490	$20,490	225,393
2	0	22,539	22,539	247,932
3	0	24,793	24,793	272,725
4	0	27,275*	27,275	300,000

*rounded

    B. DR Note Receivable   204,903
            CR Gain on Sale of Asset   104,903
            CR Land   100,000
        To record the sale of land for $204,903 on a four-year,
        non-interest bearing loan for $300,000.

    C. Interest revenue for the first year is $20,490 per the amortization schedule.

4. Wenner Company
    DR Loss on Disposal of Asset   15,000
        CR Equipment   15,000
    To record equipment at fair market value.

DR Note Payable	300,000	
DR Interest Payable	6,000	
DR Accumulated Depreciation	50,000	
CR Cash		100,000
CR Equipment		210,000
CR Extraordinary Gain on		
Debt Restructuring		46,000

To record settlement of debt for cash and equipment.

Bank
DR Equipment   160,000
DR Cash   100,000
DR Loss on Receivable Restructuring   46,000
CR Note Receivable   300,000
CR Interest Receivable   6,000
To record settlement of Wenner Company note for equipment and cash.

5.   A.   DR Note Payable — Commerce Bank 100,000
            DR Interest Payable   10,000
            CR Restructured Note Payable   110,000
            To record the restructure of the note to Commerce Bank
            due in two years for total payment of $120,000.

            DR Interest Expense   4,892
                CR Restructured Note Payable   4,892
            To record one year's interest at 4.447%.
            $(1 + r)^2 = \underline{\text{Future Cash Flows}} = \underline{\$120,000} = 1.090909$ Therefore r = 4.447%
                Carrying Value $110,000
                            Amortization Table

Period	Interest Payment	Interest Revenue	Amortization	Carrying Value
				$110,000
1	$0	$ 4,892	$ 4,892	114,892
2	0	5,108	5,108	120,000

                        * rounded
            DR Restructured Note Payable   114,892
            DR Interest Expense   5,108
                CR Cash   120,000
            To record payment of restructured note.

      B. DR Restructured Note Receivable   99,174
              DR Loss on Receivable Restructuring   10,826
                  CR Note Receivable   100,000
                  CR Interest Receivable   10,000
            To record restructure of the note at 10% interest.
            Present Value = Maturity $120,000 x PVIF 0.82645 = $99,174

            DR Restructured Note Receivable   9,917
                CR Interest Revenue   9,917
            To record one year's interest at 10%.

DR Cash   120,000
    CR Restructured Note Receivable   109,091
    CR Interest Revenue   10,909
To record final collection of note. Interest is 10% of
($99,174+$9,917) rounded.

CHAPTER 9

INVENTORIES

Chapter Review

FYI. . .
Expired costs become expenses on the income statement. **Unexpired costs** are assets on the balance sheet. The cost of inventory is either expired in Cost of Goods Sold or unexpired in the Inventory account.

Inventories are significant assets for retail, wholesale, and manufacturing firms. Retailers and wholesalers have one inventory account **Merchandise Inventory** on the balance sheet. Manufacturers have three inventory accounts:

1. **Raw Materials Inventory** — component materials not yet started into the manufacturing process.
2. **Work-in-Process Inventory** — unfinished products in some stage of the manufacturing process. Costs include materials, direct labor, and manufacturing overhead.
3. **Finished Goods Inventory** — products ready to sell that are equivalent to merchandise inventory for retailers and wholesalers.

For merchandising and manufacturing firms, inventories may comprise the largest asset on the balance sheet and the largest expense on the income statement. Therefore, the accounting for inventory is vitally important for the integrity of both the balance sheet and the income statement.

The **Cost of Goods Sold** section of an income statement is an equation that separates the expired inventory costs from the unexpired inventory costs:

      Beginning Inventory (unexpired costs from the prior year)
Plus **Inventory Purchases** (unexpired costs)
Equals **Goods Available for Sale** (unexpired costs)
Minus **Ending Inventory** (unexpired costs that go to the ending balance sheet)
Equals **Cost of Goods Sold** (expired costs)

FYI. . .
Determining the cost of goods sold is the major issue of inventory

The **physical flow** of goods describes how the units actually move from purchase to sale. The **cost flow assumption** describes how the accounting system assumes the units move from purchase to sale. There is no GAAP requirement for the two to coincide.

Learning Objective 1:
The two methods used to determine inventory quantities; the perpetual inventory system and the periodic inventory system.

FYI...
Scanner technology allows many firms to use perpetual inventory systems. Some firms keep only unit counts on the perpetual system for reordering and inventory control, and continue to use the periodic system for financial accounting purposes.

accounting.

If a firm began and ended each accounting period with a zero inventory, all costs would be expired costs on the income statement. Let's separate two issues. The first is the number of units and the second is the cost of those units.

Regardless of the firm's **cost flow assumption**, the number of units will not change. There are several cost flow assumptions allowed under GAAP:

1.   Specific identification — used for non-homogeneous, expensive items that often have serial numbers or other unique characteristics.
2.   First-in, First-out (FIFO) — most closely represents the physical flow of goods where the first purchases are sold first.
3.   Last-in, First-out (LIFO) — least closely resembles the physical flow of goods where the last purchases are sold first.
4.   Weighted average — used for homogeneous items to assign an average cost to each unit of inventory.

Although the number of units does not change, different cost flow assumptions will assign very different costs to the income statement and balance sheet if costs for an item change during the accounting period.

In addition to the choice of cost flow assumption, GAAP allows the choice of accounting system. A **perpetual inventory system** keeps a running record of the amount in inventory. It applies the cost flow assumption at the time of each transaction. Inventory purchases are initially recorded as an asset (Inventory) and are expensed as Cost of Goods Sold at the time of each sale. A **periodic inventory system** does not keep a running record of the amount in inventory. It applies the cost flow assumption at the end of each period. Inventory purchases are initially recorded as expenses in the Purchases account and the Inventory asset account is reconciled at the end of each period to its actual value. **(See Demonstration Problem 1.)**

A firm must select its inventory system and cost flow assumption in the first year of operation and utilize the same choice each year to protect the **consistency** and **comparability** of its financial statements. Regardless of which system a firm selects, a firm must take a **physical inventory** no less than annually to reconcile the Inventory account to the physical count and to determine the amount of inventory "gone" for reasons other than sales.

Learning Objective 2:

What specific items and kinds of costs are included in inventory.

The inventory asset includes the costs of all items to which the firm has legal title. Inventory costs are all of the costs necessary to put the merchandise in saleable condition. For a merchandising firm, inventory costs are the purchase price, sales taxes, transportation costs, insurance, and storage. For a manufacturing firm, costs include all **product** costs to make the product saleable including materials, labor, and overhead. A manufacturer does not include **period** costs in inventory. Period costs are generally selling, general, and administrative costs.

The heart of the matter . . .

To distinguish product costs from period costs for a manufacturer, the easiest method is to determine whether the cost would be present in a merchandising firm. If a merchandiser would have the same cost, such as advertising, it is probably a period cost.

The flow of production costs for manufacturing firms is:

Materials
Labor Overhead

Work in Process
Inventory

Finished Goods
Inventory

Cost of
Goods Sold

In the accounting system, destinations are debits and sources are credits. For example, to transfer
$10,000 of raw materials (source) into process (destination):

DR Work-in-Process Inventory   10,000
          CR Raw Materials Inventory   10,000

Learning Objective 3: What absorption

GAAP require that manufacturers use **absorption costing** for external reporting purposes. The only difference between **variable costing** and

costing is and how it complicates financial analysis.

absorption costing is the treatment of fixed manufacturing overhead costs such as rent, taxes, depreciation, and property insurance. Absorption costing allocates the fixed manufacturing overhead costs to the total manufacturing costs before unit inventory costs are calculated. Variable costing includes only those cost that change with the level of production so that fixed overhead costs are charged as a period cost. Critics of absorption costing complain that increases in inventory levels can increase net income by reducing the fixed costs charged against income. Likewise, large sales increases that deplete inventory mask net income increases because the inventoried fixed costs are charged through cost of goods sold in the period of the sale. **(See Demonstration Problem 2.)**

Learning Objective 4:
The difference between various cost flow assumptions — weighted average, FIFO and LIFO.

The **FIFO** cost assumption most closely resembles the physical flow of goods. Most firms used FIFO for financial reporting and LIFO for income tax accounting until Congress passed the **LIFO Conformity rule**. Why would companies use two different methods? The reasons are fundamental:

1.   In periods of rising prices, FIFO produces the highest net income and most realistic valuation of inventory on the balance sheet. FIFO leaves the newest (highest cost) purchases in the ending inventory, and expenses the oldest (lowest cost) purchases through Cost of Goods Sold.
2.   In periods of rising prices, LIFO produces the lowest net income and the most realistic valuation of the cost of sales on the income statement. LIFO leaves the oldest (lowest cost) purchases in the ending inventory and expenses the newest (highest cost) purchases through Cost of Goods Sold.

Firms quickly realized that investors like FIFO's high profits and LIFO's low taxes. LIFO firms enjoy substantial cumulative cash flow benefits from using LIFO for tax purposes. When Congress passed the LIFO conformity rule, many firms changed financial accounting practices to LIFO to maintain the tax benefits.

FYI. . .
The **weighted average** cost flow assumption produces results somewhere between LIFO and FIFO.

When input costs change for inventory, firms either profit or lose from holding inventory. If a **current cost** accounting system were permitted by GAAP, unrealized holding gains and losses for inventory would be recognized on the income statement in the current period. After such a recognition, both the income statement (Cost of Goods Sold) and the balance sheet (Inventory) would reflect the current replacement costs. Because current cost accounting is not GAAP, firms must choose between the income statement or the balance sheet to reflect current costs. LIFO places more current costs on the income statement and FIFO places more current costs on the balance sheet. FIFO recognizes the holding gains or losses in the income statement for units sold during the period.

Learning Objective 5:
How to use the LIFO reserve disclosure to estimate inventory holding gains and to transform LIFO firms to a FIFO basis.

LIFO cost flow assumptions distort the Inventory asset account by understating the value of the inventory during periods of rising prices. Recognizing this, the SEC adopted the LIFO Reserve disclosure policy in 1974. The LIFO Reserve allows readers to determine the approximate FIFO inventory for comparative purposes. The LIFO Reserve equation is:

$$\text{Inventory}_{\text{FIFO}} = \text{Inventory}_{\text{LIFO}} + \text{LIFO Reserve}$$

From the LIFO Reserve equation, we can derive an equation to compute cost of goods sold approximation as:

Cost of Goods Sold$_{\text{LIFO}}$ — Increase in LIFO Reserve
or + Decrease in LIFO Reserve = Cost of Goods Sold$_{\text{FIFO}}$
(See Demonstration Problem 3.)

The conversion of Inventory and Cost of Goods Sold from LIFO to FIFO makes comparison between firms more meaningful.

Learning Objective 6:
How LIFO liquidations distort gross profit and how to adjust for these distortions to improve forecasts.

When a LIFO firm allows its inventory units to decline, the firm liquidates LIFO layers. The older the firm, the more likely that the old LIFO layers contain much lower costs. When these costs become part of Cost of Goods Sold, net income falsely increases. The intensity of the illusory profit is directly related to the rate of price increases during the period from the LIFO layer to the present time. Obviously, LIFO liquidation profits are not sustainable income. The SEC requires that material effects of LIFO liquidation profits be disclosed in the firm's 10-K report because this is another instance when a firm's management can manipulate poor earnings into a better profit picture. By using the information in the disclosure, investors can adjust the reported income to remove illusory profits.

During a period from 1980 to 1993, approximately 10% to 20% of LIFO firms experienced LIFO liquidations. From 70% to 90% of the liquidations cause positive earnings effects that ranged from 5.7% to 15.4% of pre-tax earnings.

FYI. . .
LIFO liquidation is also called **LIFO dipping.**

Because the LIFO cost assumption increases Cost of Goods Sold and decreases the Inventory asset account, the firm's ratios involving either of these accounts are also distorted. To remove the distortion, add the LIFO Reserve to all Inventory amounts and add the pre-tax effect of the LIFO dipping to the reported Cost of Goods Sold. The resulting ratios will approximate FIFO ratios. **(See Demonstration Problem 4.)** Management can manipulate income in either direction in LIFO firms if prices have changed during the period. To decrease reported net income, simply make substantial purchases before the year end to drive up the Cost of Goods Sold. To increase reported net income, indulge in LIFO liquidation.

Learning Objective 7:

What research tells us about the economic incentives guiding the choice of inventory accounting methods.

According to an AICPA survey, less than 60% of firms use LIFO despite its tax benefits. Research indicates the main reasons that a firm does not adopt LIFO are that it has substantial loss carryforwards to reduce taxes and its inventory levels are subject to substantial fluctuations. Smaller firms avoid LIFO because of the increased cost of LIFO accounting. Although firms fear that the lower reported LIFO earnings will depress stock prices, research indicates that the market perceives that LIFO earnings are more sustainable earnings than FIFO earnings and, therefore, produce a higher quality earnings signal.

Learning Objective 8:

How to eliminate realized holding gains from FIFO income.

While LIFO puts holding gains into income only in a LIFO liquidation event, FIFO infuses holding gains into every period in which inventory costs rise. The materiality of the holding gains depends upon the degree of price changes and the rapidity of the inventory turnover. The higher the degree of change within a period and the slower the inventory turnover, the more material the income distortion. To remove the unsustainable holding gains from income, we can convert the reported Cost of Goods Sold (CGS) to replacement costs (RC) by the following formula:

$$CGS_{RC} = COGS_{FIFO} + B \times r$$

Where:
B = Beginning Inventory
r = Rate of inventory cost change

The r can be estimated from a LIFO competitor's following information:

$$r = \frac{\text{Change in LIFO Reserve}}{B_{LIFO} + \text{Beginning LIFO Reserve}}$$

The accounting constraint of **conservatism** implies that assets should not be overvalued. Applied to inventory, conservatism connotes that Inventory reported on the balance sheet should not exceed what can be realized from the asset. A firm recognizes any impairment of the asset value in the income statement as a loss from decline in the market value of inventory. Computations to determine the amount of loss are based on the following rules:

Learning Objective 9:

How to apply the lower of cost or market method and on what assumptions the choice of method rests.

1.   Market value must be determined from the following alternatives:
    a.   **Replacement cost** is the current wholesale price.
    b.   **Ceiling** is the **net realizable value** of the item or the selling price less costs of completion and disposal. Ceiling is the maximum market value.
    c.   **Floor** is the net realizable value minus a **normal profit**. Floor is the minimum market value.
2.   Determine the market value, which is always the **middle value** of the three potential market values.

3.   Compare cost to market and select the lower value.

4.   Firms may choose to apply the lower of cost or market determination to the entire inventory, to inventory classes, or to individual inventory items. As a practical matter, application to individual items provides the highest adjustment amounts. **(See Demonstration Problem 5.)**

Tax regulations preclude LIFO firms from using the lower of cost or market so that they do not receive tax advantage in times of declining prices.

FYI. . .
Lower of cost or market inventory is often abbreviated as **LCM**.

The conservatism illustrated by the lower-of-cost-or-market rule tends to reduce reported earnings. This can always be manipulated because estimates of value are required. The conservatism usually favors lenders and equity purchasers over borrowers and equity sellers. Write-downs should always be warranted and truly reflect reductions in prospective realization.

Learning Objective 10:
How the dollar value LIFO method is applied.

Application of the LIFO inventory cost assumption costs more than FIFO because of the clerical work involved — especially for perpetual inventory systems. LIFO liquidation also creates holding gain recognition that would otherwise be deferred. The dollar value LIFO technique avoids the detailed record keeping and adds layers at the beginning of year prices which reduces deferral of some of the holding gains. **(See Demonstration Problem 6.)**

Inventory errors are usually accidental but have a significant impact on the financial statements for two periods. An ending inventory error at the end of period one causes cost of goods sold and net income to be misstated on the income statement, and inventory and retained earnings to be misstated on the balance sheet. This error carries over to period two as an error in beginning inventory in the cost of goods sold computation and leads to misstatement of cost of goods sold and net income in the opposite direction from period one. Retained earnings are automatically corrected and the new ending inventory balance appears on the balance sheet. For example, if ending inventory is understated in period one, cost of goods sold will be overstated and net income will be understated. The inventory balance on the balance sheet and the retained earnings account will also be understated. In period two, the error carries over as an understatement of beginning inventory which leads to an understatement of cost of goods sold and an overstatement of net income. The retained earnings balance will automatically be corrected.

Glossary of Terms

Absorption Costing	Absorption (or full costing) is a costing method that assigns all production costs, both variable and fixed costs to inventory. It is required for financial reporting by GAAP.
Ceiling	The maximum value applied to "market" in the application of the lower of cost or market method, also equal to net realizable value.
Consignments	Goods that are physically in the possession of one firm (consignee) that actually belong to another firm (consignor).
Dollar-Value LIFO Method	An inventory costing method that measures increases and decreases in the inventory pools in dollars only and does not account for units.
Finished Goods Inventory	Represents the total costs incorporated in completed but unsold units.
First-In, First-Out Method	A method of inventory accounting that assumes that the oldest units available in inventory are the first units that are sold.
Floor	Net realizable value reduced by an allowance for a normal profit margin. The floor establishes the lowest value applicable in the application of lower of cost or market.
Last-In-First-Out Method	A method of inventory accounting that presumes that the goods purchased most recently are the first units to be sold.
LIFO Conformity Rule	U. S. tax rules specify that if a firm uses LIFO for tax reporting, it must also use LIFO for financial reporting.
LIFO Liquidation	The problem associated with a LIFO firm reducing its inventory and liquidating older LIFO layers which then results in a distortion of the net income.
LIFO Reserve Disclosure	A disclosure requirement of the SEC that requires firms using LIFO to disclose the dollar magnitude of the difference between LIFO and FIFO inventory costs.
Lower of Cost Or Market	A method for stating inventory at the current replacement cost.
Net Realizable Value	Estimated selling price of goods less reasonably predictable costs of completion and disposal.
Period Costs	Costs that are associated with the passage of time and not associated with a specific product.

Periodic Inventory	A method for reporting inventory that requires the taking of a physical count of goods on hand at the end of the accounting period.
Perpetual Inventory System	A method for maintaining a running balance or record of the amount and cost of inventory.
Product Costs	Costs that are directly associated with the products included in inventory, including costs required to obtain physical possession and to put the goods into saleable condition.
Purchase Discount	A reduction in the cost of goods purchased as a result of early payment for the goods.
Raw Materials Inventory	Goods held by the company that will be used in the manufacture of a completed product.
Specific Identification Method	A method of inventory accounting which assigns cost to inventory based on the known or actual cost of the item.
Variable Costing	A method of costing inventories which only includes variable costs and assigns all fixed costs of production as period costs. It is not permitted for financial reporting under GAAP.
Weighted Average Cost Method	A method of valuing inventory that assumes the cost of goods in inventory equals the average of the cost of all units in inventory weighted for the number of each item at a different cost.
Work-In-Process Inventory	The cost of units that have been started into production but not yet completed at the balance sheet date. The work-in-process inventory includes the cost of the raw materials, direct labor and factory overhead.

Demonstration Problems

1.   Separation of costs between Cost of Goods Sold and Ending Inventory.

Liviti Corporation has the following transactions involving Product A during the month of July:

July	1	Balance	6,500 units @ $6
	4	Purchase	250 units @ $7
	6	Sold	350 units @ $12
	8	Sold	200 units @ $13
	12	Purchase	450 units @ $8
	14	Sold	200 units @ $14

Required: Calculate the cost of the ending inventory and the cost of goods sold under each of the

following methods:
A.   Periodic Method of Inventory
      1.   FIFO
      2.   LIFO
      3.   Weighted Average
B.   Perpetual Method of Inventory
      1.   FIFO
      2.   LIFO

A. Periodic Inventory
1.   FIFO

First Step: Determine the total number of units sold and the total number of units remaining in the ending inventory. This step is the same for all three methods.

Application: Identify and total the units available for sale and the units sold for the month. The income statement format calculates ending inventory as Goods available for sale minus cost of goods sold.

Solution:	Purchases	Sales
July 1 Balance	650 units	
4 Purchase	250 units	
6 Sold		350 units
8 Sold		200 units
12 Purchase	450 units	
14 Sold	_____	200 units
Goods Available for Sale	1,350 units —	Units Sold 750 = Ending Inventory 600 units

Second Step: Determine the cost of goods sold and the ending inventory under the periodic system of inventory using FIFO.

Application: FIFO assumes that the first goods in are the first goods sold and the last goods in are the ones remaining in inventory.

Solution:	Cost of Goods Sold	Ending Inventory
July 1 Balance	650 units @ $6 = $3,900	
4 Purchase	100 units @ $7 = 700	150 units @ $7 = $ 1,050
12 Purchase		450 units @ $8 = 3,600
	Total $4,600	Total $4,650

2.   LIFO

First Step: Determine the total number of units sold and the total number of units remaining in the ending inventory. This step is the same for all three methods.

Application: Identify and total the units available for sale and the units sold for the month. The income statement format calculates ending inventory as Goods available for sale minus cost of goods sold.

Solution:	Purchases	Sales
July 1 Balance	650 units	
4 Purchase	250 units	
6 Sold		350 units
8 Sold		200 units
12 Purchase	450 units	
14 Sold	_____	200 units
Goods Available for Sale	1,350 units —	Units Sold 750 = Ending Inventory 600 units

Second Step: Determine the cost of goods sold and the ending inventory under the periodic system of inventory using LIFO.

Application: LIFO assumes that the last goods in are the first goods sold and the first goods in are the ones remaining in inventory.

Solution:	Cost of Goods Sold	Ending Inventory
July 1 Balance	50 units @ $6 = $300	600 units @ $6 = $3,600
4 Purchase	250 units @ $7 = 1,750	
12 Purchase	450 units @ $8 = $3,600	
	Total $5,650	Total $3,600

3.   Weighted Average

First Step: Determine the total number of units sold and the total number of units remaining in the ending inventory. This step is the same for all three methods.

Application: Identify and total the units available for sale and the units sold for the month. The income statement format calculates ending inventory as goods available for sale minus cost of goods sold.

Solution:	Purchases	Sales
July 1 Balance	650 units	
4 Purchase	250 units	
6 Sold		350 units
8 Sold		200 units
12 Purchase	450 units	
14 Sold	_____	200 units
Goods Available for Sale	1,350 units —	Units Sold 750 = Ending Inventory 600 units

Second Step: Determine the cost of goods sold and the ending inventory under the periodic system of inventory using the Weighted Average method.

Application: The Weighted Average method assumes that the cost assigned to ending inventory is the weighted average cost of all goods purchased and available during the period .

Solution:

July 1 Balance	650 units @ $6= $3,900
4 Purchase	250 units @ $7 = 1,750
12 Purchase	450 units @ $8 = 3,600
	1,350 $ 9,250 $9,250/1,350 = $6.852 per unit

Ending Inventory = 600 units x $6.852 = $4,111
Cost of Goods Sold = 750 units x $6.852 = $5,139

B. Perpetual Inventory
1.   FIFO

First Step: Determine the total number of units sold and the total number of units remaining in the ending inventory. This step is the same for all three methods.

Application: Identify and total the units available for sale and the units sold for the month. The income statement format calculates ending inventory as goods available for sale minus cost of goods sold.

Solution:	Purchases	Sales
July 1 Balance	650 units	
4 Purchase	250 units	
6 Sold		350 units
8 Sold		200 units
12 Purchase	450 units	
14 Sold		200 units

Goods Available for Sale   1,350 units — Units Sold 750 = Ending Inventory 600 units

Second Step: Determine the cost of goods sold and the ending inventory under the periodic system of inventory using FIFO.

Application: FIFO assumes that the first goods in are the first goods sold and the last goods in are the ones remaining in inventory. The perpetual method of calculating inventory and cost of goods sold must be carried out sequentially based on dates of sales.

Solution:		Cost of Goods Sold	Ending Inventory
July 1 Balance	650 units @ $6		
4 Purchase	250 units @ $7		
6 Sold	350 units	350 units @$6	300 units @ $6
			250 units @ $7
8 Sold	200 units	200 units @$6	100 units @ $6
			250 units @ $7
12 Purchase	450 units @ $8		100 units @ $6
			250 units @ $7
			450 units @ $8
14 Sold	200 units	100 units @$6	150 units @ $6
		100 units @$7	450 units @ $8

650 units @$6 = $3,900		150units @$7= $1,050	
100 units @$7= 700		450 units @$8=3,600	
Total	$4,600	Total	$4,650

2.   LIFO

First Step: Determine the total number of units sold and the total number of units remaining in the ending inventory. This step is the same for all three methods.

Application: Identify and total the units available for sale and the units sold for the month. The income statement format calculates ending inventory as Goods available for sale minus cost of goods sold.

Solution:	Purchases	Sales
July 1 Balance	650 units	
4 Purchase	250 units	
6 Sold		350 units
8 Sold		200 units
12 Purchase	450 units	
14 Sold	_____	200 units
Goods Available for Sale	1,350 units — Units Sold 750 = Ending Inventory 600 units	

Second Step: Determine the cost of goods sold and the ending inventory under the periodic system of inventory using LIFO.

Application: LIFO assumes that the last goods in are the first goods sold and the first goods in are the ones remaining in inventory. The perpetual method of calculating inventory and cost of goods sold must be carried out sequentially based on dates of sales.

Solution:		Cost of Goods Sold	Inventory
July 1 Balance	650 units @ $6		
4 Purchase	250 units @ $7		
6 Sold	350 units	250 units @$7	
		100 units @$6	550 units @ $6
8 Sold	200 units	200 units @$6	350 units @ $7
12 Purchase	450 units @ $8		350 units @ $7
			450 units @ $8
14 Sol	200 units	200 units @$8	350 units @ $6
			250 units @ $7
		250 units @ $7 =$ 1,750	350 units @ $6= $2,100
		300 units @ $6 = 1,800	250 units @ $8 = 2,000
		200 units @ $8 = 1,600	
		Total $5,150	Total $4,100

2.   Absorption and variable costing.

The following data is available for the Red Robin Manufacturing Corporation:

	Year 5	Year 6

Selling Price	$10 / unit	$10 / unit
Fixed Cost of Production	$300,000	$300,000
Variable Cost of Production	$5 / unit	$5 / unit
Units Produced	200,000	260,000
Units Sold	240,000	200,000

Beginning Inventory (FIFO basis) January 1, Year 4 was 150,000 units @ $6.00.

Required:

A.   Prepare an income statement for Red Robin Manufacturing Corporation for Year 5 under the absorption costing method.

B.   Prepare an income statement for Red Robin Manufacturing Company for Year 5 under the variable costing method.

A.

First Step: Prepare an income statement for the corporation using the information provided under the absorption costing method.

Application: Absorption costing assumes that both fixed and variable costs are included in the inventory and the cost of goods sold.

Solution:

Red Robin Manufacturing Corporation
Absorption Cost Income Statement
For the Year Ended December 31, Year 5

Sales Revenues	$2,400,000
Cost of Goods Sold	1,620,000**
Gross Margin	$780,000

** Beginning Inventory 150,000 @ $600	= $900,000
# From Production (240,000 — 150,000) @$8.00	= 720,000
Cost of Goods Sold	$1,620,000

# Variable Production Cost		= $5.00/unit
Fixed Production Cost	$600,000/200,000	= 3.00/unit
Total		= $8.00/unit

B.

First Step: Prepare an income statement for the corporation using the information provided under the variable costing method.

Application: Variable costing assumes that only variable costs are included in the inventory and the cost of goods sold; fixed costs are treated as period costs.

Solution: Red Robin Manufacturing Corporation
                                    Variable Cost Income Statement
                               For the Year Ended December 31, Year 5

Sales Revenues		$2,400,000
Variable Cost of Goods Sold:		
Beginning Inventory (150,000@ $6)	$ 900,000	
From Production (90,000@$5)	450,000	1,350,000
Variable Contribution Margin		$1,050,000
Less: Fixed Production Costs treated as period costs		300,000
Variable Cost Gross Margin		$750,000

3.   LIFO Reserves

The following information is available for the Clark Co.:

Beginning Inventory — LIFO	$1,400,000
Purchases	1,600000
Ending Inventory — LIFO	600,000
Beginning LIFO Reserve	850,000
Ending LIFO Reserve	790,000

Required:
A.   Determine the ending FIFO inventory.
B.   Determine the Cost of Goods Sold under FIFO.

A.
First Step: Determine the ending balance of inventory based on FIFO.
Application: Ending LIFO Inventory + Ending LIFO Reserve = Ending FIFO Inventory
Solution: Ending LIFO Inventory + Ending LIFO Reserve = Ending FIFO Inventory
              $600,000   + $790,000   = $1,390,000

B.
First Step: Determine the cost of goods sold under FIFO.
Application: LIFO Cost of Goods Sold + Decrease in LIFO Reserve = FIFO Cost of Goods Sold
Solution: LIFO Cost of Goods Sold + Decrease in LIFO Reserve = FIFO Cost of Goods Sold
              $2,400,000*   + $60,000   = $2,460,000

* Beginning Inventory $1,400,000 + Purchases $1,600,000 — 600,000 = $2,400,000

4.   LIFO liquidations

The Hayman Corporation reports the following LIFO inventory layers in its January 1, Year 10 inventory. At this time the replacement cost of the inventory was $500 per unit.

Year LIFO Layer Added	Units	Unit Cost	Total	LIFO Reserve as of January 1, Year 10
Year 7	20	$200	$4,000	($500 — 200) x 20= $6,000
Year 8	35	300	10,500	($500 — 300) x 35= 7,000
Year 9	50	350	17,500	($500 — 350) x 50= 7,500
	105		$32,000	$20,500

Hayman determines its selling price by adding a $250 per unit markup to the replacement cost at the time each unit is sold. As of January 1, Year 10, the replacement cost was $500, and it remained constant throughout the year. During Year 10 Hayman purchased 25 units at a cost of $1,000 and sold 100 units at a price of $750 per unit.

Required:
Determine the impact of LIFO dipping on the gross margin of Hayman Corporation for Year 10.

First Step: Determine the units left in ending inventory.
Application: LIFO liquidation involves reducing earlier layers.
Solution:

Units available		105
Plus: Purchases Year 10	25	
Less: Sales Year 10	100	
Total Ending Inventory	30	

Second Step: Determine the LIFO Reserve as of December 31, Year 10.
Application: LIFO liquidation involves reducing earlier layers.
Solution:

Year LIFO Layer Added	Remaining Units	Unit Cost	Ending Inventory December 31, Year 10 Total	LIFO Reserve as of December 31, Year 10
Year 7	20	$200	$4,000	($500 — $200) x 20 = $6,000
Year 8	10	300	3,000	($500 — $300) x 10 = 2,000
	30			$8,000

Third Step: Determine the LIFO Liquidation Profits.
Application: LIFO liquidation involves reducing earlier layers.
Solution:

Liquidated LIFO Layer Year Added	Units Liquidated		Current Cost	Historical Cost	LIFO Liquidation Effect on Earnings
Year 9	50	x	($500	— $350)	= $7,500
Year 8	25	x	($500	— $300)	= 5,000
a.					$12,500

5.   Lower of cost or market accounting

The Libby Co. uses the Lower of Cost or Market Method to value its inventory. The following information was available at the end of Year 1.

Product	Original Cost	Replacement Cost	Disposal Cost	Projected Sale Price	Normal Profit on Sales
AA	$10.00	$12.00	$1.50	$22.50	15%
BB	$25.00	$11.00	$1.00	$30.00	25%
CC	$27.50	$30.00	$4.50	$45.00	10%

Required:
A.   Use the Lower of Cost or Market Approach to calculate the ending inventory on an item by item basis.
B.   Use the Lower of Cost or Market Approach to calculate the ending inventory based on the total dollar amount of inventory.

First Step: Determine the market value of the inventory and compare to historical cost to determine LCM.
Application: Market is determined by comparing replacement cost with the net realizable value and floor. The middle value will be the market value to be compared with cost. Net realizable value is selling price minus costs to complete or dispose. The floor is net realizable value minus a normal profit.

Solution:

Product	Original Cost	Replacement Cost	Net Realizable Value	Floor	Market	LCM
AA	$ 10.00	$ 12.00	$ 21.00	$ 17.63	$ 17.63	$ 10.00
BB	$ 25.00	$ 11.00	$ 29.00	$ 21.50	$ 21.50	$ 21.50
CC	$ 27.50	$ 30.00	$ 40.50	$ 36.00	$ 30.00	$ 27.50
Total	$ 62.50	$ 53.00	$ 90.50	$ 75.13	$ 69.13	$ 59.00

A.   Lower of Cost or Market of the ending inventory on an item by item basis identified is $59.00.
B.   Lower of Cost or Market of the ending inventory based on the total dollar amount of inventory is $62.50.

6.   Dollar value LIFO computations

Harold Corporation decided to adopt the dollar-value LIFO inventory method on June 30, Year 6. The entire inventory represents a single inventory pool. The inventory at June 30, Year 6, was $870,000 under the dollar-value LIFO method. Information for Year 6 is as follows:

June 30, Year 7 inventory at year-end prices	$1,250,000
Price Index at year end with Year 6 as the base year	115%

Required: Using the dollar-value LIFO Method, calculate the inventory at June 30, Year 7

First Step: Determine the ending inventory at base period prices.
Application: Apply the price index at year end to convert to base year price.
Solution: Ending Inventory at Base Period Prices ($1,250,000/1.15) $1,086,956

Second Step: Determine the increase in ending inventory at base period prices.
Application: Comparison of beginning and ending inventories at base period prices.
Solution:

Beginning Inventory at Base Period Prices	$870,000
Ending Inventory at Base Period Prices ($1,250,000/1.15)	1,086,956
Inventory Increase in Base Period Prices ($1,086,956 — $870,000)	$216,956

Third Step: Determine the increase in ending inventory under dollar value LIFO.
Application: Add additional layer to beginning inventory.
Solution:

Beginning Inventory of Year 2	$870,000
Year 2 Layer ($216,956 x 1.15)	249,499
Ending Inventory Dollar Value LIFO	$1,119,499

Test Yourself

True or False Questions

T F   1.   Choice of method for allocation of costs between ending inventory and the cost of goods sold is the major issue in inventory accounting.

T F   2.   If the cost of inventory never changed, the FIFO and LIFO cost flow assumptions would yield the same results.

T F   3.   A perpetual system for inventory maintains a running record of the amount of inventory.

T F   4.   Beginning inventory minus purchases plus ending inventory equals cost of goods sold.

T F   5.   Periodic inventory systems would be used by heavy duty equipment dealers.

T F   6.   Consignment goods should be included in the inventory of the consignee.

T F   7.   Cost of inventory includes all costs to obtain physical possession and to put the merchandise in saleable condition.

T F   8.   A manufacturer of furniture would include raw materials, labor, and overhead items in the cost of inventory.

T F   9.   Manufacturing costs are called period costs.

T F   10. Another term for full costing is variable costing.

T F   11. Variable costing includes variable and fixed costs of production in inventory.

T F   12. The rationale for absorption costing is that both variable and fixed production costs are assets since both are required to produce a saleable product.

T F   13. GAAP requires the use of absorption costing in external financial statements.

T F   14. As inventory absorbs more fixed costs, net income goes down.

T F   15. When physical inventory levels are decreasing, absorption cost income tends to rise .

T F   16. Cost flow assumptions must be made to allocate goods available for sale between ending inventory and cost of goods sold.

T F   17. Accounting rules require that the cost flow assumption conform to the actual physical flow of the goods.

T F   18. LIFO method of inventory valuation matches the most oldest costs against revenues.

T F   19. Current cost accounting for inventories is permissible under GAAP.

T F   20. LIFO reports inventory at approximate current cost and cost of goods sold at historical cost.

T F   21. The SEC requires that firms using LIFO for inventory must disclose the dollar magnitude of the difference between LIFO and FIFO inventory costs.

T F   22. As a firm liquidates old LIFO layers, the firm's profits may be seriously distorted by greatly reduced profit margins.

T F   23. Ratios using inventories and cost of goods sold need to be analyzed carefully for necessary adjustments if LIFO inventory costing is used.

T F 24.   U.S. tax law specifies that if a firm uses FIFO for financial statement purposes, it must use FIFO for tax purposes.

T F 25.   Recent studies show that the market perceives LIFO earnings to be of higher quality than FIFO earnings.

T F 26.   The lower of cost or market method of inventory valuation does not allow the value of inventory to exceed the net realizable value.

T F 27.   For the lower of cost or market rule, the market value is always defined as the net realizable value.

T F 28.   A method used for inventory valuation, dollar value LIFO, was designed to overcome the cost of maintaining records and the problems with liquidation when using LIFO valuation methods.

Multiple-Choice Questions
Select the best answer from those provided.

_____ 1.   A debit to an account titled purchases would indicate the use of a /an
a. periodic inventory system.
b. job order cost system.
c. perpetual inventory system.
d. voucher system.

_____ 2.   A firm that has a small number of expensive items of inventory should prefer the use of a
a. periodic inventory system.
b. perpetual inventory system.
c. job order cost system.
d. process cost system.

_____ 3.   A consignor of goods is the
a. firm holding the goods.
b. firm that is the legal title holder of the goods.
c. firm that is trying to sell the goods to the public.
d. firm that has no legal title to the goods.

_____ 4.   If a firm wishes to minimize the amount of record keeping necessary to maintain the inventory records, the firm would most likely choose the
a.   periodic system of inventory.
b.   activity based costing system.
c.   perpetual inventory system.
d.   process cost system.

_____ 5.   The cost-benefit constraint would be a reason why which one of the following costs would not be included in inventory?
a.   Factory Overhead
b.   Direct Materials
c.   Direct Labor
d.   Advertising

_____ 6.   Product costs are costs associated with the inventory of a
a.   manufacturer.
b.   wholesaler.
c.   service firm.
d.   retailer.

_____ 7.   Direct costing is synonymous with which one of the following terms?
a.   absorption costing.
b.   fixed costing.
c.   period costing.
d.   variable costing.

_____ 8.   When recording inventory costs using the absorption costing method,
a.   only variable costs are included.
b.   only fixed costs are included.
c.   both fixed and variable production costs are included.
d.   both fixed and variable period costs are included.

_____ 9.   Which one of the following is an example of an item inventoried under variable costing?
a.   Advertising Expense
b.   Officers' Salaries
c.   Rent on the manufacturing facility
d.   Raw materials used to produce goods

_____ 10.   As the inventory of a manufacturing concern absorbs more fixed costs using the absorption costing method, the gross profit of the firm will
   a.   remain unchanged.
   b.   decrease.
   c.   increase.
   d.   become highly volatile.

_____ 11.   Financial analysts should be aware that manipulations of income by management are allowed by the
   a.   LIFO method of inventory.
   b.   FIFO method of inventory.
   c.   Weighted Average method of inventory.
   d.   Specific Identification method of inventory.

_____ 12.   The failure to match current costs with current revenues is a serious deficiency of the
   a.   LIFO method of inventory.
   b.   FIFO method of inventory.
   c.   Weighted Average method of inventory.
   d.   Specific Identification method of inventory.

_____ 13.   The requirement that companies disclose information about the LIFO reserve was the original mandate of the
   a.   State Boards of Accountancy.
   b.   SEC.
   c.   National Association of Securities Dealers.
   d.   New York Stock Exchange.

_____ 14.   The LIFO reserve disclosure attempts to approximate the ending inventory at
   a.   Market.
   b.   Lower of Cost or Market.
   c.   FIFO.
   d.   Weighted Average.

_____ 15.   The distortion caused in the current ratio by the under LIFO inventory costing methods may be adjusted or corrected by
   a.   subtracting the LIFO reserve from total assets
   b.   subtracting the LIFO reserve from current assets.
   c.   adding the LIFO reserve to the quick assets.
   d.   adding the LIFO reserve to current assets.

_____ 16.   When a firm uses the lower of cost or market method to value the inventories on the balance sheet at year end, the firm is departing from the principle of
a. going concern.
b. cost-benefit.
c. matching.
d. historical cost.

_____ 17.   The principle of conservatism is employed when a firm adopts the method of inventory valuation known as
a. LIFO.
b. Lower of Cost or Market.
c. FIFO.
d. Specific Identification.

_____ 18.   Net realizable value is equal to the expected selling price less
a. the cost to complete and dispose of the item.
b. a normal profit.
c. advertising expense.
d. freight out.

_____ 19.   When applying the lower of cost or market method the floor is equal to the net realizable value
a. plus a normal profit.
b. less a normal profit.
c. less advertising costs.
d. Plus advertising costs.

_____ 20.   Recognizing a probable loss in the period in which it is sustained is an attempt to apply the
a. conservatism principle.
b. cost-benefit principle.
c. matching principle.
d. going concern principle.

_____ 21.   The dollar-value LIFO method of inventory uses a price index, which utilizes the comparison of current year inventory prices with
a. the previous year prices.
b. an estimate of next year's inventory prices.
c. base year prices.
d. the current year budget figures for inventory.

_____ 22.   The base period is the time at which
  a. a firm switches to FIFO.
  b. a firm adopts dollar-value LIFO.
  c. a firm adopts dollar-value FIFO.
  d. the lower of cost or market method is adopted.

_____ 23.   The liquidation of LIFO layers is less likely to take place when inventory records are kept on a/an
  a. total inventory basis.
  b. item-by-item basis.
  c. specific identification basis.
  d. lower-of-cost-or-market basis.

_____ 24.   The Cost of Goods Sold under LIFO minus the increase in LIFO Reserve is equal to
  a. Cost of Goods Sold under Specific Identification Inventory costing.
  b. Cost of Goods Sold under Weighted Average Inventory costing.
  c. Cost of Goods Sold under FIFO costing.
  d. Ending Inventory under FIFO costing.

_____ 25.   An overstatement of ending inventory in period one will lead to?
  a. Understatement of net income in period one.
  b. Understatement of net income in period two.
  c. Understatement of cost of goods sold in period two.
  d. Understatement of retained earnings in period two.

Exercises

Table 9-1

The White Company had the following transactions for the month of July:		
	Purchases	Sales
July 1 (Beginning Inventory)	200@$2.40	July 3 100@ $7.00
5	700@ 4.20	6 400@ 7.00
8	300@ 4.60	10 300@ 6.00
25	400@ 5.00	30 200@ 8.00

1.   Refer to Table 9-1. Assume White uses a periodic inventory system.

   Required:
   A. Calculate the LIFO basis ending inventory.
   B. Calculate the FIFO basis ending inventory.

_____

_____

_____

_____

_____

_____

_____

_____

2.   Refer to Table 9-1. Assume White Company uses a perpetual inventory.

        Required:
        A. Calculate the LIFO basis ending inventory.
        B. Calculate the FIFO basis ending inventory.

_____

_____

_____

_____

_____

_____

_____

3.   Refer to Table 9-1. Assume White Company uses a periodic inventory system.

        Required:
        A. Calculate the Cost of Goods Sold under LIFO.
        B. Calculate the Cost of Goods Sold under FIFO.

_____

_____

_____

_____

_____

_____

_____

_____

4.   The Spring Corporation is a calendar year corporation. The financial statements for years 6 and 7 contain the following errors:

	Year 6	Year 7
Ending Inventory	$10,000 overstated	$24,000 understated
Depreciation Expense	$12,000 understated	$17,000 overstated

Required:

A.   Assume no correcting entries were made at the end of Year 6. By how much will retained earnings be overstated or understated at the end of Year 7?

B.   Assume no correcting entries were made at the end of Year 6 or Year 7 and no additional errors occurred in Year 8. By how much will working capital be overstated or understated at the end of Year 8?

_____

_____

_____

_____

_____

_____

_____

_____

_____

_____

_____

5.   The Phil Collins Company reported a LIFO reserve of $100,000 at the end of the current fiscal year. The beginning LIFO Reserve was $85,000. Collins reported Cost of Goods Sold under LIFO for the year of $575,000.

Required: Determine the Cost of Goods Sold under FIFO.

_____

_____

_____

_____

_____

_____

6.   The Agra Company uses the lower of cost or market method to value its inventory. The
        inventory consisted of 200 units of Product Koi. The inventory had an historical cost basis
        of $500. The replacement value was $400. Product Koi had a total expected selling price
        of $600 and a cost to complete the inventory of $50. The product had a normal profit of
        10%.

        Required:
        A. Calculate the net realizable value of Product Koi.
        B. Calculate the "floor" value of Product Koi.
        C. Calculate the lower of cost or market for Product Koi.

_____

_____

_____

_____

_____

_____

_____

_____

_____

_____

_____

7.   The Young Corporation uses the dollar-value LIFO method for valuing inventory. The
        company provides the following information at year-end:

Year	Year End Price	Price Index
1	$600,000	100
2	780,000	110
3	500,000	115

Required:
  A. Determine the dollar-value LIFO ending inventory at the end of Year 2.
  B. Determine the dollar-value LIFO ending inventory at the end of Year 3.

_____
_____
_____
_____
_____
_____
_____
_____
_____
_____
_____
_____
_____

Solutions

Answers to True or False Questions

True Answers: 1, 2, 3, 7, 8, 12, 13, 16, 21, 23, 25, 26, 28
False answers explained:
  4.   Beginning inventory plus purchases minus ending inventory equals cost of goods sold.
  5.   Perpetual inventory systems would be used by heavy equipment dealers.
  6.   Consignment goods should be included in the inventory of the consignor.
  9.   Manufacturing costs are called product costs.
  10.   Another term for full costing is absorption costing.
  11.   Variable costing includes only variable costs of production in inventory.
  14.   As inventory absorbs more fixed costs then net income goes up.
  15.   When physical inventory levels are decreasing absorbtion cost income tends to fall.
  17.   Accounting rules do not require that the cost flow assumption conform to the actual physical flow of the goods.
  18.   LIFO matches the most recently incurred costs against revenues.
  19.   Current cost accounting for inventories is not permissible under GAAP because it is a departure from historical cost.
  20.   FIFO reports inventory at approximate current cost and cost of goods sold at historical cost.
  22.   As a firm liquidates old LIFO layers the profits of the firm may be seriously distorted by greatly

inflating profit margins.

24.   U.S. tax law specifies that if a firm uses <u>LIFO</u> for financial statement purposes, it must use <u>LIFO</u> for tax purposes.

27.   Market value is the <u>middle value</u> of replacement cost, net realizable value, or net realizable value less a normal profit margin.

Answers to Multiple-Choice Questions

1.	A	6.	A	11.	D	16.	D	21.	C
2.	B	7.	D	12.	B	17.	B	22.	B
3.	B	8.	C	13.	B	18.	A	23.	A
4.	A	9.	D	14.	C	19.	B	24.	C
5.	D	10.	B	15.	D	20.	C	25.	B

Answers to Exercises

1.   A.   Ending Inventory:

Purchases	1,500 units
Sales	1,000 units
Ending Inventory	500 units

LIFO Inventory	200 units @ $2.40 =	$480.00
	300 units @ $4.20 =	1,260.00
Total LIFO Inventory		$1,740.00

B.

FIFO Inventory	400 units @ $5.00 =	$2,000.00
	100 units @ $4.60 =	460.00
Total FIFO Inventory		$2,460.00

2.   A.   Ending Inventory - LIFO Perpetual Method

	100 units @ $2.40 =	$240.00
	200 units @ $4.20 =	840.00
	200 units @ $5.00 =	1,000.00
Total LIFO Inventory		$2,080.00

B.   Ending Inventory - FIFO Perpetual Method

FIFO Inventory	400 units @ $5.00 =	$2,000.00
	100 units @ $4.60 =	460.00
Total FIFO Inventory		$2,460.00

3.   A.   Cost of Goods Sold

	LIFO	400 units @ $5.00 =	$ 2,000.00
		200 units @ $4.60 =	920.00
		400 units @ $4.20 =	1,680.00
	Total LIFO Cost Of Goods Sold		$4,600.00

      B.   Cost of Goods Sold

	FIFO	200 units @ $2.40 =	$480.00
		700 units @ $4.20 =	2,940.00
		100 units @ $4.60 =	460.00
	Total FIFO Cost of Goods Sold		$3,880.00

4.   A.   At the end of Year 7 Retained Earnings is overstated $29,000 as a result of the overstatement to ending inventory and the understatement to depreciation. ($24,000 + $5,000).   The easiest way to verify this is to use hypothetical information from an income statement. It does not make any difference what numbers are used, if you keep true to the parameters of the problem.

	Year 6		Year 7	
	As Reported	As Corrected	As Reported	As Corrected
Sales	$100,000	$100,000	$100,000	$100,000
COGS				
Beginning Inventory	0	0	20,000	10,000
Purchases	60,000	60,000	50,000	50,000
Goods Available	60,000	60,000	70,000	60,000
Ending Inventory	20,000	10,000	16,000	40,000
COGS	40,000	50,000	54,000	20,000
Gross Profit	60,000	50,000	46,000	80,000
Depreciation	20,000	32,000	30,000	13,000
Net Income	$ 40,000	$ 18,000	$ 16,000	$ 67,000

Net Income As Reported Year 6 and 7	$56,000
Net Income As Corrected Year 6 and 7	85,000
Retained Earning Understatement	$29,000

      B.   There is no working capital effect in Year 8 because the inventory errors are counterbalancing errors and Year 8 has no inventory error.

5.   LIFO CGS $575,000 ─── Increase in LIFO Reserve $15,000 = FIFO CGS $560,000

6.   A.   Net Realizable Value $550 = Expected Selling Price $600 ─── Cost to Complete $50

      B.   Floor $490 = Net Realizable Value $550 ─── Normal profit Margin [10% x $600]

      C.   Lower of Cost or Market:

Replacement Cost = $400   Market = $490
Cost = $500   Lower of Cost or Market = $490

7.   A.   Year 2 = $780,000/1.10 = $709,091
            Year 1 Layer   600,000 x 1.00= $600,000
            Year 2 Layer   109,091 x 1.10 =   120,000
                        Total $720,000

      B.   Year 3 = $500,000/1.15 = $434,782
            Year 1 Layer   434,782 x 1.0 = $434,782

CHAPTER 10

LONG-LIVED ASSETS AND DEPRECIATION

Chapter Review

Learning Objective 1:
What measurement base is used in accounting for long-lived assets and why this base is used.

Long-lived assets are expected to provide benefits to the firm for more than one year or one operating cycle, whichever is longer. Long-lived assets include both **tangible** (physical) assets and **intangible** assets (contractual rights) of which the firm has absolute control. Theoretically, there are two ways to measure the future economic benefits of long-lived assets:

1. **expected benefits approaches** that measure the **net realizable value** if sold or the **discounted present value** of the future cash inflows the asset will generate.
2. **economic sacrifice approaches** that measure the **historical cost** or **replacement cost**.

Although there are many reasons to use any of the four approaches to measure asset carrying values, GAAP use historical cost. The following qualitative characteristics of accounting information justify this position. Asset values should be:

1. **reliable** — not prone to manipulation or opinion.
2. **objective** — historical cost is verifiable.

Both expected benefits approaches are subjective estimates of value that are neither reliable nor objective. Even replacement cost is subjective because many long-lived assets are special use assets without ready market replacements.

If we return to the concept that assets are unexpired costs, the historical cost of long-lived assets represents the unused portion of the cost of the asset, not its market value.

FYI...
Capitalized costs are included in assets on the balance sheet.

Learning Objective 2:
What specific costs can be capitalized and how joint costs are allocated among assets.

Long-lived asset costs include all of the costs to acquire the asset and make it ready for use. Capitalized costs include:

1. purchase price, including transportation costs and insurance in transit;
2. installation labor and materials to make the asset usable;
3. training costs for employees to utilize the asset; and

4.   capitalized interest for self-constructed assets.

FYI...
When all relative values of the assets purchased jointly are known, use the **proportional** method to allocate joint costs. When all but one relative value is known, use the **incremental** method to allocate joint costs.

When a group of assets is purchased for a lump sum without any allocation of cost among the assets, the purchaser must determine a relative value for each item. Value should be allocated based upon a defendable apportionment. Bases available are relative sales value, fair market value, appraised value, or at last resort either original cost or current book value of the seller.

Expenditures made subsequent to purchase are capitalized when the expenditure:
1.   extends the useful life of the asset.
2.   increases the capacity of the asset.
3.   increases the efficiency of the asset.
4.   increases the future service potential value of the asset
When none of these conditions are met, the item becomes an expense on the income statement.

Specialized rules apply to self-constructed assets, the most common of which is building construction. Because land is not depreciable, the separation of costs between land and building affects both asset values and future net income.
Land costs include:
1.   land purchase price
2.   destruction of existing structures less any salvage received
3.   preparation of land for its intended use
4.   legal, title, and recording fees to acquire the land.
Building costs include:

FYI...
GAAP's proprietary view of the firm does not allow the capitalization of interest on contributed ownership capital.

1.   any structure acquired with the land that is used as part of the final structure
2.   materials, labor, and other construction costs
3.   excavation costs for the structure
4.   interest costs during construction from funds borrowed from outsiders, limited to avoidable interest.

Capitalized interest costs increase reported net income in the year(s) capitalized because the amounts would otherwise be deducted from income as an operating expense. Tax rules parallel financial reporting principles, including the capitalization of interest. For tax purposes, most firms seek to minimize amounts charged to land and capitalized as interest. **(See Demonstration Problem 1.)**

Learning Objective 3:
How GAAP measurement rules complicate both trend analysis and cross-company analysis and how to avoid misinterpretations.

One of the limitations of historical cost accounting for long-lived assets comes to light when examining a firm's rate of return on assets. As long as a firm continuously updates its long-lived assets, net income reflects sustainable income. However, when a firm ceases to update its long-lived assets, the rate of return on assets will continue to rise even if there is little change in net income. This income increase is not sustainable and can be misleading. Comparisons between companies should only be made for firms within the same industry because each industry's rate of capital investment is unique.

Learning Objective 4:
Why balance sheet carrying amounts for internally developed intangibles usually differ from their real value.

An **intangible asset** conveys contractual future benefits or rights to its owner. A purchased intangible asset is subject to amortization for its useful life, similar to the depreciation of a tangible asset, to allocate its cost to the periods benefited under the matching principle. Developed intangible assets present a problem of comparability. *SFAS No. 2* requires the immediate expensing of **research and development costs**. Regardless of external value, the cost of internally developed patents, copyrights, and trademarks is limited to the associated legal costs. Similarly, *SFAS No. 86* requires that software developers expense research and development costs until the product exhibits **technological feasibility.** This is established when all activities are completed that establish the product can be produced within its design specifications. Once technological feasibility is established, the firm capitalizes the remaining development costs. Comparisons between a firm with purchased intangible assets and another firm with developed intangibles is difficult at best.

Research findings seem to indicate that existing GAAP for research and development, and software development costs is too conservative. Required disclosures of expended R and D, and unamortized software assets, amortizations and write-downs each period, and expensed development costs prior to technological feasibility provide analysts with an ability to reconstruct values of these assets.

The United Kingdom follows similar financial reporting standards for intangibles. However, there is a difference in the application of historical cost accounting of long-lived assets. U.K. standards allow companies to write long-lived asset values up when market values exceed cost. A small number of U.K. firms increased the carrying value of brands (trademarks) to market value to match this treatment of tangible assets.

Oil and gas producers can choose between two different GAAP methods for capitalization of exploration cost:

1. The full-cost approach capitalizes all costs of well completion, including dry-hole costs, and recovers cost through depletion.
2. The successful-efforts approach capitalizes only the land cost and the drilling costs on successful wells and recovers those costs through depletion. The cost of drilling dry holes is expensed when holes are determined to be non-productive.

Small companies tend to favor the full-cost approach to prevent a volatile earnings pattern. FASB tried to require the successful-efforts approach in SFAS No. 19, but was forced to rescind it later due to SEC pressure. Comparison among firms with different capitalization approaches is difficult.

Learning Objective 5:	Conservatism dictates that assets not be overstated. When the fair value of an asset falls materially below book value, should a firm write down the asset? ***SFAS No. 121*** sets forth rules to judge when an asset becomes impaired and the amount of the write-down.
When long-lived asset impairment exists and how it is recorded.	1. Management should review a suspected asset if external events raise the possibility of an impairment.

1. Management should review a suspected asset if external events raise the possibility of an impairment.
2. Determine the impairment threshold — the undiscounted net cash flows expected from the asset's use. If the fair value of the asset is <u>below</u> the undiscounted net cash flows, an impairment has occurred.
3. The impairment loss is the difference between the asset's fair value and its carrying value.
4. Record the loss in the continuing operations section of the income statement.
5. Once an asset is written down, it cannot later be written up to restore any of the write-down. **(See Demonstration Problem 2.)**

Management can manipulate income with the timing of asset impairment recognition. One research study found that write-offs were often made during economically difficult times. This move would get the bad times behind a firm, to make subsequent periods at least appear to be better. International Accounting Standards permit reversals of recognized improvement losses when there has been a change in the estimates that were previously used to determine the loss.

Learning Objective 6:
How different depreciation methods are computed.

The matching principle requires that costs associated with the revenue production be matched with the income produced. A long-lived asset's cost must be allocated to the periods in which it produces revenue. The allocation process (cost expiration) is **depreciation** for tangible assets, **amortization** for intangible assets, and **depletion** for wasting assets such as mineral deposits or timber. Cost allocation is unrelated to the decline in market value.

FYI. . .
Salvage value is often called **residual value**.

Depreciation expense requires the selection of a **depreciation method** and the estimation of the asset's **useful life** and **salvage value**. Firms select depreciation methods, much like inventory methods, and use them consistently to protect the **comparability** and **consistency** of the financial statements. The major depreciation methods are:

1. **Straight-line** (SL) depreciation recognizes depreciation evenly over the useful life of the asset based on the depreciable base. The **depreciable base** is the original cost minus the salvage value (constant rate x constant base).

2. **Double-declining balance** (DDB) depreciation allocates cost more heavily in the early years of the asset's life and declines until it reaches the salvage value. DDB is computed by doubling the straight-line rate and multiplying it times the asset's carrying value (constant rate x changing base).

FYI. . .
To compute the sum-of-the-years digits denominator use the following formula:
n(n+1)/2
where n = the number of years of useful life.

3. **Sum-of-the-years digits** (SYD) depreciation is another accelerated method. The percentage used as the multiplier of the depreciable base is calculated as a ratio of the remaining life in years divided by the sum-of-the-years digits (changing rate x constant base).

4. **Production methods** allocate the depreciable base over the number of hours used, the number of units produced, the number of miles driven, or some other relevant measure.

Regardless of method, depreciation never exceeds the depreciable base and is the same amount over the life of the asset for assets held for the expected useful life. The only difference caused by method selection is the timing of the expense recognition. **(See Demonstration Problem 3.)**

Most U.S. companies use straight-line depreciation for financial reporting purposes and required income tax methods (accelerated depreciation) for tax purposes.

Many firms dispose of assets before the useful life expires due to changes in technology. When the firm disposes of the asset, the difference between the carrying value and the sales price is an ordinary gain or loss on the disposition of an asset. **(See Demonstration Problem 4.)**

Learning Objective 7: How analysts can adjust for different depreciation assumptions and improve interfirm comparisons.	Comparisons among firms which use different useful lives for assets require adjustments to equalize earnings for comparisons. Footnotes to financial statements often provide information about the average useful life assumptions. When the footnotes omit this information, the analyst can estimate the lives used by a simple formula: $$\text{Average useful life} = \frac{\text{Depreciable Base}}{\text{SL Depreciation}}$$
Learning Objective 8: How long-lived asset accounting and depreciation practices differ internationally.	Not all countries use the same basis for depreciation of long-lived assets. Financial reporting in countries such as Germany are heavily influenced by tax laws. German companies can depreciate up to 30% above normal depreciation, even in excess of the historical cost. To qualify for the tax benefits, the deductions must be shown in the published annual report. But the tax deduction will reverse in subsequent years. In the United Kingdom, long-lived assets can be revalued periodically and assets can be written up to market value. Revaluation equity is credited to an account called **Revaluation Reserve** and shown as a separate line item in owners' equity. Future depreciation is based on the revalued amounts. **International accounting** standards advocate an approach similar to the U.K. approach.

Glossary of Terms

Amortization	The term applied to the matching process, or the allocation of costs, of intangible assets.
Asset Impairment	A situation that occurs when the future value expected to be generated by an asset falls below its net book value.
Capitalization of Interest	The process of adding interest costs to the cost of assets when borrowing is undertaken to finance construction of assets that require a long construction period.

Depletion	The term applied to the matching process, or the allocation of costs, of natural resources.
Depreciation	The term applied to the matching process, or the allocation of costs, of fixed assets.
Double-Declining Balance Method	A method of depreciation that applies a constant percentage rate to the declining book value of an asset. This method produces a decreasing annual amount of depreciation over the estimated life of the asset.
Economic Sacrifice Approaches	Approaches to asset measurement that focus on the amount of resource expenditures necessary to acquire an asset.
Expected Benefit Approaches	Approaches to asset measurement that reflect the asset's value in the output market. These approaches attempt to measure various definitions of future cash inflows attributable to the asset.
Full-Cost Approach	A method of accounting applied in the exploration industries where the costs for unsuccessful ventures are capitalized.
Intangible Assets	Assets, mostly comprised of contractual rights, characterized by a lack of physical existence and having a great degree of uncertainty concerning future benefits.
Long-Lived Assets	Operating assets that are expected to yield economic benefits or service potential over a period longer than one year.
Reserve Recognition Accounting	A method of accounting in the oil and gas industry whereby a company reports the value of oil or gas on the balance sheet and income statement as soon as the oil or gas is discovered.
Salvage Value	The estimated value to be received at the time an asset is sold or taken out of service.
Straight-Line Method	A method of depreciation that assumes periodic depreciation is equal each year of its useful life.
Successful Efforts Approach	A method of accounting for exploration costs in the extractive industries where only the capitalization of successful efforts occurs.
Sum-of-Years Digits Method	A method of depreciation that results in decreasing annual depreciation charges. The method applies a decreasing fraction to a constant base.

Demonstration Problems

1. **Apportionment of joint costs, self-constructed assets, and capitalized interest.**

Donny Corporation manufactures computer equipment. The corporation purchased a parcel of land for $4,200,000 containing a building to be used as a manufacturing facility and a building that needed to be removed to construct an addition to the manufacturing building. The appraised value of the manufacturing building was $3,200,000, the second building was $600,000 and the land was $1,000,000. Donny borrowed $1,000,000 at 10% for the added construction costs of the manufacturing building.   Construction began on January 2, and was completed on December 31. Donny paid construction costs of $400,000 on January 2, $300,000 on April 1, $200,000 on October 1, and the balance on December 31. Donny had other borrowing of $1,000,000 at 11% for the entire year. The company incurred the following costs in addition to the purchase price:

Cost of razing of old building	$ 22,000
Legal fees for title investigation on land	6,000
Construction costs of building addition	1,200,000
Sales of salvaged materials from razed building	(14,000)
Grading of land to prepare for construction	16,000
Excavation of footings for building	12,000
Permanent landscaping	14,000
Total Additional Costs	$1,256,000

Required:
A. Determine the original cost assigned to land and building upon the purchase.
B. Determine the assignment of additional costs to the building and the land.

A. Original apportionment
First Step: Apportion the cost on basis of appraisal value between the land and building.
Application: Use the proportional method to allocate costs between the land and building based on appraisal values. The building to be torn down is added to the cost of the land.

Solution:	Appraisal Value	Cost	
Land	$1,600,000 / $4,800,000 x	$4,200,000 =	$1,400,000
Building	$3,200,000 / $4,800,000 x	$4,200,000 =	$2,800,000

B. Assign additional costs to land and building
First Step: Determine construction period interest assigned to cost of building.
Application: Interest paid on outside borrowing is based on weighted average expenditures.

Solution:

Date	Amount	Portion of Year	Cumulative Weighted Average Expenditures
January 2	$400,000	3/12	$ 100,000
April 1	700,000	6/12	350,000
October 1	900,000	3/12	225,000
December 31	1,256,000	0	$675,000

Second Step: Determine the interest to be capitalized.

Application: Capitalized interest is the avoidable interest limited to the actual interest paid. Compare calculated avoidable interest with total interest paid and capitalize the lower of the two amounts.

Solution: Avoidable Interest $675,000 x 10% = $67,500   Capitalized interest.

          Actual Interest:

Construction Loan	$1,000,000 x 10% =	$100,000
Other Borrowing	$1,000,000 x 11% =	110,000
		$210,000

Third Step: Analyze each item of cost to determine its allocation.

Application: Review each item and determine appropriate classification based on the rules. Land costs include preparing the land for its intended use, legal and title fees, razing old buildings, landscaping, minus salvage proceeds. Building costs include excavation, building materials and labor, and capitalized interest costs.

Solution:

	Land	Building
Original Cost (See A)	$1,400,000	$2,800,000
Razing old building	22,000	
Title Investigation	6,000	
Construction Costs		1,200,000
Sale of salvaged materials	(14,000)	
Grading of land	16,000	
Excavation for construction		12,000
Permanent landscaping	14,000	
Construction period interest		67,500
Total Cost	$1,444,000	$4,079,500

2.   Asset Impairment

Seven years ago Rich Corporation acquired a machine for use in its aircraft manufacturing operations at a cost of $6,000,000. The firm expected the machine to have a twelve-year useful life and a zero salvage value. The company used the straight-line method to depreciate the asset. Due to the rapid rate of technological change in the industry, at the end of the seventh year, Rich estimates that the machine is capable of generating undiscounted future cash flows of $4,000,000. Based on the quoted market prices of similar assets, Rich estimates the machine has a fair market value of $2,500,000.

Required:
A.   Does the asset qualify for a write-down due to impairment? If so, how much?
B.   If the expected undiscounted future cash flows are $1,000,000, does the asset qualify for a write-down due to impairment? If so, how much?

First Step: Determine the accumulated depreciation of the asset.
Application: Accumulated Depreciation = Cost — Salvage Value x Years Asset Used
                                                                   Years of Life
Solution: Cost $6,000,000 — Salvage Value $0   x 7 years = $6,000,000   x 7 = $3,500,000
                       Years of Life 12   12

Second Step: Determine the carrying value of the asset.
Application: Carrying value = Cost — Accumulated Depreciation
Solution: Cost $6,000,000 — Accumulated Depreciation $3,500,000 = $2,500,000 Book Value

Third Step: Determine qualification of asset for impairment treatment.
Application: If an external event indicates a possible impairment, and the undiscounted future cash flows are below the asset carrying value, an impairment has occurred.
Solution:
A. Technological change has occurred, but the undiscounted future cash flows of $4,000,000 exceed the carrying value of $2,500,000. Therefore, the asset does not qualify for impairment treatment.
B. Technological change has occurred, and the undiscounted future cash flows of $1,000,000 are below the carrying value of $2,500,000. Therefore, the asset does qualify for impairment treatment.

Fourth Step: Determine the amount of asset impairment loss.
Application: Impairment loss is the difference between the fair value and the carrying value of the asset.
Solution:
A. The asset is not eligible for impairment write-down.
B. Impairment loss = Carrying Value $2,500,000 — Fair Market Value $1,000,000 = $1,500,000

3.   **Alternative Depreciation Methods.**

On January 2, Year 1, Jones Corporation purchased a truck for $39,000. The truck has a 5-year estimated life and a $3000 estimated salvage value. Jones expects to drive the truck 100,000 miles during its useful life. During Year 2, the truck was driven 17,500 miles.

Required:
Calculate depreciation expense for Year 2 (the second year of ownership) for the truck for each method listed.

- A.   Straight-line
- B.   Double-declining balance
- C.   Sum-of-years-digits
- D.   Units of production

A. Straight-Line Method

First Step: Determine straight-line depreciation.

Application: Straight Line Depreciation = $\dfrac{\text{Cost} - \text{Salvage Value}}{\text{Useful Life in Years}}$

Solution: $\dfrac{\text{Cost } \$39,000 - \text{Salvage Value } \$3,000}{\text{Useful Life in Years } 5} = \dfrac{\$36,000}{5} = \underline{\$7,200}$

B. Double-declining balance Method

First Step: Determine the straight-line rate of depreciation.

Application: $\dfrac{100\%}{\text{Years of Life}}$

Solution: $\dfrac{100\%}{\text{Years of Life } 5} = 20\%$

Second Step: Calculate the double-declining-balance rate.

Application: Straight Line Rate of Depreciation x 2

Solution: Straight Line Rate (from First Step) 20% x 2 = 40%

Third Step: Calculate double-declining-balance depreciation.

Application: The carrying value of the asset is multiplied each year by the double-declining rate.

Solution:

	Beginning Carrying Value	Rate	Current Depreciation	Ending Carrying Value
Year 1	$39,000	40%	$15,600	$23,400
Year 2	$23,400	40%	$9,360	$14,040

C. Sum-of-Years-Digits Method

First Step: Determine the denominator of the fraction.

Application: Apply formula: $\dfrac{n(n+1)}{2}$ where n = number of years of life

Solution: 5(5+1) / 2   =   30 / 2 =   15

Second Step: Compute the sum-of-years-digits depreciation.
Application: Multiply the depreciable base times the fraction for each year where the numerator is the remaining number of year of life and the denominator is the sum of the years (from First Step).
Solution:

Years Remaining	Fraction	Depreciation
Year 1 5	5/15	$12,000
Year 2 4	4/15	$9,600

D. Units of Production Method

First Step: Determine rate of depreciation per unit.
Application: Unit depreciation = $\dfrac{\text{(Cost — Salvage Value)}}{\text{Total units of production}}$

Solution: $\dfrac{\text{(Cost \$39,000— Salvage Value \$3,000)}}{\text{Total units of production}} = \dfrac{(\$39,000 — \$3,000)}{100,000 \text{ miles}} = \$.036$ cents per mile

Second Step: Compute units of production depreciation.
Application: The annual depreciation is the units of production times the unit depreciation rate.
Solution: Units of production 17,500 miles   x   rate per unit $.036 = $6,300

4.   Long-Lived Asset Disposition

The Stervil Corporation sold, for $12,000, a long-lived asset that was purchased seven years ago at a cost of $40,000. Stervil established a salvage value of $10,000 with an estimated 10 year life. Stervil uses straight-line depreciation.

Required: Determine the gain or loss on the sale.

First Step: Determine the accumulated depreciation to date.
Application: $\dfrac{\text{(Cost — Salvage Value)}}{\text{Useful Life}}$ x   Years Used

Solution: $\dfrac{\text{(Cost \$40,000 — Salvage Value \$10,000)}}{\text{Useful Life 10}}$ x   Years Used 7 = $21,000

Second Step: Determine the carrying or book value at date of sale.
Application: Book value = Cost — Accumulated Depreciation.
Solution: Book Value $19,000 = Cost $40,000 — Accumulated Depreciation $21,000

Third Step: Determine the gain or loss on sale.
Application: Gain or loss on sale is the difference between the net book value of the asset and proceeds.

Solution: Net Book Value $19,000
                    Proceeds   12,000
                    Loss on Sale $7,000

Test Yourself

True or False Questions

T F   1.   Operating assets expected to yield economic benefits over a period longer than one year are called long-lived assets.

T F   2.   The dominant measurement method for long-lived assets under GAAP is the discounted present value method.

T F   3.   Reliability relates to the verifiability of accounting numbers.

T F   4.   Financial statement users should expect the balance sheet numbers for long-lived assets to approximate their real economic worth.

T F   5.   Costs included in the long-lived asset accounts are referred to as capitalized costs.

T F   6.   All costs incurred for long-lived assets that are necessary to acquire the assets and make them ready for use are included in the asset accounts.

T F   7.   When common stock is sold to raise capital for the purchase of long-lived assets, the cost of the capital in the form of imputed interest should be added to the cost of the assets.

T F   8.   Financial reporting allocates costs between land and building on the basis of which item generated which cost.

T F   9.   An expenditure on a long-lived asset which increases the capacity or the efficiency of an asset should be expensed.

T F   10. Analysis of a firm's financial statements may be distorted by an aging asset base and increasing costs and prices.

T F   11. Items such as patents, copyrights, and trademarks are all tangible assets.

T F   12. The FASB requires the immediate expensing of research and development costs unless they are reimbursed by some outside group.

T F   13. Financial analysis is enhanced by the understatement of internally generated intangible assets.

T F   14.   Financial rules concerning intangibles are different in the U.K. as compared to the U.S..

T F   15.   Oil and gas producing companies are required to use the full-cost approach for accounting.

T F   16.   When the future undiscounted net cash flows are higher than the carrying amount of the asset, no write-down for impairment is necessary.

T F   17.   An impairment loss is the difference between the fair value of the asset and the carrying amount of the asset.

T F   18.   Apportionment of the cost of an asset such as a piece of equipment is called amortization.

T F   19.   The matching process applied to intangible assets is called depreciation.

T F   20.   The matching process for long-lived assets requires the reporting entity to determine the useful life of the asset, the expected salvage value, and the depreciation pattern to be used.

T F   21.   Straight-line depreciation is the predominant method used for financial statement purposes.

T F   22.   Depreciation of long-lived assets is intended to track an asset's declining market value.

T F   23.   Cost minus salvage value divided by the estimated life of the asset is the formula for straight-line depreciation.

T F   24.   The sum-of-years digits method of depreciation ignores salvage value except as a limit to the amount of depreciation taken.

T F   25.   The financial reporting rules for long-lived assets are the same around the world.

Multiple-Choice Questions
Select the best answer from those provided.

_____   1.   The use of the discounted present value method to value long-lived assets is an example of the
    a.   expected benefit approach.
    b.   historical cost approach.
    c.   economic sacrifice approach.
    d.   current replacement value.

_____   2.   The predominant approach to the measurement of long-lived assets is the
    a.   present value approach.
    b.   historical cost approach.
    c.   lower of cost or market approach.
    d.   current replacement cost approach.

_____ 3.   If the numbers on the financial statements are verifiable, then the numbers are
a. objective.
b. qualitative.
c. subjective.
d. accurate.

_____ 4.   When a cost of a long-lived asset is capitalized, it is included in the
a. expenses.
b. assets.
c. liabilities.
d. retained earnings.

_____ 5.   The cost of razing a structure, before the construction of a new building may occur, is added to the cost of the
a. old building.
b. new building.
c. land.
d. equipment necessary to destroy the old building.

_____ 6.   When a firm constructs its own long-lived assets, the firm must capitalize interest on the construction cost only if the firm has borrowed from
a. insiders.
b. stockholders.
c. management.
d. outsiders.

_____ 7.   When an expenditure is made on a long-lived asset that increases the capacity of the asset, the expenditure should be
a. capitalized.
b. ignored.
c. expensed.
d. written off in the current period.

_____ 8.   An aging asset base is a factor considered by financial analysts that makes it
a. easy to use trend analysis.
b. impossible to use trend analysis .
c. difficult to use trend analysis.
d. easy to use analytical procedures.

_____ 9.   If reinvestment in fixed assets is sporadic and prices are unstable, distortions of financial data are
a. maximized.
b. minimized.
c. avoided.
d. non-existent.

_____ 10.   Research and development costs associated with an internally generated patent or other asset should be
a. capitalized.
b. expensed.
c. ignored.
d. charged directly to retained earnings.

_____ 11.   Advertising costs associated with creative development expenditures are currently
a. expensed.
b. charged to retained earnings.
c. capitalized.
d. ignored.

_____ 12.   The successful efforts approach used in the oil and gas industry capitalizes
a. the exploration costs of all wells.
b. the exploration costs of unsuccessful wells.
c. the exploration costs of productive wells.
d. no exploration costs.

_____ 13.   The reserve recognition approach used in the oil and gas industry is a method used to account for exploration costs that measures
a. the estimated worth of discoveries.
b. the estimated worth of dry holes.
c. the cost of dry holes.
d. the cost of productive wells.

_____ 14.   A long-lived asset is impaired in value if the asset's remaining expected future value
a. rises above its net book value.
b. falls below its net book value.
c. remains the same as its net book value.
d. rises above its current fair market value.

_____ 15.   An impairment loss is classified on the income statement as a/an
    a.   discontinued operation.
    b.   ordinary item.
    c.   cumulative effect.
    d.   extraordinary item.

_____ 16.   The ability of management to manipulate earnings as a result of asset impairments
    has been
    a.   enhanced by the FASB.
    b.   hampered by the FASB.
    c.   encouraged by the FASB.
    d.   encouraged by the SEC.

_____ 17.   When a firm systematically apportions the cost of a trademark or patent to future
    periods using amortization, the firm is following the
    a.   historical cost principle.
    b.   going-concern principle.
    c.   revenue recognition principle.
    d.   matching principle.

_____ 18.   The systematic apportionment of the cost of oil deposits to future periods is
    commonly referred to as
    a.   depreciation.
    b.   amortization
    c.   allocation.
    d.   depletion.

_____ 19.   Financial analysts have the most difficult time adjusting for differences in long-
    lived assets on the balance sheets of various companies because the companies
    may use different
    a.   amortization methods.
    b.   depreciation methods.
    c.   estimated lives.
    d.   cost bases.

_____ 20.   The formula expressed as

$$\frac{\text{gross property, plant, and equipment} - \text{salvage value}}{\text{straight-line depreciation}}$$

is the formula to determine the
a. total useful life of long-lived assets.
b. average useful life of long-lived assets.
c. average useful life of current assets.
d. total useful life of current assets.

_____ 21.   A report on financial statements that indicates the financial statements present a "true and fair view" is most likely from the
a. United States.
b. United Kingdom.
c. Japan.
d. Germany.

_____ 22.   The formula expressed as "Cost minus Salvage value / Estimated life" is the formula for
a. declining-balance depreciation.
b. sum-of-years digits depreciation.
c. straight line depreciation.
d. composite depreciation.

_____ 23.   Once a software product establishes technological feasibility, development costs are
a. expensed.
b. capitalized as tangible assets.
c. capitalized as intangible assets.
d. charged to retained earnings.

_____ 24.   The cost of architectural plans for a new manufacturing plant are classified as
a. cost of the building.
b. cost of the land.
c. expenses.
d. revenues.

_____ 25.   The cost of freight to obtain a new piece of equipment is
a. expensed.
b. ignored.
c. charged to retained earnings.
d. capitalized.

Exercises

1.   The Kollar Corporation purchased new machinery on January 4, Year 1 for $600,000. The equipment had an estimated four-year useful life and a $40,000 salvage value. Management estimated that the machine can operate for 40,000 hours.

Required:

    A. Calculate the depreciation for all four years of life using straight-line depreciation.

    B. Calculate the depreciation for all four years of life using sum-of-years digits depreciation.

    C. Calculate the depreciation for all four years of life using double declining balance depreciation.

    D. Calculate the depreciation for all four years of life using units of production depreciation assuming the following rates of production: Year 1 - 10,000 hours, Year 2 - 8,000 hours, Year 3 - 16,000 hours, Year 4 - 4,000 hours.

2.   The Walsh Grain Corporation acquired a new piece of equipment at the start of Year 10. The corporation paid the following additional costs for the machine:

Freight charges for delivery	$1,500
Insurance on machine while in transit	500
Costs of installation	1,000
Costs of testing the new machine	250

Required: Assuming the invoice price of the equipment was $100,000, determine the capitalized equipment cost.

_____

_____

_____

_____

_____

_____

3.   Rock Brewery Corporation purchased a parcel of land on which it decided to construct a new facility. The corporation paid $200,000 for the parcel of land with a building the corporation decided must be removed. Rock spent $50,000 to remove the building and was able to sell remnants of the razed building for $10,000. After the building was removed Rock spent another $5,000 to grade the land and get it ready for construction. The cost of the building plans was $6,000 and the construction cost of the building was $1,000,000.

Required:
1.   Determine the cost of the land.
2.   Determine the cost of the building.

_____

_____

_____

_____

_____

_____

_____

_____

_____

_____

_____

4.   During Year 7, the Jones Corporation acquired three trucks from one of its competitors. Hall paid $60,000 for the trucks. The following information is available for the three trucks:

	Current Appraised Value
Truck #1	$25,000
Truck #2	30,000
Truck #3	20,000
Total Appraised Value	$75,000

Required: Determine the cost to be assigned to Truck #2.

_____

_____

_____

_____

5.   Kunkel Corporation purchased a new product patent for $390,000. The patent had an expected useful life of 15 years. After 5 years, a new product was developed that reduced the expected useful life of Kunkel's patent to a total of 7 years.

Required: Determine the amount of patent amortization to be charged against income in the seventh year of life of the patent.

_____

_____

_____

6.   Falcon Corporation incurred the following costs during Year 8:

Research and development services performed by Ford, Inc. for Falcon	$1,000,000
Costs of testing in search of new products	200,000
Design of prototypes	300,000
Construction of prototypes	150,000
Testing of pre-production prototypes	100,000

Required: Determine the amount that Falcon Corporation should deduct on the income statement for Research and Development Expense.

_____

_____

_____

_____

_____

_____

_____

Solutions

Answers to True or False Questions

True Answers: 1, 5, 6, 8, 10, 12, 14, 16, 17, 20, 21, 23
False answers explained:
2.   The dominant measurement method for long-lived assets under GAAP is the <u>economic sacrifice</u> approach.
3.   <u>Objectivity</u> relates to the verifiability of accounting numbers.
4.   Financial statement users should <u>not</u> expect the balance sheet numbers for long-lived assets to approximate their real economic worth because these assets predominantly are carried at depreciated historical costs.
7.   Capitalization of interest is limited to interest arising from <u>actual borrowing from outsiders</u>.
9.   An expenditure on a long-lived asset which increases the capacity or the efficiency of an asset should be <u>capitalized</u>.
11. Items such as patents, copyrights, and trademarks are all <u>intangible</u> assets.
13. Financial analysis is <u>hindered</u> by the understatement of internally generated intangible assets.
15. Oil and gas producers may use <u>either</u> the successful efforts approach or the full-cost approach for accounting purposes.
18. Apportionment of the cost of an asset such as a piece of equipment is called <u>depreciation</u>.
19. The matching process applied to intangible assets is called <u>amortization</u>.
22. Depreciation is <u>not</u> intended to track an asset's declining market value.
24. The <u>double-declining balance</u> method has a built in salvage value.
25. There is <u>much disparity</u> around the world in accounting for long-lived assets.

Answers to Multiple-Choice Questions

1.	A	6.	D	11.	A	16.	B	21.	B
2.	B	7.	A	12.	C	17.	D	22.	C
3.	A	8.	C	13.	A	18.	D	23.	C
4.	B	9.	A	14.	B	19.	C	24.	A
5.	C	10.	B	15.	B	20.	B	25.	D

Answers to Exercises

1. A. Straight-Line Depreciation

$$\frac{\$600,000 - \$40,000}{4} = \$140,000 \text{ each year}$$

    B. Sum of Years Digits Depreciation
Year 1 ($600,000 — $40,000) x 4/10 = $224,000
Year 2 ($600,000 — $40,000) x 3/10 = $168,000
Year 3 ($600,000 — $40,000) x 2/10 = $112,000
Year 3 ($600,000 — $40,000) x 1/10 = $56,000

    C. Double Declining Balance Depreciation
Year 1 $600,000 x 50% = $300,000
Year 2 $300,000 x 50% = $150,000
Year 3 $150,000 x 50% = $75,000
Year 4 $ 75,000 x 50% = $35,000
Depreciation is limited based on the salvage value.

    D. Units of Production Depreciation

$$\frac{\$600,000 - \$40,000}{40,000 \text{ hours}} = \$14.00 \text{ per machine hour}$$

Year 1	10,000 hours	x $14	=	$14,000
Year 2	8,000 hours	x $14	=	$112,000
Year 3	16,000 hours	x $14	=	$224,000
Year 4	4,000 hours	x $14	=	$56,000

2.

Invoice Price	$100,000
Freight	1,500
Insurance	500
Installation Costs	1,000
Costs of Testing	250
Total Cost	$103,250

3.   A.   Land Cost $200,000
            Raze Old Building   50,000
            Salvage   (10,000)
            Grading   5,000
            Total Land Cost $245,000

      B.   Building $1,000,000
            Plans   6,000
            Total Building Cost $1,006,000

4.   Cost Assigned to Truck #2 based on the relative sales value method equals:
            $30,000/$75,000 x $60,000 = $24,000

5.   Cost of Patent/Years of Life
      $390,000/15 = $26,000 per year
      $26,000 x 5 years = $130,000
      $390,000 — $130,000 = $260,000 Remaining Cost to be written off over two years.
      $260,000/2 = $130,000 per year for years 6 & 7

6.   Research and Development Expense
      ($1,000,000 + $200,000 + $300,000 + $150,000 + $100,000) = $1,750,000

CHAPTER 11

FINANCIAL INSTRUMENTS AS LIABILITIES

Chapter Review

Liabilities are probable future sacrifices of economic benefits arising from present obligations of a particular entity to transfer assets or provide services to other entities in the future as a result of past transactions or events. *(SFAC NO. 6)*

FYI. . .
Liabilites are either **determinable** or **contingent**. Determinable liabilities contain evidence to determine precise valuation. Contingent liabilities depend upon future events for definition of amounts.

A liability has three important characteristics that must **all** be present to be considered a liability at a specific point in time:
1. It must be a **present** obligation.
2. It must be **unavoidable**.
3. It must be due to a **past transaction**.

A liability that requires cash payment is a **monetary liability**. A **nonmonetary** liability is one that will be satisfied by the delivery of goods or services in the future. Monetary liabilities should be recorded at the **discounted present value** of the future cash outflows required to settle the debt. Current liabilities (amounts due within one year or within the company's operating cycle whichever is longer) are not discounted, due to the **materiality** constraint. Nonmonetary liabilities are recorded at the present value when incurred.

Bonds are promissory notes to repay principal and interest according to the term of a **bond indenture**, a contract between the borrowers and lenders which contains the terms and conditions of the lending agreement. Bonds come in many forms:
1. **Debentures** are unsecured bonds.
2. **Mortgage bonds** are secured by real property.
3. **Serial bonds** have a series of different maturity dates or pay principal in installments.
4. **Zero coupon bonds** pay no interest and are issued at deep discounts. U. S. savings bonds are zero coupon bonds.

255

FYI...
Bonds have unique terminology that one must understand to analyze the balance sheet competently, and to participate in the bond markets.

FYI...
Interest rates consist of three elements:
1. the pure cost of interest (usually 3%);
2. the risk of inflation; and
3. individual risk of default.

Bonds have a **principal** amount that is due upon maturity. Principal can be called the **par value**, **maturity value**, or **face value**. The bond requires the firm to pay interest (except for zero coupon bonds) that is fixed on the bond certificate. This interest rate is called the **stated** rate, the **coupon** rate, the **face** rate, or the **nominal** rate. Firms make cash payments of interest equal to the principal (face value) times the stated (nominal) rate.

Bond interest = Principal x Stated rate

The bond indenture sets forth the dates of interest payments, usually semi-annually, annually, or quarterly. The number of interest payments made per year defines the compounding periods for present value calculations. The bond's market values are based on interest yield. Unlike stock valuation, which investors base on a number of criteria including future earnings or cash flow, bond valuation is simply a matter of determining the required interest rates for certain levels of risk.

The heart of the matter...
Remember these simple truths about bond terminology:
Firms "sell" or issue bonds — but in reality firms borrow money.
Investors "buy" bonds — but in reality they lend money to firms.
Therefore, the seller is the borrower and the buyer is the lender.

Learning Objective 1:

How to compute a bond's issue price from its effective yield to investors.

A firm issues a bond (and initially records it in the accounting records) at market price, which is equal to the discounted present value of the bond at the effective yield. The **effective rate** is also called the **market rate** or **yield rate**. We can compute the bond's issue price in a two-step calculation based upon the present value of the maturity and the present value of the stream of cash inflows for interest.

    Present value of the maturity (PVIF x maturity value)
 + Present value of the interest (PVIFA x cash interest payments)
 = Present value of a bond

The effective (market) rate and the number of interest payments are used to determine the present value interest factors. **(See Demonstration Problem 1A.)**

FYI...
When bonds sell at par, the **market interest** rate is equal to the **nominal interest** rate and the **present value** of the bonds is equal to the **maturity value** of the bonds.

The heart of the matter . . .
The life cycle of bonds is simple:
1. Bonds are sold.
2. Interest is paid.
3. Bonds are repaid.

Journal entries to record bond transactions follow a predictable pattern.

To issue bonds at par:
DR Cash
       CR Bonds Payable

To accrue interest expense:
DR Interest Expense
       CR Interest Payable

To pay interest: To repay the bonds at maturity:
DR Interest Payable   DR Bonds Payable
       CR Cash   CR Cash

Although the bond concept is simple, reality complicates the bond process. Bonds do not sell at par because market interest changes between the time of initiation of the SEC approval process and market issuance. Bonds with nominal interest lower than investors' requirements sell at a discount, or less than the par value. Bonds with nominal interest greater than investor's requirements sell at a premium, or more than par value. If a firm issues $100,000 of 10%, five-year bonds which pay interest annually, the firm will pay out the following amounts in the five-year period:

Principal repayment at maturity	$100,000
Annual interest ($100,000 x 10% x 5 years)	50,000
Total payments	$150,000

Total interest expense for any loan is the difference between the proceeds of the loan and the amount paid back. Look at three different scenarios for the bonds.

	Discount	Par	Premium
Cash received from investors	$92,790	$100,000	$105,911
Cash payments by the firm	150,000	150,000	150,000
Firm's total interest expense	$ 57,210	$ 50,000	$ 44,089

If the bonds are issued at par, the interest for five years is $50,000. The

FYI. . .
When a 10% bond sells to yield 8.5%, bond investors will pay more than par for the bond. When a 10% bond sells to yield 12%, the bond investors will pay less than par for the bond.

discount raises the interest expense and the premium lowers the interest expense. Therefore, discounts and premiums change the effective interest paid by the firm and received by the investors. Premiums and discounts change the entry made at issuance. Consider these entries for bonds sold to yield 12% (a discount) or 8.5% (a premium):

	Discount	Premium
DR Cash	92,790	105,911
DR Bond Discount	7,210	
CR Bond Premium		5,911
CR Bonds Payable	100,000	100,000

Learning Objective 2:
How to construct an amortization table for calculating bond interest expense and net carrying value of the debt.

GAAP requires the use of the effective interest method to recognize interest expense and amortize any bond discount or premium. The first step to determine these amounts necessitates completion of an amortization table. The table consists of five columns:

A   Cash interest paid = Par value of the bonds x nominal interest rate

B   Interest expense = Carrying value of the bonds at the end of the prior period (E) x effective interest rate

C   Amortization of bond premium or discount = Column A - Column B

D   Bond premium (or discount) balance = Prior balance - Column B

E   Bond carrying value = Prior balance - Column B for premiums
     or   = Prior balance + Column B for discounts

(See Demonstration Problem 1C.)
The bond carrying value in Column E should correspond with the net amount of Bonds Payable on the balance sheet at that date.

Learning Objective 3:
Why and how bond interest expense and net carrying value change over time.

The following bond amortization tables for the premium and discount situations illustrate several points:

	A	B (8.5% x E)	C (A — B)	D (D — C)	E (E — C)
Period	Cash Interest	Effective Interest	Amortization	Unamortized Premium	Carrying Value
0				$5,911	$105,911
1	$10,000	$ 9,002	$998	4,913	104,913
2	10,000	8,918	1,082	3,831	103,831
3	10,000	8,826	1,174	2,657	102,657
4	10,000	8,726	1,274	1,383	101,383
5	10,000	8,617	1,383	0	100,000
Total	$50,000	$44,089	$5,911		

	A	B	C	D	E

Period	Cash Interest	(12% x E) Effective Interest	(B — A) Amortization	(D — C) Unamortized Discount	(E + C) Carrying Value
0				$7,210	$ 92,790
1	$10,000	$11,135	$1,135	6,075	93,925
2	10,000	11,271	1,271	4,804	95,196
3	10,000	11,424	1,424	3,380	96,620
4	10,000	11,594	1,594	1,786	98,214
5	10,000	11,786	1,786	0	100,000
Total	$50,000	$57,210	$7,210		

Notice that the totals in the tables agree with the total interest expense we calculated for the bond issues. The carrying value for the premium bond issue falls from the issue amount to the maturity value during the life of the bond as the premium amortizes. The carrying value of the discount bond issue rises from the issue amount to the maturity amount as the discount amortizes. The carrying value represents the **amortized historical cost** of the bonds. The carrying value does not equal the market price of the bonds. Bond markets fluctuate over the life of the bonds and the market value of the bonds is often different that the carrying value. Realistically, the Bonds Payable account represents the **net present value** and market value of the bonds on two dates, the issue date and the maturity date.

Learning Objective 4:
How and when floating-rate debt protects lenders.

Once the firm issues its bonds, market fluctuations have no impact on its income or financial reporting. Market changes subject bond investors to gains or losses on their investments. **Floating-rate debt** protects investors from market fluctuations by transferring the risk of interest rate increases to the debtor. On the other hand, the debtor transfers the risk of interest rate decreases to the investors. Floating-rate bonds usually sell at par so the accounting entries are simple. The only changes during the bond life are the amounts of interest paid each period. The bond carrying value stays at par so the accounting entries are simple. The only changes during the bond life are the amounts of interest paid each period. The bond carrying the value stays at par, which equals the market value.

Learning Objective 5:
How debt extinguishment gains and losses arise, and what they mean.

Firms issue bond debt with maturity dates of 10 to 30 years. During the bond life, corporate strategies change, interest rates fluctuate, and the firm's financing needs change. For any of these reasons, management may decide to extinguish the old debt and reissue new debt that better satisfies corporate needs. To accomplish this, a firm can buy its own bonds in the open market to retire the debt. Some bond indentures include terms, called **call provisions**, that allow the issuer to recall the debt at a specified price, usually above par. Whenever bonds are retired, the difference between the settlement price and the bond's amortized historical cost (carrying value) is a gain or loss on debt extinguishment.

Carrying Value — Repurchase Price = Gain or Loss on Debt Extinguishment

SFAS No. 4 requires that **debt extinguishment** gains and losses, by definition, be treated as extraordinary items on the income statement if the amount is material, even though the rules for extraordinary items are not met. FASB believes that inclusion of debt extinguishment gains and losses in income from continuing operations is potentially misleading because such items do not represent recurring events. **(See Demonstration Problem 2.)**

FYI...
Gains on debt at retirement arise when the firm pays less than the carrying value to redeem the bonds. Losses occur when the firm pays more than the carrying value to redeem the bonds.

Firms can also engage in **debt-for-debt swaps** and **debt-for-equity swaps**. When bond market values fall below the carrying value, the firm can extinguish debt at a gain. Firms can arrange to swap the old debt for new debt with the same current value and future cash outflows. The economic difference is nil, but the firm still reports a gain on the income statement that represents unreported market interest fluctuations from prior periods. Since the firm and its investors are left in the same position, the motivation for the transaction might be earnings enhancement. In reality, most debt-for-debt swaps require **sweeteners** (or inducements) to persuade debt-holder actions which reduce gains. Gains are generally taxable.

Debt-for-equity swaps are equally suspicious. Low market value bonds are traded for high market value stock. The book value of the bonds is much higher than the market value of the stock, which generates a large gain on debt extinguishment. Despite the cash flow benefits of not having to repay the maturity value, the common stock issue dilutes existing ownership shares and lowers earnings per share. Both of these consequences reduce the share values in the market.

Both debt-for-debt and debt-for-equity swaps have the potential to reduce pressure on restrictive loan covenants, improve ratio numbers, and improve reported earnings. Because of this, *SFAS No. 107* requires footnote disclosure of the market value of all financial asset instruments and financial liability instruments.

Learning Objective 6:
How to find the future cash payments for a company's debt.

SFAS No. 47 requires footnote disclosure of scheduled debt repayments for each of the five years following the balance sheet date. The footnote information provides readers with the financing cash outflows for the following five years. In addition, the reader can determine the approximate amounts of interest expense payments for each of those years. To estimate future interest expense, first determine the average interest rate with this formula:

$$\text{Interest rate} \; = \; \frac{\text{Interest Expense}}{\text{Average outstanding debt}} \; = \; \frac{\text{Interest Expense}}{\frac{\text{Beginning debt} + \text{Ending debt}}{2}}$$

Multiplying the interest rate by the ending debt will predict next year's interest cash outflow. An analyst or lender can predict cash flow requirement for the next five years to service a firm's debts.

Learning Objective 7:
Why statement readers need to beware of off-balance sheet financing and loss contingencies.

Restrictive financial debt covenants give management incentive to reduce the amount of debt on the balance sheet to comply with required ratios concerning the amount of debt (debt-to-tangible-assets or debt-to-equity). Managers use a variety of financing schemes to keep liabilities off the balance sheet. **Off-balance sheet financing** can be accomplished through the creative use of operating leases, unconsolidated subsidiaries, and joint ventures. Leasing will be discussed in Chapter 12. Investments in unconsolidated subsidiaries (where ownership is exactly 50% or less) are reported using the equity method so only the investment — not the subsidiary's debts — appears on the parent firm's financial statements. The same holds true for a joint venture partnership. Therefore, a company can join another firm to complete a substantial project requiring debt financing, and by each firm owning exactly 50% of a newly created entity, keep the project debt off both companies' financial statements.

Learning Objective 8:
How futures, swaps, and options contracts are used to hedge financial risk.

Firms constantly have exposure to financial market risks — changes in interest rates, foreign currency exchange rates, and commodity prices. Many business organizations engage in **hedging** to protect against financial market risk by use of **derivative securities**. Derivative securities have no inherent value but represent a claim against some other asset. Common derivatives are:

1.   A **futures contract** sets a price today to purchase or sell an asset or commodity at a future date.

2.   A **swap contract** is an arrangement through a swap dealer to trade fixed-rate interest payments for floating-rate interest receipts.

3.   A **foreign exchange currency swap** is similar to an interest rate swap except the parties are trading currencies.

4.   A **call option** is a unilateral agreement to purchase an asset in the future for a price specified today. This protects prices for the option holder because if prices rise above the option price, the holder is protected. If prices fall below the option price, the holder does not exercise the option and buys at the lower price.

5.   A **put option** gives its holder the option to sell at a specified price during a specified period of time.

Learning Objective 9:
When hedge accounting can be used, and how it works to reduce earnings volatility.

Current GAAP for derivatives is based on the following:

1) All derivatives must be carried at fair value on the balance sheet.
2) Changes in the fair value of a derivative must be recognized in income when they occur with a hedge transaction being an exception.
3) A derivative security used to hedge financial risk can be accounted for applying special rules that eliminate or reduce the earnings volatility from reporting the derivatives at fair value.
   a. In some cases the change in the fair value of the derivative offsets an adjustment to the carrying value of the asset of liability being hedged.
   b. In other cases, the change in the fair value of derivative is reported as "other comprehensive income, in the stockholders' equity section of the balance sheet."

These are three general categories:

1. **Fair value hedge** – hedges exposure to variability of an asset, liability or firm commitment. The gain (loss) on the derivative is recognized in earnings as an offset to the gain (loss) of the hedged item.

2. **Cash flow hedge** – hedges exposure to variability in cash flows of an existing asset, liability or forecasted transaction. The gain (loss) on the derivative is recognized in "other comprehensive income" and later recognized in earnings, when the future transaction occurs.

3. **Foreign currency exposure hedge** - hedges exposure to changes in currency exchange rates of an unrecognized firm commitment, available for sale securities, a forecasted transaction, or a net investment in foreign operations. The gain (loss) is recognized in "other comprehensive income" as part of the cumulative transaction adjustment.

Loss contingencies present special problems for financial statement preparers and readers. The most critical step for preparers is determining when a loss contingency requires inclusion on financial statements, or disclosure in footnotes, or should be ignored. Once the contingency meets the three requirements of a liability, two additional requirements must be met:

1. the loss must be **probable**, and
2. the amount of the loss must be **reasonably estimable**.

If one, but not both conditions are met, the firm must disclose the contingency in the footnotes to the financial statement.

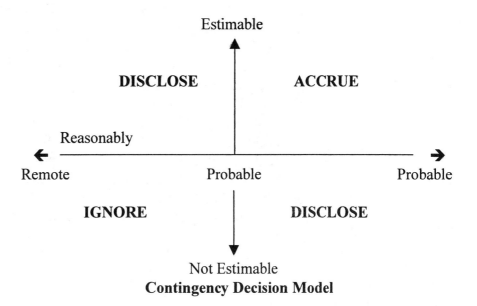

Contingency Decision Model

SFAS No. 5 requires disclosure of loss contingencies when the loss is reasonably possible and estimable. The contingency decision model gives an approximation of actions for contingent losses. The upper right quadrant is where both conditions are met for accrual. The lower left quadrant is where there is little substance to the contingency and it can be ignored. The remainder is left to professional judgment to properly disclose the contingency in the footnotes.

Firms encounter several types of contingencies:

1.   Routine contingencies include provisions for uncollectible accounts, warranties, sales returns.
2.   Lawsuits are filed for a variety of reasons ranging from nuisance suits to serious matters of liability.
3.   Violations of federal and local laws in areas of pollution, safety, and product liability.

Management estimates routine contingencies which normally are both probable and estimable and require accrual. Lawsuits and violations require study by legal counsel and accountants to determine both the probability and the estimability of the possible loss. When a loss is probable, the most likely amount of loss is accrued and any additional liability is disclosed. When the loss is reasonably probable and estimable, the loss is disclosed.

For an ongoing contingency, legal counsel's opinion may change during the course of settling the dispute. If in Year 1, a customer sues Fast Food Giant for $2,000,000, counsel believes that chances of a loss are remote. Fast Food Giant is not required to disclose the lawsuit. In Year 2, legal counsel decides that there is a possibility that the plaintiff will prevail but believes that the maximum collectible is $500,000. In Year 2, Fast Food Giant discloses the lawsuit in a note to the financial statement that indicates that legal counsel believes chances are reasonably possible that the plaintiff will prevail up to $500,000 in the $2,000,000 lawsuit. In Year 3, counsel decides that Fast Food will probably lose this lawsuit in the amount of $1,000,000. Fast Food must accrue $1,000,000 and disclose the remaining $1,000,000 in the footnotes.

Glossary of Terms

Bond Principal   An amount that will be repaid to the investor at the maturity date of the bond. (Also referred to as the par value, maturity value, or face value.)

Call Option   An option contract giving the holder the right to buy a specific underlying asset at a specified price during a specified time.

Cash Flow Hedge   A hedge of cash flow exposure of a planned transaction.

Consolidation   The presentation of combined financial statements for a parent company and its subsidiaries. (This will be covered in greater detail in Chapter 15.)

Current Liabilities	Obligations due within one year or within the company's operating cycle, whichever is longer.
Debt-for-Debt Swap	An exchange of existing debt for new debt issued by the entity.
Derivative Security	A security having no inherent value, but represents a claim against some other asset. (Futures contracts, and swap contracts are examples of derivative securities.)
Discount	The term applied when the issue price of a bond is below the face value. A bond discount is a liability valuation account.
Discount Amortization	The process of spreading the discount on bonds to increase interest expense over the life of the bonds.
Effective Yield	The true rate of return. Also called market yield or market rate.
Equity-for-Debt Swap	Exchange of existing debt for a company's common stock.
Equity Method	A method of accounting for the investment in a subsidiary. (This will be covered in Chapter 15.)
Extinguishment of Debt	The accounting gain or loss at retirement of debt when there is a difference between the book value and the cash paid to extinguish the debt. Extinguishment gains or losses are treated as extraordinary items.
Fair Value Hedge	A hedge of the fair value exposure of an existing asset, liability, or a firm commitment.
Floating-Rate Debt	Debt with a stated interest rate that fluctuates in tandem with some interest rate benchmark.
Foreign Currency Exposure Hedge	A hedge of the risk arising from a company's net investment in a foreign operation.
Futures Contracts	A type of derivative security that requires each party to engage in the agreed upon transaction. Two parties agree to the sale of some asset on some future date at a price specified today.
Hedging	A business transaction designed to protect a company from commodity price, interest, or exchange rate risk.
Interest	The price charged for the privilege to delay payment.
Investment Banker	A financial intermediary who purchases bonds or stocks and resells them to institutional investors.

Liabilities	Probable future sacrifices of economic benefits arising from present obligations of an entity to transfer assets or provide services to other entities in the future as a result of past transactions.
Loss Contingency	The possibility of a loss occurring that must be accrued or disclosed in the financial statements. The loss contingency is accrued if it meets two conditions: 1. It is probable that an asset has been impaired or a liability has been incurred at the balance sheet date. 2. The amount of loss can be reasonably estimated.
Monetary Liabilities	Liabilities that are satisfied by payment in cash.
Nonmonetary Liabilities	Liabilities that are satisfied by delivery of goods or services other than cash.
Option Contract	A type of derivative security which provides the holder the right, but not the obligation, to do something.
Par Value of Bonds Payable	The face value of a bond. The term applied when a bond is sold at face value.
Premium	The term applied when the issue price of a bond is greater than the face value of the bond.
Premium Amortization	The process of spreading the premium on bonds to decrease interest expense over the life of the bonds.
Put Option	An option contract giving the holder the right to sell a specific underlying asset at a specified price during a specified time.
Stated Interest Rate	The rate of interest that a company agrees to pay on the issued bond. (Also called the coupon rate or nominal rate.)
Swap Contract	A type of futures contract that is used to hedge interest rate and foreign exchange risk.

Demonstration Problems

1.   Bond Pricing, Issuance, Amortization, and Journal Entries.

On July 1, Year 7, Roth Company issued $3,000,000 of 8%, 20-year bonds with a yield of 9%. The bonds pay interest semi-annually on June 30 and December 31 of each year. Roth Company closes its books on December 31.

Present value information:	4%	4.5%
PVIF (40 periods)	0.20829	0.17193
PVIFA (40 periods)	19.79277	18.40158

Required:
A.   Determine the bond issue price.
B.   Record the issuance of the bonds.
C.   Using the effective interest method, prepare an amortization schedule for each of the first four semi-annual interest payment periods.
D.   Prepare journal entries to record the first two interest payments.
      Record the entry to repay the bonds on July 1, Year 27

A.
First Step: Determine the present value interest factors (PVIF) to use in calculations.
Application: Use the PVIF for the effective interest rate.

Solution: Use the PVIF for 40 periods at 4.5% (one-half of 9%) for the maturity value = 0.17193
        Use the PVIFA for 40 periods at 4.5% for the interest payments = 18.40158

Second Step: Compute the amount of the semi-annual interest payments.
Application: Interest payments = Maturity value x semi-annual effective interest rate
Solution:
Interest payments=Maturity value $3,000,000 x semi-annual effective interest rate 4% = $120,000

Third Step: Compute the issue price of the bond.
Application: Compute the present value of the maturity value and the present value of the interest payments. Add the two present values to get the present value of the bonds.
Solution: Maturity $3,000,000 x PVIF   0.17193 = $ 515,790.00
          Interest $120,000 x PVIFA 18.40158   =   2,208,189.60
          Selling Price $2,723,979.60

B.
First Step: Prepare the entry to record the issuance of bonds.
Solution: DR Cash   2,723,979.60
          DR Discount on Bonds Payable   276,020.40
              CR Bonds Payable   3,000,000.00

C.
First Step: Prepare the amortization schedule.
Application: Utilize the bond amortization schedule model.

Solution:

	A	B	C	D	E
		(4.5% x E)	(B — A)	(D — C)	(E + C)
	Cash	Effective		Unamortized	Carrying
Period	Interest	Interest	Amortization	Discount	Value
0				$276,020.40	$2,723,979.60
1	$120,000	$122,579.08	$2,579.08	273,441.32	2,726,558.68
2	120,000	122,695.04	2,695.04	270,246.28	2,729,253.22
3	120,000	122,816.42	2,816.42	267,429.86	2,732,070.14
4	120,000	122,943.16	2,943.16	264,486.70	2,735,013.30

D.

First Step: Prepare the journal entries for the interest payments.

Application: Use the effective interest amortization schedule to determine the entries. Column A provides the cash paid, Column B the interest expense, and Column C the amortization of discount.

Solution:

Year 7	DR	Interest Expense	122,579.08	
December 31	CR	Bond Discount		2,579.08
	CR	Cash		120,000.00
Year 8				
June 30	DR	Interest Expense	122,695.04	
	CR	Bond Discount		2,695.04
	CR	Cash		120,000.00

Second Step: Prepare the journal entry to repay the bonds.

Application: On the maturity date, the Bond Discount account will be zero.

Solution:

Year 27			
July 1	DR Bonds Payable	3,000,000	
	CR Cash		3,000,000

2.   Retirement of Bonds

On January 1, Year 7, Davis Company issued $4,000,000 of 9%, ten-year bonds to yield 12%. The bonds pay interest annually on December 31 of each year. The company closes its books on December 31.

Required:

A.   Prepare the journal entry to record the issue of the bonds.

B.   What is the book value of the bonds on January 1, Year 8?

C.   On January 1, Year 8, the market interest rate for bonds of this type is 11%. What is the market value of the bonds on this date?

D.   The bonds were repurchased for cash on January 1, Year 8 at the market price. Ignoring taxes, prepare the journal entry that the company would make to record the debt retirement.

A.

First Step: Determine the issue price of bond (See Demonstration 1, A & B)
Application: Use the present value of the of the yield rate of interest applied to maturity value and interest

Solution:

DR Cash	3,321,959	
DR Bond Discount	678,041	
CR Bonds Payable		4,000,000

Maturity $8,000,000 x PVIF 0.32197 =	$1,287,880
Interest $720,000 x PVIFA 5.65022 =	2,034,079
Bond Issue Price	$3,321,959

B.

First Step: Prepare amortization schedule
Application: Calculate effective interest to determine carrying value (See Demonstration 1, C)
Solution:

Year	Cash Interest	Effective Interest	Amortization	Unamortized Discount	Carrying Value
0				$678,041	$3,321,959
1	$360,000	$398,635	$38,635	639,406	3,360,594

C.

First Step: Calculate current market price using present value factors for current interest rate.
Application: Use present value factors for current interest rate.
Solution:

Maturity $8,000,000 x PVIF 0.39092 =	$1,563,680
Interest $720,000 x PVIFA 5.53705 =	1,993,338
Bond Market Price	$3,557,018

D.

First Step: Prepare the entry for retirement.
Application: The difference between the carrying value of the bonds and the cash paid for retirement is a gain or loss on debt extinguishment.
Solution:

DR Bonds Payable	4,000,000	
DR Extraordinary Loss on Debt Retirement	196,424	
CR Bond Discount		639,406
CR Cash		3,557,018

Test Yourself

True or False Questions

T   F   1.   Liabilities that are to be paid in cash are called monetary liabilities.

T   F   2.   Noncurrent monetary liabilities are initially recorded at present value when incurred.

T   F   3.   When the issue price of a bond is below the face value, the bond is sold at a premium.

T   F   4.   The coupon rate of a bond is the true rate of return.

T   F   5.   When bonds are issued at par value, the coupon rate is equal to the effective yield earned by bond investors.

T   F   6.   The bond discount account is an asset valuation account.

T   F   7.   Amortization of bond discount is the process of spreading the discount on bonds to decrease interest expense over the life of the bonds.

T   F   8.   When bonds are sold at a premium, the amortization of the premium increases interest expense.

T   F   9.   The issue price of a bond is determined by management.

T   F   10.   GAAP requires bonds payable to be carried on the books at amortized historical cost.

T   F   11.   On the maturity date of a bond, the book value and the market value are equal.

T   F   12.   Gains and losses from the extinguishment of debt are treated as ordinary items on the income statement.

T   F   13.   Debt-for-debt swaps are attempts by management to manage the reported earnings and balance sheet numbers.

T   F   14.   Derivative securities are used to insulate companies from exchange rate risk.

T   F   15.   Off-balance sheet financing involves methods that enable management to minimize reported financial statement liabilities.

T   F   16.   Derivative securities get their name from the fact that they have a high inherent value.

T   F   17.   Option contracts provide that each party is required to engage in the agreed-upon transaction.

T F 18.   A put option gives the holder the right to buy a specific underlying asset at a specified price during a specified time.

T F 19.   A loss contingency arises when there is an event which raises the future possibility of a loss.

T F 20.   A loss contingency must be probable and reasonably estimable to be accrued on the balance sheet.

T F 21.   Footnote disclosure is the preferred treatment for loss contingencies in all cases.

T F 22.   Footnote disclosure is preferable when a loss contingency is only reasonably possible.

T F 23.   Investors and analysts have a difficult time analyzing financial statements when a firm uses off-balance sheet financing.

Multiple-Choice Questions
Select the best answer from those provided.

_____   1.   A monetary liability is satisfied through the payment of
   a.   inventory.
   b.   cash.
   c.   long-lived assets.
   d.   intangible assets.

_____   2.   A non-monetary liability is satisfied through the
   a.   provision of services.
   b.   payment of cash.
   c.   payment of cash equivalents.
   d.   discounting of accounts receivable.

_____   3.   A bond issue's terms are found in the
   a.   articles of incorporation.
   b.   stockholders minutes.
   c.   bond indenture agreement.
   d.   board of directors minutes.

_____   4.   The principal amount of a bond is also referred to as the
   a.   face value.
   b.   discounted value.
   c.   present value.
   d.   future value.

_____ 5.   A bond that sells at a premium has a nominal rate of interest that is
        a.   above the market rate of interest.
        b.   below the market rate of interest.
        c.   equal to the market rate of interest.
        d.   the same as the discount rate of interest.

_____ 6.   When a bond sells at par or face value the effective yield of the bond is
        a.   greater than the coupon rate.
        b.   less than the coupon rate.
        c.   equal to the coupon rate.
        d.   greater than the discount rate.

_____ 7.   A bond that has a coupon rate of 5% when the market rate of interest is 7% will
        sell at
        a.   par value.
        b.   face value.
        c.   a premium.
        d.   a discount.

_____ 8.   The premium on bonds payable must be allocated to interest expense using the
        a.   bond yield method.
        b.   effective interest method.
        c.   cash method.
        d.   discounted yield method.

_____ 9.   A bond that sells at a premium has an effective interest rate that is
        a.   above the coupon rate.
        b.   below the coupon rate.
        c.   equal to the coupon rate.
        d.   below the coupon rate for the first year and then above the coupon rate.

_____ 10.   Generally Accepted Accounting Principles require that Bonds Payable be reported
        on the balance sheet at
        a.   present value.
        b.   discounted future value.
        c.   amortized historical cost.
        d.   future value.

_____ 11. A decline in the value of a bond is brought about by a
a. fall in the market rate of interest.
b. rise in the market rate of interest.
c. rise in the coupon rate of interest on the bond.
d. fall in the coupon rate of interest on the bond.

_____ 12. Lenders may protect themselves from losses that arise as a result of increases in the market interest rate by using
a. level-rate debt.
b. floating-rate debt.
c. same-day-rate debt.
d. discounted-rate debt.

_____ 13. The use of floating-rate debt benefits investors when the market rates of interest
a. increase.
b. decrease.
c. remain static.
d. fall.

_____ 14. The gain or loss on the extinguishment of debt is classified as a /an
a. ordinary item on the income statement.
b. extraordinary item on the income statement.
c. discontinued item on the income statement.
d. prior period adjustment to retained earnings.

_____ 15. Some financial analysts believe that it is easier for management to manipulate the accounting numbers if
a. debt is reported at current value.
b. debt is reported at discounted present value.
c. debt is reported at amortized historical cost.
d. debt is reported at amortized current value.

_____ 16. A debt-for-debt swap should be reviewed carefully to ensure that there is an underlying
a. loss.
b. gain.
c. economic loss.
d. economic benefit.

_____ 17.   An early warning signal concerning deteriorating credit worthiness may be
             detected by
             a. debt premiums.
             b. debt discounts.
             c. financial covenants.
             d. impairments.

_____ 18.   The use of unconsolidated subsidiaries gives management the opportunity to
             a. maximize reported liabilities.
             b. minimize reported liabilities.
             c. understate equity.
             d. understate net assets.

_____ 19.   A company that tries to protect itself from exchange rate risk is engaging in the
             practice of
             a. factoring.
             b. assigning.
             c. hedging.
             d. trading.

_____ 20.   A derivative security has
             a. inherent value.
             b. no claim against another asset.
             c. value in and of itself.
             d. no inherent value.

_____ 21.   An options contract is an example of a derivative
             a. debt.
             b. security.
             c. liability.
             d. equity.

_____ 22.   Contingencies that are probable with an amount of loss that is reasonably
             estimable should be
             a. disclosed in the financial statements' footnotes.
             b. accrued on the financial statements.
             c. ignored on the financial statements.
             d. reported as an adjustment to retained earnings.

_____ 23. Contingencies that are reasonably possible with an amount of loss that is
            reasonably certain should be
            a. disclosed in the financial statement's footnotes.
            b. accrued on the financial statements.
            c. ignored on the financial statements.
            d. reported as an adjustment to retained earnings.

_____ 24. A loss that is remote and inestimable should be
            a. ignored.
            b. footnoted.
            c. accrued.
            d. charged directly to retained earnings.

_____ 25. A loss that is reasonably possible and estimable should be
            a. ignored.
            b. accrued.
            c. disclosed.
            d. charged directly to retained earnings.

Exercises

1. Constable Company sold $1,000,000 face value, ten-year bonds on July 1, Year 9. The stated
    annual interest rate is 6% per year, payable annually on June 30. These bonds were sold to yield
    8%.

Present value information:	6%	8%
PVIF (10 periods)	0.55839	0.46319
PVIFA (10 periods)	7.36009	6.71008

    Required: Compute the selling price of the bonds on July 1, Year 9.

    _____

    _____

    _____

    _____

    _____

    _____

2. Adam Corporation and Eve Corporation form a partnership to manufacture and distribute tribbles.
    Each corporation contributes $575,000 cash and receives 50% of the partnership. The partnership
    borrows $6 million from a consortium of banks and uses the money to build its manufacturing and
    distribution facilities. The loan is made on December 31, Year 1, and is fully guaranteed by both
    Adam Corporation and Eve Corporation.

Required:

A.   How much of the $6 million debt appears on Adam Corporation's December 31, Year 1 balance sheet?_____

B.   Explain why the amount in A. appears (or does not appear) on the balance sheet.

_____

_____

_____

_____

3.   On January 1, Year 5, Baily Incorporated, issued $6,000,000 of 6%, ten-year bonds for a yield of 8%. The bonds pay interest semi-annually on June 30 and December 31. Damien Incorporated closes its books on December 31.

Required:
A. Determine the bond issue price.
B. Using the effective interest method, prepare an amortization schedule for each of the first four semi-annual interest payment periods.
C. Prepare journal entries to record the first two interest payments.

_____

_____

_____

_____

_____

_____

_____

_____

_____

_____

_____

_____

_____

_____

_____

_____

_____

_____

_____

_____

_____

_____

_____

_____

_____

_____

_____

_____

_____

_____

_____

_____

4.   On January 1, Year 5, Ferris Corporation issued $15,000,000 of 9%, ten-year bonds to yield 12%. The bonds pay interest annually on December 31 of each year. The company closes its books on December 31.

Required:
   A.   Prepare the journal entries to record the issue of the bonds.
   B.   What is the book value of the bonds on January 1, Year 6?
   C.   On January 1, Year 6, the market interest rate for bonds of this type is 11%. What is the market value of the bonds on this date?
   D.   The bonds were repurchased for cash on January 1, Year 6 at the market price. Ignoring taxes, prepare the journal entry that the company would make to record the debt retirement.

Solutions

Answers to True or False Questions

True answers: 1, 4, 5, 10, 11, 13, 14, 15, 19, 20, 23
False answers explained:

2.   Non-current monetary liabilities are initially recorded at <u>present value</u> when incurred.
3.   When the issue price of a bond is below the face value, the bond is sold at a <u>discount</u>.
6.   The bond discount account is a <u>liability</u> valuation account.
7.   Amortization of bond discount is the process of spreading the discount on bonds to <u>increase</u> interest expense over the life of the bonds.
8.   When bonds are sold at a premium, the amortization of the premium <u>decreases</u> interest expense.
9.   The issue price of a bond is determined by <u>market forces</u>.
12.   Gains and losses from the extinguishment of debt are treated as <u>extraordinary</u> items on the income statement.
16.   Derivative securities get their name from the fact that they have a <u>low</u> inherent value.
17.   Option contracts provide that each party <u>has an option</u> to engage in the agreed-upon transaction.
18.   A put option gives the holder the right to <u>sell</u> a specific underlying asset at a specified price during a specified time.
21.   Footnote disclosure is the preferred treatment for loss contingencies in <u>some</u> cases.
22.   Footnote disclosure is preferable when a loss contingency is <u>only</u> reasonably possible.
24.   Gains (losses) from hedge transactions are included as other comprehensive income <u>some</u> of the time.

Answers to Multiple-Choice Questions

1.	A	6.	C	11.	B	16.	D	21.	D
2.	C	7.	B	12.	B	17.	D	22.	C
3.	C	8.	B	13.	D	18.	B	23.	A
4.	D	9.	C	14.	B	19.	A	24.	C
5.	B	10.	C	15.	C	20.	D	25.	B

Answers to Exercises

1.   Maturity $1,000,000 x PVIF   0.46319 = $463,190.00
        Interest $60,000 x PVIFA 6.71008 =   402,604.80
        Selling Price $865,794.80

2.   A.   None of the debt will appear on the balance sheet of December 31, Year 1.
        B.   The method used by Adam Corporation and Eve Corporation is an off-balance sheet method of financing that is used to move the reporting of debt off the books of the corporations involved. GAAP requires footnote disclosure of the debt guarantees to enable analysts to see the structure of the transactions and make

             appropriate decisions.

3.   A.   Maturity $6,000,000 x PVIF 0.45639 = $2,738,340.00
            Interest $180,000 x PVIFA 13.59033   =   2,446,259.40
            Selling Price $5,184,599.40

B.	Cash	Effective		Unamort.	Carrying
Year	Interest	Interest	Amortization	Discount	Value
0				$815,400.60	$5,184,599.40
1	$180,000	$207,383.98	$27,383.98	788,016.62	5,211,983.38
2.	180,000	208,479.34	28,479.34	759,537.28	5,240,462.72
3.	180,000	209,618.51	29,618.51	729,918.77	5,270,081.23
4.	180,000	210,803.25	30,803.25	699,115.52	5,300,884.48

C.
Year 5
June 30   DR   Interest Expense   207,383.98
                     CR   Bond Discount   27,383.98
                     CR   Cash   180,000.00

December 31 DR   Interest Expense   208,479.34
                     CR   Bond Discount   28,479.34
                     CR   Cash   180,000.00

4.   A.   Maturity $15,000,000 x PVIF 0.32197   = $4,829,550
            Interest $1,350,000 x PVIFA 5.65022   = 7,627,797
            Bond Issue Price $12,457,347

B.	Cash	Effective		Unamortized	Carrying
Year	Interest	Interest	Amortization	Discount	Value
0				$2,542,653	$12,457,347
1	$1,350,000	$1,494,882	$144,882	2,397,771	12,602,229

      C.   Maturity $15,000,000 x PVIF 0.39092   = $5.863,800
            Interest $1,350,000 x PVIFA 5.53705   = 7,475,018
            Bond Market Price $13,338,818

      D.   DR Bonds Payable   15,000,000
            DR Extraordinary Loss on Debt Retirement   736,589
                  CR Bond Discount   2,397,771
                  CR Cash   13,338,818

CHAPTER 12

FINANCIAL REPORTING FOR LEASES

Chapter Review

A lease is a **contract** that conveys the right to use an asset from its owner (**lessor**) to another party (**lessee**) for a specified period of time. Legal title remains with the lessor. At inception, a lease is a **mutually unperformed contract** or **executory contract**, because neither party has fulfilled its obligation under the contract.

Learning Objective 1:
The difference between capital leases and operating leases.

SFAS No. 13 details current GAAP for leases. Leases are either operating leases or capital leases. **Operating leases** conform to the nature of the executory contract and recognize events as those events become performed under the contract. Therefore, the lessee records no assets or liabilities at the inception of the lease. At the beginning of each month (or lease period), rent expense and rent revenue is recorded for the cash payment as:

Lessee's Books	Lessor's Books
DR Rent Expense	DR Cash
CR Cash	CR Rental Revenue

The lessor continues to depreciate the asset and record any interest expense related to a mortgage on the property. **(See Demonstration Problem 1.)**

Learning Objective 2:
Lessee's incentives to keep leases off the balance sheet.

Lessees prefer operating lease treatment because the liability for the lease obligation remains off the balance sheet. This affords the lessee benefits in its profitability and solvency ratios by keeping both debts and assets low. Low debt amounts protect the debt-to-equity ratio, and low assets reduce the denominator of the return on assets ratio, making the firm appear to be more profitable.

GAAP require footnote disclosure of future cash outflows arising from operating leases to enable statement readers to find a lease's "hidden" asset and liability. Prior to FASB's release of *SFAS No. 13*, most leases were treated as operating leases. The SEC, in *ASR No. 147*, urged adoption of a **property rights** approach to lease accounting but made no requirements to adopt that approach. *SFAS No.13* defined operating and capital leases and required strict classification based on four criteria.

Learning Objective 3:

Following the theory advanced by the SEC that leases convey **property rights**,

The criteria used to classify leases on the lessee's books.

FASB established four criteria, any one of which, establish a lease as a **capital lease**:

1. The lease transfers ownership to the lessee at the end of the lease term.
2. The lease contains a bargain purchase option.
3. The noncancellable lease term is 75% or more of the economic life of the leased asset.
4. The present value of the minimum lease payments equals or exceeds 90% of the leased asset's fair value.

FYI. . .
A firm must carefully construct leases to avoid capital lease criteria if it desires operating lease treatment.

Criterion 1 requires that the substance of the transaction, a transfer of ownership in an installment sale, prevail over its form as a lease. Criterion 2 is similar because a bargain purchase insures that a transfer will take place. Criterion 3 establishes that if most of the useful life will be consumed by the lessee, the lessee receives significant property rights. With criterion 4, the recovery of investment criterion, the lessor recovers the bulk of its investment which indicates the substantial transfer of ownership. If any of the four criteria are met, the lessee <u>must</u> record the lease as a capital lease. If none of the criteria is met, the lessee must record the lease as an operating lease.

FYI. . .
Asset purchases are never recorded at amounts in excess of **fair market value**.

A lessee records the lease as a purchase of an asset in exchange for a liability.

The following rules apply to **lessee accounting**:

1. The lessee records its **leased asset** at the lower of the fair market value of the asset or the present value of the minimum lease payments required by the lease. The discount rate used to compute the present value of the lease payments is the <u>lower</u> of the **lessee's incremental borrowing rate** or the lessor's rate of return implicit to the lease.

FYI. . .
The **lessee's incremental borrowing rate** is the rate the lessee would pay if it obtained a secured loan with similar repayment terms.

2. The lessee records the **lease liability** at the same value as the leased asset. The liability is amortized like a normal loan under the **effective interest method** based on the discount rate that equates the lease payments with the asset value recorded. Sometimes the lessor has to impute this rate.

3. The lessee depreciates the leased asset over the term of the lease based on the most appropriate depreciation method for the asset, except that there may not be any salvage value.

Learning Objective 4:
The treatment of executory costs, residual values and other aspects of lease contracts.

4. **Executory costs** are operating costs of using the assets such as maintenance, taxes, and insurance. Sometimes the lessee pays executory costs to the lessor in addition to the lease payments. Often the lessee pays the executory costs directly. All executory

costs represent normal operating costs and are recorded as such.

5. Lessors sometimes protect the asset value by requiring a **residual value guarantee** at the end of the lease. If the asset is not worth the guaranteed residual value at the end of the lease, the lessee must pay the lessor the difference. The lessee must include the guaranteed residual value in the computation of the present value of the minimum lease payments and use the guaranteed residual value as a salvage value when computing depreciation. At the end of the lease term, the Obligation under Lease Liability account and the Leased Asset (net) will both be equal to the residual value.

6. If the lessee has to reimburse the lessor for any deficiency in the guaranteed residual value, the lessee records a Loss on the Residual Value Guarantee. **(See Demonstration Problem 2.)**

Learning Objective 5:
The effects of capital lease versus operating lease treatments on lessees' financial statements.

The financial statement treatments of operating and capital leases are quite different during the lease term — but identical by the end of the lease. All costs of a lease end up as a reduction of retained earnings because the costs all flow through the income statement as expense. Look at the example in Demonstration Problem 2:

Lease Payments	$ 30,866.87
Term	4 years
Guaranteed Residual Value	10,000.00
Total Interest	26,384.48
Loss on Guaranteed Residual Value	1,000.00
Depreciation Expense	97,083.00

Total charges to expense for operating lease:
Rental Expense (4 x $30,866.87)	$123,467.48
Loss on Guaranteed Residual Value	1,000.00
Total Expenses	$124,467.48

Total charges to expense for capital lease:
Depreciation Expense	$97,083.00
Interest Expense	26,384.48
Loss on Guaranteed Residual Value	1,000.00
Total Expenses	$124,467.48

The timing of the expenses is different:

Year	Operating Lease	Capital Lease

1	$ 30,866.87	$ 33,908.22
2	30,866.87	31,997.59
3	30,866.87	29,914.97
4	_31,866.87	28,646.72
	$124,467.48	$124,467.50

In both instances, the total payments made to the lessor reduced Retained Earnings during the four years, although the capital lease records expenses at an accelerated rate. (Capital lease treatment would accelerate at a faster rate if the lessee used accelerated depreciation.) Managers prefer not to front-end load expenses because it impacts bonus computations based on income performance. Most industries effectively keep leases off the balance sheet by carefully constructing contracts to avoid the four criteria for a capital lease. This is not true in the utility industry because public utility rates are based on the amount of invested capital.

The operating lease treatment never involves the balance sheet except for Cash and Retained Earnings. The capital lease treatment records a leased asset and liability that diminish to zero over the lease period. So public utility companies benefit by having the leased asset included in the rate base.

Learning Objective 6: How analysts can adjust for ratio distortions from off-balance sheet leases when comparing firms.

SFAS No. 13 requires the following footnote disclosures for **lessees:**

1.   Minimum lease payments required in each of the next five fiscal years after the balance sheet date and the total required after those five years for both capital leases and operating leases net of sublease rental income.

2.   For capital leases, a breakdown of executory costs and interest included in the minimum lease payments to arrive at the short-term and long-term lease obligations.

Some firms voluntarily include a comparison of expenses recognized under capital leases and the minimum lease payments.

Disclosures help analysts compare firms that use difference types of leases. When firms have relatively stable lease portfolios, income statement differences are seldom significant. But capital lease treatments cause changes in the lessee's balance sheet that worsen key ratios. By adding a long-term asset and both a short-term and long-term

liability, the following ratios change with a capital lease:
1.   Current ratio — The increase in the short-term liability (for minimum principal payments due within one year) decreases the current ratio. The principal portion increases each year so the current ratio suffers more in later years than early years.
2.   Debt-to-Equity ratio — The increase in liabilities increases the numerator of the equation and increases the debt ratio.
3.   Return on Assets ratio — The increase in assets reduces the profitability because the denominator of the equation increases.

Lessees report operating lease costs as operating outflows on the cash flow statement and capital leases as financing outflows. Therefore, operating leases lower cash flow from operations.

Learning Objective 7: That lessors also classify leases either as capital leases or as operating leases but that their reporting incentives are very different from those of lessees'.

Lessors classify leases in one of three ways:
1.   Operating leases transfer no property rights or contain uncertainty about the ultimate collection of lease amounts.
2.   Sales-type leases represent disguised installment sales. A manufacturer or dealer uses the lease as a financing arrangement for sale.
3.   Direct financing leases represent financing arrangement between a finance company and a customer.
Lessors remove the asset from the books in a capital lease situation because the lessor recognizes the lease as a sale. Lessors retain the asset on the books for operating leases — just the opposite of lessee accounting.

SFAS No. 13 requires lessors to meet two types of tests to qualify for capital lease treatment. Lessors must meet *at least one* of the same four tests (called Type I Characteristics) as a lessee in proving the transfer of property rights. In addition, lessors must meet *both* of the Type II Characteristics:
1.   The collectibility of the minimum lease payments is reasonably predictable.
2.   There are no important uncertainties surrounding the amount of unreimbursable costs yet to be incurred by the lessor under the lease.

The Type II characteristics conform to revenue recognition rules. When one of Type I and both of Type II conditions are met, the lease must be treated as a capital lease. If none of Type I or only one of Type II are

treated as a capital lease. If none of Type I or only one of Type II are met, the lease must be treated as an operating lease. The additional requirements in Type II characteristics indicate that a lessee could treat a lease as a capital lease and the lessor might have to treat the same lease as an operating lease.

Learning Objective 8: The differences among sales-type, direct financing, and operating lease treatment by lessors and the criteria for choosing the accounting treatment.

Lessor accounting for operating leases consists of the following:
1.   Lease payments are recorded as income when receivable and earned.
2.   The leased asset remains on the lessor's books and is depreciated under the method selected by the lessor.

Lessor accounting for direct financing leases consists of the following:
1.   The lessor uses its implicit rate of return in accounting for the lease.
2.   To record the lease:
DR Gross Investment in Leased Assets
         CR Asset (cost)
         CR Unearned Financing Income — Leases
The Gross Investment in Leased Assets equals the total minimum lease payments over the life of the lease plus the guaranteed residual value. The unearned revenue account is the difference between gross investment and the cost of the asset sold under the lease.
3.   The lessor records payments received from the lessee:
DR Cash
         CR Gross Investment in Leased Asset
4.   The lessor recognizes financing income as the interest portion of the lease payment.
DR Unearned Financing Income — Leases
         CR Financing Income — Leases
5.   At the end of the lease, the Gross Investment in Leased Assets will either be zero, if the lessee keeps the asset, or the amount of the residual value. If a residual value exists and the lessor takes back the asset, the lessor records:
DR Equipment — Residual Value
         CR Gross Investment in Leased Assets

(See Demonstration Problem 3.)

Lessor accounting for sales-type leases consists of the following rules:
1.   The lessor separates the profit into two components:

a. Profit on the sale — equal to the cash sales price minus the cost of goods sold.

b. Financing profit — equal to the total gross inflows from the lease minus the cash sales price.

2.   To record the lease:

DR Gross Investment in Leased Assets

DR Cost of Goods Sold

       CR Inventory

       CR Sales Revenue

       CR Unearned Financing Income — Leases

The Gross Investment in Leased Assets and Unearned Financing Income — Leases are the same as for a direct financing lease. Sales Revenue is credited with the cash sales price. Cost of Goods Sold and Inventory are recorded at the leased asset's cost.

3.   All other accounting is the same as for a direct financing lease.

(See Demonstration Problem 4.)

Learning Objective 9: How the different lessor accounting treatments can affect income and net asset balances.	Just as in lessee accounting, the income the lessor recognizes for an operating lease is the same as for a capital lease over the life of the lease, but the timing of revenue recognition is different. Direct financing leases front-end load revenue recognition. Lessors seldom oppose a capital lease because it improves the return on asset ratio in the early years of the lease. The current ratio also improves because the current portion of the Gross Investment in Leased Assets includes the next lease payment's principal amount.
Learning Objective 10: Sale/leaseback arrangements and other special leasing situations.	To raise capital, firms sometimes sell assets and lease them back from the buyers. In doing so, the seller creates income or loss on the sale (the difference between the carrying value and the sales price). Losses are recognized immediately under the conservatism constraint. Gains on sale are deferred and recognized over the life of the lease. Without this deferral mechanism, firms could sell assets at inflated prices and artificially increase income, only to reduce income in the future with higher leasing costs. A **leverages lease** is a special leasing situation where the lessor obtains nonrecourse financing for the leased asset from a third party. The lessor uses the direct financing approach with special details.
Learning Objective 11:	*SFAS No. 13* requires lessors to disclose separately for capital leases and operating leases:

How to use footnote disclosures to estimate the increase in assets and liabilities that would ensue if operating leases had been capitalized instead.

1. The minimum future lease payments for each of the next five years after the balance sheet date and a total for later years.
2. The components of the net investment in capital leases (minimum lease payments, residual values, allowance for doubtful accounts, and deferred income) for comparative years.
3. The cost and accumulated depreciation of operating leases for comparative years.

The easiest way to compare companies with different levels of operating and capital leases is to convert operating leases to capital leases. To accomplish this, use the footnote disclosure and other elements from the financial statements to estimate leased assets and obligations under capital leases. Add these to the balance sheet and recompute the financial ratios to compare the companies.

Glossary of Terms

Capital Lease

A lease which meets certain criteria and is then recorded as an asset and related liability on the books of the lessee.

Direct Financing Lease

A capital lease in which the lessor is a financial institution such as a bank, insurance firm, or financing company.

Executory Contract

A mutually unperformed contract.

Executory Costs

Certain operating costs of using assets, such as maintenance, taxes, and insurance.

Gross Investment in Leased Assets

The sum of the minimum lease payments plus the guaranteed residual at the end of the lease term.

Lessee

A party to a lease contract which has the right to use some asset.

Lessor

A party to a lease contract which has ownership of an asset.

Leveraged Lease

A lease in which the lessor borrows to finance the transaction using nonrecourse financing from a third party. Leveraged leases must be treated as direct financing leases.

Mutually Unperformed Contract	The legal term applied to a contract when neither party to the contract has yet performed any of the duties called for by the contract.
Off-Balance Sheet Financing	The term that applies to the fact that a lessee has financed the acquisition of asset services without recognizing a liability on the financial statement.
Operating Lease	A lease arrangement in which the asset remains on the books of the lessor and the lessee does not record a liability for the future stream of payments called for by the contract.
Residual Value Guarantee	A provision in a lease contract in which the lessee guarantees that the leased asset will have a certain value at the end of the lease.
Sale and Leaseback	A situation in which a company sells an asset to another company and immediately leases it back.
Sales-Type Lease	A capital lease that exists when the lessor is a manufacturer or dealer.
Unearned Financing Income	The unearned portion of future revenues of a lessor generated by a capital lease.

Demonstration Problems

1.   Operating Lease Accounting

Hatfield Company leased a machine from McCoy Company on July 1, Year 1, with the following terms:

Lease term	5 years
Annual rental payment at start of each lease year	$20,000
Useful life of machine	10 years
Implicit interest rate	12%
Annual Depreciation	$13,000

Hatfield must return the machine at the end of the lease on July 1, Year 5.
The lease is an operating type lease.

Required:
A.   Prepare all the journal entries on the lessee's books for Years 1 and 2, assuming a fiscal year end of December 31.
B.   Prepare all the journal entries on the lessor's books for Year 1 and Year 2, assuming a fiscal year end of December 31.

A.   Prepare entries for the lessee for Years 1 and 2
First Step: Identify entries to be made by lessee.

Application: The lessee must record the rental expense on the accrual basis.

Solution: Year 1

July 1	DR Rent Expense	10,000	
	DR Prepaid Rent	10,000	
	CR Cash		20,000

Year 2

January 1	DR Rent Expense	10,000	
	CR Prepaid Rent		10,000
July 1	DR Rent Expense	10,000	
	DR Prepaid Rent	10,000	
	CR Cash		20,000

B.   Prepare entries for the lessor for Years 1 and 2

First Step: Identify entries to be made by lessor.

Application: Lessor should record the rental revenue and depreciation expense on the accrual basis.

Solution: Year 1

July 1	DR Cash	20,000	
	CR Rental Revenue		10,000
	CR Unearned Rental Revenue		10,000
December 31	DR Depreciation Expense	13,000	
	CR Accumulated Depreciation		13,000

Year 2

January 1	DR Unearned Rental Revenue	10,000	
	CR Rental Revenue		10,000
July 1	DR Cash	20,000	
	CR Rental Revenue		10,000
	CR Unearned Rental Revenue		10,000
December 31	DR Depreciation Expense	13,000	
	CR Accumulated Depreciation		13,000

2.   Capital Lease Accounting

Yankee Corporation enters into a four-year noncancelable lease with the Met Corporation on January 1, Year 5. The lease begins on this date. Facts that bear on this lease transaction are as follows:

1.   The lease calls for four payments of $30,866.87 to be made at the end of the year.
2.   The leased asset has a fair market value of $100,000 on January 1, Year 5.
3.   The lease has a guaranteed residual value of $10,000. At the end of the lease the value is $9,000.
4.   The leased asset has an expected economic life of five years.

5.   Assume that this lease qualifies as a capital lease.
6.   Assume the following present value factors:
      PVIF 4 years at 9% = .70843
      PVIFA 4 years at 9% = 3.23972
      PVIFA 4 years at 10% = 3.16986
      PVIF 4 years at 10% = .68301
7.   The lessor's rate of interest is 9% and the lessee's incremental borrowing rate is 10%.

Required :
A. Prepare all the journal entries required on the lessee's books in the first year of the lease.
B. Prepare all the journal entries required on the lessee's books in the last year of the lease.

A.
First Step: Determine the journal entries to be made on the lessee's books in the first year of the lease.
Solution: Lessee must record the initial payment for the asset, the first year's payment, and the depreciation expense.

Second Step: Identify the interest rate to be used in the computation of the leased asset cost.
Application: The lessee should use the lower of the lessee's incremental borrowing rate or the lessor's implicit rate.
Solution: The lessee should use the lessor's rate of 9% since it is lower than the lessee's incremental borrowing rate of 10%.

Third Step: Compute the capitalized value of the leased asset.
Application: Apply the appropriate present value factors to the payment and the residual value to determine the asset cost basis to the lessee.
Solution: PVIFA at 9% 3.23972 x Lease Payment $30,866.87   = $100,000.00
              + PVIF at 9%   0.70843 x Residual Value $10,000   =   <u>   7,083.00</u>
                                                                             <u>$107,083.00</u>

Fourth Step: Prepare the journal entry to record the asset.
Application: Use the capitalized asset cost developed in step 3.
Solution:
      DR Leased Asset — Capital Lease   107,083.00
          CR Obligation Under Capital Lease   107,083.00

Fifth Step: Prepare amortization schedule.
Application: The amortization schedule is based on the effective interest method.

Solution:

Period	Interest	Principal	Carrying Value

			$107,083.00
1	$9,637.47	$21,229.40	85,853.60
2	7,726.82	23,140.05	62,713.55
3	5,644.22	25,222.65	37,490.90
4	3,375.97	27,490.90	10,000.00

Sixth Step: Prepare the entry to record the first year's payment.
Application: Utilize the information presented in the amortization schedule.
Solution:

DR Liability Under Capital Lease	21,229.40	
DR Interest Expense	9,637.47	
CR Cash		30,866.87

Seventh Step: Compute the amount of depreciation expense.
Application: Apply the depreciation formula: $\dfrac{\text{Cost} - \text{Residual Value}}{\text{Years of Life}}$

Solution: $\dfrac{\text{Cost } \$107{,}083.00 - \text{Residual Value } \$10{,}000}{\text{Years of Life } 4} = \dfrac{\$97{,}083.00}{4} = \$24{,}270.75$

Eighth Step: Prepare the entry for depreciation expense.
Application: Utilize information in the previous step to develop the journal entry.
Solution:

DR Depreciation Expense	24,270.75	
CR Accumulated Depreciation		24,270.75

B.

First Step: Determine the journal entries to be made on the lessee's books in the last year of the lease.
Solution: Lessee must record the depreciation expense for the year, the final payment, and the return of the asset to the lessor.

Second Step: Prepare the journal entry for depreciation.
Application: See Step A. 7
Solution:

DR Depreciation Expense	24,270.75	
CR Accumulated Depreciation		24,270.75

Third Step: Record the final payment and return of the asset.
Application: Review the amortization schedule for the necessary information to prepare the final entry. The lessee must reimburse the lessor for the deficiency in the guaranteed residual value of $1,000.

Solution:

DR Obligation Under Capital Lease	37,490.90	
DR Loss on Return	1,000.00	
DR Interest Expense	3,375.97	
DR Accumulated Depreciation	97,083.00	
CR Cash		31,866.87
CR Leased Equipment — Capital Lease		107,083.00

3.   Financing Type Lease

Yankee Corporation enters into a four-year non-cancelable lease for equipment with the Met Corporation on January 1, Year 5. The lease begins on this date. The lessor is neither a manufacturer nor a dealer. Facts that bear on this lease transaction are as follows:

1. The lease calls for four payments of $30,866.87 to be made at the end of the year.
2. The leased asset has a present value of lease inflows of $107,083.00 on January 1, Year 5, which is also the cost of the leased asset.
3. The lease has a guaranteed residual value of $10,000.
4. The leased asset has an expected economic life of five years.
5. Assume that this lease qualifies as a capital lease.
6. Assume the following present value factors:

   PVIF 4 years at 9% = .70843
   PVIFA 4 years at 9% = 3.23972
   PVIFA 4 years at 10% = 3.16986
   PVIF 4 years at 10% = .68301

7. The lessors' implicit rate of return on the lease is 9%.
8. The collectibility of the lease payments is reasonably predictable.
9. The residual value equals the fair market value at the end of the lease and the asset reverts to the lessor.

Required:
A.   Prepare all journal entries on the lessor's books during the first year regarding the lease and first payment.

First Step: Determine the entries to be made.
Solution: Record entries for the Gross Investment in Leased Assets, the entry to record the receipt of the first payment, and the entry to record the physical repossession of the asset.

Second Step: Determine the lessor's Gross Investment in Leased Assets.
Application: Calculate the sum of the minimum lease payments plus the residual value.

Solution:
   (Minimum Lease Payments $30,866.87 x Years of Life 4) + Guaranteed Residual Value

$10,000 = $123,467.48 + $10,000 = $133,467.48

Third Step: Prepare an amortization schedule.
Application: Use the effective interest method.
Solution:

Current Period	Receipt	Interest Income	Principal Reduction	Remaining Principal Amount
				$107,083.00
1	$ 30,866.87	$9,637.47	$21,229.40	85,853.55
2	30,866.87	7,726.82	23,140.05	62,713.55
3	30,866.87	5,644.22	25,222.65	37,490.90
4	30,866.87	3,375.97	27,490.90	10,000.00
Total	$123,467.48	$26,384.48	$97,083.00	

Fourth Step: Prepare the journal entry to record the Gross Investment in Leased Assets.
Application: Use the information in the amortization schedule.
Solution:

DR Gross Investment in Leased Assets	133,367.48	
CR Equipment		107,083.00
CR Unearned Financing Income — Leases		26,384.18

Fifth Step: Record the first annual payment.
Application: Use the information in the amortization schedule.
Solution:

DR Cash	30,866.87	
CR Gross Investment in Leased Assets		30,866.87
DR Unearned Financing Income — Leases	9,637.47	
CR Financing Income — Leases		9,637.47

4. Sales Type Lease

The Unis Auto Dealership leased autos to Hertz, Inc., on July 1, Year 15. The lease is appropriately accounted for as a sale by Unis and as a purchase by Hertz. The lease expires on June 30, Year 20 and requires 5 equal payments of $340,000 beginning July 1, Year 15. Unis purchased the equipment for $1,100,000 on January 1, Year 15, and established a list selling price of $1,500,000 on the autos. The present value of at July 1, Year 15, of the lease payments discounted at 10% is $1,420,000.

Required:

A. Prepare the journal entries to record the signing of the lease by Unis.
B. Prepare the journal entry to record the financing revenue for the year ended June 30, Year 17.

A.

First Step: Determine the gross investment in the leased assets.

Application: Multiply the lease payment by the number of payments.
Solution: Lease payment $340,000 x 5 = $1,700,000

Second Step: Determine the sales price and cost of sales to be recorded.
Application: Identify the present value of the lease payments and the cost paid by the lessor. The sales amount is the present value of the lease payments.
Solution: Present value is given as $1,420,000 and the cost of the goods is $1,100,000.

Third Step: Record the journal entries.
Application: Utilize information identified in steps 1 and 2.
Solution:

DR Cash	340,000	
DR Gross Investment in Leased Asset	1,360,000	
CR Sales		1,420,000
CR Unearned Financing Income — Leases		280,000
DR Cost of Goods Sold	1,100,000	
CR Inventory		1,100,000

B.

First Step: Calculate the interest revenue.
Application: Prepare the amortization schedule.
Solution:

Payment Date	Payment	Interest (10%)	Principal	Carrying Value
				$1,420,000
7-1-YR15	$340,000	$ 0	$340,000	1,080,000
7-1-YR16	340,000	108,000	232,000	848,000
7-1-YR17	340,000	84,800	255,200	592,800

Interest Revenue for Year 17 is $84,800.

Second Step: Prepare the journal entry to record receipt of the payment.
Application: Refer to the amortization table in the first step.
Solution:

DR Cash	340,000	
CR Gross Investment in Leased Asset		340,000
DR Unearned Financing Income — Leases	84,800	
CR Financing Income — Leases		84,800

Test Yourself

True or False

T F 1.   The party to a lease contract who owns the asset is the lessee.

T F 2.   The party to a lease contract who has the right to use the asset is the lessor.

T F 3.   A lease contract is called an executory contract.

T F 4.   The operating lease method does not reflect the cumulative liability for all future lease payments on the balance sheet of the lessee.

T F 5.   A capital lease is an example of off-balance sheet financing.

T F 6.   A lease that transfers the ownership of asset to the lessee by the end of the lease term is a capital lease.

T F 7.   A lease that contains a bargain purchase element is an operating lease.

T F 8.   When the non-cancelable lease term is 75% or more of the estimated economic life of the leased asset, the lease is a capital lease.

T F 9.   If the present value of the minimum lease payments equals or exceeds 80% of the fair value of the leased asset, the lease is a capital lease.

T F 10.   Each criterion for a capital lease represents a condition under which property rights in the leased asset have been transferred to the lessee.

T F 11.   Maintenance costs incurred for the use of a leased asset are capitalized costs.

T F 12.   A residual value guarantee is a lease contract clause that requires the lessor to pay the lessee the difference between the actual market value and the residual value if the actual value is less than the residual value.

T F 13.   Leased assets seldom revert to the lessor at the end of the lease term.

T F 14.   For mature firms, the income statement effects of capital versus operating leases are usually not significantly different.

T F 15.   Accounting for leases using the capital lease approach usually has a negative impact on the current ratio of the lessee.

T F 16.   A sales-type lease is a capital lease in which the lessor is a financial institution.

T F 17.   A direct financing lease is a capital lease in which the lessor is a dealer.

T F 18.   The lessor will treat a lease as an operating lease if the lease transfers property rights to the lessee and allows accurate estimates of lease net cash flows and their collectibility.

T F 19.   When at least one of the Type I characteristics and both of the Type II characteristics are met, the lessor's criteria for a capital lease are met.

T F 20.   Capital lease treatment accelerates the timing of income recognition for lessors.

T F 21.   When a lessor borrows from a bank using nonrecourse financing for the leased asset, the lessor has a leveraged lease.

T F 22.   A sale and leaseback transaction occurs when one firm sells an asset to another company and immediately leases it back.

Multiple-Choice Questions

Select the best answer from those provided.

_____ 1.   The term applied to a lease that is legally binding is a/an
        a. mutually performed contract.
        b. executed contract.
        c. unilateral contract.
        d. executory contract.

_____ 2.   The amount recorded on the balance sheet to represent an operating lease should be
        a. zero.
        b. the present value of the lease.
        c. 75% of the value of the lease.
        d. the fair market value of the lease.

_____ 3.   The future cash outflows arising from operating leases are required to be
        a. recorded on the income statement.
        b. recorded on the balance sheet.
        c. disclosed in the financial statement's footnotes.
        d. adjusted directly to retained earnings.

_____ 4.   Off-balance sheet financing may be accomplished with a/an
        a. capital lease.
        b. operating lease.
        c. property right lease.
        d. capital lease for an automobile.

_____ 5.   Lessees often believe that an operating lease serves to protect the firms'
a. borrowing capacity.
b. earnings capacity.
c. liabilities.
d. property rights.

_____ 6.   When a lessee meets none of the criteria of *SFAS No. 13* for the treatment of a lease, the lease is properly treated as a/an
a. operating lease.
b. capital lease.
c. either a capital lease or an operating lease.
d. other form of business arrangement.

_____ 7.   When a firm has a capital lease in force, it recognizes the expense as
a. rent expense.
b. interest and depreciation expense.
c. interest and amortization expense.
d. lease expense.

_____ 8.   The leased asset in a capital lease must be
a. amortized.
b. depreciated.
c. immediately expensed.
d. charged to retained earnings.

_____ 9.   The discount rate used to value a capital lease on the lessee's books is the lower of the lessor's implicit rate or the
a. prime rate.
b. discounted prime rate.
c. lessee's incremental borrowing rate.
d. lessor's incremental borrowing rate.

_____ 10.   Any executory costs associated with a lease should be treated as
a. interest costs.
b. operating expenses.
c. deferred expenses.
d. a prior period adjustment.

_____ 11.   When a lease contract contains a residual value guarantee, the lessee must
a.   add the present value of the guaranteed amount to the present value of the minimum lease payments.
b.   add the guaranteed amount to the present value of the minimum lease payments.
c.   add the guaranteed amount to the present value of the minimum lease payments if the lessee intends to keep the asset at the end of the lease.
d.   ignore the residual value.

_____ 12.   The total expenses charged to income over the life of a lease are
a.   greater for a capital lease.
b.   greater for an operating lease.
c.   identical for either type of lease.
d.   less for an operating lease.

_____ 13.   Lease expenses charged under an operating lease are usually
a.   lower than a capital lease in the early years and higher than a capital lease in the later years.
b.   equal to the capital lease expenses in each month of the existence of the lease.
c.   higher than a capital lease in the early years and lower than a capital lease in the later years.
d.   lower than a capital lease throughout the life of the lease.

_____ 14.   For ease of financial statement manipulation, lessee's management prefers that leases be treated as though they were
a.   long-term leases.
b.   short-term leases.
c.   capital leases.
d.   operating leases.

_____ 15.   Financial statement analysts must rely on which one of the following to adjust for distortions that arise from off-balance sheet financing?
a.   Income Statement
b.   Balance Sheet
c.   Cash Flow Statement
d.   Footnotes to the Financial Statements.

_____ 16.   The capitalization of a lease contract causes the deterioration of the
a.   current ratio.
b.   return on equity ratio.
c.   accounts receivable turnover ratio.
d.   merchandise inventory turnover ratio.

_____ 17.   A manufacturer of equipment that sells the equipment to customers or leases the
             equipment to credit-worthy customers would treat these leases as
             a. direct-financing leases.
             b. sales-type leases.
             c. operating leases.
             d. an outright sale.

_____ 18.   A Type I characteristic associated with the lessor's treatment of leases is linked to
             a. the critical event criteria for asset recognition.
             b. the critical event criteria for revenue recognition.
             c. measurement of the lease expense.
             d. measurement of yearly lease income.

_____ 19.   A Type II characteristic associated with the lessor's treatment of leases is linked to
             a. the critical event criteria for revenue recognition.
             b. measurement of the lease expense.
             c. measurement of yearly lease income.
             d. measurement of collectibility for revenue recognition.

_____ 20.   The Gross Investment in Leased Asset is classified on the lessor's balance sheet as
             a/an
             a. long-lived asset.
             b. long-term liability.
             c. intangible asset.
             d. current liability.

_____ 21.   The lessor must treat a leveraged lease as a/an
             a. sales-type capital lease.
             b. direct financing capital lease.
             c. sales-type operating lease.
             d. operating lease.

_____ 22.   The easiest way to make a number of lessee firms' balance sheet data comparable
             is to treat all leases as
             a. sales-type leases.
             b. operating leases.
             c. capital leases.
             d. direct financing leases.

___ 23.   Since the effective interest on lease transactions is always higher in the early years and declines in later years, most capital leases without up-front payments have
   a. less liability than asset book value.
   b. more liability than asset book value.
   c. liability equal to asset book value.
   d. no liability.

Exercises

1.   United Corporation leased a machine from Nevada Corporation on July 1, Year 5, with the following terms:

Lease term	10 years
Annual rental payment at start of each lease year	$65,000
Useful life of machine	10 years
Implicit interest rate	12%
Present value of an annuity due of $1 for 10 periods at 12%	6.32825
Present value of $1 due at the end of 10 periods at 14%	0.32197

   United may purchase the machine on July 1, Year 15, for $70,000, which approximates the expected fair value of the machine on that date.

   Required: Determine the amount of the capitalized leased asset on July 1, Year 15.

_____

_____

_____

_____

2.   Deck Trucks leased trucks to Orleans, Inc., on July 1, Year 10. The lease is appropriately accounted for as a sale by Deck and as a purchase by Orleans. The lease expires on June 30, Year 15 and requires 5 equal payments of $230,000 beginning July 1, Year 10. Deck purchased the trucks for $700,000 on January 1, Year 10, and established a list selling price of $750,000 on the trucks. Assume that the present value at July 1, Year 10, of the rent payments over the lease term discounted at 10% (the approximate interest rate) was $900,000.

   Required:
   A. Prepare the journal entries Deck should make to record the signing of the lease.
   B. How much interest revenue should Deck record for the year ended June 30, Year 11?
   C. How much interest revenue should Deck record for the year ended June 30, Year 12?

_____

_____

_____

_____

_____

_____

_____

_____

_____

_____

_____

3.   Penn, Inc. leased a milling machine from Teller Equipment Leasing for 10 years at $140,000 annually with the first payment due upon execution of the lease. The lease specifies a 12% interest rate and a purchase option of $140,000 at the end of the tenth year when the machine's estimated value is $160,000. Penn's incremental borrowing rate is 10%.

The present value of an annuity paid at the start of each period:

10% for 10 years	6.75902	12% for 10 years	6.32825

The present value of $1 at:

10% in 10 years	0.38554	12% in 10 years	0.32197

Required:

A. Is this lease an operating or capital lease?

B. Determine the amount of lease liability to be recorded at the beginning of the lease term.

_____

_____

_____

_____

4.   On December 31, Year 9, Rio, Inc. sold equipment to Gold Coast Co. and simultaneously leased it back for 10 years. The terms of the lease are:

Sales price	$825,000
Equipment book value	650,000
Estimated remaining economic life	12 years

Required:

A.   Prepare the journal entries to record the sale and leaseback of the equipment on December 31, Year 9 on Rio's books.

B.   Record the journal entries if the sales price was $525,000.

_____

_____

_____

_____

_____

_____

_____

_____

_____

_____

_____

_____

_____

Solutions

Answers to True or False Questions

True answers: 3, 4, 6, 8, 10, 14, 15, 19, 20, 21, 22
False answers explained:
1. The party to a lease contract who owns the asset is the <u>lessor</u>.
2. The party to a lease contract who has the right to use the asset is the <u>lessee</u>.
5. An <u>operating</u> lease is an example of off-balance sheet financing.
7. A lease that contains a bargain purchase element is a <u>capital</u> lease.
9. If the present value of the minimum lease payments equals or exceeds <u>90%</u> of the fair value of the leased asset then the lease is a capital lease.
11. Maintenance costs are executory costs.
12. A residual value guarantee in a lease contract that requires the <u>lessee to pay the lessor</u> the difference between the actual market value and the residual value if the actual value is less than the residual value.
13. Leased assets <u>often</u> revert to the lessor at the end of the lease term.
16. The lessor is a <u>manufacturer</u> in a sales-type lease.
17. A direct financing lease is a capital lease in which the lessor is a <u>financial institution</u>.
18. The lessor will treat a lease as a <u>capital</u> lease if the lease transfers property rights to the lessee and allows accurate estimates of lease net cash flows and their collectibility.

Answers to Multiple-Choice Questions

1.	D	6.	A	11.	A	16.	A	21.	A
2.	A	7.	B	12.	C	17.	B	22.	C
3.	C	8.	B	13.	A	18.	B	23.	B
4.	B	9.	C	14.	D	19.	D		
5.	A	10.	B	15.	D	20.	A		

Answers to Exercises

1.   PVIFA 6.32825 x Annual Payment $65,000 = Leased Asset $411,336.25

2.   A.   DR Gross Investment in Lease Asset   1,150,000
                CR Sales   900,000
                CR Unearned Financing Income — Leases   250,000

            DR Cost of Goods Sold   700,000
                CR Inventory   700,000

     B.

Payment Date	Payment	Interest (10%)	Principal	Carrying Value
				$900,000
7-1-YR10	$230,000	$ 0	$230,000	670,000
7-1-YR11	230,000	67,000	163,000	507,000
7-1-YR12	230,000	50,700	179,300	

            Interest Revenue for Year 11 is $67,000

     C.   Interest Revenue for Year 12 is $50,700

3.   A.   This is a capital lease because it contains a bargain purchase option.
     B.   The lessee uses the lower of the specified interest rate or the lessee's incremental
            borrowing rate.
            PVIFA 6.75902 x Lease Payments $140,000 = Lease Liability $946,262.80

4.   A.   DR Cash   825,000
                CR Deferred Gain   175,000
                CR Equipment   650,000

            DR Leased Asset — Capital Lease   825,000
                CR Obligation Under Capital Lease   825,000

     B.   DR Cash   525,000
            DR Loss on Sale of Equipment   125,000
                CR Equipment   650,000
            DR Leased Asset — Capital Lease   525,000
                CR Obligation Under Capital Lease   525,000

CHAPTER 13

INCOME TAX REPORTING

Chapter Review

Learning Objective 1:
The different objectives underlying income determination for financial reporting (book) purposes versus tax purposes.

The rules of income tax accounting and financial accounting differ in most countries primarily because each type of accounting has different objectives. Financial income (**book income**) reflects increases in a firm's net assets which meet accrual accounting revenue and expense recognition criteria. Financial income is computed according to accrual accounting, which does not match cash flows in all instances. **Taxable income** adopts the theory of "constructive receipt" or the "ability to pay" doctrine that bases taxation on the ability to pay from the cash flow that taxable transactions provide. Therefore, GAAP and IRS regulations diverge on definitions of income and expense, creating complications in reporting income tax expense on GAAP financial statements.

Learning Objective 2:
The distinction between temporary (timing) and permanent differences and the items that cause each of these differences, and how each affects book income versus taxable income.

Because of the disparity between book income and taxable income, two types of differences arise:
1.   **temporary** or **timing** differences and
2.   **permanent** differences
Temporary differences arise when the timing of cash flows and accrual revenue and expense recognition do not coincide. They are temporary because they eventually reverse themselves. For example, a lease defines rental income of $20,000 over four years and the lessor accounts for it on an accrual basis. If the rent is prepaid in Year 1, it creates $20,000 of taxable income in Year 1 (an **originating timing difference**), but only $5,000 is income for financial purposes. In Years 2, 3 and 4, financial income is $5,000 (**reversing timing differences**), but taxable income is zero. For both tax and financial purposes, there is a total of $20,000 of revenue. The only difference is the timing of the recognition. By the end of Year 4, both tax and financial income have recognized the full $20,000.
Temporary differences which cause income recognition to be deferred for tax purposes create **deferred tax liabilities**. Temporary differences which cause income recognition to be accelerated for tax purposes create **deferred tax assets**. The following are the major temporary differences between GAAP and U. S. taxable income:

1. Depreciation Expense – Accelerated depreciation is used for tax purposes and straight-line depreciation is used for book purposes. Useful lives are determined under the Modified Accelerated Cost Recovery System (MACRS) for tax purposes and economic lives are used for book purposes.

2. Bad Debt Expense — IRS requires direct write-off recognition and GAAP prohibits direct write-off in favor of the allowance method.

3. Warranty Expense — IRS allows only actual expenditures and GAAP requires an estimated expense recognition.

4. Prepaid Expenses — IRS allows deductions when paid but accrual-basis accounting requires proper matching of expenses to revenues.

5. Pension and Postretirement Benefit Expenses — GAAP requires recognition of pension and postretirement benefit costs as accrued. IRS allows deduction only for pension costs as funded and postretirement benefits as paid.

6. Purchased Goodwill — IRS allows amortization over 15 years under certain conditions but GAAP does not allow amortize goodwill. For book purposes purchased goodwill is subject to periodic impairment tests.

7. Installment Sales — Financial accounting allows installment recognition when there is uncertainty as to ultimate collection. IRS allows installment recognition for goods sold on the installment basis.

8. Long-term Construction Contracts — GAAP requires percentage-of-completion method (with exceptions) and taxpayers may choose either percentage-of-completion or completed-contract method.

9. Revenues Received in Advance — IRS requires reporting when received and GAAP requires recognition when earned.

10. Equity in Undistributed Earnings of Investees — For tax purposes, income from ownership interests greater than 20% is limited to the dividends received (subject to a special deduction). For GAAP, income recognition is computed under the equity method as the percentage ownership times the net income of the investee. Dividends are not income but a return of capital.

Permanent differences between taxable and financial income arise from:
1. items that affect financial income but never affect taxable

income, and

2.   items that affect taxable income but never affect financial income.

Permanent differences create no deferred tax assets or liabilities because they will never reverse.

Examples of permanent differences are:
1.   Items recognized for financial purposes but **not** for tax purposes:
     a.   Interest on state and municipal bonds is not taxable.
     b.   Fines levied due to violation of laws are not deductible for tax purposes.
     c.   Goodwill amortization is not deductible for tax purposes except in special circumstances.
     d.   Insurance premiums for policies on the lives of executives in which the corporation is the beneficiary are not deductible nor are the proceeds taxable
     e.   Compensation for certain employee stock options is not deductible for tax purposes.
2.   Items recognized for tax purposes but not for financial purposes:
     a.   Tax laws allow statutory depletion that may be in excess of the cost basis of the asset. The excess of depletion over cost is a permanent difference.
     b.   U.S. corporations receive a deduction for domestic dividends that range from 70% to 100% of the dividends. **(See Demonstration Problem 1.)**

Learning Objective 3:
The distortions created when the deferred tax effects of temporary differences are ignored.

Setting tax expense equal to current taxes payable ignores the future tax liability that results from temporary (timing) differences between book and taxable income. To avoid the disparity between GAAP financial income tax expense and current taxes payable, the income statement reflects both taxes currently due and any liability for future taxes that result from temporary differences that reverse in future periods. Under *SFAS No. 109,* income tax expense equals the total of the current taxes owed plus or minus the change in deferred tax liability.

When tax rates do not change from year to year, GAAP deferred income tax accounting overcomes the problems that exist if one simply measured tax expense as cash taxes paid. The liability for future taxes is explicitly recognized, and reported tax expense is exactly equal to the tax rate times pre-tax book income plus or minus any permanent differences between book and taxable income.

In some instances, the originating timing differences generate deferred income tax assets (because income is recognized as taxable income before it is earned and recognized under GAAP revenue recognition) and taxable income will be lower than book income in future periods, when the differences reverse. In this situation the debit to income tax expense is a net amount representing the sum of current taxes payable and any change in the amount of the deferred tax asset. The opposite situation occurs when income recognition is delayed for tax purposes. That situation creates a deferred tax liability.

Learning Objective 4:
How tax expense is determined with interperiod tax allocation.

Using inter-period tax allocation,

> **Income Taxes Payable (computed from tax return)**
> + /— <u>**Increase or Decrease in Deferred Tax Liability (computed)**</u>
> = **Income Tax Expense**

This results in a tax expense number that is matched with the revenue and expenses recognized for financial accounting purposes.

A temporary difference that results in future tax return income being higher than future book income is a *future taxable amount* (deferred tax liability) according to *SFAS No.109*. A temporary difference that results in future tax return income being lower than future book income is a *future deductible amount* (**deferred tax asset**). **Deferred tax assets** are anticipated future benefits that arise from situations where future taxable income is expected to be less than future financial book income due to temporary timing differences. The realization of tax benefits that derive from deferred tax assets depends on the firm having future taxable income. If management believes that the probability of future taxable income is better than 50%, deferred tax assets can be recognized in their entirety. If management believes that it is more likely than not that that some portion of the tax benefit will not be realized in its entirety, SFAS No. 109 requires a valuation allowance account sufficient to reduce the deferred tax asset to the amount that is realizable.

Learning Objective 5:
How changes in tax rates are measured and recorded.

Under *SFAS NO.109,* when the tax rates change, the additional tax benefits or costs are recognizd as an adjustment to tax expense in the year that the tax rate changes are *passed,* not when the tax rate change is *realized*. Financial analysts often have a difficult time detecting these earnings effects since they are reported as part of the tax expense on the income statement. A careful reading of the tax footnote which reconciles the book-effective tax rate with the marginal tax rate may help reveal the size of earnings increases or decreases due to changes in the tax rates. **(See Demonstration Problem 2.)**

Learning Objective 6:
The reporting rules for net operating loss carrybacks and carryforwards.

Since a firm pays taxes in profitable years, it seems unfair to deny it some tax relief during unprofitable years. United States' tax laws allow firms to offset operating losses against taxable income. A firm may elect to carry back losses up to two years and to carry unused losses forward 20 years, or the firm may elect only to carry forward the loss up to 20 years. Any adjustment for the tax benefit associated with the loss carryback or carryforward is recorded as an adjustment to income tax expense in the year of the loss.
(See Demonstration Problem 3.)

Learning Objective 7:
How to read and interpret tax footnote disclosures and how these footnotes can be used to enhance interfirm comparability.

Disclosures contained in the financial statements concerning income tax expense provide a wealth of information to the readers. Footnote disclosures usually contain three items:
1. A breakdown of the provision for income taxes between the current tax expense and the deferred tax expense.
2. A reconciliation between the provision for income taxes and income taxes determined by applying the federal statutory rate to income before income taxes. This is the only disclosure required by GAAP.
3. The aggregate federal and foreign deferred income tax balance, representing the tax effect of the temporary differences.

Increases in the deferred tax liability balances result from a widening excess of book income over taxable income. A continual increase in the deferred income tax liability represents a potential danger signal for analysts, because it may be an indication of deteriorating earnings quality. The analyst needs to understand the reasons why the tax deferral is increasing. A firm can decide to extend the useful lives of its long-lived assets and not disclose this fact in the financial statement footnotes, hiding behind the concept of **materiality**. Because the materiality guidelines are arbitrary and mainly based on professional judgment, management can deliberately keep such changes below materiality thresholds and avoid disclosure. This may enable management to subtly manipulate or smooth income. Careful scrutiny of the income tax footnote provides financial analysts with a method of detecting subtle changes that indicate a deterioration of earnings quality.

It is possible for financial analysts to remove the differences in financial reporting choices across firms by examining the income tax footnotes to improve inter-firm comparisons. Detailed analysis of differences in depreciation methods, useful lives, and inventory valuation methods enables analysts to improve inter-firm comparability.

Learning Objective 8:
How tax footnotes can be used to evaluate the degree of conservatism in firms' book (GAAP)

Financial analysts should compute the degree of conservatism in a firm's set of accounting choices to assess a firm's earnings quality. Conservative choices, such as accelerated depreciation, decrease earnings and asset values, relative to more liberal techniques like straight-line depreciation. All things being equal, the more conservative the accounting choices, the higher the earnings quality.

accounting choices.   The tax footnote contains information necessary to assess the degree of earnings conservatism. The earnings conservatism (EC) ratio is stated as:

$$EC = \frac{\text{Pre-tax book income}}{\text{Taxable income per return}}$$

The closer the EC ratio is to 1.0, the more conservative the firm's financial reporting choices. The EC ratio can be computed for one company over time to monitor overall earnings conservatism. The EC ratio has three primary limitations:

1.   EC ratio comparisons for a single company over time can be misleading if the tax law changes during the period of comparison.
2.   Comparisons across companies in different industries should be made cautiously. The impact of tax burdens can vary because of differences in capital intensity between industries or specific tax rules which affect only certain industries.
3.   Earnings deterioration arising from LIFO dipping is not reliably captured in the EC ratio.

Glossary of Terms

Book Income	A measure of the increases in a firm's "well-offness," including all increases in net assets which meet the GAAP criteria for revenue recognition and costs that have expired according to the expense matching principle.
Deferred Income Tax Accounting	An accounting method that avoids the distortions caused by the differences between book income and taxable income.
Deferred Income Tax Asset	The result of a temporary difference that provides for a future deductible amount since future tax income will be lower than future book income.
Deferred Income Tax Liability	The result of a temporary difference that provides for future taxable amounts since future tax return income will be higher than future book income.
EC Ratio	A ratio to help determine the level of earnings conservatism. EC = Pre-tax book income/Taxable income per tax return.
Interperiod Tax Allocation	See "Deferred Income Tax Accounting."
Originating Timing Difference	The original book income versus taxable income differences.
Permanent	A situation that arises when book income and taxable income permanently

| Differences | differ in what is considered a revenue or expense. |

| Reversing Timing Difference | The title applied to the reversal of the originating timing differences. |

| Taxable Income | A measure of income governed by the constructive receipt/ability to pay doctrine. |

| Temporary Differences | See "Timing Differences." |

| Timing Differences | A revenue (gain) or expense (loss) that enters into the determination of book income in a different period than it does for tax purposes. These are considered temporary differences because they eventually reverse themselves. |

Demonstration Problems

1.   **Timing Differences**

The Bach Corporation reported $1,000,000 in income before income tax for book purposes in Year 7, the first year of operation. The tax depreciation exceeded its book depreciation by $120,000. The tax rate for Year 7 and all future years is 40%.

Required:
A.   Calculate the amount of deferred income tax liability that Bach reported in its December 31, Year 7, balance sheet.
B.   Calculate the amount of income taxes payable that Bach reported in its December 31, Year 7, balance sheet assuming that Bach paid no estimated income taxes.
C.   Calculate the amount of income tax expense that Bach reported on the income statement for Year 7.
D.   Record the journal entry that Bach prepared to record the taxes at December 31, Year 7.

A.
Step One: Identify the temporary timing differences for the corporation.
Application: Temporary differences cause taxable income to be higher or lower than book income in future periods, giving rise to a deferred tax asset or liability.
Solution: The temporary difference results from the $120,000 difference between book and tax depreciation.

Step Two: Calculate the amount of deferred tax liability.
Application: Deferred tax liability = Temporary Difference x Tax Rate
Solution: Deferred tax liability = Temporary Difference $120,000 x Tax Rate 40% = $48,000

B.

Step One: Determine the taxable income.

Application: Taxable income = Book Income + or - Temporary and Permanent Differences.

Solution: Taxable Income = Book Income $1,000,000 - Temporary Difference $120,000 = $880,000

Step Two: Determine the amount of income taxes payable.

Application: Income Taxes Payable = Tax Rate   x Taxable Income

 Solution: Income Taxes Payable = Tax Rate 40% x Taxable Income $880,000 = $352,000

C.

Step One: Calculate the income tax expense.

Application: The Income Tax Expense formula is:

        Income Taxes Payable (computed from tax return)
  + / -   Increase or Decrease in Deferred Tax Liability (computed)
  =   Income Tax Expense

Solution: Income Taxes Payable $352,000 + Deferred Taxes Payable $48,000 = $400,000

D.

Step One: Prepare the journal entry to record the income taxes for the year.

Application: Utilize the information in sections A, B, and C to develop the entry.

Solution:

DR Income Tax Expense	400,000	
CR Income Taxes Payable		352,000
CR Deferred Income Taxes Payable		48,000

2.   Deferred Tax Assets and Liabilities, with Tax Rate Changes.

Southridge Corporation began to manufacture widgets on January 2, Year 5. In Year 5, Southridge reported a pretax book income of $900,000 and had taxable income of $1,200,000. Southridge Corporation had a temporary difference relating to accrued product warranty costs which are expected to be paid in the following manner:

        Year 6 $180,000
        Year 7 $90,000
        Year 8 $30,000

The enacted tax rates are 35% for Years 5 & 6 and 40% for Years 7 & 8.

Required:

A.   Calculate the amount of the timing difference for Year 5.

B.   Calculate the amount of the Income Taxes Payable at the end of Year 5.

C.   Compute the amount of the Deferred Tax Asset at the end of Year 5 assuming no other timing differences occurred in Year 6, Year 7, or Year 8.

D.   Calculate the amount of Income Tax Expense for Year 5.

A.

Step One: Determine the timing differences.

Application: Temporary differences cause taxable income to be higher or lower than book income in future periods, giving rise to a deferred tax asset or liability. When taxable income is higher than book income, a deferred tax asset is created.

Book Income - Taxable Income = Timing Difference.

Solution: Book Income $900,000 - Taxable Income $1,200,000 = Timing Difference $(300,000)

B.

Step One: Calculate the Income Taxes Payable.

Application: Income Taxes Payable = Taxable Income x Current Tax Rate

Solution: Income Taxes Payable =Taxable Income ($1,200,000) x Current Tax Rate (35%) = $420,000

C.

Step One: Compute the amount of the Deferred Tax Asset.

Application: The deferred tax asset is the timing difference times the tax rates in effect for each year.

Solution:

Period	Timing Difference	Rate	Deferred Tax Asset
Year 6	$180,000	35%	$63,000
Year 7	90,000	40%	36,000
Year 8	30,000	40%	12,000
Total Deferred Tax Asset			$111,000

or alternative calculation:

Timing Difference $300,000 x Current Rate 35% = $105,000
Subject to Change $120,000 x Rate Change 5% = 6,000
Total Deferred Tax Asset $111,000

D.

Step One: Compute the income tax expense.

Application: Income Tax Expense = Income Taxes Payable - Deferred Tax Asset Increase

Solution: Income Tax Expense $309,000 = Income Taxes Payable $420,000 - Deferred Tax Asset Increase $111,000

3.   Loss Carrybacks and Carryforwards

The Bowa Corporation reported the following operating income figures for its first three years of operations:

Year 1	$1,500,000
Year 2	(3,300,000)
Year 3	5,400,000

Bowa has a tax rate of 40% and in Year 2 elected to carryback the maximum amount of loss. Bowa Corporation has no deferred taxes in any year.

Required:

A.   Calculate the amount of Bowa Corporation's income tax expense reported on the income statement for each year.

B.   Calculate the amount of tax Bowa must pay to the Internal Revenue Service in Year 3.

A.

Step One: Calculate the amount of tax expense for each year.
Application: Operating Income x Tax Rate = Income Tax Expense
Solution:

Year	Income	Tax Rate	Income Tax Expense
1	$1,500,000	40%	$ 600,000
2	(3,300,000)	40%	(1,320,000)
3	5,400,000	40%	2,160,000

B.

Step One: Calculate the amount of loss carryback available for Year 3.
Application: Cox elected to carryback the loss first, then carry forward any unused amount. Since Cox has only one prior year, the loss is carried back to Year 1.
Solution:

Amount of Carryback Available from Year 2	$(3,300,000)
Amount Used in Year 1	1,500,000
Available to carry forward for use in Year 3	$ (1,800,000)

Step Two: Calculate the amount of taxable income for Year 3.
Application: Taxable Income = Year 3 Income — Loss Carryforward
Solution:

Year 3 Income	$5,400,000
Less: Carryforward	(1,800,000)
Taxable Income in Year 3	$3,600,000

Step Three: Determine the tax liability for Year 3.
Application: Taxable Income x Tax Rate = Income Tax Liability
Solution:

Taxable Income:	$3,600,000
Tax Rate	40%
Income Tax Liability	$1,440,000

Test Yourself

True or false questions:

T F 1.   Book income includes all increases in net assets which meet the GAAP criteria for revenue recognition.

T F 2.   Book income is governed by the "constructive receipt/ability to pay" doctrine.

T F 3.   Intraperiod income tax allocation is the GAAP solution for avoiding distortions caused by differences between financial income and U. S. taxable income.

T F 4.   A reversing timing difference causes book income to be greater than or less than taxable income in future periods.

T F 5.   A temporary difference that causes taxable income to be higher than book income in future periods gives rise to a deferred tax liability.

T F 6.   A permanent difference may create a deferred tax asset or liability.

T F 7.   Rent revenue received in advance is an example of a permanent difference.

T F 8.   Interest received on state and municipal bonds is a temporary difference.

T F 9.   Financial analysts must be alert to how tax changes can impact earnings in the year Congress enacts new tax rates.

T F 10. The liability approach of *SFAS No. 109* recognizes the full change in the amount of future tax liability as an increase or decrease in tax expense in the year the tax rate becomes known.

T F 11. Deferred income tax assets always generate future benefits.

T F 12. When a company determines that it is likely that a portion of future tax benefits will not be realized, a valuation allowance account must be established.

T F 13. The tax benefit associated with a loss carryback or carryforward is recorded as an adjustment to tax expense in the year of the loss.

T F 14. A detailed analysis of deferred income tax balances is important in the determination of earnings quality.

T F 15. A comparison of pre-tax accounting income with the estimate of taxable income allows analysts to develop a rough index of the degree of conservatism in the set of GAAP accounting choices.

T   F   16.   Tax footnotes provide information to help analysts assess the earnings quality of the firm.

T   F   17.   Deferred income tax accounting is used whenever permanent differences exist between book and tax income.

T   F   18.   *SFAS No. 109* specifies the use of the liability method for deferred tax accounting.

T   F   19.   The more aggressive the set of accounting choices for a given firm, the higher the quality of earnings.

T   F   20.   When computing the EC ratio, any "permanent differences" should be included in the numerator.

Multiple-Choice Questions

Select the best answer from those provided.

_____   1.   A firm's recognized revenue for financial purposes includes
   a.   all earned inflows of cash.
   b.   all earned inflows of net liabilities.
   c.   all unearned inflows of net cash.
   d.   all earned inflows of net assets.

_____   2.   The doctrine of "constructive receipt/ability to pay" is a determining factor for
   a.   accrued income.
   b.   book income.
   c.   taxable income.
   d.   not-for-profit institutions.

_____   3.   The term interperiod tax allocation is synonymous with the term
   a.   intraperiod tax allocation.
   b.   deferred income tax accounting.
   c.   book income allocation.
   d.   constructive income allocation.

_____   4.   Intraperiod income tax allocation is the allocation of the tax cost or benefit
   a.   across accounting periods.
   b.   across components of book income between different accounting periods.
   c.   across components of book income within a given period.
   d.   between several accounting periods.

_____ 5.   A temporary timing difference is a timing difference that will
a.   eventually reverse.
b.   never reverse.
c.   become a permanent difference.
d.   always results in a tax refund.

_____ 6.   A deferred tax asset arises as a result of a temporary difference that causes taxable income to be
a.   higher than book income in future periods.
b.   lower than book income in future periods.
c.   the same as book income in future periods.
d.   lower than book income in prior periods.

_____ 7.   Interest received on municipal bonds is an example of a/an
a.   temporary timing difference.
b.   partial timing difference.
c.   permanent timing difference.
d.   future timing difference.

_____ 8.   Depreciation expense is an example of a/an
a.   temporary timing difference.
b.   permanent timing difference.
c.   past-due timing difference.
d.   partial timing difference.

_____ 9.   An originating timing difference causes book income to be greater than or less than taxable income
a.   one year after it is recorded.
b.   two years after it is recorded.
c.   when it is initially recorded.
d.   in total at the end of the term of the timing difference.

_____ 10.   A reversing timing difference is one that causes book income to be greater than or less than taxable income
a.   when it is initially recorded.
b.   in future periods.
c.   in past periods.
d.   when the tax rates change.

_____ 11.   The failure of a firm to take temporary timing tax differences into account violates the
a.   matching principle.
b.   historical cost principle.
c.   going concern principle.
d.   conservatism principle.

_____ 12.   The liability approach presented in *SFAS No. 109* calls for the full change in the amount of future liability to be recognized as an increase or decrease in income tax expense in the year the tax rate is
a.   proposed.
b.   known.
c.   effective.
d.   discussed.

_____ 13.   A corporation that incurs a net operating loss must
a.   must carryback the loss for tax purposes.
b.   may elect to carryback the loss for tax purposes.
c.   may elect to carryforward the loss for tax purposes.
d.   may elect to both carryback and carryforward the loss for tax purposes.

_____ 14.   The net operating loss incurred by a corporation may be
a.   carried forward 25 years.
b.   carried back 2 years and carried forward 20 years.
c.   carried back 3 years and carried forward 15 years.
d.   carried back 5 years and carried forward 20 years.

_____ 15.   The determination of the necessity for a valuation allowance, when it is likely that not all of a deferred tax asset will be used, requires
a.   stockholder approval.
b.   board of director approval.
c.   subjective assessment.
d.   objective judgment.

_____ 16.   Financial analysts learn a great deal about the financial affairs of a firm when they study information about the income taxes contained in the
a.   balance sheet.
b.   footnotes to the financial statements.
c.   income statement.
d.   cash flow statement.

_____ 17. Taxable income equals pre-tax book income plus or minus
   a. depreciation.
   b. amortization.
   c. permanent tax differences.
   d. contingent gains.

_____ 18. Temporary timing differences give rise to
   a. deferred tax assets or deferred tax liabilities.
   b. deferred tax assets but not deferred tax liabilities.
   c. deferred tax liabilities only.
   d. permanent tax differences.

_____ 19. The potential deterioration of earnings quality arises as a result of
   a. increases in deferred tax liability.
   b. decreases in deferred tax liability.
   c. no change in deferred tax liability.
   d. decrease in prepaid tax liability.

_____ 20. Sudden changes in deferred tax asset or liability accounts should always be
   a. adjusted.
   b. corrected.
   c. investigated.
   d. ignored.

_____ 21. The earnings conservatism ratio is defined as the ratio of pre-tax book income to
   a. the deferred tax assets.
   b. the deferred tax liabilities.
   c. taxable income per the tax return.
   d. the prior year tax return.

_____ 22. A primary limitation associated with the earnings conservatism (EC) ratio is that the
   a. temporary timing differences are ignored.
   b. permanent timing differences are ignored.
   c. earnings conservatism deterioration that arises from LIFO dipping is not reliably captured in the EC ratio.
   d. earnings conservatism deterioration that arises from LIFO dipping is captured in the EC ratio.

_____ 23.   By removing the permanent differences from the numerator of the earnings
            conservatism (EC) ratio, the ratio is
            a.   strengthened.
            b.   weakened.
            c.   not affected.
            d.   no longer useful.

Exercises

1.   On January 2, Year 1, Grant Company acquired a machine for $340,000 with a useful life of 5
     years and a residual value of $40,000. Grant uses straight-line depreciation for financial
     accounting purposes. Tax-basis depreciation for Year 1 was $150,000 and $90,000 for Year 2.
     Grant's Year 2 income before taxes and depreciation expense is $375,000 with a tax rate of 30%.

     Required: If Grant made no estimated tax payments during Year 2, how much is the tax liability
     on the December 31, Year 2 balance sheet?

2.   Barber, Inc. opened on January 1, Year 1. Barber recognizes revenue on the accrual method but recognizes revenue on the installment method for tax purposes. Barber's gross profit for each method is:

Year	Accrual Basis	Installment Basis
Year 1	$ 300,000	$175,000
Year 2	850,000	550,000

Enacted income tax rates are 30% for Year 1 and 25% thereafter. There are no other temporary differences.

Required: How much is Barber's December 31, Year 2 balance sheet asset or liability for deferred income taxes?

_____

_____

_____

_____

_____

_____

_____

_____

_____

_____

3.   Royal Ship Construction, Inc. recognizes revenues under the percentage-of-completion method for financial reporting purposes and chooses to employ the completed-contract method for tax purposes. The first three years' income under both methods were as follows:

Year	Percentage of Completion	Completed Contract
1	$100,000	$ 0
2	325,000	150,000
3	362,500	337,500

Tax rates for all current and future years is 40% and there are no other timing differences.

Required: Determine the appropriate balance sheet recognition of any deferred tax asset or liability at the end of Year 3.

_____

_____

_____

_____

4.   At December 31, Year 20, Chevy, Inc. had a loss carryforward of $500,000 available to offset future taxable income at a time in which company officials believe that Chevy will have future earnings. The tax rate is 40%.

Required: Indicate the proper income statement treatment of this information on the Year 20 income statement.

5.   The following is a summary of Wrangler's operating income for its first three years:

Year 1	$800,000
Year 2	(1,500,000)
Year 3	1,6000,000

There are no deferred taxes in any year. Wrangler has a tax rate of 30% and in Year 2 elected to carryback the maximum amount of loss.

Required:
A. What is the amount of Wrangler's income tax expense reported on the income statement for each year?
B. How much of a refund did Wrangler receive for the loss carryback to Year 1?
C. How much must Wrangler pay the government in Year 3?

6.   Stratis, Inc. included the following reconciliation of income per books with the income per tax return for Year 9:

Financial income before income taxes	$4, 800,000
Add: Temporary difference for construction contract which will reverse in Year 10	700,000
Deduct: Temporary difference for depreciation which will reverse in equal amounts over the next three years	(1,200,000)
Taxable Income	$ 4,300,000

Stratis' income tax rate is 30% for Year 9 and future years.

Required:

A.   How much is the current provision for income taxes on the Year 9 income statement?

B.   Prepare the journal entry to record the income tax expense for Year 9.

C.   With no additional temporary differences, how much will Stratis report on the Year 10 income statement for deferred income taxes?

_____
_____
_____
_____
_____
_____
_____
_____

Solutions

Answers to True or False Questions

True answers: 1, 4, 5, 9, 10, 12, 13, 14, 15, 16, 18
False answers explained:
2.   <u>Taxable</u> income is governed by the constructive receipt/ability to pay doctrine.
3.   <u>Interperiod</u> income tax allocation is the GAAP solution for avoiding distortions caused by differences between financial income and U. S. taxable income.
6.   A permanent difference <u>never</u> affects taxable income.
7.   Rent revenue received in advance is an example of a <u>temporary</u> difference.
8.   Interest received on state and municipal bonds is a <u>permanent</u> difference.
11.   Deferred income tax assets <u>do not</u> always generate future benefits.
17.   Deferred income tax accounting is used whenever <u>temporary</u> differences exist between book and tax income.
19.   The more <u>conservative</u> the set of accounting choices for a given firm, the higher the quality of earnings.
20.   Permanent differences should be <u>removed</u> from the numerator of the EC rates.

Answers to Multiple-Choice Questions

1.	D	6.	B	11.	A	16.	B	21.	C
2.	C	7.	C	12.	B	17.	C	22.	C
3.	B	8.	A	13.	D	18.	A	23.	A
4.	C	9.	C	14.	B	19.	A		
5.	A	10.	B	15.	C	20	C		

Answers to Exercises

1. Tax Liability at December 31, Year 2:
    Straight-Line Depreciation = $340,000 — $40,000/5 years = $60,000
    Excess of Tax Depreciation over Book Depreciation = $90,000 — $60,000 = $30,000
    Net Income $375,000 — Timing Difference $30,000 = Taxable Income $345,000 x Tax Rate 30% = $103,500

2. Deferred Income Tax Liability at December 31, Year 2:

Deferred Tax Year 1 ($300,000 — $175,000) x 25%	=	$31,250
Deferred Tax Year 2 ($850,000 — $5500,000) x 25%	= +	75,000
Deferred Tax Liability		$106,250

3.
Income reported under Percentage of Completion	$787,500
Income reported under Completed Contract	487,500
Timing Difference	$300,000
Tax Rate	x .40
Deferred Tax Liability	$ 120,000

4. For Year 20, the income statement will show a deferred tax asset of $200,000
    (40% x $500,000) = $200,000

5. A.
	Income	Income Tax Expense
Year 1	$800,000	$240,000
Year 2	(1,500,000)	(450,000)
Year 3	1,600,000	480,000

    B.   Refund = Carryback $800,000 x Tax Rate 30% = $240,000

    C.
Amount of carryback	$(1,500,000)
Amount Used in Year 1	800,000
Available for carry forward to Year 3	$(700,000)
Year 3 Income	$ 1,600,000
Less: Carryforward from Year 2	(700,000)
Taxable Income in Year 3	$ 900,000
Tax Rate	.30
Liability on Tax Return	$ 270,000

6.   A.   Current Provision for Income Taxes for Year 9 = Financial Income x Tax Rate
              $4,800,000 x .30 = $1,440,000

       B.   DR Income Tax Expense   1,440,000
                  CR Deferred Tax Liability   150,000
                  CR Income Taxes Payable   1,290,000

              Current tax   = $2,400,000 x 30%   = $720,000
              Payable   = $2,150,000 x 30%   = $645,000
              Deferred tax   = $210,000 x 30%   = $75,000

       C.   Year 10 Deferred Taxes:
              Timing difference — construction contract $(700,000)
              Timing difference — depreciation ($1,200,000 / 3 years)   400,000
              Net difference $(300,000)
              Tax rate   .30
              Net decrease in deferred tax liability $ (90,000)

CHAPTER 14

PENSIONS AND POST-RETIREMENT BENEFITS

Chapter Review

Learning Objective 1:
The difference between defined contribution and defined benefit pension plans.

Firms that seek to attract and retain quality employees often establish pension plans to provide income to employees when they retire. Pension plans are either **defined contribution** plans or **defined benefit** plans. Each plan is unique to its employer, so that no two plans are identical.

Defined contribution plans define the amount the employer contributes each year for the employees' pension account. Contributions are often a percentage of the employees' wages or of the firm's net income. Upon retirement, the employee has an accumulated amount in the pension plan value and receives payments based on the valuation at retirement. The plan provides no guarantee of benefits and the employee bears the risk of benefit adequacy. Defined contribution plans present no accounting problems because the required contribution is an expense each year for financial reporting purposes.

FYI. . .
The **vesting** period is the required service years before an employee is entitled to full pension benefits. Once an employee vests, the pension benefits become the asset of the employee in case of death or termination of employment.

Defined benefit plans define the employee's benefit upon retirement. Defined benefit plans rely upon present value calculations to determine the contributions needed today to provide the promised benefits in the future. Actuaries provide accountants with much of the information needed to compute current pension expense and liability. To derive this data, actuaries must seek the following information:

1. Plan specified benefits to retirees, death and disability benefits if any, and **vesting** formula.
2. Age, sex, current salary, service years, and life span of each employee.
3. Anticipated salary increases between today and retirement.
4. Anticipated employee turnover rates.
5. Anticipated earnings rate on the plan assets.
6. Appropriate discount rate for present value calculations.

Learning Objective 2:
What the components of pension expense are and their relation to pension assets and the pension

SFAS No. 87 and *SFAS No. 132* govern GAAP for pension and postretirement benefits. Pension accounting is complicated mainly because it contains many off-balance sheet elements that must be considered for the financial accounting numbers. Let's try to simplify it as much as possible.
Pension costs contain six elements that either increase or decrease the

liability.

FYI...

Actuaries compute pension benefits for each employee from an employee census using the exact age, expected life, service years, and salary information. Amounts are totaled for the entire plan to compute pension costs and liability.

expense:

	Cost type	Increase or decrease
1.	Service cost	Increase
2.	Interest cost	Increase
3.	Expected return on plan assets	Decrease
4.	Recognition of gains or losses	Increase or decrease
5.	Amortization of unrecognized Transition asset or obligation	Increase or decrease
6.	Recognized prior service cost	Increase or decrease

Service cost is the increase in the discounted present value of the benefits ultimately payable that is attributable to an additional year's employment. As each employee adds a year's service to the employer, the ultimate benefits increase because benefit formulas are often based on a fixed percentage of ending salary for each year of service. Vesting also contributes to service cost.

Interest cost is the increase in the present value of the benefits due to the passage of time. The actuary computes an individual employee's expected retirement benefit for years of service and salary, and discounts the anticipated benefit back to the present value. Each year as the employee approaches retirement, the present value of the benefits grows. Interest cost is the growth of the present value of the pension liability from year to year.

Expected return on plan assets reduces the pension cost. In a perfect world, the interest cost and expected return on plan assets would be equal each year. Successful pension planning would find them nearly equal over a long period of time.

Recognized gains or losses are not recognized each year. Realizing that the expected return on plan assets and interest cost are not equal each year, FASB instituted a smoothing device to stabilize pension costs over time. Differences between interest cost and actual return on plan assets are accumulated and not recognized until the balance reaches a threshold called the corridor. Then portions of the accumulated gains or losses are recognized as appropriate from year to year.

Learning Objective 3: The requirements for funding pension plans, computing the return on plan assets, and the role of the plan trustee.

Amortization of unrecognized transition assets or obligations comes from the adoption of *SFAS No. 87*. If at that time, the plan was overfunded or underfunded, *SFAS No. 87* required that the resulting transition asset (overfunding) or liability (underfunding) be amortized over the greater of the average remaining service life of the employees or 15 years.

Recognition of prior service costs smooths the cost of changes in the plan benefits over the average remaining service life of the employees. For many reasons, employers elect to increase or decrease pension benefits as time passes. Changes in plan benefits mean that prior contributions are now either insufficient or excessive. The prior service costs (or reductions) are spread over the remaining years of the plan to prevent income shocks in one year.

The employer is the **plan sponsor** who transfers funds to the **plan trustee** who holds the pension plan funds in a **pension trust**. The pension funds are not included in the financial statements of the employer, but in the balance sheet of the pension trust. The plan trustee must protect the assets and invest the assets wisely to provide benefits to the retired employees who are the **plan beneficiaries**.

Where do the **accounting numbers** come from to compute pension cost?

1. **Service Cost** — The service cost amount is provided by the actuary.

2. **Interest Cost** — *SFAS No. 87* requires that the **settlement rate** be used to compute interest cost. The settlement rate is the rate at which the pension benefits could be settled. The settlement rate is used to determine interest cost and the service cost. Interest cost is computed by multiplying the settlement rate times the **projected benefit obligation** (PBO). The PBO is the discounted present value of the pension obligation based on assumed future compensation levels.
   Interest cost = PBO x settlement rate

3. **Expected Return on Plan Assets** — Firms are free to select an expected return on plan assets that may or may not be the same as the settlement rate. Typically, expected rates of return are higher than the settlement rates.
   Expected return = Beginning plan assets x expected rate

4. **Recognized Gains or Losses** — Expected rates of return on

FYI. . .
Actual rates of return on plan assets in the long-run are usually higher than the discount rates used in estimated pension costs and liabilities. This is an example of **conservatism** at work. The lower the discount rate used, the higher the pension costs and liability.

FYI. . .
Pension costs are reduced when nonvested employees terminate their employment. The costs previously allocated for future benefits are no longer necessary.

plan assets are determined for the long run. There is no way that a plan can earn exactly the same percentage each year. Notice that the deduction from pension costs is the **expected** return. So each pension cost calculation includes this section with sample numbers:

Less:

Actual return on plan assets	$(10,000)
Unrecognized gain (loss)	1,000
Expected return on plan assets	(9,000)

The unrecognized gains and losses should, theoretically, net out to zero over time. Gains and losses arise from three causes:

a. Differences between actual and expected earnings on plan assets.
b. Differences between actual experience and actuarial assumptions such as salary increases, longevity, and turnover.
c. Changes in assumptions such as the settlement rate due to market factors.

Learning Objective 4:
How GAAP smoothes the volatility inherent in pension estimates and forecasts.

SFAS No. 87 provides the **corridor approach** to compute recognition of unexpected gains and losses. The corridor approach contains the following steps:

a. Compute **10 %** of the balance at the beginning of the plan year for the **larger** of the PBO or the market-related value of the pension plan assets. This becomes the **threshold**.

Threshold = 10% x > Beginning PBO or Plan Assets Market Value

b. Compare the absolute value of the accumulated gains or losses to the threshold. If the absolute value of the accumulation exceeds the threshold, *recognition is triggered.*

c. Divide the excess of the accumulated gains and losses over the corridor by the average remaining service life of the employees to compute the recognized gain or loss.

Recognition =   Threshold — Accumulated gains or losses
                    Average remaining service life

5. **Amortization of Unrecognized Transition Assets or Obligation** — *SFAS No. 87* attempted to close an abuse of plans being overfunded or underfunded. Upon adoption of *SFAS No. 87*, firms had to determine if the plans were overfunded (producing an off-balance sheet **transition asset**) or underfunded (causing an off-balance sheet **transition obligation**). The transition asset or obligation must be amortized over the remaining average service life of the employees. If the average service life remaining is less than 15 years, the firm may elect to use 15 years instead. Transition assets will reduce future pension expense and transition obligation will increase future pension expense.

    Amortization = Transition asset or obligation
    Average remaining service life

6. **Recognized Prior Service Cost** — When employers increase (or decrease) pension benefits, it creates additional (or reduced) pension costs and liability. Firms usually increase benefits to attract and retain quality personnel or be more competitive in the job market. The change adds a "shock" to the pension liability for the accumulated costs that would have been recognized and funded in the past. The actuary provides the amount of the prior service costs (PSC) or the increase to the PBO for the change in benefits. Divide the change in the PBO by the average remaining service life of the employees for the annual adjustment.

    Recognition of PSC = Increase (decrease) in PBO
    Average remaining service life

Learning Objective 5:
The determinants of the pension funding decision.

The journal entries to record pension expense are very straightforward. Debit Pension Expense for the computed pension cost and, if fully funded, credit Cash. Firms may contribute amounts different from the pension cost each year. If a firm overcontributes, it creates an asset called Prepaid Pension Expense. If a firm contributes less than the pension expense, it creates a liability called Unfunded Accrued Pension Cost. **(See Demonstration Problem 1.)**

When plans are underfunded, the employees are left unprotected if the company fails. Under the Employees Retirement Income Security Act (ERISA) of 1974, firms must contribute a minimum of the service cost each year unless the plan is overfunded at the beginning of the year. IRS also encourages employer funding because only the amounts contributed each year are deductible. Firms face four competing forces in making pension funding decisions:

1.   **Tax incentives** encourage funding when tax rates are high.
2.   **Finance incentives** encourage funding when capital is available for contributions.
3.   **Labor incentives** encourage funding, especially in a strong unionized work force.
4.   **Contracting/political costs incentives** stifle pension contributions because payments of cash lower some important financial ratios.

Learning Objective 6:
How to analyze the
funded status footnote
and reconciliation of
pension asset and
liability accounts and
how to use this
information.

SFAS No. 132 details the requirements for the pension disclosure footnote. GAAP require two major sections of information:

1.   Reconciliation of the off-balance sheet assets and liabilities to the on-balance sheet pension asset or liability including:
     a.   funded status reconciliation and
     b.   reconciliation to the net pension asset or liability.
2.   Disclosure of the six pension expense components.

The **funded status reconciliation** provides information that reconciles off-balance sheet information from the pension trust to the employer's records. Plans are categorized in three ways:

1.   **Overfunded plans** have a greater fair value of plan assets than PBO.
2.   **Underfunded plans** have a greater PBO than fair value of plan assets, but the fair value of plan assets exceeds the ABO.
3.   **Severely underfunded plans** have a greater ABO than the fair value of the plan assets.

The plan assets, PBO and ABO are off-balance sheet assets and liabilities of the pension plan. Plan assets are kept at fair value. The PBO is computed each year by an actuary. The **accumulated benefit obligation** is the actuarial present value of the pension benefits based on current salary levels. To determine funded status for the footnote, complete the following information:

Vested benefit obligation	$
Nonvested benefit obligation	+ _____
Accumulated benefit obligation	= $
Effect of future compensation levels	+ _____
Projected benefit obligation	= $
Fair value of plan assets	- _____
Funded status	= $

From the funded status, the second part of the reconciliation continues:

Unrecognized prior service cost	+ or -
Unrecognized transition asset (or liability)	+ or -
Unrecognized net gain (or loss)	+ or -
Accrued pension asset or liability	$_____

To compute the numbers required for this reconciliation, the off-balance sheet data for the pension plan must be computed.

1. **Plan assets** consist of the following elements:

	Beginning plan assets at fair value
+	Actual return on plan assets
+	Contributions made by the plan sponsor
-	Benefits paid to beneficiaries
=	Ending plan assets at fair value

2. **Pension benefit obligation** (PBO) consists of the following elements:

	Beginning balance of the PBO
+	Service cost for the period
+	Interest cost for the period
+	Changes in the benefits from plan amendments
+	Changes in actuarial assumptions
-	Benefits paid to beneficiaries
=	Ending balance of PBO

(See Demonstration Problem 2.)

Learning Objective 7: When a minimum balance sheet pension liability must be recognized.

SFAS No. 87 requires that a minimum balance sheet liability be recorded when a pension plan is severely underfunded. The minimum balance sheet liability is equal to the excess of the ABO over the fair value of the plan assets.

	Accumulated benefit obligation
-	Plan assets at fair value
=	Minimum balance sheet liability

The minimum liability is shown on the balance sheet as Additional Pension Liability with an offsetting asset called Intangible Asset (deferred pension cost).

(See Demonstration Problem 2.)

Severely underfunded pension plans should warn statement readers of future requirements of cash flow to solve the funding problems.

Learning Objective 8:
The financial reporting rules for other postretirement benefits.

Until FASB issued *SFAS No. 106* in 1990, postretirement benefits were recognized on a pay-as-you-go basis mainly because the cost of the benefits prior to 1980 were minimal. *SFAS No. 106* accorded postretirement benefits the same accounting treatment as pension expenses with several differences:

1.   Postretirement benefits need not be funded.
2.   Postretirement benefits have no projected benefit obligation because postretirement benefits are based not on salary, but on insurance and service costs.
3.   Only plans that are funded have computations for expected return on plan assets.

Upon adoption of *SFAS No. 106*, firms with postretirement benefits had the option to

1.   select immediate recognition of the transition asset or obligation; or
2.   amortize the transition obligation or asset over the longer of 20 years or the average remaining service life of active plan participants.

Computations and disclosures for the accrued postretirement benefit cost are similar to those for pension plans. **(See Demonstration Problem 3.)**

Learning Objective 9:
What research tells us about the usefulness of the detailed pension and other postretirement benefits disclosures.

Research indicates that investors value the service cost, interest cost, and expected return on plan assets components of the pension and postretirement benefits expenses as part of sustainable earnings. The other components of pension and postretirement benefits expenses are viewed as more transitory. As a result, the information contained in the footnote disclosures required under *SFAS No. 87* and *SFAS No. 106* helps investors in their decisions because investors give different components different share price implications.

The pension footnote gives information from off-balance sheet sources and reconciles that information to the balance sheet's pension assets and liabilities. The footnote includes information concerning the fair value of the plan assets, the **vested benefit obligation** (VBO), the ABO, and the PBO. All of these values are closely associated with stock price, much more than the on-balance sheet pension asset and liability accounts.

The postretirement benefit footnote also gives information from off-balance sheet sources and reconciles that information to the balance sheet's postretirement assets and liabilities. But due to the uncertainty surrounding the ultimate future health care costs and Medicare reimbursements, analysts find the accounting information on postretirement benefits to be less reliable than pension information.

Glossary of Terms

Accumulated Benefit Obligation	The present value of pension obligations based on current compensation levels.
Defined Benefit Plan	An agreement that specifies the formula for determining the amount that will be paid out to the employee after retirement rather than the amount that will be paid into the plan.
Defined Contribution Plan	An agreement that specifies the amount of cash that the employer puts into the plan for the benefit of the employee.
Expected Return on Plan Assets	A target return chosen by the firm that it expects to achieve in the long term.
Interest Cost	The component of pension expense that arises from the passage of time.
Market-Related Value	Either the fair market value of pension plan assets or a moving-average smoothed value that recognizes changes in value more slowly.
Pension Plan	An agreement by an organization to provide a series of payments to employees when they retire.
Plan Beneficiaries	Employees of the plan sponsor.
Plan Sponsor	The firm that establishes the pension plan.
Plan Trustee	The legal entity that has custody of the plan assets.
Prior Service Cost	The dollar amount of the increase in the projected benefit obligation due to a retroactive increase in the pension plan.
Projected Benefit Obligation	The present value of pension obligations based on assumed future compensation levels.
Return on Plan Assets	The amount earned on plan assets that reduces pension expense.

Service Cost	The increase in the discounted present value of the pension benefits ultimately payable attributable to an additional year's employment.
Settlement Rate	The rate of return at which the pension benefits of employees can effectively be fulfilled.
Transition Asset or Liability	The difference between the amount of the pension liability and the pension plan assets.
Vesting	The term that applies to the employees qualifying for benefits under a pension plan.

Demonstration Problems

1.   **Pension expense, off-balance accounts, funded status, and minimum pension liability.**

Beaves, Inc. has a defined benefit pension plan with the following information available for the current year:

Beginning fair value of plan assets	$800,000
Beginning projected benefit obligation	760,000
Ending accumulated benefit obligation	895,200
Beginning unrecognized losses	160,000
Service costs for current year	120,000
Actual return on plan assets	64,000
Pension benefits paid during the year	80,000
Settlement rate	7%
Changes in actuarial assumptions	90,000
Changes in plan benefits	100,000
Employer contributions	90,000
Beginning minimum pension liability	-0-
Average remaining service life of employees	20 years

Required:
> A. Determine the pension expense for the year.
> B. Determine the funded status of the plan at year end.
> C. Determine the minimum liability for the year-end balance sheet.

A.
First Step: Determine the interest cost for the year.
Application: Interest cost = Beginning PBO x Settlement rate
Solution: Interest cost = Beginning PBO $760,000 x Settlement rate 7% = $53,200

Second Step: Determine the expected return on the plan assets.

Application: Expected return on plan assets = Beginning plan assets   x   Settlement rate

Solution: Expected return on plan assets=Beginning plan assets $800,000 x Settlement rate 7% =$ 56,000

Third Step: Determine if there are unrecognized losses to amortize.

Application: Unrecognized losses are recognized if the accumulated losses exceed the larger of 10% of the beginning PBO or the beginning fair value of plan assets.

Solution: Beginning PBO $760,000   x 10% $76,000

            Beginning fair value of plan assets $800,000 x 10% $80,000

The beginning unrecognized losses are $160,000, which exceed 10% of the fair value of the plan assets.

Fourth Step: Compute the amount of loss recognition.

Application: Recognition = Threshold   —   Accumulated gains or losses
                            Average remaining service life

Solution: Recognition = Threshold $80,000   —   Accumulated losses $(160,000) = $4,000
                            Average remaining service life 20 years

Fifth Step: Compute the pension expense.

Application: Pension expense is computed as follows:

+	Service Cost
+	Interest Cost
-	Expected Return on Plan Assets
+	Amortization of Unrecognized Gains and Losses
+	Amortization of Prior Service Costs
+	Amortization of Transition Asset or Liability
=	Pension Expense

Solution:

Service Cost		$120,000
Interest Cost from Step 1		53,200
Less: Actual Return on Plan Assets	$64,000	
Deferred Gain	(8,000)	
Expected Return on Plan Assets from Step 2		(56,000)
Amortization of Unrecognized Losses		4,000
Pension Expense		$121,200

B.

First Step: Compute the ending fair value of plan assets.

Application: Plan assets consist of the following elements:

         Beginning plan assets at fair value

+   Actual return on plan assets
+   Contributions made by the plan sponsor
-     Benefits paid to beneficiaries
=   Ending plan assets at fair value

Solution:

Beginning plan assets at fair value	$800,000
Actual return on plan assets	64,000
Contributions made by the plan sponsor	90,000
Benefits paid to beneficiaries	(80,000)
Ending plan assets at fair value	$874,000

Second Step: Compute the Ending balance of the PBO.
Application: PBO consists of the following elements:

Beginning balance of the PBO
+   Service cost for the period
+   Interest cost for the period
+   Changes in the benefits from plan amendments
+   Changes in actuarial assumptions
-     Benefits paid to beneficiaries
=   Ending balance of PBO

Solution:

Beginning balance of the PBO	$760,000
Service cost for the period	120,000
Interest cost for the period	53,200
Changes in the benefits from plan amendments	100,000
Changes in actuarial assumptions	90,000
Benefits paid to beneficiaries	(80,000)
Ending balance of PBO	$1,043,200

Third Step: Determine the funded status of the pension plan.
Application: The funded status equals:

+   Accumulated benefit obligation
+   Effect of future compensation levels
=   Projected benefit obligation
-     Fair value of plan assets
=   Funded status

Solution:

Accumulated benefit obligation	$(895,200)	
Effect of future compensation levels	(148,000)	(plugged number)
Projected benefit obligation	(1,043,200)	

Fair value of plan assets	874,000
Funded status (underfunded)	$(169,200)

C.

First Step: Determine the ending balance sheet minimum liability.
Application: The formula for the minimum pension liability is:

+   Fair value of plan assets
-   Accumulated benefit obligation
=   Minimum pension liability

Solution:

Fair value of plan assets	$ 874,000
Accumulated benefit obligation	(895,200)
Minimum pension liability	$ (21,200)

or

PBO	$(1,043,200)
Fair value of plan assets	874,000
Underfunded status	(169,200)
Unrecognized losses	148,000
Minimum pension liability	$(21,200)

2. Pension expense and liability disclosures.

The Koller Corporation provides the following information on its pension plan for the year:

Ending accumulated benefit obligation	$812,500
Ending projected benefit obligation	937,500
Accrued pension liability	47,500
Fair value of plan assets	725,000
Net unrecognized obligation at *SFAS No. 87* adoption	125,000
Unrecognized prior service cost	135,000

Required: Determine the net minimum pension liability at year end.

First Step: Determine the minimum pension liability.
Application: The formula for the minimum pension liability is:

+   Fair value of plan assets
-   Accumulated benefit obligation
=   Minimum pension liability

Solution:

Fair value of plan assets	$725,000
Accumulated benefit obligation	812,500
Minimum pension liability	$ 87,500
or	

Pension benefit obligation	$937,500
Fair value of plan assets	725,000
	$ (212,500)
Unrecognized transition obligation	125,000
Unrecognized prior service cost	135,000
Adjustment to recognize minimum liability	(135,000)
Net liability on balance sheet	$ (87,500)

3.   Postretirement benefit expense and liability disclosures.

Mitro Corporation always extended its healthcare benefits to retirees. Upon the adoption of *SFAS No. 16* five years ago, the corporation had an unrecognized transition obligation of $480,000 for the unfunded plan, with an average remaining service years of 15 years. Information for the current year follows:

Service cost	$ 86,000
Benefit payments	42,000
Unrecognized prior service cost (12 years remaining)	168,000
Contributions by Mitro	100,000
Beginning accumulated postretirement benefit obligation	740,000
Settlement rate	7%

Required:
A. Determine the postretirement benefit expense for the current year.
B. Determine the ending accumulated postretirement benefit obligation.

A.
First Step: Determine the interest cost.
Application: Interest cost = Beginning APBO x Settlement rate
Solution: Interest cost = Beginning APBO $740,000 x Settlement rate 7% = $51,800

Second Step: Determine the amortization of unrecognized prior service cost.
Application: Recognition of PSC = Increase (decrease) in PSC
                                     Average remaining service life

Solution: Recognition of PSC = Increase (decrease) in PSC $168,000 = $14,000

Average remaining service life 12 years

Third Step: Determine the amortization of transition obligation.
Application: Amortization = <u>Transition asset or obligation</u>
                              Average remaining service life

Solution: Amortization = <u>Transition asset or obligation $480,000</u> = $32,000
                              Average remaining service life 15 years

Fourth Step: Compute the postretirement benefit expense
Application: The formula for postretirement benefit expense with unfunded plans is:
    +   Service Cost
    +   Interest Cost
    +   Amortization of Prior Service Costs
    +   Amortization of Transition Asset or Liability
    =   Postretirement Benefit Expense
Solution:
    Service cost $86,000
    Interest cost from Step 1   51,800
    Amortization of unrecognized PSC from Step 2   14,000
    Amortization of transition obligation from Step 3 <u>32,000</u>
    Postretirement benefit expense $<u>183,800</u>

B.
First Step: Determine the ending APBO balance.
Application: The formula to compute the APBO is:
              Beginning balance of the APBO
    +   Service cost for the period
    +   Interest cost for the period
    +   Changes in the benefits from plan amendments
    +   Changes in actuarial assumptions
    -    Benefits paid to beneficiaries
    =   Ending balance of APBO

Solution: Beginning balance of the APBO $740,000
              Service cost for the period   86,000
              Interest cost for the period   51,800
              Changes in the benefits from plan amendments   0
              Changes in actuarial assumptions   0

Benefits paid to beneficiaries	(42,000)
Ending balance of APBO	$835,800

Test Yourself

True or False Questions

T   F   1.   A defined benefit plan specifies the formula for determining the amount of cash that will be paid out to an employee after retirement.

T   F   2.   In a defined contribution pension plan, the employee is always required to contribute to the plan.

T   F   3.   Funding is the term that applies to the employee qualifying for pension benefits.

T   F   4.   The increase in the discounted present value of the pension benefits attributable to an additional year's employment is the service cost.

T   F   5.   The trustee funds the pension plan by transferring assets to the legal entity that has custody of plan assets.

T   F   6.   The plan sponsor distributes pension payments to retired plan beneficiaries.

T   F   7.   *SFAS No. 87* requires the same interest rate be used for computing both the service cost and interest cost components of pension expense.

T   F   8.   Assumed discount rates should reflect the rates at which pension benefits could effectively be settled.

T   F   9.   The actual return on pension plan assets is always the same as the expected return in any given year.

T   F   10.   The impact of asset gain or loss deferral is to reduce or increase pension expense by the unexpected return differential.

T   F   11.   The projected benefit obligation is the discounted present value of the expected pension payments over future years.

T   F   12.   The prior service cost is the dollar amount of increase in the projected benefit obligation due to plan amendments.

T   F   13.   *SFAS No. 87* uses a smoothing device by deferring initial adjustments for pension adjustments and bringing them into pension expense over a series of years.

T F 14. Legislation and income tax rules have little influence on pension plan funding.

T F 15. The pension plan assets and liability appear on the balance sheet of the sponsor.

T F 16. When a pension plan is seriously underfunded and has insufficient funds to pay retirees, the Pension Benefit Guarantee Corporation pays the promised benefits.

T F 17. The projected pension benefit obligation is the present value of the pension liability without considering future pay raises.

T F 18. The inclusion of the underfunded amount of pension liability in the balance sheet is a red flag regarding potential cash flow problems.

T F 19. *SFAS No. 106* addressed the issue of the off-balance sheet liabilities for other post-retirement benefits such as health care.

T F 20. The FASB permitted adoption of *SFAS No. 106* by allowing the amortization of the transition obligation on a straight-line basis over the shorter of the average remaining service period of active participants or 20 years.

T F 21. Pension expense consists of service cost, interest cost, return on plan assets, and net amortization and deferral.

T F 22. The reporting rules for postretirement benefit plans are completely different than pension accounting rules.

Multiple-Choice Questions
Select the best answer from those provided.

_____ 1. An IRS approved pension plan that allows the firm to contribute a percentage of an employee's salary to the plan is a
   a. defined benefit pension plan.
   b. defined contribution pension plan.
   c. government provided pension plan.
   d. defined postretirement benefit plan.

_____ 2. An IRS approved pension plan that allows the firm to make contributions to provide for payment to each employee based on a percentage of salary times the number of years of service is a
   a. ꞏ defined benefit pension plan.
   b. defined contribution pension plan.
   c. government provided pension plan.
   d. defined postretirement benefit plan.

_____ 3.   The application of the matching principle to the expensing of pension costs is
           complicated by
           a. the historical cost principle.
           b. materiality.
           c. periodicity.
           d. uncertainty.

_____ 4.   The determination of specific expense accruals for defined benefit pension plans
           rely upon actuarial assumptions and
           a. future values.
           b. future cash flows.
           c. present values.
           d. corporate profits.

_____ 5.   A change in the pension liability caused by one additional year of employee
           service is
           a. interest cost.
           b. service cost.
           c. amortization cost.
           d. return on plan assets.

_____ 6.   The beginning liability of the pension plan times the assumed earning rate of the
           plan is the
           a. interest cost component.
           b. service cost component.
           c. annual fee component.
           d. present value component.

_____ 7.   The reduction in pension expense created by the expected earnings of the plan is
           the
           a. interest cost component.
           b. service cost component.
           c. annual fee component.
           d. return on plan assets component.

_____ 8.   The pension plan trustee
           a. funds the plan.
           b. disburses pension benefits.
           c. is liable for making plan contributions.
           d. receives benefits upon retirement of employees.

_____ 9.   The pension plan sponsor
a. funds the plan.
b. disburses pension plan benefits.
c. receives benefits upon retirement of employees.
d. reports the assets and liabilities of the plan.

_____ 10.   According to *SFAS No. 87,* the discount rate used for pension plans is required to
be the
a. prime rate of New York banks.
b. current Treasury Bill rate.
c. rate at which pension benefits could be effectively settled.
d. future prime rate.

_____ 11.   Pension expense may be smoothed over time and this process is
a. prohibited by the SEC.
b. prohibited by GAAP.
c. illegal.
d. allowed through amortization and deferral.

_____ 12.   When a corporation amends a pension plan to increase benefits to employee plan
participants, the amendment creates
a. transition asset.
b. transition liability.
c. future service cost.
d. prior service cost.

_____ 13.   A transition asset is created if the fair value of the plan assets at the time of
adoption of *SFAS No. 87*
a. exceeds the pension benefit obligation.
b. is equal to the pension benefit obligation.
c. is below the pension benefit obligation.
d. is below the accumulated benefit obligation.

_____ 14.   A plan sponsor is required to fund annually a minimum of the
a. pension expense.
b. service cost.
c. interest cost.
d. pension liability.

_____ 15.   The assets and liabilities of a pension plan are reported on the balance sheet of the plan trustee at
  a. historical cost.
  b. discounted future value.
  c. market value.
  d. present value.

_____ 16.   When pension expense exceeds pension funding, a/an
  a. accrued pension asset arises.
  b. accrued pension liability arises.
  c. deferred pension asset arises.
  d. deferred pension liability arises.

_____ 17.   Disclosure of the funded status of a pension plan in the form of footnotes is
  a. required by GAAP
  b. encouraged by GAAP.
  c. suggested by GAAP.
  d. optional.

_____ 18.   Cash flow problems of a corporation may be suggested when the firm's pension plan is
  a. overfunded.
  b. slightly overfunded.
  c. underfunded.
  d. approved.

_____ 19.   If the accumulated benefit obligation exceeds the present value of plan assets, the plan is
  a. severely overfunded.
  b. severely underfunded.
  c. slightly underfunded.
  d. slightly overfunded.

_____ 20.   Postretirement benefit plans are
  a. not required to be funded.
  b. required to be funded up to 50% of the projected benefit obligation.
  c. required to be funded up to 75% of the projected benefit obligation.
  d. required to be funded.

_____ 21.   The postretirement benefits expense of any postretirement plan must be based upon
a. past salary amounts of the employees.
b. future salary amounts of employees.
c. current benefit amounts for employees.
d. future benefit amounts for employees.

_____ 22.   The immediate recognition of the transition asset or transition obligation under *SFAS No. 106* is classified as a/an
a. extraordinary gain or loss item.
b. ordinary gain or loss item.
c. cumulative effect of a change in accounting principle.
d. discontinued operation.

_____ 23.   The amortization of the transition asset or obligation under *SFAS No. 106* takes place over
a. 20 years.
b. the greater of 20 years or the average remaining service period of active plan participants, on a straight-line basis.
c. the lesser of 20 years or the average remaining service period of active plan participants, on a straight-line basis.
d. 25 years.

_____ 24.   Studies have shown that a more reliable indicator of security prices for firms with pension plans is the
a. accumulated pension assets.
b. projected benefit obligation.
c. accumulated benefit obligation.
d. vested benefit obligation.

Exercises

1.   Treasury International created a defined benefit pension plan in its fifth year of operation. The following information is available for the plan in Year 9:

Service cost	$143,000
Actual and expected gain on plan assets	12,500
Expected return on plan assets	29,000
Amortization of unrecognized prior service costs	4,500
Annual interest on pension obligation	42,500

Required: Compute Treasury's pension expense for the Year 9 income statement.

2.   Green Incorporated, provided the auditors with the following information concerning the defined benefit pension plan for Year 4:

Service cost	$590,000
Interest cost	398,000
Actual return plan assets	172,000
Beginning of the year fair value of plan assets	1,350,000
Accumulated unrecognized losses	(200,000)
Settlement rate	7%
Average remaining service years	10

Required: Compute Green's pension expense for the Year 8 income statement.

_____

_____

_____

_____

_____

_____

_____

3.   Rossi Corporation instituted a defined benefit pension plan soon after organization. The following information is available for the current year:

Beginning projected benefit obligation	$990,000
Service costs for current year	214,000
Actual return on plan assets	146,000
Pension benefits paid during the year	98,000
Settlement rate	6%
Changes in actuarial assumptions	(54,000)
Changes in plan benefits	330,000
Employer contributions	400,000

Required: Compute the ending projected benefit obligation at year-end.

_____

_____

_____

_____

_____

_____

4.   Rose Industries has a defined benefit pension plan with the following information available for the current year:

Beginning fair value of plan assets	$387,500
Service costs for current year	25,000
Actual return on plan assets	24,000
Pension benefits paid during the year	20,500
Settlement rate	8%
Changes in actuarial assumptions	12,500
Changes in plan benefits	15,000
Employer contributions	47,500

Required: Determine the fair value of the plan assets at year-end.

5.   Kent International provides postretirement benefits for its employees.   The following information is for the current year:

Service cost	$160,000
Benefit payments for beneficiaries	47,000
Interest on accumulated postretirement benefit obligation	28,000
Unrecognized transition obligation balance (10 yrs. remaining)	87,500

Required: Determine Kent's current postretirement benefit expense.

Solutions

Answers to True or False Questions

True answers: 1, 4, 7, 8, 10, 11, 12, 13, 16, 18, 19, 21
False answers explained:

2. In a defined contribution pension plan, the employee is <u>sometimes</u> required to contribute to the plan.
3. <u>Vesting</u> is the term that applies to the employee qualifying for pension benefits.
5. The <u>sponsor</u> funds the pension plan by transferring assets to the legal entity that has custody of plan assets.
6. The <u>trustee</u> distributes pension payments to retired plan beneficiaries.
9. The actual return on pension plan assets <u>can differ markedly from</u> the expected return in any given year.
14. Legislation and income tax rules have <u>a strong</u> influence on pension plan funding.
15. The pension plan assets and liability appear on the balance sheet of the <u>plan trustee</u>.
17. The <u>accumulated</u> pension benefit obligation is the present value of the pension liability without considering future pay raises.
20. The FASB permitted adoption of *SFAS No. 106* by allowing the amortization of the transition obligation on a straight-line basis over the <u>longer</u> of the average remaining service period of active participants or 20 years.
22. The reporting rules for postretirement benefit plans <u>closely parallel</u> pension accounting rules.

Answers to Multiple-Choice Questions

1.	B	6.	A	11.	D	16.	B	21.	D
2.	A	7.	D	12.	D	17.	A	22.	C
3.	D	8.	B	13.	A	18.	C	23.	B
4.	C	9.	A	14.	C	19.	B	24.	C
5.	B	10.	C	15.	D	20.	A		

Answers to Exercises

1.
Service Cost	$143,000
Interest Cost	42,500
Expected Return on Plan Assets	(29,000)
Net Amortization of Prior Service Costs	4,500
Pension Expense	$161,000

2.   Service Cost $590,000
      Interest Cost   398,000
      Less: Actual Return on Plan Assets $172,000
      Deferred Gain   (77,500)
      Expected Return on Plan Assets ($1,350,000 x .07)   (94,500)
      Amortization and Deferral of Unrecognized Losses   (6,500)*
      Pension Expense $887,000
      *Corridor is 10% of $1,350,000 = $ 135,000
      Prior Losses   (200,000)
       Subject to Amortization $ (65,000) / 10 Years = $(6,500)

3.   Beginning balance of pension benefit obligation $990,000
      Service cost   214,000
      Interest cost ($990,000 x .06)   59,400
      Changes in benefits   330,000
      Changes in actuarial assumptions   (54,000)
      Benefits paid to retirees   (98,000)
      Ending balance of pension benefit obligation $1,441,000

4.   Beginning balance of plan assets $387,500
      Actual return on plan assets   24,000
      Contributions by employer   47,500
      Benefits paid to retirees   (20,500)
      Ending balance of plan assets $438,500

5.   Service cost $160,000
      Interest cost   28,000
      Net amortization of transition obligation   8,750
      Postretirement Benefits Expense $196,750

CHAPTER 15

FINANCIAL REPORTING FOR OWNERS' EQUITY

Chapter Review

Owner's equity represents the claims of the owners on assets. Owners' equity is comprised of:

1. contributions by owners
2. net earnings generated by the entity's operating activities
3. gains and losses on investing and financing activities
4. distributions to owners.

The **entity view** of the firm is:
Assets = Liabilities + Equity
Capital deployed = Capital sources

Prevailing GAAP hold the **proprietary view** of the firm:
Assets - Liabilities = Equity
Net Capital deployed = Owners' capital

Learning Objective 1: Why some financing transactions - like debt repurchases - generate reported gains and losses while others - like stock repurchases - do not.

Under the proprietary view of the firm, owners are undistinguished from the entity. Therefore, there can be no gains or losses from transactions with owners or insiders. Consequently, dividends are not expenses and treasury stock transactions do not produce a gain or loss. Transactions with outsiders, such as lenders, can produce revenues, gains, expenses, or losses. While dividends paid to insiders (owners) are not expenses, interest payments to bondholders (outsiders) are expenses.

Financing transactions can be either debt or equity. We looked at debt financing in Chapter 11. Equity financing takes two basic forms:

1. Common stock
2. Preferred stock

Common stock represents the basic residual ownership in a corporation. Common shareholders usually have voting rights, enjoy **limited**

liability, and experience a limitation of loss equal to the original investment if the stock was issued at **par value** or above. Firms place an arbitrary par value on the stock upon issue, which has no relationship to market value.

The journal entry to record a common stock issue is:

DR Cash	= cash proceeds from issue
CR Common Stock	= par value x shares issued
CR Paid-in Capital in Excess of Par Value	= cash - par value

If the firm later reacquires the stock, it becomes **treasury stock**. This entry records the reacquisition:

DR Treasury Stock	= cost of the treasury shares
CR Cash	= amount paid by the firm to the shareholder

The **Treasury Stock** account is a **contra-stockholders' equity account**, not an asset. It always has a debit balance that is equal to the cost of any stock held. If the stock is reissued, the following entry occurs:

DR Cash	= cash received
CR Treasury Stock	= cost of treasury stock shares
CR Paid-in Capital in Excess of Par	= cash — cost

There is no gain or loss recorded upon the purchase or resale of treasury stock because such transactions are with insiders or owners of the corporation. Many companies repurchase stock. (**See Demonstration Problem 1**)

Firms repurchase common stock for a various reasons:
1.   To protect surplus cash from **corporate raiders**.
2.   To return cash to stockholders at capital gains rates instead of ordinary tax rates.
3.   To take advantage of undervalued shares.
4.   To increase the earnings per share.
5.   To distribute shares to executives in **stock option plans**.
6.   To distribute shares to employees in **employee stock option plans** (ESOPs).

Corporations accomplish treasury stock purchases several ways.
1. The most common is an **Open Market Repurchase** where the company purchases treasury stock in the open market.

2. **Fixed-price** offer — the firm announces both the number of shares it desires to repurchase and the price it is willing to pay.

3. **Dutch auction** — the firm announces the number of share it desires to repurchase and a range of prices it is willing to pay. Shareholders

respond with the number of shares they are willing to sell at a specific price. The firm selects the lowest price that will deliver the number of shares desired. All stocks are repurchased at the same price.

Firms typically repurchase stock at 23% higher than market value but after the repurchase, the stock tends to increase by 45% more than the market over the next four years. There is a cash drain when the company repurchases stock and distributes the shares to employees through ESOPs because the firm pays more than market for the stock and resells it to employees at amounts below market value.

Firms also issue preferred stock. Preferred stockholders enjoy two preferences over common stockholders — preference in dividends and liquidation. However preferred stock usually does not have voting rights. Preferred dividends must be paid in full before the corporation pays common dividends. In a liquidation, the preferred shareholders must be paid at least the stated value of shares before common shareholders receive any distribution.

Preferred stock usually has these characteristics:
1.   **Cumulative** preferred stock — If for any reason a dividend is not declared, the dividends accumulate and must be paid in full before any common dividends are paid. If a dividend is passed with noncumulative preferred stock, it will never be paid.
2.   **Nonparticipating** stock — Dividends are limited to the stated dividend rate. **Participating** stock can share in profits above the stated dividend rate with the common stockholders or can be **adjustable-rate** preferred for which the rate is adjusted based on some market factor.

Investors buy preferred stock because:
1.   preferred stock offers a fixed return that is usually above money market or CD rates; and
2.   corporate investors can exclude 70% to 80% of domestic dividends from taxable income, but interest earned on debt securities is fully taxable.

Corporations issue preferred stock because:
1.   Poorer corporations consider preferred stock less risky than debt because preferred dividends can be skipped without precipitating bankruptcy.

2.   Companies with a history of operating losses do not need tax deductions for interest payments.

3.   Preferred stock is equity capital and improves solvency ratios. Preferred stock can be issued if the corporation cannot issue additional debt.

Learning Objective 3:
Why some preferred stock resembles debt, and how preferred stock gets reported on financial statements.

Preferred stock's fixed dividends, preference in dividends and liquidation, and nonvoting status give it some characteristics of debt. **Mandatorily redeemable preferred stock** is even more like debt — so much so that the SEC requires that redeemable preferred stock not be listed as equity on the balance sheet. It is shown on a separate line between liabilities and equity. *SFAS No. 47* requires firms to disclose the amount of redemption requirements for each of the five years following the balance sheet date, similar to the requirements for long-term debt. Some redeemable preferred stock is convertible into common stock, so it may contain elements of equity.

A trust preferred security is a new form of mandatorily redeemable preferred stock that enables a corporation to obtain the tax deduction associated with interest expense while making dividend payments. The conduit for such activity is a business trust.

Learning Objective 4:
How and when retained earnings limits a company's distribution to common stockholders.

State law governs corporate distributions to protect creditors' and others' claims against a corporation. Remember that stockholders are afforded limited liability in the corporate form. The distinction between **contributed capital** and **earned capital** becomes important when deciding dividend policy. Some states allow only earned capital to be paid in dividends, and others allow earned capital plus paid-in capital in excess of par value. Many states have adopted the **1984 Revised Model Business Corporation Act,** which allows dividends to be paid as long as the corporation is **solvent.** This act defines **solvency** as a condition when the fair value of the assets exceeds the fair value of the liabilities after a distribution to stockholders. A company could be insolvent on the balance sheet and still meet the requirements under the 1984 act. To judge the firm's legal ability to pay dividends might now require current value information not provided in GAAP financial statements.

FYI...

Stock dividends and splits also play a role in cash dividend distributions. Stock dividends reduce retained earnings exactly like cash dividends, but stock splits do not. **Small stock dividends** (of less than 25% of the outstanding number of shares) reduce retained earnings by the fair value of the stock issued. Large stock dividends or splits (more

A wise board of directors considers two factors before declaring dividends — first the legality of the distribution and second the cash available to pay the dividend.

Learning Objective 5:
How to calculate basic earnings per share (EPS) and fully diluted earnings per share (EPS), and whether EPS is a meaningful number.

FYI. . .
Stock options arise from employee compensation. **Stock warrants** are often "sweeteners" used to sell bonds or preferred stock.

FYI. . .
Securities are only included in diluted EPS when they are dilutive. **Anti-dilutive** issues are ignored. As a rule, a security is anti-dilutive when its option price is above the current market price.

than 25% of the outstanding shares) can be treated as a dividend or a split. A **large stock dividend** reduces retained earnings by the par value of the distributed shares. A **stock split** reduces the par value and increases the number of shares proportionately. Stock dividends reduce the capacity to pay cash dividends in the future. **(See Demonstration Problem 2.)**

Earnings per share (EPS) is one of the most often quoted ratios of a firm. Analysts view firm value from a share perspective and earnings per share is important to the per share valuation. Two EPS calculations are made — **basic earnings per share** and **diluted earnings per share**. A **simple capital structure** exists when a corporation has no convertible debt or preferred stock and no outstanding options or warrants. A simple capital structure requires only the computation of basic EPS. A **complex capital structure** exists when there are either **convertible securities** or outstanding **options** or **warrants**. A complex capital structure requires computation of both basic and diluted EPS.
To compute **basic earnings per share**:

$$\text{EPS} = \frac{\text{Net income — preferred dividends}}{\text{Weighted average number of common shares outstanding}}$$

The three steps to compute basic earnings per share are:
1. Determine net income.
2. Determine the preferred dividend requirement.
3. Compute the weighted average number of common shares outstanding.

To compute **diluted earnings per share**:

$$\text{Diluted EPS} = \frac{\text{Net income - preferred dividends + After-tax adjustments due to dilutive instruments}}{\text{Weighted average number of common shares outstanding + Newly issuable shares due to dilutive financial instruments}}$$

(See Demonstration Problem 3.)
Common stockholders enjoy a preemptive right to have their ownership percentage protected. Stockholders waive this right to allow convertible bonds and convertible preferred stock or stock options and warrants to be issued. These securities will lower or dilute the ownership percentage of the existing stockholders. Before these conversion privileges or options are exercised, the dilutive effect of the securities is not included in basic earnings per share. That is why we compute diluted earnings per share — to warn potential investors of the "worst case scenario" if

all of the options and conversions were made. All conversions and option exercises are assumed to happen at the beginning of the year under *SFAS No. 128*'s **if converted method**.

Various dilutive securities change the equation in the following ways:
1.   Convertible preferred stock:
    a. Numerator — The preferred dividend becomes zero.
    b. Denominator — Add the number of common shares that result from the conversion to the weighted average shares outstanding.
2.   Convertible bonds:
    a. Numerator — Add the after-tax interest expense back to net income, because "if converted" at the beginning of the year there would be no interest expense.
    b. Denominator — Add the number of common shares that result from the conversion to the weighted average shares outstanding.
3.   Options and Warrants:
    a. Numerator — No effect.
    b. Denominator — Add the number of common shares created by the options or warrants. Subtract the amount of treasury stock the firm could purchase (at market price) with the proceeds of the option or warrant exercise. This is the **treasury stock method**.
(See Demonstration Problem 4.)

Earnings per share is one of the most often quoted statistics for a firm but suffers from several problems:
1.   EPS is not related to the amount of capital required to produce it.
2.   EPS is not comparable among companies because each have different capital structures.
3.   EPS does not reflect the profitability of the firm relative to revenue.
4.   EPS is subject to manipulation with treasury stock repurchases and reissues.

Learning Objective 6:
What GAAP says about

employee stock options, and why GAAP's accounting treatment has been controversial.

Contractual agreements to purchase equity shares in a firm at a specified price (usually below market value) are **stock options**. U. S. corporations often compensate executives and other employees with a combination of cash and stock options. The typical employee stock option provides the employee the right to purchase a specified number of common shares at a specified price (**exercise price**) over some specified time period. The exercise price is usually greater than or equal to the market price of the underlying shares at the time the options are issued.

Companies use stock options to augment cash compensation for several reasons:
1.   Options help align employees' interests with those of the stockholders.
2.   "Start-up" high-growth companies are often "cash starved" and cannot afford to pay competitive cash salaries.
3.   As long as the exercise price is equal to or greater than the stock price when the option is issue, the compensation is not taxable to the employee until the option is exercised.

APB No. 25 offered no mechanism for estimating the value of stock options granted as compensation to employees. Options issued with an exercise price equal to or above the market price of the underlying common shares were assumed to have no value for compensation expense purposes. During the 1970s the Black-Scholes option pricing theory evolved into practice. Despite this development, stock options issued as compensation were generally treated as valueless except in rare instances. Many financial experts considered the presumptions of *APB No. 25* to be incorrect. These beliefs triggered the FASB to reconsider the accounting for stock options in 1984.

Sentiment in the business community soon shifted to strong and widespread opposition to the FASB initiative when it became clear that the initiative would require expenses to be recognized on the income statement when stock options were granted. Critics cited four issues:
1.   appropriate income measurement;
2.   compliance with contract terms and restrictions;
3.   legality of corporate distributions to owners; and
4.   linkage to equity valuation.

The widespread opposition to the FASB proposal caused the FASB to allow a choice of accounting methods:
1. Companies could continue using the *APB No. 25* approach and rarely if ever recognize the compensation expense.
2. Companies could measure the fair value of the stock option and charge this amount to expense.

SFAS No. 123 represents a political compromise. The FASB was unanimous in its belief that expenses are incurred when companies grant stock options to employees as a part of a compensation package. Nevertheless, companies are not required to record this expense in the financial statements. Instead, the compromise allows firms to disclose the fair amount of stock-based compensation in a footnote to the financial statements. **(See Demonstration Problem 5.)**

Learning Objective 7: How and why GAAP understates the true cost of convertible debt, and what to do about this understatement.

APB No. 14 permits companies to record debt conversion either by the:
1. book value method which records the newly issued stock at the book value of the debt retired; or
2. market value method which records newly issued shares at their current market value. Any difference between the market value and the conversion privilege is recognized as a loss or (gain) on conversion.

Convertible debt provides investors the upside potential of common stock and the safety net of debt. Interest rates on convertible debt are very low for this reason. The option value of the conversion feature compensates for the lower interest paid to the investors. Interest expense may therefore be understated because GAAP ignores the value of the conversion option.

Learning Objective 8: Why employee stock ownership plans (ESOPs) have become popular, and what they mean for statement readers.

An employee stock ownership plan (ESOP) is an employee benefit pension plan that invests primarily in the common stock of the employer company. To establish an ESOP, the company first sets up a trust to hold the ESOP assets and typically makes contributions of up to 25% of payroll for employees into the plan. Stock contributed to, or purchased by the trust, is allocated to the accounts of employees who have met certain eligibility requirements.

ESOPs are attractive to employer companies for the following reasons:
1. ESOPs have considerable tax advantages.
2. ESOPs can provide a source of low-cost debt financing for firms.
3. ESOPs have been widely used as a takeover defense since the

shares are impervious to a buyout.

Financial statement readers must be alert for the following points when examining ESOPs:

1.   ESOP debt is not hidden in financial statement footnotes as an off-balance sheet item because it is shown on the balance sheet like any other debt.

2.   ESOP accounting produces an unusual balance sheet item called the Employee Stock Plan for undistributed shares held by the trust.

3.   Some analysts argue that ESOP accounting understates the true cost of employee compensation because dividends paid on the ESOP held stock are not recorded as an expense.

Glossary of Terms

Additional Paid-in Capital

The difference between the issue price and the par value of a share of stock.

Basic Earnings per Common Share

EPS is equal to net income minus preferred dividends divided by weighted average number of common shares outstanding.

Call Option

An option that provides the holder with the right to buy shares at a fixed price before a specified date in the future, usually three to nine months.

Complex Capital Structure

A financing structure that includes either securities that are convertible into common stock, or options and warrants which entitle holders to obtain common stock under specified conditions.

Contributed Capital

All increases to shareholders' equity from owners.

Conversion Price

The dollar value at which debt or preferred stock can be converted into common stock.

Convertible Securities

Corporate securities, usually preferred stock or bonds, that are exchangeable for a set number of another security (usually common shares) at a prestated exchange rate.

Cumulative Preferred Stock

Cumulative preferred stock's dividend accumulates if not declared so that all undeclared past and current preferred dividends must be paid before the common stockholders are entitled to a dividend.

Diluted Earnings Per Share	A conservative measure of the earnings flow to each share of stock, presuming the maximum possible new share creation, and the minimum earnings flow to each share.
Dutch Auction	A method for repurchasing a company's shares in which the company announces the number of shares it is willing to repurchase and a range of prices within which it is willing to pay.
Earned Capital	Earned capital is the retained earnings of the corporation.
Employee Stock Option	A call option that is often three to five years in duration.
Entity View	The view of the firm that the assets owned by the firm are important, not whether the resource was provided by owners or creditors. The entity view is expressed by the equation: Assets = Liabilities + Owners' Equity.
Fixed-Price Offer	A method for repurchasing company shares in which the company announces both the number of shares it wishes to repurchase and the price it is willing to pay.
Grant Date	The date when the terms are mutually agreed upon and stock options are awarded to individual employees.
Paid-in Capital in Excess of Par Value	The difference between the issue price and the par value of a share of stock.
Participating Preferred Stock	Participation entitles preferred shareholders to share in profits above and beyond their declared dividend by sharing with the common stockholders.
Par Value	Refers to the nominal or face value of a security, having no relation to the market value of the security.
Preferred Stock	An equity instrument that has preferences to dividend payments and the distribution of corporate assets in liquidation.
Proprietary View	The view of the firm that the firm and its owners are the same. The proprietary view is expressed by the equation: Assets - Liabilities = Owners Equity.
Simple Capital Structure	A capital structure in which a company has no convertible securities and no options or warrants outstanding.
Subscription Warrant	A security issued with a bond or preferred stock, that entitles the holder to buy a specified number of shares of common stock at a specified price.
Treasury Stock	Shares of a company's own stock that have been bought back by the company.

Demonstration Problems

A. Recording stock transactions.

Haley Corporation was organized on January 2, Year 1 with 1,000,000 shares of $2 par value common stock authorized. Haley also had 500,000 shares of $10 par value, 10% cumulative preferred stock authorized. During Year 1 the company completed the following transactions:

January 10	Issued 200,000 shares of common at $12 per share
March 12	Issued 50,000 shares of common at $15 per share
March 18	Issued 150,000 shares of preferred stock at $18 per share
June 15	Sold subscriptions to 50,000 shares of common at $20 per share
August 30	Purchased 20,000 shares common stock in the open market at $16 per share
December 23	Sold the 20,000 shares purchased on August 30, at $22 per share
December 30	Collected the subscriptions receivable and issued the stock.

Required: Prepare the journal entries to record the stock transactions.

First Step: Analyze each transaction. Prepare the entries to record original stock issues.
Application: Record each transaction according to GAAP. Record common stock into the Common Stock account at par value. Amounts paid for the stock over the par value are recorded into the Paid-in-Capital in Excess of Par Value account.
Solution: <u>Year 1</u>

January 10	DR Cash	2,400,000	
	CR Common Stock		400,000
	CR Paid-in Capital in Excess of Par Value — Common		2,000,000
March 12	DR Cash	750,000	
	CR Common Stock		100,000
	CR Paid-in Capital in Excess of Par Value — Common		650,000
March 18	DR Cash	2,700,000	
	CR Preferred Stock		1,500,000
	CR Paid-in Capital in Excess of Par Value — Preferred		1,200,000

Second Step: Prepare the entries to record the subscription of stock.
Application: Subscribed stock is recorded as a receivable and the par value is recorded in an account titled Common Stock Subscribed, an adjunct stockholders' equity account. When fully paid for, the stock is issued and the par value is credited to the Common Stock account and

removed from the Common Stock Subscribed account.

Solution: <u>Year 1</u>

June 15	DR Subscriptions Receivable	1,000,000	
	CR Common Stock Subscribed		100,000
	CR Paid-in Capital in Excess of Par Value — Common		900,000
December 30	DR Cash	1,000,000	
	CR Subscriptions Receivable		1,000,000
December 30	DR Common Stock Subscribed	100,000	
	CR Common Stock		100,000

Third Step: Prepare the entries to record the treasury stock transactions.

Application: Treasury stock is recorded at cost in the contra-equity account Treasury Stock. When resold, the cost of the treasury stock is credited to the Treasury Stock account and any excess of reissue price over cost is credited to Paid-in Capital in Excess of Par Value.

Solution: <u>Year 1</u>

August 30	DR Treasury Stock	320,000	
	CR Cash		320,000
December 23	DR Cash	440,000	
	CR Treasury Stock		320,000
	CR Paid-in Capital in Excess of Par Value — Common	120,000	

B. Dividend distributions.

The Unis Company reported the following stockholders' equity at January 2, Year 8:

Preferred Stock, $50 par value, 10%, cumulative, 50,000 shares issued and outstanding	$2,500,000
Common Stock, $1 par value, 1,000,000 shares issued and outstanding	1,000,000
Additional Paid-In Capital	3,000,000
Retained Earnings	4,500,000
Total Stockholders' Equity	$11,000,000

The Unis Company reported net income of $6,000,000 for Year 8. The company declared and paid the preferred dividend for the year and also declared and paid a $1 per share dividend on the common stock. The preferred stock had no dividends in arrears. Later, the company declared and paid a 10% stock dividend. At the time of the stock dividend, the market price of the stock was $7 per share.

Required:

A.   Prepare journal entries to record the three different dividend declarations and payments.

B.   Assume the preferred stock had two years dividends in arrears. Prepare the entries for the preferred stock dividend assuming that the arrears dividends would be paid along with the current year's dividends.

A.

First Step: Analyze the preferred dividend to be paid and prepare the entry to record the declaration of the preferred dividend.

Application: When the dividend is declared, reduce retained earnings and recognize a current liability for the par value of the preferred times the dividend rate times the number of shares outstanding.

Solution:

DR Retained Earnings	250,000	
CR Preferred Dividends Payable		250,000

$50 x 10% x 50,000 shares = $250,000

Second Step: Prepare the entry to record the payment of the preferred dividend.

Application: Payment of the dividend reduces the current liability.

Solution:

DR Preferred Dividends Payable	250,000	
CR Cash		250,000

Third Step: Analyze the common dividend to be paid and prepare the entry to record the declaration of the common dividend.

Application: When the dividend is declared, reduce retained earnings and recognize a current liability for the dividend amount times the number of shares outstanding.

Solution:

DR Retained Earnings	1,000,000	
CR Common Dividends Payable		1,000,000

1,000,000 shares x $1 per share.

Fourth Step: Prepare the entry to record the payment of the common dividend.

Application: Payment of the dividend removes the current liability.

Solution:

DR Common Dividends Payable	1,000,000	
CR Cash		1,000,000

Fifth Step: Analyze the common stock dividend to be declared.

Application: Small stock dividends are dividends of less than 25 % of the outstanding stock. This 10% dividend is a small stock dividend and should be recorded at market value. To compute the number of shares to be issued, multiply the outstanding number of shares times 10%.
Solution:
> 10% of 1,000,000 shares = 100,000 shares x $7 = $700,000

Sixth Step: Prepare the entry to record the declaration of the common stock dividend.
Application: Debit Retained Earnings for the market value of the stock dividend and record Common Stock Dividend Distributable (an adjunct stockholders' equity account) for the par value and Paid-in Capital in Excess of Par Value for the difference between the market value and par.
Solution:

DR Retained Earnings	700,000	
CR Common Stock Dividend Distributable		100,000
CR Paid-in Capital in Excess of Par Value — Common		600,000
100,000 shares x $7 = $700,000		

Seventh Step: Record the common stock distribution.
Application: To record the distribution, credit Common Stock for the par value and debit Common Stock Dividend Distributable.
Solution:

DR Common Stock Dividend Distributable	100,000	
CR Common Stock		100,000

B.
First Step: Determine the total amount of the dividends in arrears.
Application: Dividends in Arrears = Dividend per Year x Number of Years in Arrears.
Solution: Dividends in Arrears=Dividend per Year $250,000 x Number of Years 2 = $500,000

Second Step: Determine the amount available for dividends.
Application: Review the amount of dividends declared and compare to the Retained Earnings account.

Solution:	
Preferred dividends in arrears	$ 500,000
Current preferred dividend	250,000
Common dividend	1,000,000
Total dividends	$1,750,000

Retained Earnings are sufficient for dividends in arrears and the current year's dividend.

Third Step: Record the journal entry to record the declaration of the preferred dividends.
Application: When the dividend is declared, reduce retained earnings and recognize a current liability.

Solution:

DR Retained Earnings	750,000	
CR Preferred Dividends Payable		750,000

$50 x 10% x 50,000 shares x 3 years = $750,000
(Three years for the 2 years in arrears and the current year.)

Fourth Step: Record the journal entry to record the payment of the dividends.
Application: Payment of the dividend reduces the current liability.
Solution:

DR Preferred Dividends Payable	750,000	
CR Cash		750,000

C. Basic and diluted earnings per share.

The following information is from the year-end balance sheet and income statement of Southridge, Inc. for Year 4:

8% Bonds Payable (at par)	$14,000,000
Common Stock, $10 Par value	16,000,000
9% Preferred stock, $50 Par value	8,000,000
Treasury Stock (50,000 shares at cost)	(6,000,000)
Net Income	4,400,000

The only change in common shares during Year 4 was a sale of 200,000 shares on June 1 and the repurchase of the treasury stock on October 1. Each $1,000 bond is convertible into 20 shares of common stock. The common stock had a market value of $65 per share at the end of the year. There are no preferred dividends in arrears. Southridge experiences a 40% tax rate.

Required:
A.   Compute basic and diluted earnings per share.
B.   If each preferred stock is convertible into four shares of common, compute basic and diluted earnings per share.

A.
First Step: Determine the weighted average number of common shares issued and outstanding for basic earnings per share.
Application: Multiply the number of common shares x the portion of the year outstanding. Sum the total.

Solution:

Weighted average number of shares for basic earnings per share:

January 1	600,000 x 5/12	250,000
June 1	800,000 x 3/12	200,000
September 1	750,000 x 4/12	250,000
	Total Weighted Average Shares	700,000

Second Step: Determine the weighted average number of common shares issued and outstanding for diluted earnings per share.

Application: Calculate the number of shares outstanding as if the bonds were converted at the first of the year and add that total to the weighted average number of common shares outstanding from Step One.

Solution:

Weighted average number of shares for diluted earnings per share:

Basic weighted average number of shares	700,000
Add: As-if converted bonds 1,400 x 20	280,000
Total Weighted Average Shares	980,000

Third Step: Calculate basic earnings per share.

Application: Apply the formula for basic earnings per share: $\dfrac{\text{Net Income} - \text{Preferred Dividends}}{\text{Basic Weighted Average Common Shares Outstanding}}$

Solution: EPS $= \dfrac{\text{Net Income \$4,400,000} - \text{Preferred Dividends \$720,000*}}{\text{Basic Weighted Average Common Shares Outstanding 700,000 shares}}$

$= \dfrac{\$3,680,000}{700,000} = \$5.26$ per share

*\$8,000,000 x 9%

Fourth Step: Calculate diluted earnings per share.

Application: Apply the formula for diluted earnings per share:

$$\frac{\text{Net Income} - \text{Preferred Dividends} + \text{After-tax interest}}{\text{Diluted Weighted Average Common Shares Outstanding}}$$

Solution:

EPS $= \dfrac{\text{Net Income \$4,400,000} - \text{Preferred Dividends \$720,000} + \text{After-tax interest (.6 x \$1,120,000)}}{\text{Diluted Weighted Average Common Shares Outstanding 840,000 shares}}$

$= \dfrac{\$4,400,000 - \$720,000 + \$672,000}{980,000} = \dfrac{\$4,352,000}{980,000} = \$4.44$ per share

B.

First Step: Calculate basic earnings per share.

Application: Basic earnings per share is the same as in part A.

Solution: Refer to part A. Basic earnings per share is $5.26 per share.

Second Step: Calculate weighted average number of shares for diluted earnings per share.
Application: Weighted average number of shares for diluted earnings per share:

Basic weighted average number of shares	700,000
Add: As-if converted bonds 14,000 x 20	280,000
As-if converted preferred stock 160,000 x 4	640,000
Total Weighted Average Shares	1,620,000

Third Step: Calculate diluted earnings per share.
Application: Apply the formula: EPS $= \dfrac{\text{Net Income} - \text{Preferred Dividends} + \text{After-tax Interest}}{\text{Diluted Weighted Average Common Shares Outstanding}}$

Solution: EPS $= \dfrac{\text{Net Income } \$4,400,000 - 0 + \text{After-tax Interest } (.6 \times \$1,120,000)}{\text{Diluted Weighted Average Common Shares Outstanding } 1,620,000}$

$= \dfrac{\$4,400,000 + (.6 \times \$1,120,000)}{1,160,000}$

$= \dfrac{\$5,072,000}{1,620,000} = \$3.13$ per share

4.   **Basic and diluted earnings per share using the Treasury Stock Method.**

The Diller Corporation had outstanding 100,000 stock options at $30 per share when the average market value of the stock was $50 per share. Diller Corporation reported earnings for the year of $6,000,000, and it had 1,000,000 shares of common stock outstanding for the full year.

Required: Calculate the basic earnings per share and the diluted earnings per share for the Diller Corporation.

First Step: Determine the weighted average number of common shares issued and outstanding for basic earnings per share.
Application: Multiply the number of common shares x the period of time they are outstanding.
Solution: Number of common shares 1,000,000 x entire year = 1,000,000

Second Step: Determine the weighted average number of common shares issued and outstanding for diluted earnings per share.
Application: Using the Treasury Stock method, calculate the number of shares outstanding as if the options were converted at the first of the year, add the number of common shares created by the options and subtract the amount of treasury stock the firm could purchase (at market price) with the proceeds of the option exercise.

Solution:

Weighted average number of shares for diluted earnings per share:

Basic weighted average number of shares	1,000,000
Add: number of common shares created by the options	100,000

Subtract: amount of treasury stock the firm could purchase at market

$$\frac{100,000 \times \$30}{\$50} = \frac{\$3,000,000}{\$50} = 60,000 \text{ shares} \qquad (60,000)$$

Total Weighted Average Shares for diluted EPS   1,040,000

Third Step: Calculate basic earnings per share.

Application: EPS $= \dfrac{\text{Net Income}}{\text{Basic Weighted Average Common Shares Outstanding}}$

Solution: EPS $= \dfrac{\text{Net Income } \$6,000,0000}{\text{Basic Weighted Average Common Shares Outstanding } 1,000,000 \text{ shares}}$

$= \dfrac{\$6,000,000}{1,000,000} = \$6.00 \text{ per share}$

Fourth Step: Calculate diluted earnings per share.

Application: Apply the formula for diluted earnings per share:

$$\frac{\text{Net Income - Preferred Dividends + After-tax interest}}{\text{Diluted Weighted Average Common Shares Outstanding}}$$

Solution:

EPS $= \dfrac{\text{Net Income} \quad \$6,000,000 - 0 + 0}{\text{Diluted Weighted Average Common Shares Outstanding } 1,040,000 \text{ shares}}$

$= \dfrac{\$6,000,000}{1,040,000} = \$5.77 \text{ per share}$

5.   **Employee stock options.**

On January 2, Year 10, Eppley Corporation granted to an employee, Martin Long, an option to buy 5,000 shares of Eppley's common stock at $60 per share. The option was exercisable for three years from December 31, Year 10. Long exercised his option on December 31, Year 12 and sold the shares on January 31, Year 13. The service period was deemed to be three years for Years 10, 11, and 12. The market prices for Eppley Corporation stock at various dates were:

January 2, Year 10	$60 per share
December 31, Year 10	$70 per share
December 31, Year 12	$85 per share
January 31, Year 13	$95 per share

Required: Determine the additional compensation expense that the company should recognize in Year 10 as a result of the option granted to Long by the Eppley Corporation if Eppley elects to follow:

A.   *APB No. 25.*

B.   *SFAS No. 123* if the value of each option is $15 on the grant date.

A.

First Step: Determine the amount of compensation under *APB No. 25* for Year 10.

Application: Under *APB No. 25* the granting of stock options gives no rise to compensation when the option price is not less than the fair market price on the grant date.

Solution: Compensation is zero because the fair market value of the stock is the same as the option price on the grant date.

B.

First Step: Determine the amount of compensation under *SFAS No. 123* for Year 10.

Application: Under *SFAS No. 123,* compensation is measured as the option value times the number of options. Annual compensation is the total compensation divided by the number of service years.

Solution: Option value $15 x Number of options 5,000 = $75,000 compensation

$$\frac{\$75,000}{3 \text{ years of service}} = \$25,000 \text{ for Year 10}$$

Test Yourself
True or False Questions

T F 1.   Under the proprietary view of an entity, the assets of the entity are what is important, not the resources used to obtain them.

T F 2.   Under the entity view of the entity, the firm and its owners are the same.

T F 3.   Par value of common stock is equal to its market value.

T F 4.   Accounting gains and losses are recognized on repurchases of an entity's own stock.

T F 5.   One reason for the repurchase of a company's own stock is to distribute excess cash to stockholders.

T F 6.   Financial analysts believe that the popularity of preferred stock may be explained by its potential use in avoiding various contractual constraints.

T F 7.   The distinction between debt and preferred stock is not always clear.

T F 8.   A firm that issues mandatorily redeemable preferred stock is precluded from reporting this as an item of equity by the SEC.

T   F   9.   The SEC requires that mandatorily redeemable preferred stock be shown as a liability on the balance sheet.

T   F   10.   Under the 1984 Revised Model Business Corporation Act, as long as the fair value of assets exceeds the fair value of liabilities after a distribution of assets, the firm is considered to be solvent.

T   F   11.   When a corporation has no convertible securities and no options or warrants outstanding, the company has a complex capital structure.

T   F   12.   *SFAS No. 128* requires companies with a complex capital structure to compute diluted earnings per share.

T   F   13.   EPS is a very useful tool for measuring a company's profit performance.

T   F   14.   The FASB expressed the belief that expenses are incurred when companies grant stock options to employees as part of a compensation package.

T   F   15.   Companies are required to record compensation expense for employee stock options under *SFAS No. 123.*

T   F   16.   A subordinated debenture is one in which the claims of senior creditors must be partially settled before any payments will be made to holders of subordinated debentures in the event of insolvency or bankruptcy.

T   F   17.   Financial analysts can easily estimate the future cash flow implications of convertible debt.

T   F   18.   Employee Stock Ownership Plans can provide a source of low-cost debt financing for firms.

T   F   19.   In a leveraged ESOP, the trust borrows funds from a financial institution to purchase the securities of the employer company.

T   F   20.   In a nonleverageable ESOP, the plan contains no provision for the use of borrowed funds.

T   F   21.   ESOP debt is hidden in financial statement footnotes as an off-balance sheet item.

Multiple-Choice Questions

Select the best answer from those provided.

_____ 1. The importance of which one of the following is stressed by the proprietary view of a firm?
    a. Owner's Equity
    b. Assets
    c. Expenses
    d. Revenues

_____ 2. The payment of dividends by a corporation represents a /an
    a. distribution of earnings to the stockholders.
    b. liability of the corporation.
    c. expense of the corporation.
    d. contra liability account.

_____ 3. The par value of common stock is
    a. equal to the market value of the stock.
    b. established by the state government.
    c. another measure of the value of the common stock.
    d. established by the corporation.

_____ 4. When a stockholder sells shares of a firms' stock back to the firm, the stockholder is
    a. not taxed on any gain.
    b. taxed at ordinary rates.
    c. taxed at capital gains rates.
    d. subject to a special tax.

_____ 5. Corporations issue preferred stock rather than debt because they believe that the preferred stock is
    a. less risky than debt.
    b. riskier than debt.
    c. less risky than common stock.
    d. always treated as debt.

_____ 6. The SEC requires that mandatorily redeemable preferred stock be treated as a/an
    a. liability.
    b. asset.
    c. separate line item between assets and liabilities.
    d. separate line item between liabilities and shareholders' equity.

_____ 7. Distributions to shareholders of corporations are governed by
   a. the SEC.
   b. federal law.
   c. state law.
   d. management.

_____ 8. Generally Accepted Accounting Principles call for a reduction in which one of the following accounts for the payment of a stock dividend?
   a. Retained Earnings
   b. Common Stock
   c. Revenues
   d. Expenses

_____ 9. A simple capital structure occurs when a corporation has
   a. options outstanding.
   b. warrants outstanding.
   c. convertible securities.
   d. no convertible securities, options, or warrants outstanding.

_____ 10. The formula used to calculate earnings per share for a corporation with a simple capital structure is referred to as
   a. basic earnings per share.
   b. simple earnings per share.
   c. complex earnings per share.
   d. fully-diluted earnings per share.

_____ 11. The denominator in the formula to calculate basic earnings per share is
   a. Preferred Stock outstanding.
   b. Common Stock outstanding.
   c. weighted average number of preferred shares outstanding.
   d. weighted average number of common shares outstanding.

_____ 12. If a corporation has securities that are convertible into shares of the firms' common stock, it has a
   a. complex capital structure.
   b. basic capital structure.
   c. simple capital structure.
   d. superior capital structure.

_____ 13. To enable employees to build wealth and postpone taxes, a firm may provide its employees with
   a. a current bonus.
   b. stock options.
   c. current salary increases.
   d. current salary reductions.

_____ 14. If the option price of a stock is greater than or equal to the market price of the stock at the grant date of a stock option plan, the options
   a. have no value under *APB No. 25.*
   b. have great value under *APB No. 25.*
   c. are recorded at fair market value under *APB No. 25.*
   d. are capitalized at the net present value of the options.

_____ 15. According to *SFAS No. 123,* a corporation should measure the fair market value of stock options at the
   a. payment date.
   b. exercise date.
   c. restructure date.
   d. grant date.

_____ 16. Today, most corporations
   a. have adopted *SFAS No. 123.*
   b. still follow *APB No. 25.*
   c. follow the SEC guidelines for stock options.
   d. follow the NYSE guidelines for stock options.

_____ 17. Financial analysts can find a lot of information about a firm's stock options in the
   a. balance sheet.
   b. income statement.
   c. footnotes to the financial statements.
   d. cash flow statement.

_____ 18. A convertible bond is usually a
   a. real estate bond.
   b. subordinated debenture.
   c. junior bond.
   d. guaranteed bond.

_____ 19.   When a corporation is in a period of falling stock prices, convertible debt offerings
a. increase.
b. decrease.
c. remain the same.
d. are nonexistent.

_____ 20.   *APB No. 14* requires the issuance of convertible bonds to be recorded at the value of the
a. debt only.
b. debt minus interest.
c. debt plus interest.
d. fair market value of the conversion feature.

_____ 21.   Corporate managers may protect against recognizing losses on the conversion of convertible bonds by using the
a. temporal method to record the transaction.
b. current-value method to record the transaction.
c. book value method to record the transaction.
d. fair market value to record the transaction.

_____ 22.   A corporation is protected against extreme stock price increases by having
a. call provisions on convertible bonds.
b. interest expense on convertible bonds.
c. interest income on convertible bonds.
d. interest free convertible bonds.

_____ 23.   The amount of capital required to generate a given level of earnings per share is
a. prominent in EPS.
b. comparable between all companies.
c. prominent in diluted EPS.
d. ignored by EPS.

_____ 24.   A reverse stock split has the effect of
a. increasing the number of shares of stock issued and outstanding.
b. keeping the number of shares of common stock issued and outstanding the same.
c. decreasing the number of shares of stock issued and outstanding.
d. decreasing the number of shares authorized.

Exercises

1.   Derry Corporation has 10,000,000 shares of common stock authorized. The par value of the stock is $10 per share and 7,000,000 shares are outstanding. The corporation received $15 per share from the sale of the stock to the public.

Required:
A. What is the book value of the Common Stock account and the Paid-in Capital in Excess of Par Value account?
B. Record the entry to book the sale of the common shares.

2.   The Wilson Company was organized on January 1, Year 1 with 1,000,000 shares of $2 par value common stock authorized. During Year 1 the company completed the following transactions:

January 5	Issued 250,000 shares at $30 per share
April 4	Issued 100,000 shares at $38 per share
June 5	Issued 50,000 shares at $50 per share
June 25	Purchased 20,000 shares at $40 per share
December 1	Sold the 20,000 shares purchased on June 25 at $60 per share

Required:
Determine the balances of the Common Stock account and the Paid-in Capital in Excess of Par Value account at December 31, Year 1.

_____

_____

_____

_____

_____

3. Bristol Company was organized on January 2, Year 5. The company issued 600,000 shares of common stock with a par value of $1 per share for $20 per share. The company was authorized to issue 750,000 shares of common stock. From January 2, Year 5 through December 31, Year 7, Bristol reported a total of $750,000 net income and paid out cash dividends of $400,000. On January 31, Year 7, Bristol acquired 50,000 shares of its common stock for $16 per share. On December 31, Year 7, Bristol sold the 50,000 shares at $24 per share.

    Required:
    Determine the book value of total stockholders' equity at December 31, Year 7.

_____

_____

_____

_____

_____

_____

_____

_____

_____

4. The Marshall Corporation posted $700,000 in net income for the current year. Marshall's capital structure consists of 100,000 shares of common stock and 16,000 shares of $100 par value, 7% preferred stock outstanding for the entire year. Each share of preferred stock is convertible into 3 shares of common.

    Required:
    A. Compute basic and diluted earnings per share.
    B. Compute the basic and diluted earnings per share, if Marshall had 10,000 stock options outstanding at $20 per option when the average market price of the stock is $25.

5.   On January 2, Year 9 Harris Company granted to an employee, Bruce Stern, an option to buy 6,000 shares of Harris' common stock at $55 per share. The option was exercisable for three years from the date of the grant. Stern exercised his option on December 1, Year 12 and sold the shares on December 29, Year 12. The market prices for Harris Company's stock during Year 9 were as follows:

January 2	$40 per share
December 1	$60 per share
December 31	$75 per share

Required:
Determine the additional compensation expense that the company should recognize in Year 9 as a result of the option granted to Stern. Assume that Harris Company elects to follow *APB No.25.*

Solutions

Answers to True or False Questions

True answers: 5, 6, 7, 8, 10, 12, 13, 14, 18, 19, 20
False answers explained:

1.   Under the <u>entity</u> view of a company the assets of the entity are what is important, not where they came from.
2.   Under the <u>proprietary</u> view of the entity, the firm and its owners are the same.
3.   Par value of common stock <u>has no relation</u> to its market value.
4.   Accounting gains and losses are not recognized on repurchases of a company's own stock.
9.   The SEC requires that mandatorily redeemable preferred stock be shown <u>on a separate line between liabilities and shareholders' equity</u>.
11.   When a corporation has no convertible securities and no options or warrants outstanding, the company has a <u>simple</u> capital structure.
15.   Companies are <u>not</u> required to record compensation expense for employee stock options.

16. A subordinated debenture is one in which the claims of senior creditors must be <u>completely</u> settled before any payments will be made to holders of subordinated debentures in the event of insolvency or bankruptcy.

17. Financial analysts <u>have a difficult time estimating</u> the future cash flow implication of convertible dept.

21. ESOP debt is <u>not</u> hidden in financial statement footnotes as an off-balance sheet item, but carried as a long-term liability.

Answers to Multiple-Choice Questions

1.	A	6.	D	11.	D	16.	B	21.	C
2.	A	7.	C	12.	A	17.	C	22.	A
3.	D	8.	A	13.	B	18.	B	23.	D
4.	C	9.	D	14.	A	19.	B	24.	C
5.	A	10.	A	15.	D	20.	A		

Answers to Exercises

1. A. Shares Issued and Outstanding 7,000,000 x $10=$70,000,000 Balance in Common stock account.
    Shares Issued and Outstanding 7,000,000 x $5 = $35,000,000 Balance in Paid-In Capital in Excess of Par Value account.

    B. DR Cash   105,000,000
            CR Common Stock   70,000,000
            CR Paid-In Capital in Excess of Par Value   35,000,000

2.

	Common Stock	Paid-In Capital in Excess of Par Value
Jan. 5 Sold 250,000 at $30	$500,000	$7,000,000
Apr. 4 Sold 100,000 at $38	200,000	3,600,000
June 5 Sold 50,000 at $50	100,000	2,400,000
June 25 Purch. 20,000 at $40	No Effect	No Effect
Dec. 1 Sold 20,000 at $60	No Effect	400,000
Balance 12 -31	$ 800,000	$13,600,000

3.

	Common Stock	PIC>Par	Retained Earnings	Treasury Stock
Sale of 600,000 shares of Common	$600,000	$11,400,000		
Purchase of Treasury Stock				$(800,000)
Earnings			$750,000	
Dividends			(400,000)	
Sale of Treasury Stock	-0-	400,000		800,000
Total Stockholders' Equity	$600,000 +	$11,800,000 +	$350,000 +	0 =
			$12,750,000	

4.   A.   Basic EPS = $\dfrac{\text{Net Income — Preferred Dividends}}{\text{Weighted Average Common Shares Outstanding}}$

= $\dfrac{\text{Net Income \$700,000 — Preferred Dividends (16,000 x \$100 x 7\%)}}{\text{Weighted Average Common Shares Outstanding 100,000}}$

= $\dfrac{\$700,000 - \$112,000}{100,000}$ = $\dfrac{\$588,000}{100,000}$ = \$5.88 per share

Diluted EPS = $\dfrac{\text{Net Income}}{\text{Weighted Average Shares Outstanding + Converted Shares}}$

= $\dfrac{\text{Net Income \$700,000}}{\text{Weighted Average Shares 100,000 + Converted Shares (3 x 16,000)}}$

= $\dfrac{\$700,000}{148,000}$ = \$4.73 per share

B.   Basic EPS = \$5.88 (the same as part A.)

Diluted EPS = $\dfrac{\text{Net Income}}{\text{Diluted Weighted Average Shares Outstanding}}$

Weighted Average number of Shares for diluted earnings per share:

Basic weighted average number of shares		100,000
Add: number of shares created by conversion of preferred		48,000
Add: number of common shares created by the options	10,000	
Subtract: amount of treasury stock the firm could purchase at market		
$\dfrac{10,000 \times \$20}{\$25}$ = $\dfrac{\$200,000}{\$25}$ = 8,000 shares	(8,000)	
Total Weighted Average Shares for diluted EPS		150,000

$\dfrac{\text{Net Income \$700,000}}{\text{Diluted Weighted Average Shares 150,000}}$

$\dfrac{\$700,000}{150,000}$

=\$4.67 per share

5.   Under *APB No. 25*, granting of stock options gives no rise to compensation when the option price exceeds or equals the current market price.

CHAPTER 16

INTERCORPORATE EQUITY INVESTMENTS

Chapter Review

Learning Objective 1:
How a company benefits from owning another company's common stock.

One corporation purchases equity shares of another corporation to earn a return on the investment or to gain a competitive advantage. The return on investment arises from increases in share prices or from dividends. When a company attempts to gain a competitive advantage by investing in a competitor or supplier, the return comes from increased operating profits and growth.

A **minority interest** is any ownership percentage that is 50% or below. A **majority financial interest** is an ownership interest that exceeds 50%. For financial reporting purposes, minority investments fall into one of two categories:
1.   **minority passive investments**, or
2.   **minority active investments**.

Learning Objective 2:
How an investor's ownership share is used to determine the accounting treatment of equity investments, and why.

Under existing GAAP, the method of accounting for intercorporate investments depends on the size of the ownership share in the investee corporation. Ownership shares are defined as follows:

Minority Passive Investment — less than 20% ownership.
1.   Trading Securities — The firm intends to sell within one year.
       a. Mark-to-market on the balance sheet.
       b. Unrealized gains (losses) are recognized as income.
2.   Available-for-sale Securities — The firm intends to hold for more than one year, but is willing to sell them whenever appropriate.
       a. Mark-to-market for the balance sheet.
       b. Unrealized gains (losses) are recorded in stockholders' equity.

FYI. . .
A minority interest is also called a noncontrolling interest.

Minority Active Investment — ownership between 20% and 50%.
1.   The minority active investment provides the investor the ability to influence management.
2.   The minority active investment requires use of the equity method.

Majority Investment — more than 50% ownership.
1.   The majority active investment provides the investor effective control.

2.   Accounting for a majority investment requires full consolidation and the use of either the purchase or pooling method to value the investment on the investor's books.

Learning Objective 3:
How the accounting for short-term speculative investments differs from the accounting for long-term investments.

Trading securities are actively managed to achieve trading gains. Under *SFAS No. 115*, trading securities are reported at fair market value or marked-to-market at each balance sheet date. The **Market Adjustment** valuation account carries a debit balance when the market price of securities is greater than the cost and a credit balance when the cost exceeds the securities' market value. Utilize a two step process to compute the year end market adjustment.

1.   The first step compares the securities' cost to the fair market value.

2.   Any difference between the two figures becomes the **target balance** for the market adjustment account. The market adjustment account must be increased or decreased to equal its target balance, and the unrealized gain or (loss) for the same amount is recorded.

Available-for-sale securities are usually shown as noncurrent investments. The accounting entries to record the purchase, dividend, and mark-to-market adjustment entries are virtually identical to the entries for trading securities. The major difference is that the mark-to-market adjustment is not included in income. The upward or downward adjustment to reflect fair value for available-for-sale securities is a direct (net of tax) credit or debit to a special owners' equity account. **(See Demonstration Problem 1.)**

Learning Objective 4:
The equity method and when to use it.

When an investors' ownership share exceeds 20%, GAAP presume the investor can exert influence over the company, and the ownership percentage implies a continuing relationship between the two companies. Once the ownership percentage becomes large enough for investor influence, the simple accounting system used for passive investments is no longer suitable. Minority passive accounting treatment allows the investor the ability to manipulate its reported income. To preclude this from occurring, GAAP requires the use of the equity method of accounting for minority active investments.

Under the **equity method,** the original investment is recorded at cost, but the investment account is increased for the investors' proportionate share of the investee's income and decreased when the investor company receives dividends. Based on the equity method of accounting, dividends declared and paid by the investee company have no effect on the income of the investor because the dividends are viewed as a return of capital.

An investment made at a price that exceeds the book value of the subsidiary company requires additional analysis. One possible explanation for the excess purchase price is the fair market value of the assets acquired exceeds historical cost, and the second reason is goodwill. The investor must analyze why the cost exceeds book value. The elements consist of the:

1.   historical book value,
2.   excess of fair market value over cost, and
3.   goodwill.

The parent company is required to amortize the cost of shares that exceeds book value attributable to inventory, depreciable assets, or goodwill. Amortization is recorded as a debit to investment income and a credit to the investment account. **(See Demonstration Problem 2.)**

Learning Objective 5:
What consolidated financial statements are and how they are compiled.

When one company owns more than 50% of the voting shares of another, the parent controls the subsidiary. When this condition exists, the financial statements of the subsidiary and the parent are combined on a line-by-line basis in a consolidation process. Consolidated financial statements are required only when the parent company owns more than 50% of the subsidiary. If exactly 50% of the voting shares are owned, the equity method is used and no line-by-line consolidation is necessary. Consolidated financial statements are designed to portray the economic activities of a group of legal entities controlled by a single management. The purpose of the consolidation process is to combine the economic entities and to avoid double counting. When the parent acquires the subsidiary company for cash, the purchase method of accounting is used.

Learning Objective 6:
What goodwill is and when is it shown on the financial statements.

Under the purchase method of accounting, the parent company must analyze the investment account to determine the price paid for book value, the fair market value paid for other assets, and any goodwill acquired.   **Goodwill** is the excess of the purchase price paid over the fair market value of the net assets acquired. The entry to eliminate the investment account on the books of the parent and the book value of the equity on the books of the subsidiary must be made to avoid double counting. The consolidation process also requires that adjustments must be made to avoid any double counting of internal business transactions like parent-subsidiary investments, loans, or sales. **(See Demonstration Problem 3.)**
Prior to 2002, goodwill acquired in a purchase transaction was

amortized to income over a period not to exceed 40 years. *SFAS No. 142* no longer permits the amortization of goodwill for purchase transactions. Instead good will must be tested for impairment annually and then written down if impaired. A two stepimpairment test is imposed:

1. Determine if there is impairment of goodwill by seeing if the book value of the unit's net assets exceed their fair value.
2. The amount of the impairment charge is the difference between the implied goodwill and the goodwill reported on the balance sheet.

Learning Objective 7: How business acquisitions and mergers are recorded and why the recording method matters to statement readers.

Prior to the issuance of *SFAS No. 141,* GAAP allowed a second method of accounting for business combinations known as the **pooling-of-interests** method. When a business combination takes place that involves a stock for stock exchange, the combination should be accounted for as a pooling of interests provided that all twelve of the necessary requirements for pooling treatment are met. Under existing GAAP, no buyout occurs in a pooling of interests. The entry to record a pooling of interests consolidation is to eliminate the investors' investment account and the subsidiary's equity accounts. Unlike a purchase of one firm by another, a pooling of interests is a merger of two entities into one. Because the pooling of interests assumes there is no buyout, there is no recognition of the fair value of assets acquired or goodwill. The book values of the previously separate companies are carried forward to the consolidated financial statements.

The pooling of interests method of accounting permits companies to record business acquisitions at artificially low amounts — using book values rather than fair market values. This method makes the rate-of-return ratios and other financial performance measures appear higher than they should. This is why the pooling method is only used when the required conditions are met. Purchase accounting avoids these distortions by recording the acquisition at fair market value. **(See Demonstration Problem 4.)**

Learning Objective 8: How foreign subsidiaries are treated when financial statements in U.S. dollars are prepared.

All majority-owned subsidiaries — foreign and domestic — must be consolidated. A complication arises when consolidating foreign subsidiaries. The numbers on the foreign subsidiary's financial statements must be converted into the parent's currency units before the consolidation process begins. *SFAS No. 52* specifies one of two procedures, depending upon the operating characteristics of the foreign subsidiary:

1. Foreign subsidiaries that are not self-sufficient (non-free-standing) are translated using the **temporal method**.
2. Foreign subsidiaries that are essentially self-contained units are translated using the **current rate method**.

Those units that are non-free-standing, engage in a series of foreign currency transactions. Accounting for assets and liabilities arising from foreign currency transactions varies on the basis of the nature of the item.

1. Translate foreign currency monetary assets and liabilities using the current rate of exchange in effect at the balance sheet date.
2. Translate foreign currency nonmonetary assets and liabilities using the historical rate of exchange in effect at the time the asset was acquired or the liability was incurred.

Non-free-standing subsidiaries are treated as though they were invented for the purpose of facilitating foreign currency transactions. The consolidation of a non-free-standing subsidiary includes numbers that are identical to the numbers included if the subsidiary did not exist and the parent engaged directly in the foreign currency transactions. The translation exchange rates under the temporal method use the current rate for monetary assets and liabilities, the historical rate for nonmonetary assets and liabilities, and for cost of sales and depreciation. The rate at the time of the transaction is used for all revenue and expense accounts other than cost of sales and depreciation.

The problem that arises with self-contained foreign subsidiaries is that the ultimate exchange rate effects on U.S. dollar cash flows are uncertain. The FASB decided that these subsidiaries should be translated using the current rate method and that any debit or credit arising from translation gains or losses should be put directly into the owners' equity account and not recognized as income. This is a comprehensive income item.

Glossary of Terms

Available-for-Sale Securities	Equity investments of less than 20 percent that are not trading securities.
Consolidation	The process of combining line-by-line the financial statements of the investor and investee companies.
Current Rate Method	The method used to re-express, in dollars, foreign currency amounts for foreign

subsidiaries that are free-standing economic units.

Equity Method	A method of accounting for an investment in equity securities that calls for increasing or decreasing the investment account for the owner's share of profits or losses and a further decrease in the investment account for the receipt of earnings in the form of dividends.
Foreign Currency Transactions	Any business transaction denominated in units of a foreign currency.
Goodwill	The excess of the amount paid for a company over and above the fair market value of the company. Goodwill also represents the "extraordinary" earnings potential of the entity.
Historical Exchange Rate	The exchange rate in effect at the time of a particular transaction.
Minority Active Investment	One shareholder owns a proportion of the voting shares of another company, and the percentage of ownership is large enough for shareholder influence.
Minority Passive Investment	One shareholder owns a small proportion of the voting shares of another company, and the shareholder has no ability to influence the decisions of that company.
Parent Company	A company that owns more than 50% of the voting stock of another company (subsidiary).
Pooling of Interests Method	A method of accounting used for mergers accomplished using a "stock-for-stock" exchange.
Purchase Method	Equity securities designated by the investor to be held for a short period of time.
Subsidiary	A company who has more than 50% of its voting stock owned by another company (parent).
Temporal Method	A method of accounting used when one company buys another company for cash, stock, debt, or any other form of consideration..
Trading Securities	The method used to re-express, in dollars, foreign currency amounts for foreign subsidiaries that are mere extensions of the U.S. parent with no self-sufficiency.

Demonstration Problems

1.   Minority Passive Ownership

The following information relates to the Stewart Corporation's investments in marketable equity securities.

		Market Value at Year End		Dividends Received	
	Cost	Year 8	Year 9	Year 8	Year 9
Trading	$300,000	$200,000	$315,000	$1,000	$1,500
Available-for-sale	300,000	335,000	275,000	2,500	2,000

Required:

A.   Prepare the journal entry to record the purchase of the securities.

B.   Prepare the journal entry to record the receipt of dividends in Year 9.

C.   Calculate the amount of unrealized holding gains and losses in the Year 9 income statement and prepare the journal entry at the end of Year 9 to record the adjustment for the holding gain or loss.

D.   Calculate the amount of unrealized holding gains and losses in the Year 9 balance sheet and prepare the journal entry at the end of Year 9 to record the adjustment for the holding gain or loss.

A.

Step One: Prepare the journal entry to record the acquisition of investment securities.

Application: Record the entry based on the historical cost of the investment.

Solution:

DR Trading Securities	300,000	
DR Available-for-sale Securities	300,000	
CR Cash		600,000

B.

Step One: Prepare the journal entry to record the dividends received in Year 8.

Application: Record the dividends as dividend income according to the rules for minority passive investments.

Solution:

DR. Cash	3,500	
CR Dividend Income		3,500

C.

Step One: Determine which group of the securities reports holding gains and losses on the income statement.

Application: GAAP require that the holding gains and losses of trading securities are to be reported on the income statement.

Solution: The holding gains and losses of the trading securities are to be reported on the income statement.

Step Two: Determine the holding gains and losses for the trading securities for Year 8.
Application: Compare the Year 8 total cost of trading securities to the market value at the end of Year 8 and determine by how much the market value exceeds or is below the cost basis. Any difference becomes the target balance of the market adjustment.
Solution: Cost $300,000 — Market $200,000 = Holding Loss (Target Balance) $100,000

Step Three: Prepare the adjusting entry.
Application: Increase or decrease the market adjustment account to equal its target balance and record an unrealized gain or loss for the same amount.

Solution:

> **DR** Unrealized Holding Loss on Trading Securities (Income Statement)   100,000
>   **CR** Market Adjustment — Trading Securities   100,000

Step Four: Determine the holding gains and losses for the trading securities for Year 9.
Application: Compare the Year 9 cost balance of trading securities to the market value at the end of Year 9 and determine by how much the market value exceeds or is below the cost basis. Any difference becomes the target balance of the market adjustment account.
Solution: Cost $300,000 - Market $315,000 = Holding Gain (Target Balance)($15,000)

Step Five: Determine the adjustment required in Year 9.
Application: Compare the target balance in step three with the market adjustment account from Year 8.
Solution: Target Balance ($15,000) - Balance from Year 8($100,000) = $115,000 Adjustment

Step Six: Prepare the entry to record the unrealized holding gain or loss at the end of Year 9.
Application: Based on the information in step four, record the unrealized holding gain.
Solution:

> **DR** Market Adjustment - Trading Securities   115,000
>   **CR** Unrealized Holding Gain on Trading Securities (Income Statement) 115,000

D.
Step One: Determine which group of the securities reports holding gains and losses on the balance sheet.
Application: GAAP require that the holding gains and losses of available-for-sale securities are to be reported on the balance sheet.
Solution: The holding gains and losses of the available-for-sale securities are to be reported on the income statement.

Step Two: Determine the holding gains and losses for the available-for-sale securities for Year 8.
Application: Compare the Year 8 total cost of available-for-sale securities to market value at the end of Year 8 and determine by how much the market value exceeds or is below the cost basis. Any difference becomes the target balance of the market adjustment.
Solution: Cost $300,000 - Market $335,000 = Holding Gain $35,000

Step Three: Prepare the adjusting entry.
Application: Increase or decrease the market adjustment account to equal its target balance and record an unrealized gain or loss for the same amount.

Solution:
        DR Market Adjustment - Available-for-Sale Securities   35,000
              CR Unrealized Holding Gain on Available-for-Sale Sec. (Balance Sheet) 35,000

Step Four: Determine the holding gains and losses for the available-for-sale securities for Year 9.
Application: Compare the Year 9 cost balance of trading securities to market value at the end of Year 9 and determine by how much the market value exceeds or is below the cost basis. Any difference becomes the target balance of the market adjustment account.
Solution: Cost $300,000 - Market $275,000 = Holding Loss $25,000

Step Five: Determine the adjustment required in Year 9.
Application: Compare the target balance in step three with the market adjustment account from Year 8.
Solution: Target Balance $(25,000) - Balance from Year 8 $35,000 = $60,000 Holding Loss

Step Six: Prepare the entry to record the unrealized holding gain or loss at the end of Year 9.
Application: Based on the information in Step Four, record the unrealized holding loss.
Solution:
DR Unrealized Holding Loss on Available-for-Sale Securities (Balance Sheet)   60,000
    CR Market Adjustment - Available-for-Sale Securities   60,000

2.   Minority Active Ownership — The Equity Method

The Nee Corporation acquired a 40% interest in the Luffy Corporation for $1,200,000 cash on January 2, Year 5. Luffy Corporation had net assets with a book value of $1,900,000 and a fair market value of $2,400,000. The excess of fair value over the book value of net assets relates to equipment being depreciated over its remaining useful life of 10 years. Luffy's net income for Year 5 was $300,000, and the corporation declared and paid $80,000 in dividends.

Required: Prepare all the journal entries required on the books of Nee Corporation for Year 5 related to the acquisition of its interest in the Luffy Corporation using the equity method.

Step One: Prepare the journal entry to record the initial investment.
Application: Record the journal entry to record the acquisition.
Solution:

DR Investment in Luffy	1,200,000	
CR Cash		1,200,000

Step Two: Calculate the investee's share of Luffy Corporation's net income.
Application: Multiply the net income of Luffy Corporation by 40%.

Solution: Net Income $300,000 x 40% = $120,000

Step Three: Prepare the journal entry to recognize the investee's net income for the year.
Application: Using the information from step two, record the appropriate entry.
Solution:

DR Investment in Luffy	120,000	
CR Income from Affiliate		120,000

Step Four: Calculate the investee's share of Luffy Corporation's dividends..
Application: Multiply the dividends of Luffy Corporation by 40%.
Solution: Dividends $80,000 x 40% = $32,000

Step Five: Prepare the journal entry to recognize the investee's dividends for the year.
Application: Using the information from step four, record the appropriate entry.
Solution:

DR Cash	32,000	
CR Investment in Luffy		32,000

Step Six: Calculate the excess of the fair market value of the assets over the book value assigned to fixed assets.
Application: Subtract the book value of the net assets from the fair market value of the assets acquired.
Solution: Fair market value of the assets acquired ($2,400,000 x 40%) — Book value of the net assets ($1,900,000 x 40%) = $960,000 — $760,000 = $200,000

Step Seven: Calculate the amount of the amortization associated with the equipment.
Application: The excess assigned to equipment is divided by the estimated remaining life of the identified equipment.

Solution: <u>Excess Assigned $200,000</u> = $20,000
              10 Years

Step Eight: Prepare the journal entry to record the amortization for excess cost related to equipment.
Application: Use the information in step seven to prepare the journal entry.
Solution:

> **DR** Income from Affiliate   20,000
>   **CR** Investment in Luffy Corporation   20,000

Step Nine: Calculate the excess of the purchase price over the fair market value of the net assets.
Application: Subtract the fair market value of the net assets from the purchase price.

Solution: Purchase price of the investment $1,200,000 — Fair market value of the equity in net assets
($2,400,000 x 40%) = ($960,000) = $240,000 Goodwill

3.   Majority Ownership — Purchase Method

The Nee Corporation acquired a 100% interest in the Luffy Corporation for $2,600,000 cash on January 2, Year 5. Luffy Corporation had net assets with a book value of $1,900,000 and a fair market value of $2,400,000. The excess of fair value over the book value of net assets relates to equipment being depreciated over its remaining useful life of 10 years. (This situation is independent of Demonstration Problem 2.)

Required:

A.   Analyze the Investment in the Luffy Corporation account into its major components.

B.   Prepare the entry to eliminate the investment in the Luffy Corporation account.

A.
Step One: Analyze the Investment account
Application: Subtract the book value of the net assets from the fair market value of the assets acquired.
Solution: Fair market value of the assets acquired ($2,400,000 x 100%) — Book value of the net assets ($1,900,000) = ($2,400,000 x 100%) = $2,400,000 — $1,900,000 = $500,000 Excess of Cost over Book Value

Step Two: Calculate the excess of the purchase price over the fair market value of the net assets.
Application: Subtract the fair market value of the net assets from the purchase price.

Solution: Purchase price of the investment $2,600,000 — Fair market value of the equity in net assets ($2,400,000 x 100%) = ($2,400,000) = $200,000 Goodwill

Final Solution:
    Purchase Price Breakdown:

Recorded Value of Luffy's net assets	$ 1,900,000
Unrecorded Difference between fair value and book value of Luffy's fixed assets	500,000
Unrecorded value of Luffy's goodwill	200,000
Purchase Price	$2,600,000

B.

Step One: Prepare the consolidation entry to avoid double-counting the book value of Luffy's assets and its owners' equity.

Application: Use the information in the Final Solution above to generate the journal entries.

Solution:

DR Common Stock	1,900,000	
CR Investment in Luffy		1,900,000

Step Two: Prepare the consolidation entry to reclassify the excess purchase price between fixed assets and goodwill.

Application: Use the information in the Final Solution above to generate the journal entries.

Solution:

DR Fixed Assets	500,000	
DR Goodwill	200,000	
CR Investment in Luffy		700,000

4.   Majority Ownership — Pooling of Interests Method

The Nee Corporation acquired a 100% interest in the Luffy Corporation on January 2, Year 5. The transaction qualified for pooling of interests treatment. Luffy Corporation had net assets with a book value of $1,900,000 and a fair market value of $2,400,000. The excess of fair value over the book value of net assets relates to equipment being depreciated over its remaining useful life of 10 years. Nee issued stock valued at $1,900,000 in exchange for the stock of Luffy Corporation.

Required: Prepare the consolidation journal entry to eliminate the potential double counting of Luffy's net assets.

Step One: Prepare the journal entry to eliminate the investment account.

Application: In a pooling of interests, only the book value of Luffy is eliminated. This is equal to the Investment account on Nee's books.

Solution:

DR Common Stock   1,900,000
     CR   Investment in Luffy   1,900,000

FYI . . .
Please note that under the pooling of interests method, there is never a write-up of assets nor is there ever any goodwill recorded.

Test Yourself

True or False Questions

T F 1.   A minority investor in a corporation never has the ability to influence company decisions.

T F 2.   A minority active investment represents an ownership percentage large enough for shareholder influence.

T F 3.   Equity securities that an investor to hold for less than one year are classified as trading securities.

T F 4.   Trading securities are reported at cost value at each balance sheet date.

T F 5.   Bond investments made to generate short-run trading gains are classified as trading securities and accounted for in an identical manner to equity securities in the trading portfolio.

T F 6.   Equity securities acquired for their long-term investment potential are treated as trading securities.

T F 7.   Unrealized gains and losses on available-for-sale securities affect income in the period of the market value change.

T F 8.   Minority active investments are accounted for using the equity method.

T F 9.   The book value of equity investments recorded under the equity method is marked-to-market.

T F 10.   Goodwill exists because successful companies are frequently worth more than the sum of their individual net assets.

T F 11.   Ownership of between 20 percent and 50 percent of the stock of another company requires the use of the equity method.

T F 12.   Ownership of less than 20 percent of another company requires the use of the equity method of accounting.

T F 13.   When the investee company is controlled by another company, the financial statements must be consolidated.

T F 14.   If exactly 50 percent of the voting shares of one company are owned by another entity, consolidation of financial statements is required.

T F 15.   The adjustments made in preparing consolidated financial statements are designed to avoid double counting.

T F 16.   Pooling of interests accounting is used when one company exchanges equity shares with the stockholders of another company, and the combination meets the remaining conditions of pooling.

T F 17.   Under the pooling of interests accounting treatment, a buyout is considered to have taken place.

T F 18.   The write up of existing assets to fair market value takes place under the purchase method.

T F 19.   There are twelve conditions that must be met to qualify for the purchase method.

T F 20.   Almost 90 percent of all business combinations use pooling of interests accounting.

T F 21.   Pooling of interests accounting causes the rate of return ratios and other financial performance measures to appear higher than they should.

T F 22.   When a majority-owned foreign subsidiary operates independently from the parent, its financial statement accounts are translated into dollars using the current rate method.

T F 23.   Foreign currency translation gains and losses for self-contained foreign subsidiaries are put directly into the owners' equity account.

Multiple-Choice Questions
Select the best answer from those provided.

_____ 1.   When an investor owns less than 20% of another company, the investor is a
   a.   majority investor.
   b.   minority active investor.
   c.   minority passive investor.
   d.   major investor.

_____ 2.   When an investor owns shares of another company that total more than 20% but less than 50% of the investee company, the investor is a
   a.   majority investor.
   b.   minority passive investor.
   c.   minority active investor.
   d.   majority passive investor.

_____ 3.   Available-for-sale securities are securities that the investor plans to hold for
   a.   more than one year.
   b.   at least 30 days.
   c.   less than one year.
   d.   no more than 30 days.

_____ 4.   Trading securities are securities held by an investor for
   a.   more than one year.
   b.   less than one year.
   c.   more than two years.
   d.   more than five years.

_____ 5.   An investor who owns more than 50% of the shares of the investee corporation is a
   a.   minority owner.
   b.   majority owner.
   c.   minority active investor.
   d.   minority passive investor.

_____ 6.   The equity method of accounting is required to be used when an investor has
   a.   a minority active ownership interest.
   b.   a 10% interest in the investee company.
   c.   a minority passive ownership interest in the company.
   d.   between a 10% and 20% ownership interest.

_____ 7.   The adjustment to recognize holding gains or losses on available-for-sale securities is recorded in the
a.   cash flow statement.
b.   income statement.
c.   balance sheet.
d.   footnotes to the financial statements.

_____ 8.   Unrealized holding gains and losses that arise from available-for-sale securities are a component of
a.   cash flow.
b.   the income statement.
c.   retained earnings.
d.   comprehensive income.

_____ 9.   A majority investment is accounted for by the
a.   cost method.
b.   equity method.
c.   lower of cost or market method.
d.   cost or equity method.

_____ 10.   When an investor in a corporation pays more for the company than the fair market value of the net assets acquired, the investor recognizes the existence of
a.   goodwill.
b.   negative goodwill.
c.   organization cost.
d.   trademarks.

_____ 11.   Consolidated financial statements are required to be prepared if the parent company owns more than
a.   50% of the subsidiary.
b.   40% of the subsidiary.
c.   30% of the subsidiary.
d.   20% of the subsidiary.

_____ 12.   If a parent and subsidiary company engage in intercompany transactions, an entry to eliminate the intercompany transactions is required based on the
a.   historical cost principle.
b.   cost-benefit constraint.
c.   matching principle.
d.   economic entity concept.

_____ 13.   Managers would prefer to record all business combinations based on pooling of interests treatment because the pooling of interests method of recording business combinations
a.   overstates consolidated income.
b.   understates consolidated income.
c.   overstates extraordinary items.
d.   understates extraordinary items.

_____ 14.   If a parent company owns a foreign subsidiary that is an extension of the parent company, the foreign subsidiary's financial statements must be translated using the
a.   temporary method.
b.   current rate method.
c.   present value method.
d.   temporal method.

_____ 15.   If a parent company owns a foreign subsidiary that is a self-contained unit, the foreign subsidiary's statements must be translated using the
a.   temporary method.
b.   temporal method.
c.   current rate method.
d.   present value method.

_____ 16.   Financial analysts must use caution when evaluating companies that have been acquired by a parent using the pooling of interests method because the pooling of interests method tends to inflate
a.   current ratio.
b.   quick-ratio.
c.   cash flow ratios.
d.   rate of return ratios.

_____ 17.   Goodwill is reported under
a.   the purchase method.
b.   the pooling of interests method.
c.   both the pooling of interests and purchase method.
d.   neither the purchase method nor the pooling of interests method.

_____ 18.   The purpose underlying the adjustments made to consolidate financial statements is to
   a. follow the SEC guidelines.
   b. avoid double counting transactions.
   c. obey federal laws.
   d. obey state laws.

_____ 19.   The investment account representing ownership of a subsidiary may contain an element of
   a. the present value of net assets.
   b. the future value of net assets.
   c. goodwill.
   d. the present value of gross assets.

_____ 20.   In a business combination that qualifies for pooling of interests treatment a
   a. stock-for-stock exchange must take place.
   b. cash-for-cash exchange must take place.
   c. cash-for-assets exchange must take place.
   d. cash-for-stock exchange must take place.

Exercises

1.   The following information applies to Woods Company's investments in marketable equity securities.

		Market Value at Year End	
	Cost	Year 2	Year 3
Trading	$650,000	$550,000	$490,000
Available-for-sale	600,000	640,000	475,000

Required:
A.   How much should Woods report as unrealized holding gains and losses in its Year 3 income statement?
B.   How much should Woods report as net unrealized loss on available-for-sale securities on its December 31, Year 3 statement of stockholders' equity?

2. In January, Year 4, the Ira Corporation acquired 25% of the outstanding common stock of George Company for $800,000. This investment gave Ira the ability to exercise significant influence over George. The book value of these shares was $675,000. The excess of cost over book value was attributed to an identifiable tangible asset, which had a remaining useful life of ten years. For the year ended December 31, Year 4, George reported net income of $600,000 and paid cash dividends of $160,000 on its common stock.

Required:
A. How much would Ira Corporation's income increase in Year 4 as a result of its investment in George Company?
B. What is the carrying value of Ira's investment in George Company at December 31, Year 4?

_____

_____

_____

_____

_____

_____

_____

_____

_____

3.   Southern Company bought 48% of Northern Company's outstanding common stock on January 2, Year 8, for $1,300,000. The carrying amount of Northern's net assets on the purchase date totaled $1,900,000. Fair values and carrying amounts were the same for all items except equipment, for which the fair value exceeded its carrying amount by $400,000. The equipment has a 12-year life. During Year 8, Western reported net income of $284,000 and paid a $90,000 cash dividend.

Required:
A.   How much should Southern report on its income statement from the Northern investment for the Year 8?
B.   How much should Southern report on the Year 8 balance sheet for the Northern investment?

_____

_____

_____

_____

_____

_____

_____

_____

4.   On January 1, Year 6, the Boone Company purchases for cash, 35% of the 100,000 shares of voting common stock of the Daniel Company for $750,000. At this time, 35% of the underlying equity in the net assets of Daniel was $600,000. Of the total excess cost, $35,000 relates to the excess of fair market value over the book value of inventory, which Daniel accounts for using FIFO. An additional $60,000 of excess cost is attributed to under-valuation of depreciable assets with an average remaining life of 10 years. As a result of this transaction, Boone has the ability to exercise significant influence over the operating and financial policies of Daniel. Daniel's net income for the year ended December 31, Year 6, is $250,000. During Year 6, Daniel pays $95,000 in dividends to its stockholders.

Required:

A. How much income would Boone report on its Year 6 income statement for its investment in Daniel?

B. What would be the balance in the investment in the Daniel Company account on December 31, Year 6?

_____

_____

_____

_____

_____

_____

_____

_____

_____

_____

Solutions

Answers to True or False Questions

True answers: 2, 3, 5, 8, 10, 11, 13, 15, 16, 18, 21, 22, 23.

False answers explained:

1. A minority investor in a corporation <u>usually has no</u> ability to influence company decisions.
4. Trading investments are reported at <u>fair market value</u> at each balance shut date.
6. Equity securities acquired for their long-term investment potential are treated as <u>available-for-sale</u> securities.
7. Unrealized gains and losses on available-for-sale securities <u>do not</u> affect income in the period of the price change.
9. The book value of equity investments recorded under the equity method is <u>not</u> marked-to-market.
12. Ownership of less than 20 percent of another company requires the use of <u>mark-to-market</u> accounting.
14. If exactly 50 percent of the voting shares of one company are owned by another entity, consolidation of financial statements is <u>not</u> required.
17. Under the pooling of interests approach, <u>no</u> buyout is considered to have taken place.
19. There are twelve conditions that must be met to qualify for the <u>pooling of interests</u> method.
20. Almost 90 percent of all business combinations use <u>purchase</u> accounting.

Answers to Multiple-Choice Questions

1.	C	6.	A	11.	A	16.	D
2.	C	7.	C	12.	D	17.	A
3.	A	8.	D	13.	A	18.	B
4.	B	9.	D	14.	D	19.	C
5.	B	10.	A	15.	C	20.	A

Answers to Exercises

1. A. Holding Gain or Loss - Income Statement
        Trading Securities
        Year 2 ($650,000 — $550,000) = $100,000 Holding Loss
        Year 3 ($550,000 — $490,000) = $60,000 Holding Loss

    B. Holding Gain or Loss - Balance Sheet
        Available-for-Sale Securities
        Year 2 ($600,000 — $640,000) = $40,000 Holding Gain
        Year 3 ($640,000 — $475,000) = $165,000 Holding Loss

2. A. Ira Corporation-Income (Equity Method) .25 x $600,000 = $150,000
        Less: Cost over Book Value Amortization ($800,000 — $675,000/10)   (12,500)
        Total increase in income $137,500

    B. Investment Balance January 1, Year 4 $ 800,000
        Equity in Income   150,000
        Amortization   (12,500)
        Dividends   (40,000)
        Investment Balance December 31, Year 4 $ 897,500

3. Investment in Northern Co. $1,300,000 Cost
                    48% x $1,900,000   (912,000) Book Value
                                            388,000 Excess
                                           (192,000)Equipment
                                           $196,000 Goodwill acquired

    A. Year 5 Income Statement:
        Share of Income ($284,000 x .48) $136,320
        Amortization of Equipment ($192,000 / 12) (16,000)
        Total Income Recognized $120,320

B.   Year 5 Balance Sheet:

Beginning Investment	$1,300,000
+ Income	136,320
— Amortization	16,000
— Dividends	43,200
Ending Investment Balance	$1,377,120

4.

Investment	$750,000
Book Value	600,000
Excess of Cost over Book	$150,000
Less: Inventory	(35,000)
Equipment	(60,000)
Remaining Cost in Excess (Goodwill)	$ 55,000

A.   Boone's income for Year 6 based on investment:

		$250,000
		x .35
		$ 87,500
Less Amortization:		
Inventory	$35,000	
Depreciation ($60,000 / 10)	6,000	(41,000)
Total		$ 46,500

B.

Beginning Investment account	$750,000
+ Income	46,500
— Dividends ($95,000 x .35)	33,250
Ending Investment account	$762,250

CHAPTER 17

STATEMENT OF CASH FLOWS

Chapter Review

Learning Objective 2:
Why accrual net income and operating cash flows differ and the factors that explain this difference.

Positive cash flow is a critical attribute of successful companies. In the operations of a firm, two realities exist — a performance reality and a cash reality. The income statement measures the performance reality with all of the flaws of the accrual method of accounting. The **cash flow statement** describes the reality of the cash position. Significant differences between these two realities may be a "red flag" for manipulations of reported income or impending financial difficulties. No matter what the profit picture of a firm is, sound cash management is imperative. Profits are wonderful, but only cash pays the bills.

There are a number of reasons why the reality of accrual income and cash differ:
1. The income statement is prepared on an accrual basis of accounting and not all operating transactions are cash transactions. Accrual accounting contains a number of estimates and one-time write-offs made from subjective judgments. Management can manipulate accrual income numbers.
2. Some changes in cash arise from transactions with owners, which never become part of the income statement.
3. Some non-cash investments are made directly from borrowings or stockholders' transfers and never involve cash. The amortization of costs however, becomes part of the income statement.

Learning Objective 1:
The major sources and uses of cash reported in the operating, investing and financing sections of the statement of cash flows.

A firm's activities exist in three critical areas:
1. It **operates** to produce revenues.
2. It **invests** resources to enable the firm to operate.
3. It **finances** the investments from owner or lender provided resources.

The cash flow statement classifies the cash inflows and outflows in terms of the firm's **operating**, **investing**, and **financing** activities.

FYI. . .
Operating cash flow is the only **renewable** source of cash. The primary investing source of cash is the sale of assets. Firms have a finite quantity of assets to sell. The primary sources of financing cash flows is borrowing and stock sales. Firms can only borrow a finite amount from creditors and the market will only purchase a finite amount of stock. Operating cash flow is limited only to the amount of goods or services the company can sell within a given time period.

FYI. . .
For a healthy company, operating cash flows should be consistently positive and sufficient to service debt and dividend needs. Investing cash flows are usually negative. Positive investing flows indicate that a company is divesting assets. Financing cash flows can be either positive or negative. Negative indicates payment of dividends and retirement of debt. Positive can indicate either sale of stock or

The heart of the matter. . .
Here is an easy way to remember the classifications of cash flows. If the item you are considering has to do with the highlighted items, it is probably part of operating activities.

Balance Sheet   Income Statement

Current Assets: Current Liabilities:
  Cash   Accounts Payable
  Accounts Receivable   Taxes Payable
  Inventory   Wages Payable
  Prepaid Expenses   Accrued Liabilities
  Notes Receivable
  Marketable Securities   Notes Payable
Long-Term Assets   Long-Term Liabilities
Intangible Assets   Stockholders' Equity

Investing activities are found in the rest of the assets as highlighted.

Balance Sheet

Current Assets: Current Liabilities:
  Cash   Accounts Payable
  Accounts Receivable   Taxes Payable
  Inventory   Wages Payable
  Prepaid Expenses   Accrued Liabilities
  Notes Receivable
  Marketable Securities   Notes Payable
Long-Term Assets   Long-Term Liabilities
Intangible Assets   Stockholders' Equity

Financing activities pertain to the borrowed and invested resources highlighted below.

Balance Sheet

Current Assets   Current Liabilities:
Long-Term Assets   Accounts Payable
Intangible Assets   Accrued Liabilities
                                           Notes Payable
                                           Long-Term Liabilities
                                           Stockholders' Equity

SFAS No. 95 outlined the preferred format for the Statement of Cash Flows. The operating section delineates the sources and amounts of operating cash inflows and the sources and amounts of operating cash outflows using the **direct approach**. In particular, this includes:

1.   cash collected from customers;
2.   interest and dividends received;
3.   other operating receipts;
4.   cash paid to employees and suppliers;

borrowing.

5.   interest paid;
6.   income taxes paid;
7.   other operating cash payments.

In addition, *SFAS No. 95* specified that a reconciliation schedule be included that reconciles the differences between accrual net income and cash flow from operating activities. This reconciliation is also called the **indirect approach**. The indirect approach reverses all of the accrual adjustments made to cash-basis income statements to create accrual-basis income statements. <u>For both methods, the investing and financing activities are identical.</u>

SFAS No. 95 gave statement preparers the option of using either method with these additional rules.

1.   If the direct approach is chosen, a supplemental schedule, "Reconciliation of Net Income to Cash Flow from Operations," must be included.

2.   If the indirect approach is chosen, a supplemental schedule must indicate "the amount paid for interest and income taxes."

3.   For both methods, a schedule of "Significant Non-Cash Investing and Financing Activities" must be included. This schedule alerts readers to non-cash transactions that might have future cash implications. For example, if bonds are converted into common stock, the bonds will not require future cash to retire the debt, but future common dividend requirements will rise.

For most firms, the choice is simple. The direct approach requires preparation of both the direct and indirect approach, and the indirect approach only requires preparation of the indirect approach. In addition, the indirect approach is easier to prepare from existing accrual accounting information. Therefore, only two or three percent of companies use the direct approach.

Learning Objective 3:
The difference between the direct and indirect method of determining cash flows from operations.

FYI. . .
To prepare a statement of cash flows, one needs comparative balance sheets, the income statement that bridges them, and a good understanding of the transactions that cause balance sheet accounts to change.

Learning Objective 4:
How to prepare a Statement of Cash Flows from comparative balance sheet data, income statement data, and other financial information.

The cash flow statement details the changes in the balance sheet between two points of time in terms of cash. If you think about it, most transactions involve cash. Therefore, we can anticipate the cash effect of any changes in the balance sheet. Statement preparation involves these steps:

1.   Take a comparative balance sheet and add a third column that computes, for each account, the increase or decrease from the beginning to the end of the year.

2.   Visualize the net entries that caused that account to change. For

example, Sales increase Accounts Receivable and Cash payments from customers decrease it.

3. Determine whether changes in the account are from operating, investing, or financing activities.

4. Using the cash flow statement format, add the change in each account to the appropriate place on the statement.

5. Total the statement entries, and be sure the net change in cash is the net change in the cash account between the beginning and ending balance sheet. **(See Demonstration Problem 1.)**

The heart of the matter. . .

One method to promote understanding of the accounting system and to simplify preparation of the Statement of Cash Flows is to draw T-accounts for many of the balance sheet accounts. By clearly delineating what transactions change each account, you gain understanding of both the accounting system and the cash flow effect. For example, look at the Accumulated Depreciation account:

Accumulated Depreciation		
	130,000	Beginning Balance
A/D of assets sold 12,000	50,000	Current depreciation
	168,000	Ending Balance

If the net change in the Accumulated Depreciation account is an increase equal to the current depreciation expense from the income statement, it might be a clue that no depreciable assets were sold during the year.

Learning Objective 5:
Why changes in balance sheet accounts over a year may not reconcile to the corresponding account changes included in the statement of cash flows.

One of the reasons it is important to know the transactions that affect accounts is because the net change in an account does not always agree with the increase or decrease presented in the cash flow statement. The differences are attributable to at least three causes:

1. Asset write-offs due to impairment, corporate restructuring, or retirement;

2. Translation adjustments on assets held by foreign subsidiaries; and

3. Acquisitions and divestitures of other companies.

4. Simultaneous investing and financing activities not directly affecting cash.

Inventory may have discrepancies between the net change in inventory on the cash flow statement and the balance sheet:

1. **Restructuring write-offs** are non-cash transactions that are not included in the inventory change on the direct approach to the

cash flow statement.

2.   **Foreign currency translation adjustments** differ between the balance sheet and the cash flow statement. The balance sheet computes the exchange rates at the current rates for the balance sheet dates. The cash flow statement records a series of exchange rates.

3.   **Acquisitions and divestitures** include inventories in the acquired or divested companies. The cash flow statement presents the cash amount of the acquisition or the divestiture, but does not separate the inventories from that amount. The inventories are included in the consolidated Inventory account so that the net change does not reconcile with the cash flow presentation.

The investing section of the cash flow statement contains the changes in Plant, Property, and Equipment. It is seldom one amount.

1.   **Asset purchases** are recorded in the cash flow statement as the amount of cash paid during the period, not the historical cost of the assets acquired. Firms do not pay cash for all purchases, such as leased and financed assets.

2.   **Asset retirements** show up in the investing section as the amount of cash received for the asset. The long-lived asset account is credited with the original cost of the asset upon retirement.

3.   An **asset impairment write-down** is not reflected in the investing section of the cash flow statement because it is not a cash transaction.

4.   **Foreign currency translation adjustments** for long-lived assets vary depending upon the fluctuations in the current exchange rates from year to year, and are no longer required disclosures in the financial statements.

5.   **Acquisitions and divestitures** include plant, property, and equipment. The cash flow statement presents the cash amount of the acquisition or the divestiture, but does not separate the tangible assets from that amount. The tangible assets are included in the consolidated Plant, Property, and Equipment accounts, which creates another discrepancy between the net changes in the balance sheet and cash flow statement.

Learning Objective 6:
What "cash burn rates" are and how

The ability to generate positive operating cash flow is critical to the survival of any company. The cash burn rate is a measure that assesses

they can be used to evaluate the financial viability of Internet companies

how quickly an Internet firm is using up its cash reserves. The "months to burnout" estimates how much longer a company can survive without an infusion of external capital.

Cash burn rate is calculated as:

$$\frac{\text{Cash used for operations} + \text{net cash used for capital expenditures and purchases}}{\text{Number of months covered by cash flow statements}}$$

Or

$$\frac{\text{Earnings before interest, taxes, depreciation and amortization net of non-recurring items}}{\text{Number of months covered by the income statement}}$$

Months to burnout is calculated as:

$$\frac{\text{Cash} + \text{cash equivalents} + \text{short-term marketable securities}}{\text{Cash burn rate}}$$

Glossary of Terms

Cash burn rate A measure which assesses how quickly a firm is using up its cash reserves.

Cash Flow Statement A statement required by FASB which explains the sources and uses of cash.

Direct Approach A method of preparing the cash flow statement prescribed by *SFAS No. 95* that lists the sources and uses of operating cash.

Financing Cash Flows Cash flows that arise from an entity selling its own stock or bonds, paying dividends, borrowing money, repaying amounts borrowed, or repurchasing its own shares.

Funds A generic term used to describe liquid assets — those which are readily convertible into cash or cash equivalents.

Indirect Approach A method of preparing the cash flow statement prescribed by *SFAS No. 95* that reconciles net income to cash flow from operations.

Investing Cash Flows Cash flows that result from the purchase or sale of productive assets such as plant and equipment, buying and selling of marketable securities, and acquisitions and divestitures of other companies.

Operating Cash Flows Cash flows that result from events or transactions that enter into the determination of net income.

Working Capital   The current assets minus the current liabilities of an entity.

Demonstration Problem

1.   **Preparing an Indirect Approach Cash Flow Statement.**

Sergeant Corporation
Comparative Balance Sheets
December 31, Year 5 and Year 6

Assets	Year 5	Year 6
Cash	$ 40,000	$ 12,000
Accounts Receivable	80,000	140,000
Inventory	460,000	420,000
Prepaid Expenses	20,000	48,000
Plant & Equipment (net)	900,000	980,000
Total Assets	$1,500,000	$1,600,000
Liabilities and Stockholders' Equity		
Accounts Payable	$ 72,000	$ 48,000
Accrued Liabilities	12,000	40,000
Long-term Debt	300,000	260,000
Common Stock	600,000	700,000
Retained Earnings	516,000	552,000
Total Liabilities and Stockholders' Equity	$1,500,000	$1,600,000

Sergeant Corporation
Income Statement
For Year Ended December 31, Year 6

Sales		$1,100,000
Cost of Goods Sold		650,000
Gross Profit		450,000
Selling Expenses	$ 50,000	
Administrative Expenses	220,000	
Depreciation Expense	40,000	
Income Tax Expense	60,000	
Total Expenses		370,000

Net Income		$ 80,000

Required: Prepare the Cash Flow Statement for Year 6 for the Sergeant Corporation.

First Step: Compute the net change in each balance sheet account from Year 5 to Year 6.
Application: Subtract the amount of Year 5 from Year 6 for each account.
Solution:

Assets	Year 5	Year 6	Increase (Decrease)
Cash	$ 40,000	$ 12,000	$ (28,000)
Accounts Receivable	80,000	140,000	60,000
Inventory	460,000	420,000	(40,000)
Prepaid Expenses	20,000	48,000	28,000
Plant & Equipment (net)	900,000	980,000	80,000
Total Assets	$1,500,000	$1,600,000	$100,000

Liabilities and Stockholders' Equity			
Accounts Payable	$ 72,000	$ 48,000	$ (24,000)
Accrued Liabilities	12,000	40,000	28,000
Long-term Debt	300,000	260,000	(40,000)
Common Stock	600,000	700,000	100,000
Retained Earnings	516,000	552,000	36,000
Total Liabilities and Stockholders' Equity	$1,500,000	$1,600,000	$100,000

Second Step: Determine which balance sheet accounts provide information for the operating section of the cash flow statements.
Application: Current assets (except investments and loans to non-customer) and current liabilities (except for Notes Payable) will provide information necessary for computing cash flow from operations.

Solution:

Assets	Year 5	Year 6
Cash	$ 40,000	$ 12,000
Accounts Receivable	**80,000**	**140,000**
Inventory	**460,000**	**420,000**
Prepaid Expenses	**20,000**	**48,000**
Plant & Equipment (net)	900,000	980,000
Total Assets	$1,500,000	$1,600,000

Liabilities and Stockholders' Equity		
Accounts Payable	**$ 72,000**	**$ 48,000**
Accrued Liabilities	**12,000**	**40,000**

Long-term Debt	300,000	260,000
Common Stock	600,000	700,000
Retained Earnings	516,000	552,000
Total Liabilities and Stockholders' Equity	$1,500,000	$1,600,000

Third Step: Determine other information needed to compute the operating cash flows.
Application: Preparing the indirect approach operating section of the cash flow statement requires net income and depreciation (or amortization and depletion) from the income statement.
Solution: Net income is $80,000 and depreciation expense is $40,000.

Fourth Step: Prepare the operating section of the cash flow statement.
Application: Use the format for the indirect approach for the operating section of the cash flow statement.
Solution:

Sergeant Corporation
Statement of Cash Flows
For the Year Ended December 31, Year 6

Operating Cash Flows:

Net Income		$80,000
Plus: Depreciation	$ 40,000	
Decrease in inventory	40,000	
Increase in accrued liabilities	28,000	108,000
Minus: Increase in accounts receivable	$(60,000)	
Increase in prepaid expenses	(28,000)	
Decrease in accounts payable	(24,000)	(112,000)
Cash Flows from Operations		$76,000

Fifth Step: Identify the balance sheet accounts that contain evidence of investing activities.
Application: Investing activities describe changes in long-term assets, investments, and loans made to non-customers.
Solution:

Assets	Year 5	Year 6
Cash	$ 40,000	$ 12,000
Accounts Receivable	80,000	140,000
Inventory	460,000	420,000
Prepaid Expenses	20,000	48,000
Plant & Equipment (net)	**900,000**	**980,000**
Total Assets	$1,500,000	$1,600,000

Sixth Step: Compute the cash flow from investing activities.
Application: Determine the change in the net plant and equipment account.

Solution: Prepare a T-account to analyze the change in net plant and equipment.

Plant & Equipment (net)			
Beginning Balance	900,000		
Purchase of Assets	120,000		
(computed)		40,000	Year 6 Depreciation
Ending Balance		980,000	

Determine the purchase of assets with the following computation:

Beginning Balance - Current Depreciation = Ending Balance - Purchases

$ 900,000 - $40,000   = $ 980,000 - Purchases

Therefore: Purchases = $980,000 - $900,000 + $40,000   = $120,000

   Investing Cash Flows:

   Purchase of long-term assets $(120,000)

   Cash Outflows from Investing Activities $(120,000)

Seventh Step: Determine the balance sheet accounts that contain evidence of financing activities.

Application: Financing activities describe changes in loans, other long-term liabilities, and stockholders' equity.

Solution:

Liabilities and Stockholders' Equity	Year 5	Year 6
Accounts Payable	$ 72,000	$ 48,000
Accrued Liabilities	12,000	40,000
Long-term Debt	**300,000**	**260,000**
Common Stock	**600,000**	**700,000**
Retained Earnings	**516,000**	**552,000**
Total Liabilities and Stockholders' Equity	$1,500,000	$1,600,000

Eighth Step: Determine other items of information needed to prepare the financing section of the cash flow statement.

Application: Analyze the changes in the highlighted accounts. Analyze the change in the Retained Earnings account to determine the dividends declared and paid.

Solution:

The decrease in long-term debt is evidently a repayment of the debt. The increase in common stock indicates a new issuance of common stock. The change in retained earnings is a combination of net income and dividends paid. Prepare a T-account to analyze the change in retained earnings.

Retained Earnings			
Beginning Balance		516,000	
		80,000	Net Income
Dividends Declared	44,000		

Ending Balance   552,000

Determine the dividends declared with the following computation:
         Beginning Balance + Net Income = Ending Balance + Dividends
              $516,000   + $80,000   = $552,000   + Dividends
Therefore: Dividends = $516,000 + $80,000 - $552,000 = $44,000

Ninth Step: Prepare the financing section of the statement of cash flows.
Application: Use the format for the financing section of the cash flow statement.
Solution:
     Financing Cash Flows:
              Repayment of long-term loans $(40,000)
              Issuance of common stock   100,000
              Payment of dividends   (44,000)
              Cash Flow from Financing Activities $ 16,000

Tenth Step: Prepare the Statement of Cash Flows
Application: Consolidate the three major categories of the cash flow statement based on work completed in previous steps and complete the statement.

Final Solution:

Sergeant Corporation
Statement of Cash Flows
For the Year Ended December 31, Year 6

Operating Cash Flows:
     Net Income $ 80,000
     Plus: Depreciation $ 40,000
             Decrease in inventory   40,000
             Increase in accrued liabilities   28,000   108,000
     Minus: Increase in accounts receivable $(60,000)
             Increase in prepaid expenses   (28,000)
             Decrease in accounts payable   (24,000)   (112,000)
     Cash Flows from Operations   76,000

Investing Cash Flows:
     Purchase of long-term assets   (120,000)

Financing Cash Flows:
     Repayment of long-term loans $(40,000)
     Issuance of common stock   100,000
     Payment of dividends   (44,000)

Cash Flow from Financing Activities	16,000
Net Change in Cash	(28,000)
Cash Balance at the Beginning of the Year	40,000
Cash Balance at the End of the Year	$ 12,000

Test Yourself
True or False Questions

T F 1. Working capital is defined as current assets minus long-term liabilities.

T F 2. When a company sells its own stock to investors for cash it creates an investing activity.

T F 3. The purchase of marketable securities for cash is an example of a financing activity.

T F 4. The direct approach to the preparation of the cash flow statement requires that firms report the major classes of gross cash receipts and gross cash payments.

T F 5. The indirect approach to the preparation of the cash flow statement begins with the accrual basis net income.

T F 6. Depreciation and amortization must be added back to net income when using the direct method to prepare the cash flow statement.

T F 7. When there is an increase in accounts receivable for the year the increase must be subtracted from the accrual basis income to reconcile cash provided by operations.

T F 8. *SFAS No. 95* requires firms that use the indirect approach for cash flow statements to separately disclose income taxes paid.

T F 9. Simultaneous non-cash financing and investing transactions do not need to be disclosed for cash flow statement purposes.

T F 10. An increase in the accounts payable account results in a subtraction from the accrual-basis net income in the indirect approach of the cash flow statement.

T F 11. The repurchase of one's own stock is an example of an operating activity.

T F 12. An increase in deferred income taxes is added back to net income to derive cash flow from operations.

T F 13. *SFAS No. 95* requires that acquisition of other companies be shown separately as an investing activity as "acquisitions net of cash acquired".

T F 14. The year to year changes in comparative balance sheet accounts always coincide with the amounts reported on the statement of cash flows.

T   F   15.   Firms that consistently generate strong positive cash flows from operations are considered better credit risks by lenders.

Multiple-Choice Questions

Select the best answer from those provided.

_____   1.   Liquid assets may be identified as
   a.   non-monetary assets.
   b.   monetary assets.
   c.   intangible assets.
   d.   funds.

_____   2.   The difference between current assets and current liabilities is identified as
   a.   working capital.
   b.   operating cash flow.
   c.   investing cash flow.
   d.   liquid assets.

_____   3.   Cash flows arising from the sale of assets used to manufacture a product are cash flows from
   a.   operating activities.
   b.   investing activities.
   c.   financing activities.
   d.   development activities.

_____   4.   Cash flows that arise from the purchase or sale of treasury stock are cash flows from
   a.   operating activities.
   b.   financing activities.
   c.   investing activities.
   d.   development activities.

_____   5.   Cash flows that arise from interest received and interest paid are classified as
   a.   operating activities.
   b.   financing activities.
   c.   investing activities.
   d.   development activities.

_____ 6. On a cash flow statement, amortization and depreciation expense are
a. subtracted from net income under operating activities.
b. added to net income under operating activities.
c. subtracted from net income under investing activities.
d. added to net income under investing activities.

_____ 7. Most business entities prepare the cash flow statement based on the
a. indirect approach.
b. funds flow approach.
c. direct approach.
d. expense approach.

_____ 8. Financial analysts believe that they can obtain more relevant information about the quality of a firm's earnings from a cash flow statement prepared by the
a. direct approach.
b. revenue approach.
c. funds flow approach.
d. indirect approach.

_____ 9. The reason that the cash flow statement does not provide for the allocation of income taxes paid based on operating, financing, and investing activities is the
a. matching principle.
b. materiality constraint.
c. cost-benefit constraint.
d. historical cost concept.

_____ 10. If a firm engages in a financing transaction that does not directly and immediately involve cash flow, the transaction should be
a. ignored.
b. reported on a funds flow statement.
c. included in a supplemental schedule to the cash flow statement.
d. reported on the retained earnings statement.

_____ 11. A decrease in a current asset for the year will cause a
a. decrease in cash flow from investing activities.
b. decrease in cash flow from financing activities.
c. increase in cash flow from operating activities.
d. decrease in cash flow from operating activities.

_____ 12.   An increase in prepaid insurance expense for the year will cause a
   a.   decrease in cash flow from investing activities.
   b.   decrease in cash flow from financing activities.
   c.   decrease in cash flow from operating activities.
   d.   increase in cash flow from operating activities.

_____ 13.   A loss on the sale of a piece of productive equipment should be
   a.   added back to net income to determine cash flow from operations.
   b.   subtracted from net income to determine cash flow from operations.
   c.   a source of funds from financing activities.
   d.   a use of funds from investing activities.

_____ 14.   The only reliable, renewable source of cash flow is from the
   a.   financing activities.
   b.   operating activities.
   c.   investing activities.
   d.   sale of investments.

_____ 15.   Financial analysts who have trouble analyzing year-to-year changes in
         comparative balance sheets because the changes do not coincide with the amounts
         reported on the cash flow statement, must rely on the information in the operating
         section of the cash flow statement and the
   a.   footnotes.
   b.   balance sheet.
   c.   retained earnings statement.
   d.   funds flow statement.

_____ 16.   Subjective judgments used by accountants in utilizing accrual basis accounting
         often cause
   a.   measurement errors and certainty into reported earnings.
   b.   measurement errors and uncertainty into reported earnings.
   c.   nonmeasurement errors and certainty into reported earnings.
   d.   nonmeasurement errors and uncertainty into reported earnings.

_____ 17.   The two approaches used to prepare cash flow statements are the indirect
         approach and the
   a.   direct approach.
   b.   financing approach.
   c.   investing approach.
   d.   funds flow approach.

_____ 18. The indirect approach to the preparation of the operating activities section of the cash flow statement begins with the
   a. cash basis net income
   b. cash basis revenues.
   c. accrual basis net income.
   d. accrual basis revenues.

_____ 19. Income taxes paid is a category reported on a cash flow statement prepared under the
   a. direct approach.
   b. indirect approach.
   c. funds flow approach.
   d. reconciliation approach.

_____ 20. A decrease in accounts payable for the year will cause a/an
   a. increase in cash flow from operating activities.
   b. decrease in cash flow from operating activities.
   c. increase in cash flow from investing activities.
   d. decrease in cash flow from investing activities.

Exercises

1. Information for Statler Corporation is as follows:

Net Income	$180,000
Decrease in prepaid expenses	12,500
Cash paid for new plant equipment	40,000
Amortization of discount on bonds payable	4,000
Decrease in accounts payable	3,500
Increase in inventory	12,500
Depreciation expense	20,000
Increase in salaries payable	4,500
Increase in accounts receivable	20,000
Dividends paid to stockholder	10,000
Dividends declared	12,500

Required: Calculate the net cash provided by operating activities for Statler Corporation using the indirect method.

_____
_____
_____
_____
_____
_____
_____
_____
_____
_____

2.   Cramer Corporation's worksheet for the preparation of its Year 9 statement of cash flows
      included the following:

	January 1	December 31
Accounts receivable	$49,000	$46,000
Prepaid rent expense	18,000	19,000
Accounts payable	41,000	37,000

Cramer's Year 9 net income is $390,000.

Required: How much should Cramer Corporation include as net cash provided by
operating activities in the statement of cash flows?

_____
_____
_____
_____
_____
_____
_____
_____
_____
_____

3.   Allegheny Corporation is preparing a statement of cash flows for the year ended
      December 31, Year 15. Selected beginning and ending account balances are:

	Beginning	Ending
Equipment	$1,800,000	$1,902,000
Accumulated Depreciation-Equipment	380,000	516,000
Loss on sale of equipment		8,000

During Year 15, Allegheny received $178,000 for a machine that cost $198,000, and
purchased other items of equipment.

Required:
A.   How much was the depreciation on machinery for Year 15?
B.   How much were the Equipment purchases for Year 15?

4.   In preparing its cash flow statement for the year ended December 31, Year 3, Pele
      Corporation gathered the following data:

Gain on sale of machinery	$ 54,000
Proceeds from sale of machinery	270,000
Purchase of Jay, Inc. bonds (face value $1,000,000)	900,000
Amortization of bond discount	32,000
Dividends declared	112,000
Dividends paid	76,000
Proceeds from the sale of treasury stock (cost $480,000)	390,000

Required: What amount should Pele report as net cash provided or used in investing
activities?

_____

_____

_____

_____

_____

_____

_____

5.   In preparing its cash flow statement for the year ended December 31, Year 5, Schorr
      Corporation gathered the following data:

Loss on sale of machinery	$ 50,000
Proceeds from sale of machinery	120,000
Purchase of Pan Am bonds (face value $1,200,000)	1,020,000
Amortization of bond discount	12,000
Dividends declared	180,000
Dividends paid	64,000
Proceeds from the sale of treasury stock (cost $500,000)	620,000

      Required: What amount should Schorr report as net cash provided or used by financing
      activities?

_____

_____

_____

_____

_____

_____

_____

Solutions

Answers to True or False Questions

True answers: 4, 5, 7, 8, 12, 13, 15
False answers explained:
1.   Working capital for a business entity is defined as current assets minus <u>current</u> liabilities.
2.   When a company sells its own stock to investors for cash it gives rise to a <u>financing</u> activity.
3.   The purchase of marketable securities for cash is an example of an <u>investing activity</u>.
6.   Depreciation and amortization must be added back to net income when using the <u>indirect</u> method.
9.   Simultaneous financing and investing transactions that do not involve cash <u>need</u> to be disclosed for cash flow statement purposes.
10.   An increase in the accounts payable account results in <u>an addition to</u> the accrual basis net income in the indirect method for cash flows.
11.   The repurchase of one's own stock is an example of a <u>financing</u> activity.
14.   The year to year changes in comparative balance sheet accounts <u>may not</u> coincide with the changes implied from amounts reported on the statement of cash flows.

Answers to Multiple-Choice Questions

1.	D	6.	B	11.	C	16.	B
2.	A	7.	A	12.	C	17.	A
3.	B	8.	D	13.	A	18.	C
4.	B	9.	C	14.	B	19.	A
5.	A	10.	C	15.	A	20.	B

Answers to Exercises

1.   Cash Flows from Operating Activities:

Net Income		$180,000
Add:	Depreciation	20,000
	Amortization of bond discount	4,000
	Decrease in prepaid expenses	12,500
	Increase in salaries payable	4,500
Deduct:	Increase in inventory	12,500
	Increase in accounts receivable	20,000
	Decrease in accounts payable	3,500
Net Cash Inflows from Operations		$185,000

2.

Cramer Corporation
Statement Of Cash Flows
For the Year Ended December 31, Year 9

Cash Flows from Operating Activities		
Net Income		$390,000
Add:	Decrease in Accounts Receivable	3,000
Deduct:	Decrease in Accounts Payable	4,000
	Increase in Prepaid Rent	1,000
Net Cash Inflow from Operations		$388,000

3.   A.   Depreciation on Machinery for Year 9:

Proceeds of Sale of Machine	$178,000
Loss on the Sale	8,000
Book Value	$196,000
Cost	$198,000
Less: Book Value	186,000
Accumulated Depreciation	$ 12,000
Beginning Accumulated Depreciation	$380,000
Accumulated Depreciation of Asset Sold	(12,000)
Depreciation Expense for Year	148,000
Ending Accumulated Depreciation	$516,000

B.   Equipment Balance at the end of Year 10:

Beginning Equipment	$1,800,000
Asset sold	(198,000)
Equipment purchases	300,000
Ending Equipment	$1,902,000

4.

Pele Corporation
Cash Flows from Investing Activities
For Year Ended December 31, Year 3

Proceeds from Sale on Machinery	$ 270,000
Purchase of Jay, Inc. Bonds	(900,000)
Net Cash Outflow from Investing Activities	$(630,000)

5.

Schorr Company
Cash Flows from Financing Activities
For Year Ended December 31, Year 5

Dividends Paid	$ (64,000)
Sale of Treasury Stock	620,000
Net Cash Inflow from Financing	$556,000

CHAPTER 18

OVERVIEW OF INTERNATIONAL FINANCIAL REPORTING DIFFERENCES AND INFLATION

Chapter Review

International investment in equity and debt securities has grown substantially over the last decade. Factors that have caused this growth in foreign investment include:
1. the relaxation of security market regulatory rules;
2. improvements in telecommunications;
3. computer networking; and
4. the understanding by investors that global investment portfolios are less risky than those of strictly domestic securities.

The diversity of reporting rules and philosophies of other countries make global investment decisions more complex.

Learning Objective 1: Why financial reporting philosophies and detailed GAAP procedures differed across countries in the past.

There are two international financial reporting approaches:
1. Countries whose disclosures are intended to reflect the underlying **economic performance** of the reporting entity, including the United Kingdom, Ireland, Australia, New Zealand, the United States, Canada, Mexico, the Phillippines, and the Netherlands.
2. Countries whose financial reporting is not intended to capture the economic reality but instead **conform to mandated laws or tax rules**, including Italy, France, Germany, Belgium, Japan, and Switzerland.

Accounting principles in the United Kingdom require the accrual concept, the going concern concept, and consistency of application. Audited financial statements in the United Kingdom must present a **true and fair** view of the entity.

The United States influences financial reporting in Canada, Mexico, and the Philippines. The United Kingdom influences financial reporting in Ireland, Australia, New Zealand, India, and other British Commonwealth countries.

Financial reporting goals in France, Italy, and Belgium are designed to meet the requirements of national tax laws. The governments of Germany, Japan, and Switzerland define accounting with both commercial laws and tax laws. Many countries require conformity between tax income and book income to qualify for tax benefits. The requirement for such conformity is a major restriction of the ability of financial statements in these countries to reflect economic reality. The recent trend among many European multinational companies whose stock is listed on foreign exchanges is to use either International Accounting Standards or U.S. GAAP for consolidated financial statements prepared for foreign investors.

Learning Objective 2: Why financial reporting philosophies differ across countries.

GAAP in the United Kingdom and the United States attempt to capture the underlying economic events for business entities. These two nations greatly influence the financial reporting of many other countries. Investors need financial statements that project economic reality. There are many differences in the GAAP of the various countries whose underlying purpose of financial reporting is to capture the underlying economic reality, but there are also many similarities. In countries like Germany and Japan where tax and commercial laws drive financial reporting, the economic realities of entities are reported by mere coincidence. Financial reporting in these countries often falls short of investor needs.

The reporting philosophies of different countries are tied to the legal, ethical, institutional, and financial customs of the countries. In countries where the major source of financing is outside investors, the investors demand a reporting system that provides information about the underlying economic reality of the situation. In countries where the bulk of the financing is provided by a few banks or the government, either of which may yield tremendous power over the borrower, the demand for information that reflects the underlying economic reality is minimal.

Learning Objective 2: How globalization has relaxed cross-border barriers and prompted convergence of reporting standards across countries.

Globalization describes the increased mobility of goods, services, labor, and capital throughout the world. This has led to increased competition worldwide, which has made it necessary for firms to seek capital sources to finance international expansion. Firms in countries using the commercial and tax law approach to financial reporting were at a serious disadvantage to obtain the needed funds since their accounting reports did not provide investors with the information they require. Supplemental reports based on U. S. GAAP or standards issued by the

International Accounting Standards Board called **International Financial Reporting Standards (IFRS)** were necessary to provide potential investors with the information they require. Many countries have a two- tiered system of financial reporting. Parent company financial statements are prepared using the commercial tax law approach while consolidated financial statements use U. S. GAAP or IRFS to report performance to investors.

Learning Objective 3: The reasons for the increased importance of the International Accounting Standards Board (IASB).

Due to U. S. financial reporting scandals in the 2001 and 2002, U. S. GAAP has been tarnished and has less appeal to foreign investors. This has led to the increasing importance of IFRS as the way firms cope with the financial reporting demands of globalization. The European Union has adopted an "IAS Regulation" requiring all publicly traded EU companies to adopt IFRS for financial reporting in consolidated financial statements by January 1, 2005. This regulation will dramatically enhance the visibility of IFRS, the standards issued by the IASB.

The IASB was restructured from the old International Accounting Standards Committee (IASC) in 2001. The IASC had been in existence since 1973. There are more than 112 countries and more than 150 professional organizations represented in the IASB. By 2003, they have issued more than 41 International Financial Reporting Standards. The new IASB has 14 members and guidelines prohibit the Board from being dominated by any particular constituency or regional interest.

IASB standards are broader than U. S. GAAP and often provide more latitude. IFRS often permit different accounting treatments for similar economic events. One treatment is called the **benchmark treatment** while other reporting alternatives are called the **allowed alternative treatment**.

Learning Objective 4: Efforts by the FASB and IASB to converge their respective standards and facilitate cross-border financial transactions.

The FASB has undertaken a series of projects designed to further the goals of convergence of U. S. GAAP with IFRS. There have been joint projects conducted with the two groups addressing issues like revenue recognition and business combinations. The FASB has issued four exposure drafts that propose convergence in financial reporting for several issues. It is reasonable to expect this process to continue and differences between U. S. GAAP and IFRS will be narrowed in the future

Learning Objective 5: Mechanisms for coping

There are several methods designed to deal with the diversity that exists in international financial reporting. The methods include:

with reporting
differences that exist.

1. Compelling foreign issuers to use host country reporting regulations
2. Creation of bilateral arrangements between a particular host country and a particular foreign country
3. Allowing every foreign issuer to use the foreign issuer's own financial reporting rules in a host country
4. Requiring foreign issuers to use International Financial Reporting Standards.

The United States requires a foreign company that registers on its stock exchanges to reconcile the firm's accounting reports to U.S. GAAP. The various stock exchanges argue that this is a burdensome requirement for the foreign companies and causes many foreign companies not to register. The second problem is that comparability to the information provided by U. S. firms may not exist after the reconciliation is completed.

Learning Objective 6:
Factors that will help determine whether the SEC will ease rules that require foreign companies that wish to have securities traded on U. S. exchanges to reconcile their reporting methods to U. S. GAAP.

The SEC has set forth three elements that are necessary for the SEC's approval and acceptance of international accounting standards. The IASC standards must:

1. include a core set of accounting pronouncements that constitute a comprehensive, generally accepted basis of accounting;
2. be of high quality - resulting in comparability and transparency, and provide for full disclosure cost reporting model;
3. be rigorously interpreted and applied.

The IASC has developed a set of fundamental core financial reporting standards, which are currently under review by the International Organization of Securities Commission, (IOSCO) and the SEC.

Learning Objective 7:
How compliance with GAAP is monitored in different countries.

Not only do the financial reporting rules differ from country to country, but also the mechanisms to monitor compliance with accounting rules. In the United States and other industrialized countries, business entities are required to be audited by an independent auditor. In the United States, the SEC has the authority to challenge the financial reporting of publicly traded companies. The staff of the SEC is very small and often not able to scrutinize the financial statements of all the reporting entities.

Monitoring compliance in other countries may be even worse. The methods for monitoring compliance with financial reporting rules include:

1.   Audits by independent auditors;
2.   Oversight by government agencies;
3.   Oversight by private agencies.

Learning Objective 8: That companies in foreign countries with high inflation rates depart from the historical cost reporting model.

Inflation is a decline in the purchasing power of a country's currency. Inflation complicates the analysis of international accounting reports because historical cost-based financial statements are misleading and irrelevant. Financial reporting standards in countries with high rates of inflation mandate some form of inflation accounting.

Significant differences arise between average rates of inflation for the economy as a whole, and specific rates of price change for individual firms. To properly reflect economic activity, some believe that adjustments for changing prices need to be made based on the specific level of costs and prices experienced by individual firms. This approach is called **current cost accounting**. The rationale for the current cost approach is that each firm is unique and its own level of costs and prices should be reflected in the accounts. Others believe that adjustments for changing prices should be based on the general rate of inflation in the economy as a whole. This approach is called **general price-level accounting**.

Learning Objective 9: The two major approaches for adjusting financial reports for rapidly changing prices — current cost accounting and general price-level accounting.

Current cost refers to the existing market price that a firm pays to replace specific assets it owns. Current cost accounting attempts to accomplish two objectives:

1.   to reflect all nonmonetary assets at their current cost as of the balance sheet date; and
2.   to differentiate between
        a. current cost income from current operations and
        b. increases or decreases in current costs amounts (holding gains).

Current value accounting techniques periodically increase or decrease the balance sheet asset carrying amount as current cost changes and recognize the current holding gain or loss as income in that year. As the asset is sold or used up, the current cost carrying value is written off the books and matched against the sales revenue to record a realized gain or loss on sale. This separates holding gains and losses from realized gains and losses. **(See Demonstration Problem 1)**

Current cost income is designed to differentiate between operating profits and holding gains. The failure of historical cost accounting to differentiate between operating profits and holding gains is a serious disclosure limitation of the historical cost method.

During the 1970s and the 1980s current cost disclosures centered on nonmonetary assets like inventory and fixed assets. When the rate of inflation abated in the 1980s the focus on the efforts to adjust nonmonetary assets diminished. Disclosures under current GAAP for current cost on nonmonetary assets are voluntary.

In the mid-1980s, with the problems experienced by banks and savings and loans, the focus of market value disclosures began to change to certain types of monetary assets and liabilities. The reason for the change centered on the regulations that impact lending institutions, particularly **regulatory capital**. Financial institutions maintain accounting records based on historical cost, which means that the measure for regulatory capital is insensitive to changes in the assets and liabilities of financial institutions.

To provide more complete information to the financial community, the FASB now requires footnote disclosure of financial institution items such as loans and deposits and various other financial instruments.

FYI. . .
General price-level accounting and **constant dollar** accounting are synonymous terms.

General price-level accounting is another way to measure purchasing power. General price-level accounting focuses on changes in general purchasing power. **Purchasing power** of a currency establishes the real amount of goods and services that can be acquired at a given time. The general purchasing power approach relies on a price index. Historical cost statements ignore changes in the purchasing power of the currency. **(See Demonstration Problem 2)**

The objective of general price-level accounting is to make historical currency amounts expended in different periods comparable by adjusting all amounts to current purchasing power equivalents. Nominal dollar historical costs are restated into dollars of constant purchasing power.

General price-level accounting requires a clear delineation between monetary items and nonmonetary items because purchasing power changes affect each differently. Monetary items (cash, accounts receivable, accounts payable and bonds payable) are money, or a claim to receive or pay a sum of money, which is fixed in amount. These items are stated in terms of monetary units and the claim or amount remains fixed even if the price-level changes. Nonmonetary items (inventories, buildings, equipment, owners' equity, and most income statement accounts) are not fixed in amount, and the prices of these items will likely change as the price-level changes. **(See Demonstration Problem 3)**

Glossary of Terms

Current Cost Accounting
An accounting method used to account for inflation which calls for adjustments based on the specific level of costs and prices experienced by each individual firm.

General Price-Level Accounting
A method used to adjust for inflation using the general rate of inflation experienced in the economy as a whole.

Inflation
A situation in which there is a decline in the purchasing power of a country's currency.

Inflation Accounting
An accounting system developed to combat the reporting problems associated with a decline in the purchasing power of a country's currency.

International Accounting Standards Board (IASB)
An international body established to formulate and publish, in the public interest, accounting standards to be observed in the presentation of financial statements and to promote worldwide observance and acceptance. The IASB also works for the harmonization and improvement of regulations, standards, and procedures relating to the presentation of financial statements.

International Organization of Securities Commission (IOSCO)
An international body whose membership consists of the various national securities commissions. The SEC is a member.

Keiretsu
In Japan this is a loosely-interconnected corporate group.

Present Fairly
The term used in the audit report of U.S. companies meaning that the statements conform to Generally Accepted Accounting Principles.

Purchasing Power
The real amount of goods and services that may be acquired at any moment in time.

True and Fair View   The phrase used in audit reports in the United Kingdom. It represents an approach to financial reporting that expresses the notion that financial statements must reflect the underlying economic conditions experienced by the reporting firm.

Demonstration Problems

1.   **Preparing a Current Cost Income Statement.**

The Thompson Corporation's Year 5 historical cost income statement is as follows:

Sales	$1,050,000
Cost of Sales	510,000
Gross Profit	$540,000
Depreciation	110,000
Other operating expenses	216,000
Net income	$214,000

Management believes that the current cost of inventory sold is 25% higher than its historical cost at the time of sale. In addition, if equipment were valued at current costs, an additional $13,600 of depreciation would be recorded.

Required: Prepare a current cost income statement for Thompson Corporation.

First Step: Analyze the changes expected by management in the historical cost income statement.
Application: Adjust the Cost of Sales: Cost of Sales x   125%.
Solution: Cost of Sales $510,000 x 125% = $637,500

Second Step: Analyze the changes expected by management in the historical cost income statement.
Application: Adjust the Depreciation Expense: Depreciation Expense + $13,600
Solution: Depreciation Expense $110,000 + $13,600 = $123,600

Third Step: Prepare the current cost income statement.
Application: Prepare the current cost statements using the current cost figures developed in the first two steps.

Solution: Thompson Corporation
                                              Current Cost Income Statement

For the Year Ended December 31, Year 5

Sales	$1,050,000
Cost of Sales	637,500
Gross Profit	$412,500
Depreciation	123,600
Other Operating Expenses	216,000
Net Income	$ 72,900

2.   General Price-Level Accounting.

Joshua Corporation was formed on January 2, Year 10. Selected balances from the historical cost balance sheet at December 31, Year 10 were as follows:

Equipment (purchased in Year 10)	$412,500
Obligations under Product Warranties	25,000
Investment in Non-convertible Bonds (purchased in Year 10 and expected to be held to maturity)	280,000
Note Payable-Long-Term	375,000

The average Consumer Price Index was 95 for Year 10 and 118 for Year 11.

Required: In a general price-level accounting balance sheet at December 31, Year 11, at what amounts should the Land, Obligations under Product Warranties, Investment, and Long-Term Debt be shown?

First Step: Determine the items that are monetary assets and liabilities and those that are nonmonetary assets and liabilities.

Application: Monetary assets and liabilities remain fixed even if the price level changes, while nonmonetary assets and liabilities are restated.

Solution:

Equipment (purchased in Year 10)	$412,500	Nonmonetary Asset
Obligations under Product Warranties	25,000	Nonmonetary Liability
Investment in Non-convertible Bonds (purchased in Year 10 and expected to be held to maturity)	280,000	Monetary Asset
Note Payable-Long-Term	375,000	Monetary Liability

Second Step: Compute general price-level factor to be applied to nonmonetary assets.

Application: $\dfrac{\text{Year 11 General Price-Index}}{\text{Year 10 General Price Index}}$ x   Nonmonetary Assets

Solution: Equipment (purchased in Year 10) $412,500 x $\dfrac{118}{95}$ = $512,368

Third Step: Compute general price-level factor to be applied to nonmonetary liabilities.

Application: $\dfrac{\text{Year 11 General Price-Index}}{\text{Year 10 General Price Index}}$ x   Nonmonetary Liabilities

Solution: Obligations under Product Warranties $ 25,000 x $\dfrac{118}{95}$ = $31,053

3.   General Price-Level Accounting for Long-Lived Assets.

Lorus Corporation's equipment consisted of the following at December 31, Year 7.

Date Acquired	Price Index	Historical Cost
Year 5	80	$150,000
Year 6	120	124,000
Year 7	130	50,000
		$324,000

Required: Compute the amount reported on the balance sheet for the equipment if Lorus uses constant dollar accounting.

First Step: Determine the items that are monetary assets and liabilities and those that are nonmonetary assets and liabilities.
Application: Monetary assets and liabilities remain fixed even if the price level changes, while nonmonetary assets and liabilities are restated.
Solution: The problem relates to long-lived assets which are defined as nonmonetary assets.

Second Step: Compute the general price-level factors to be applied to nonmonetary assets.
Application: $\dfrac{\text{Year 7 General Price-Index}}{\text{Year 5 General Price Index}}$ x   Nonmonetary Assets

$\dfrac{\text{Year 7 General Price-Index}}{\text{Year 6 General Price Index}}$ x   Nonmonetary Assets

$\dfrac{\text{Year 7 General Price-Index}}{\text{Year 7 General Price Index}}$ x   Nonmonetary Assets

Solution:

Date Acquired	Price Index	Historical Cost	Multiplier	Restated Cost
Year 5	80	$150,000	130/80	$243,750
Year 6	120	124,000	130/120	134,333
Year 7	130	50,000	130/130	50,000
		$324,000		$428,083

Test Yourself

True or False Questions

T F 1.   Global investment decisions are complicated by the diversity of financial reporting measurement and disclosure rules in different countries.

T F 2.   Accounting principles in foreign countries either attempt to reflect underlying economic performance of the entity or simply conform to mandated laws or tax rules.

T F 3.   The Companies Act of 1985 helped to establish contemporary accounting principles in the United Kingdom.

T F 4.   The ultimate responsibility for formulating the financial reporting rules in the United States rests with the Financial Accounting Standards Board.

T F 5.   In the United States, the use of GAAP is designed to reflect economic events.

T F 6.   Financial statements produced by companies in the Netherlands are intended to reflect the underlying economic conditions of the reporting entity.

T F 7.   Financial reporting in the United States and the United Kingdom is not influenced by statutory law.

T F 8.   In many countries deductions claimed on tax returns must also appear on financial statements.

T F 9.   Financial reporting in Germany is designed to reflect economic events.

T F 10.   Japan and Germany rely almost exclusively on individual investors for financing.

T F 11.   The United States requires foreign companies who have their securities traded on the U.S. stock exchanges to reconcile their own reporting methods with U.S. GAAP.

T F 12.   The IASB began operation on July 1, 1993.

T F 13.   The decline in the purchasing power of a country's currency is referred to as inflation.

T F 14.   The current cost income statement results in a matching of actual sales revenues with the current costs in effect at year end.

T F 15.   In countries that are experiencing inflation, the use of historical cost reporting is more meaningful than inflation accounting.

Multiple-Choice Questions
Select the best answer from those provided.

_____ 1.   Investment portfolios based on a domestic investment strategy are
   a.   more risky than portfolios based on global investment strategies.
   b.   less risky than portfolios based on global investment strategies.
   c.   equally as risky as portfolios based on global investment strategies.
   d.   risk free.

_____ 2.   The United Kingdom utilizes accounting principles based on
   a.   economic performance.
   b.   requirements of Parliament.
   c.   tax laws.
   d.   determination of dividend strategy.

_____ 3.   The United Kingdom requires that financial statements be prepared on the
   a.   cash basis.
   b.   accrual basis.
   c.   modified cash basis.
   d.   modified accrual basis.

_____ 4.   The audit report presented in the United Kingdom indicates that financial statements present a/an
   a.   "correct view" of the company.
   b.   "accurate view" of the company.
   c.   "true and fair view" of the company.
   d.   "reasonable view" of the company.

_____ 5.   The SEC was granted powers to establish accounting principles by the
   a.   FASB.
   b.   state governments.
   c.   Congress.
   d.   New York Stock Exchange.

_____ 6.   In Japan a keiretsu is an associated group of companies that help each other
   a.   pay dividends.
   b.   with financing.
   c.   repay debt.
   d.   hire employees.

_____ 7.   In Germany the primary providers of capital are
           a. several large banks and the government.
           b. public investors.
           c. private investors.
           d. members of Parliament.

_____ 8.   A foreign corporation that wishes to have its stock traded on United States stock
           exchanges must present financial statements according to United States
           a. tax laws.
           b. securities laws.
           c. generally accepted accounting principles.
           d. generally accepted auditing standards.

_____ 9.   Which one of the following is a required element for acceptance of financial
           statements by the SEC based on the SEC's Statement on International Accounting
           Standards?
           a. The standards are required to be in accordance with U.S. GAAP.
           b. The standards must comply with U.S. tax laws.
           c. The standards must be rigorously interpreted and applied.
           d. The standards must comply with Japanese GAAP.

_____ 10. Security sales pursuant to financial statements of new registrants with the SEC are
           referred to as
           a. initial stock offerings.
           b. initial public offerings.
           c. initial private offerings.
           d. initial investment opportunities

_____ 11. Inflation represents a change in the purchasing power of a country's currency.
           The change is represented by a/an
           a. increase in purchasing power.
           b. decrease in purchasing power.
           c. abnormal change in purchasing power.
           d. rapid increase followed by a rapid decline in purchasing power.

_____ 12. In a country with a high inflation rate, the financial statements based on historical
           cost are
           a. misleading and irrelevant.
           b. less useful
           c. very useful.

d.   required by the SEC.

_____   13.   The Consumer Price Index is a broad overall price index used to adjust financial statements for inflation in a method referred to as
   a.   general price-level accounting.
   b.   current cost accounting.
   c.   accrual accounting.
   d.   cash basis accounting.

_____   14.   A serious disclosure problem appears in financial statements prepared under the historical cost method because of the failure to differentiate between operating profits and
   a.   recognized gains and losses.
   b.   recognized gains but not losses.
   c.   holding gains and losses.
   d.   holding gains but not losses.

_____   15.   Current cost accounting attempts to match the sales of a firm for the period with the current costs in effect at the
   a.   beginning of the year.
   b.   end of the year.
   c.   time of purchase of the goods.
   d.   time of each sale.

_____   16.   The collapse of the Savings and Loan industry in the 1980s caused a shift in the focus of market value disclosures from
   a.   monetary assets to nonmonetary assets.
   b.   nonmonetary assets to monetary assets.
   c.   long-lived assets to nonmonetary assets.
   d.   current assets to non-current assets.

_____   17.   A financial analyst reviewing the statements of financial institutions for information on loans and deposits will discover a wealth of information in the
   a.   balance sheet.
   b.   income statement.
   c.   cash flow statement.
   d.   footnotes to the financial statements.

_____   18.   The ability to make historical currency amounts expended in different periods comparable is accomplished through
   a.   general price-level accounting.
   b.   specific price-level accounting.

c. cash accounting.

d. accrual accounting.

_____ 19.   The restatement of owners' equity for a decrease in a monetary asset, under constant dollar accounting is

a. income.

b. expense.

c. an increase in equity.

d. a decrease in equity.

_____ 20.   Under historical cost accounting an attempt to separate operating profits from holding gains is attempted when a firm uses

a. straight-line depreciation.

b. LIFO inventory accounting.

c. FIFO inventory accounting.

d. accrual accounting.

Exercises

1.   Sarah Corporation reported its December 31, Year 6, income as follows:

Sales	$190,000
Cost of Sales	90,000
Gross Profit	$100,000
Depreciation	20,000
Other Operating Expenses	50,000
Net Income	$30,000

Management is concerned about the increase in inventory costs as well as the increasing costs of equipment. Management believes that the current cost of inventory sold is 40% higher than its historical cost at the time of sale. In addition, if equipment were valued at current costs, an additional $6,000 of depreciation would be recorded.

Required: Prepare a current cost income statement for Sarah Company.

_____

_____

_____

_____

_____

_____

2.   Silo Corporation was formed on January 1, Year 13. Selected balances from the historical cost
       balance sheet at December 31, Year 13 were as follows:
       Equipment (purchased in Year 13) $250,000
       Land (purchased in Year 13)   300,000
       Investment in nonconvertible bonds (purchased in Year 13
       and to be held to maturity)   115,000
       Note Payable-Long-Term   137,500

       The average Consumer Price Index was 100 for Year 13 and 140 for Year 14.

       Required: In a general price-level accounting balance sheet at December 31, Year 14, at what
       amounts should the equipment, land, investment and long-term debt be shown?

3.   Lou Corporation's equipment consisted of the following at December 31, Year 12:

Date Acquired	Price Index	Historical Cost
Year 10	100	$130,000
Year 11	125	160,000
Year 12	165	70,000
		$360,000

       Required: Compute the amount reported on the balance sheet for equipment if Lou uses constant
       dollar accounting.

Solutions

Answers to True or False Questions

True answers: 1, 2, 3, 5, 6, 8, 11, 13
False answers explained:

4.   The ultimate responsibility for formulating the financial reporting rules in the United States rests with the <u>SEC</u>.
7.   Financial reporting in the U.S. and the U.K. <u>is also</u> influenced by statutory law.
9.   Financial reporting in Germany is dominated by income tax regulations.
10.   Japan and Germany rely almost exclusively on <u>large banks and the government</u> for financing.
12.   The IASC began operation on July 1, <u>1973</u>.
14.   The current cost income statement results in a matching of actual sales revenues with the current costs in effect at <u>the time of each sale</u>.
15.   In countries that are experiencing inflation the use of historical cost reporting is <u>less</u> meaningful than inflation accounting.

Answers to Multiple-Choice Questions

1.	B	6.	B	11.	B	16.	B
2.	A	7.	A	12.	B	17.	D
3.	B	8.	C	13.	A	18.	A
4.	C	9.	C	14.	C	19.	D
5.	C	10.	B	15.	D	20.	B

Answers to Exercises

1.

Saria Corporation
Current Cost Income Statement
For the Year Ended December 31, Year 6

Sales	$190,000
Cost of Sales	126,000
Gross Profit	$64,000
Depreciation	26,000
Other Operating Expenses	50,000
Net Income	$(12,000)

2   Equipment ($250,000 x 140/100) $350,000
        Land ($300,000 x 140 / 100)   420,000
        Investment in Bonds (monetary asset)   115,000
        Notes Payable — Long-term (monetary liability) 137,500

3. | Date Acquired | Price Index | Historical Cost | Multiplier | Restated Cost |
|---|---|---|---|---|
| Year 10 | 100 | $130,000 | 165/100 | $214,500 |
| Year 11 | 125 | 160,000 | 165/125 | 214,500 |
| Year 12 | 165 | 70,000 | 165/165 | 70,000 |
| | | $360,000 | | $495,700 |